2000 Years of Jewish History

from the Destruction of the Second Bais HaMikdash until the Twentieth Century

Rabbi Chaim Schloss

Rambam

תלמוד בבלי

משנה

Rama

שלחן ערוך

Vilna Gaon

2000 Years of J

Feldheim Publishers

Jerusalem / New York

wish History

from the Destruction of the Second Bais HaMikdash until the Twentieth Century

Rabbi Chaim Schloss

ISBN 1-58330-214-X

FELDHEIM PUBLISHERS
POB 35002 / Jerusalem, Israel

202 Airport Executive Park
Nanuet, NY 10954

www.feldheim.com

Please address any questions or comments
regarding the contents of this book
to the author:
Rabbi Chaim Schloss
65 Laurel Park Rd. apt. F4
Fallsburg N.Y. 12733

10 9 8 7 6 5 4 3 2

Printed in Israel

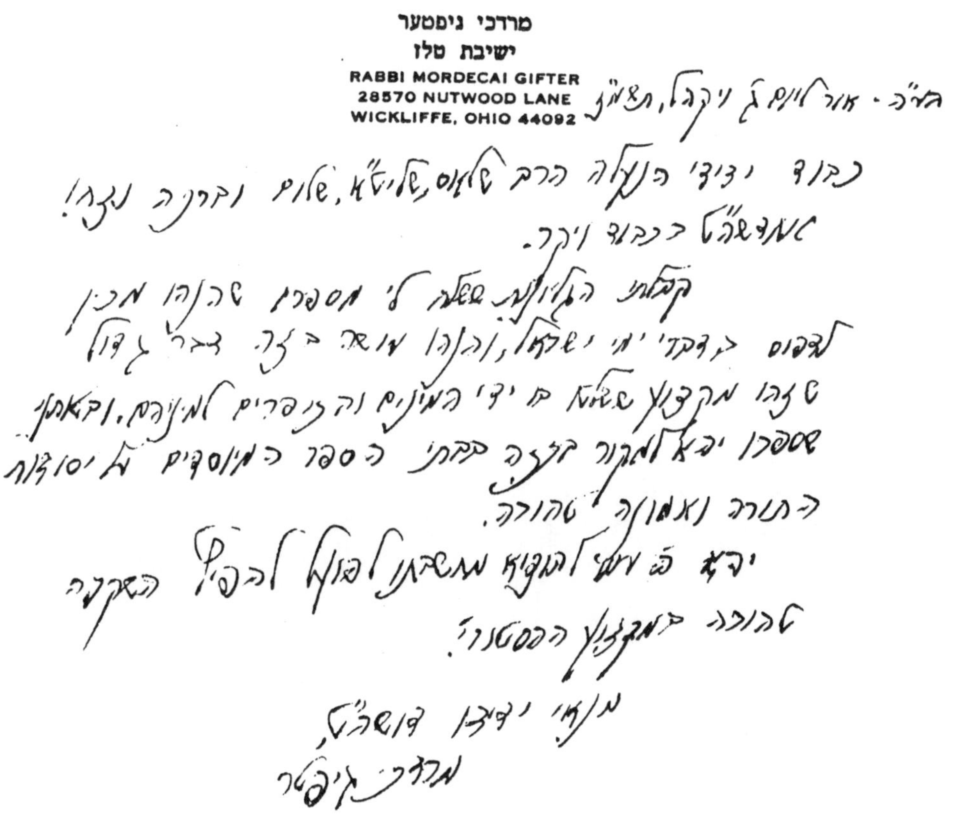

מרדכי גיפטער
ישיבת טלז
RABBI MORDECAI GIFTER
28570 NUTWOOD LANE
WICKLIFFE, OHIO 44092

[Handwritten Hebrew letter]

Dear Rabbi Schloss,

I received the excerpts of the book that you are preparing for print on the subject of Jewish history. I believe that this is a worthwhile undertaking in light of the fact that this is a subject into which many non-believers and heretics have unfortunately infiltrated. I am confident that your book will be a source of blessing for those Jewish schools that are built on the foundations of Torah and true belief.

May Hashem help you realize your intention so that pure Jewish Hashkofah can be disseminated within the study of history.

Signed,
(Rav) Mordechai Gifter

Dear Rabbi Schloss, שליט"א

    I was delighted to hear that your textbook on Jewish history is soon to appear. Jewish history is an unfortunately much neglected subject; it is a major basis for teaching השקפות התורה *on the task and mission of* עם ישראל.

    Your many years of fruitful work in חינוך *eminently qualify you to produce a text which, I am sure, will be a most suitable tool for teaching our history and elevate it to the level it deserves.*

    With all good wishes, and in old friendship, בברכת כתיבה וחתימה טובה,

Yours,
Joseph Elias

Over the past three years, I have had the opportunity to use Rabbi Schloss's history book as the basis of my course in Jewish history at Bais Yaakov of Detroit. What a welcome addition this textbook is for the teacher of Jewish history! For the first time, the Jewish history teacher has a textbook that covers the entire gamut of our history, presented in a way that is both interesting and informative.

Rabbi Schloss masterfully breaks down a dizzying array of historical events into manageable sections for the student, while pointing out the important and halachic implications of each development. In this way, Rabbi Schloss moves the study of history away from a tedious exercise in the memorization of dry facts, to a fascinating exploration of the issues and beliefs that have confronted, and continue to confront, *Klal Yisrael*. The book strikes a balance between being informative without being overwhelming, providing enough facts for the student to understand without losing the underlying theme in a myriad of details.

Rabbi Schloss's book is a welcome change to a field that has been sadly bereft of any text that thoughtfully explores our people's history from a traditional perspective. It is no longer necessary for the Jewish history teacher to search for materials, hoping to find a discussion that is intellectually stimulating, factually accurate, and consistent with traditional Jewish perspectives. A teacher can now approach any area of Jewish history with a sense of confidence and the knowledge that it will be adequately and appropriately dealt with.

I wholeheartedly and enthusiastically endorse this textbook, and look forward to the day when it will become widely available to schools throughout the country.

Sincerely,

Rabbi Shraga Rothbart
Jewish History Teacher
Bais Yaakov of Detroit

Dear Rabbi Schloss,

The Yeshiva of Spring Valley, with an enrollment of 1,400 students, has been using your textbook in a pilot program for the study of Jewish history.

I am happy to report that the material was enthusiastically received by the students of our 8th grade. The children really looked forward to their lessons, absorbing the thousands of facts with ease and satisfaction. The exceptionally high scores the students received on their final exams are a clear indication of the success of your book.

I highly recommend your book for the study of Jewish history. I am confident that any school that uses this book as part of its history curriculum will enrich the lives of both their students and teachers.

Sincerely,
Rabbi Israel Flam
Dean,
Yeshiva of Spring Valley

בס"ד

YESHIVA BETH YEHUDAH

Rabbi Nathaniel Lauer
Educational Director

Mrs. Goldie Silverstein
Mrs. Fayge Sperka
Principals

Rabbi Norman Kahn
Executive Vice President

Rabbi Eli Mayerfeld
Executive Director

Mr. Menachem Abrams
Dr. Jack Belen
Mr. Jack Blumenkopf
Rabbi Shmuel Irons
Mr. Allen Ishakis
Mr. Stephen Levitz
Dr. Elliot Samet
Mr. Larry Schon
Mr. Stuart Snider
Dr. David Weingarden
Mr. George Weiss
Rabbi Yissachar Wolf
Board of Directors

Dr. Maury Ellenberg
Chairman of the Board

Rabbi Shmuel Irons
Chairman,
Vaad HaChinuch

Mr. Gary Torgow
President

Mr. Marvin Berlin
Honorary President

כ"ח אלול תשנ"ז יום ג' לסדר "זכור ימות עולם ... זקניך ויאמרו לך..."

לכבוד האי גברא רבה רב פעלים מוהר"ר חיים שלאס שליט"א דמדילי' נפח
רוח חיים בהבנת ימות עולם, והסיר את המנעול מעל חכמת קורות עמינו
בעד נוער דורנו.

כבודו פיתח ליבן ושינן גישתו הבהירה והמקיפה בהבנת הסטורי' של
עמינו במשך עשרות שנים בכתה פה בב"י בחנכו דורות תלמידות
בדיטרויט, הוציא לאור מהדורה אחר מהדורה, כל אחת עולה על
חברתה, העביר קולמוס בשיפור הסגנון הסדר והלשון עד שב"ה זכינו היום
להוצאת חדשה שמוכן להוציא מתחת ידו - דבר הראוי לחבר כמוהו.

השתמשתי בספרו בעצמי זה כבר שנים רבות בכתה, ומצאתי את החומר
וכל מהות הספר מתאים לתלמידים ותלמידות - ואף למצוינים שבהם.

כידוע יסוד העבודה העצומה הזאת הוסד במשמר ובפקודת הגה"ח ר'
שלום גולדשטיין זצ"ל מהמיסדים והמנהל הראשון של הב"י דפה שע"י
ישיבת בית יהודה.

בזה באתי על החתום להביע רגשי הזכות בגורלי שיכולתי לעזור בזה
המפעל הנחוץ לדורנו.

באהבה ובהוקרה ובברכת כוח"ט

נתנאל לואר

---

*With greatest respect to that person of great accomplishments, our teacher,
Rabbi Chaim Schloss, Shlita; who from within himself has breathed life into the
understanding of the "days of old"; who has removed the lock from the wisdom of the antiquities of our nation for the youth of our generation.*

*The respected Rabbi has developed, perfected and honed his clear and en-
compassing approach to the understanding of our national history over decades
of his teaching generations of students here in Bais Yaakov of Detroit. He has
edited and revised, each version surpassing the previous. He has perfected the
style and the language of his work until, Thank God, we merit today the publication of a final version, one appropriate for an author of his caliber.*

*I myself used his earlier text for many years in the classroom. I found the ma-
terial and the entire book to be appropriate for students, even the most advanced.*

*As it is known, the foundation of this great work was laid under the watch-
ful eye of Hagaon Hachosid Rav Sholom Goldstein zt"l, one of the founders and
the first principal of the Bais Yaakov here, a division of Yeshiva Beth Yehudah.*

*I hereby attest to my emotions of good fortune that I too merit to assist in
this most important endeavor for our generation.*

With great respect and admiration and wishes for a Ksiva Vechasima Tova,

Nathaniel Lauer

SALLY ALLAN ALEXANDER BETH JACOB SCHOOL FOR GIRLS

14390 West Ten Mile Road • Oak Park, MI 48237 • (248) 544-9070 • Fax (248) 544-4667

BAIS SHAINDEL   בית שיינדל

High School for Girls   299 Monmouth Avenue   Lakewood, NJ 08701   (732)363-7074

לכבוד הרב שלאס, שיחי׳

As a twelfth grade הסטרי׳ teacher for six years, I search constantly for appropriate, factually correct material, presented with the proper השקפות. I have gone through many a ספר, but I have never come across a ספר like yours. It provides enough of the רוח of the times without being verbose, to feel what the תקופה was like. It is factually correct, yet not at all boring. And most of all, the views presented are Torah-true השקפות, thus assisting in fulfilling the פסוק:

״זכור ימות עולם בינו שנות דור ודור, שאל אביך ויגדך ...״

A tremendous יישר כוח for a job well-done. I look forward to the day, when this ספר will be an essential textbook of הסטרי׳, in schools worldwide.

Sincerely,
A Teacher from
Bais Shaindel High School

Dear Rabbi Schloss, Shlita,

As a teacher in the Bais Yaakov of Detroit, I have been privileged to teach Jewish history in the high school. As we use your book *2000 Years of Jewish History,* the students and I find the book interesting, informative and thought provoking.

I wish you *hatzlacha* in your tireless endeavor to enhance our young generation's appreciation of our People's *divrei y'mai olam,* and in your guiding them to realize the *Yad Hashem* in our past, present and future until the ultimate *geulah.*

Respectfully Yours,
Meir Lieberson

Acknowledgments

This book would not have been possible without the help and encouragement of many individuals:

Rabbi S.E. Cohen, former principal of Beth Jacob Schools, gave me immeasurably helpful advice on all aspects of Jewish and general history. He was always genuinely interested in the progress of this book.

Rabbi Reuven Drucker gave me his invaluable advice and friendship, along with computer assistance.

Horav Eliyahu Dov Glucksman, Dayan of K'hal Adas Yeshurun and historian of the Teacher's Seminary of K'hal Adas Yeshurun, offered his advice and critiques in two day-long sessions, going over the entire text. His suggestions were invaluable, and I made a full effort to follow his advice.

Horav Shmuel Irons spent many hours going over my book chapter by chapter, sharing with me the wealth of his historical and Talmudic background. His time and advice were invaluable.

Rabbi Nesanel Lauer, principal of Beth Jacob Schools in Oak Park, gave me his advice and encouragement. Rabbi Lauer made his staff and the technical equipment of the school available to me at all times. He supported the last years of the production of the book with great enthusiasm, and I am greatly indebted to him for his personal involvement in this project.

Horav Shimon Feder of Bnai Brak graciously allowed me to copy a number of pictures of *Gedolim* from his *sefer, Toldos Hadoros*. Agudath Israel supplied me with pictures of many *Gedolim* and leaders from their archives. Mesorah Publications allowed me to copy a paragraph in Hebrew from their *Siddur Ahavas Sholom*. CIS Publishers graciously permitted me to use paintings of the Rambam, the Rama, and the Vilna Gaon on the cover.

Many people helped bring this book to completion through editing, proofreading, computer expertise, and layout services. Mrs. Nechama Bakst edited many chapters of the book and offered continuous advice. Mrs. Hilary Drucker also edited and printed several chapters. Miss Chaya Sora Levitan tirelessly proofread and corrected errors. Mrs. Beth Applebaum contributed to the cover design and Rabbi Amos Dunst supplied the artwork for the maps, time lines, and charts. Sandra Greenberg offered graphic design and layout services. Mrs. Peninah Soleveitchik edited the entire book and rendered Rav Gabirol's *pizmon* from Hebrew into poetic English. Rabbi Menachem Stocks provided computer artwork and Susan Tawil provided proofreading and editing services. Mr. Michael Plotkin of Feldheim Publishers in Jerusalem copyedited the book. Rabbi Shraga Rothbart gave advice and did research on many facts contained throughout this book. Mrs. Elky Langer provided the flap and edited many parts of the book. Mrs. Bassie Gutman supplied arduous typesetting work, putting in time around the clock with patience and perseverence, until this publication came to its final rendition.

I would like to thank Yeshiva Beth Yehudah, the great citadel of *chinuch* in the greater Detroit community, and its Beth Jacob School Division, where I have had the opportunity to devote most of my years of teaching. Their sponsorship and encouragement throughout the years have helped bring this book to its completion.

Last but not least, I would like to express my greatest appreciation to my son Rabbi Michoel Schloss, whose perseverance and dedication to the completion and publication of this volume knew no bounds. His toil and persistence was a labor of love far beyond the parameters of *kibbud av.* "ישלם ה' פעלו."

Dedications

Jeffrey Abraham

My brother, Albert Schloss, and my sister, Miriam Baras

Mrs. Pearl Biber, in memory of Rabbi Chaim Yeshaya ben Shimon HaKohen

Mr. Arnold Carmen

Rabbi Naftali Deutsch, in memory of Reverend Phillip and Rose Hausman and Adolph and Eleanor Deutsch

Rabbi Avrohom Gold, in memory of Rabbonis Brocha Pessel bas Yehudis Kahana

Mrs. Fay Isackson, in memory of Charles N. Isackson

Paul Kohn, in memory of Esther bas Elimelech

Mr. Sam Loberman

Mr. Edward Meer, Dr. Aharon Meer, and Mr. Reuven Meer, in memory of Chana Chaya bas Mendel, Chaim ben Shlomo Moshe and Tzippora bas Ahron

Mr. Alex Saltsman, in memory of Lillian Saltsman, Sarah Saltsman, Avrohom Feldman, and Rose Feldman

Mr. Gary Torgow, in memory of Mr. Moshe ben Menachem Merzon

Dr. David Weingarden

It was when I first began teaching Jewish history many years ago that I became aware of the vital need for an English text covering the period after *Churban Bayis Sheini* until modern times.

This textbook would have to meet several criteria. It would have to lead the students from one era to the next, from one country to another, from continent to continent, from valley of tears to valley of tears, revealing in each the ever-present *Yad Hashem*—the guiding hand of Hashem in every circumstance. And more than that: it would have to teach Jewish history as a guidepost for the future. Our children are taught the basic precept of the Rambam that *Mashiach's* arrival is due at any time, and that we have to hope for and believe in that moment on any given day. The study of Jewish history can and should be an extension and a fortification of that faith, with the conviction that we are moving ever closer to the final *geulah*.

Thus was born my own version of Jewish history *al pi taharas hakodesh*: a book to stimulate the reader and, at the same time, inculcate in him proper Torah-true values. In short, the study of Jewish history should take its place within the framework of all our *limudei kodesh*.

A complete set of exercises and tests are currently in preparation, and will *b'ezras Hashem* be published in conjunction with the book itself. Yet this book is not just meant for the classroom. It is to be hoped that many of our parents and adults will acquire it and read it as well. Interspersed with many *ma'amorei Chazal,* along with examples gathered from the lives of our *Gedolim* in every generation, this book deserves its place within every Jewish library.

It is my fervent hope that this book will achieve its goal both in the classroom and in the home.

Rabbi Chaim Schloss

A Note About Dates:

Many of the dates in this book, particularly those of earlier eras, are approximate. This is the result of two circumstances that affected the recording of world history throughout the ages: the uncertainty of the calendar, and inaccurate record keeping during most of the years covered by this book.

Before modern times, calendars and dating were not consistent from country to country, or from era to era. In addition, as each new country became an important world power, it tended to impose its own version of events upon its citizens. This naturally led to inconsistencies and disagreements regarding the dates of important events.

There was also a lack of accurate record keeping, particularly in times of war and rapid change. Few people had the presence of mind to record the dates of events; often, when such records were made, they were lost in the upheaval that followed. This is even true of events that occurred less than 150 years ago; many people born at the turn of the last century, for example, are unsure of their exact date of birth.

In summary, while every effort has been made to ensure the accuracy of the dates recorded in this volume, the history of this time period is subject to the ambiguities described above.

Table of Contents

2000 Years of Jewish History

from the Destruction of
the Second Bais HaMikdash
until the Twentieth Century

Rabbi Chaim Schloss

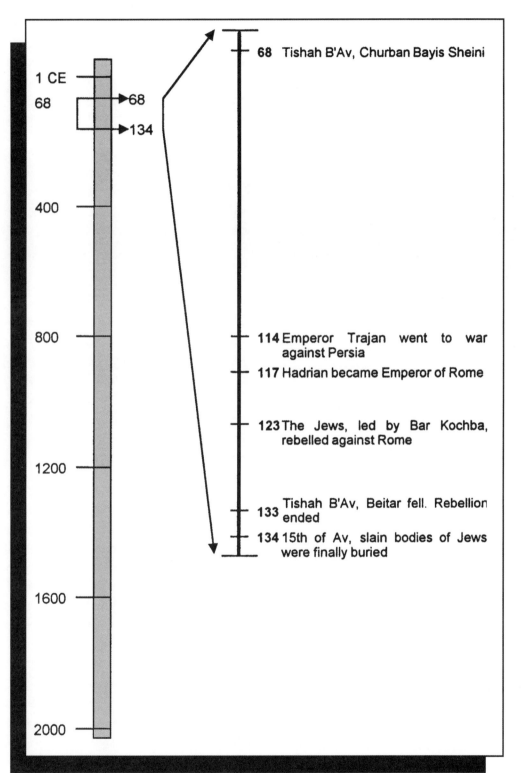

1 CE
68

400

800

1200

1600

2000

68

134

68 Tishah B'Av, Churban Bayis Sheini

114 Emperor Trajan went to war against Persia

117 Hadrian became Emperor of Rome

123 The Jews, led by Bar Kochba, rebelled against Rome

133 Tishah B'Av, Beitar fell. Rebellion ended

134 15th of Av, slain bodies of Jews were finally buried

*Only Yerushalayim,
the site of the holy
Bais HaMikdash,
remained standing*

The year was 3828 (68 C.E.).[1] The Roman Empire ruled the entire civilized world. Although it faced many rebellions, its mighty army was able to maintain iron control. There was, however, an exception—tiny Judea. It had come under the rule of procurators who were appointed by the Roman Senate. Their greed and brutality took an enormous toll in life and property, until it reached the point where Jewish zealots, an extreme group of the Jewish population, decided to rebel. Annoyed by the audacity and the arrogance of this action, coming from a relatively small nation, the Emperor took steps to crush the Jews once and for all. Battle-hardened legions marched against the small country, leaving devastated fields and smoking buildings behind them. It did not take long for Judea to fall. Only Yerushalayim, the site of the holy Bais HaMikdash, remained standing; there was little hope of preventing complete destruction.

The situation was further aggravated by the fact that the people of Judea were torn by disunity. A significant segment of the people in Yerushalayim belonged to the Sadducees, who tried to befriend the Romans because doing so served their lifestyle. The rebels had to force this influential group to persist in continuing the fight.

The Sages exhorted the people to surrender and allow the status quo to be preserved. "We still have the Bais HaMikdash," they urged. "It is not important if we become vassals of the Roman Empire, as long as we are allowed to continue living as Jews. We must surrender now! Better to live in peace than to die foolishly in battle."

Stubborn rebels refused to listen to the

1. According to Rashi, *Avodah Zarah* 9a.

wisdom of their elders. Blinded by empty visions of glory, they declared that they would rather die a splendid death in battle than live in ignominious defeat. Instead of placating the Romans, the rebels inflamed the legions with hit-and-run attacks and defiant gestures. They also burned all the storehouses of food in the city, in an effort to force the people to attack their enemies.

Yerushalayim lay in chaos. The empty warehouses mocked the starving population. Roman legions surrounded the city, ready for the final attack. The people were helpless to repel the invaders, and the Jewish nation seemed on the verge of utter ruin.

As moans and pleas for mercy filled the streets, the Sages of the era gathered to consider what steps they could take to ensure the future of the Jewish people. Looking beyond the immediate disaster, they realized that while it would be impossible to avoid the destruction completely, they could still salvage enough to rebuild the Jewish people out of the ashes.

In order for Judea to be rebuilt, a new order would need to be created. The entire sociopolitical system of the time was completely corrupt. The kings of Judea had been removed from power by Rome over sixty years before. The Kehunah, which had served as the ruling body, had degenerated through the abuse of power; at one point, the Kohen Gadol had been a non-Kohen who, through the generous application of bribery, had managed to secure the position. The Jews were divided into several different factions, which often split families apart. The Sages knew it would not be enough to continue as before; a new system would be needed to tie the people together.

The Talmud relates that when Rabban Yochanan ben Zakkai slipped out of the besieged city and reached the outskirts of Yerushalayim, he called to General Vespasian, the commander of the Roman army, "Peace unto you, Emperor."

Vespasian was shocked but flattered by the undeserved homage. "I should kill you for two reasons," he told Rabban Yochanan. "First, because I am not the Emperor, and by calling me that, you have insulted my superior, the real Emperor of Rome. Second, you have insulted me, because if I am the Emperor, why did you not come to me earlier?"

The venerable Sage replied, "Our prophets have said that the Lebanon [which refers to the Bais HaMikdash] will fall by the hands of a mighty man, meaning a king. Inasmuch as Jerusalem is practically in your hands already, you must be a king! I did not come to you earlier because the rebels have control of the city, and I was unable to leave until now."

While they were still discussing the issue, a messenger arrived from Rome. He burst into Vespasian's tent and announced, "The Emperor has died. The Senate in Rome has decided that you will be his successor!"

Vespasian was overwhelmed by the rapid fulfillment of the rabbi's words. In a flash of gratitude and good humor, he told Rabban Yochanan, "I must leave for Rome now, and someone else will take over for me here. But if you ask me for anything at this moment, I will see that you get it."

Without hesitation, Rabban Yochanan requested, "I want three things. Give me Yavneh and its wise men, give me the family of Rabban Gamliel, and give me medical help for Rabbi Zadok, who has been fasting for the last forty years for the continued existence of the Bais HaMikdash and is near death from exhaustion."

Vespasian granted Rabban Yochanan's requests, unaware that these three things would ensure the continued survival of the Jewish people.

Rabban Yochanan's three requests were the basis for the new order the Sages knew was necessary to preserve the Jewish people. With the Kehunah in tatters and the monarchy forbidden under the auspices of Rome, a new ruling body had to be created, one based on religious leadership and judicial legislation.

"Israel, the Torah and Hashem are one and inseparable." For the Jewish people to survive, the preservation of Torah learning was crucial. Thus, Rabban Yochanan asked for the city of Yavneh, which, together with its Sages, would serve as the foundation for the gigantic complex of learning centers that would uphold Torah and Klal Yisrael.

Rabban Yochanan's second request ensured the continuity of the House of David. Although Rome forbade the kings of Judea to wield power, Rabban Yochanan realized that it was vital for the Jews to maintain a bond with the ruling house of King David. Yaakov Avinu had promised Yehudah in his prophecy that "Lo yasur shevet miYehudah," that the descendants of David would never be removed from being rulers in Israel.[2] By saving the family of Rabban Gamliel, a descendant of King David, Rabban Yochanan preserved the House of David as the titular head of Klal Yisrael.

Rabban Yochanan's third request was in recognition of the changing of the times. After the destruction of the Bais

_____

2. Bereishis, 49:10.

"Israel, the Torah and Hashem are one and inseparable."

"Give me Yavneh and its wise men, give me the family of Rabban Gamliel, and give me medical help for Rabbi Zadok."

Chapter
1

After Churban Bayis Sheini:

Roots in the Ashes

Three seemingly minor things would eventually shape the destiny of Klal Yisrael.

HaMikdash, the yearning for the future redemption would be the only connection with the lost glory of the Bais HaMikdash. Without that perpetual desire to regain what once was, the memories of the former glory of the Jewish nation might fade into oblivion. Rabbi Zadok, who had fasted forty years for the continued existence of the Bais HaMikdash, was the living symbol of that perpetual yearning. Many of the prayers of today center around the longing for the Bais HaMikdash and a return to its former glory; Rabban Yochanan's insight played a major role in ensuring the memory of and the yearning for the days before the Jewish nation was exiled from Eretz Yisrael.

The Talmud relates that some felt that Rabban Yochanan could have asked Vespasian to break off the siege, end the war or spare the Bais HaMikdash. Rabban Yochanan, however, feared that if he asked for too much, Vespasian would give him nothing. Instead, he made three requests that Vespasian was sure to grant—three seemingly minor things that would eventually shape the destiny of Klal Yisrael.

Grave of Rabban Yochanan ben Zakkai

The Sanhedrin[3]

Eretz Yisrael was ravaged, trampled under the feet of marauding armies. The charred remains of the demolished Bais HaMikdash seemed to represent the destruction of the Jewish people. From a political, economic and military standpoint, the Jewish nation had collapsed. The Romans were convinced that they had finally managed to crush the stubborn Jewish spirit.

In the light of all their overwhelming successes against the Jews, it is not surprising that they paid little attention to the small pocket of Torah life that was taking root in the little city of Yavneh. The Roman attitude was basically one of disinterested contempt towards Rabban Yochanan's efforts. "Let them practice their religion," the conquerors thought dismissively. "As long as they pay their taxes and obey orders, it doesn't matter what they believe."

And so it was that Rabban Yochanan began, quietly and unobtrusively, to rebuild the Jewish nation on the basis of Torah. His first priority was to establish the Yeshivah. His second was to strengthen the power of the Sanhedrin.

The seventy-one Sages of the Sanhedrin each had *semichah,* rabbinical ordination, and were qualified to judge all matters, from financial disputes to capital offenses. Not only did the Sanhedrin function as the highest court, it also passed legislation and clarified the Oral Law when halachic problems arose. With the destruction of the Bais HaMikdash, the Sanhedrin took over the leadership of the Jewish population in Eretz Yisrael. Unlike

---

3. Throughout this book, the term "Sanhedrin" refers to the highest Rabbinic organization in each generation, with the final say on halachic questions. This does not suggest that they met the requirements that were needed for the original Sanhedrin.

the ruling body of the Kohanim, which had bogged down in a mire of corruption, the Sanhedrin's ability to govern was based on the prestige and respect the venerable Sages had earned as the undisputed teachers of Torah.

In an effort to reemphasize the leadership of the Sanhedrin, Rabban Yochanan considered the resurrection of a custom which had been in use at the time of Hillel the Elder. In Hillel's day, the Nasi, or presiding judge and head of the Court, had to be not only a scholar with superior knowledge, but also a descendant of the House of David. Fear of Roman reprisal forced Rabban Yochanan to reconsider, and it was only after his death that Rabban Gamliel, a descendant of Hillel the Elder and a descendant of the House of David, was appointed as Nasi.

Rabban Gamliel experienced some initial difficulties in his role as Nasi, especially when his views were challenged publicly by contemporary Tannaim, whom we recognize today as the outstanding scholars of all time. Among the leading scholars of the Sanhedrin at that time were the five main disciples of Rabban Yochanan ben Zakkai, who are mentioned in *Pirkei Avos*: Rabbi Eliezer ben Hurkanos, Rabbi Yehoshua ben Chananya, Rabbi Yosei the Kohen, Rabbi Shimon ben Nesanel, and Rabbi Elazar ben Arach.[4]

Rabban Gamliel, who recognized the necessity of assuring that the decisions of the Nasi remain inviolate, asserted himself with the utmost humility, but with great determination and steadfastness, as illustrated in this story brought in the Mishnah:[5]

It once happened that two witnesses testified that they saw the new moon when it should have appeared (on the thirtieth of the month) but not on the following night (on the thirty-first day). Although this testimony seemed contradictory, since the moon should have certainly been seen on the thirty-first, Rabban Gamliel accepted them as witnesses and proclaimed the new month.

Rabbi Dossa ben Harkinas objected: "How can one testify about a woman that she gave birth today and that she still looked pregnant on the next day?"

Rabbi Yehoshua said to Rabbi Dossa, "I agree with your opinion."

This was a situation that Rabban Gamliel, as Nasi, could not allow. His leadership was being challenged by his great colleagues, and he had to do something drastic to defend it; otherwise, the role of Nasi would lose its integrity.

Rabban Gamliel sent a message to Rabbi Yehoshua, saying, "I order you to come to me in your weekday clothing with your cane and money belt on the day that, according to your opinion, is Yom Kippur."

Rabbi Yehoshua was troubled by Rabban Gamliel's order, but Rabbi Akiva reassured him and said, "I can prove to you that whatever Rabban Gamliel decided, rightly or wrongly, is valid. The Torah says, 'These are the Holy Days of Hashem that you shall declare,' whether in their expected time or not.[6] Our Sages explain this verse to mean: 'I, Hashem, have no Holidays except these.'"[7]

Rabbi Yehoshua went to Rabbi Dossa ben Harkinas for additional advice, and Rabbi Dossa also brought proofs from the Torah that one must not question the decision of the Nasi of the Sanhedrin, even if one disagrees with the Nasi's ruling.

Rabban Gamliel recognized that the decisions of the Nasi must remain inviolate.

---

4. *Pirkei Avos*, 2:10.
5. *Rosh HaShanah*, Perek 2.

6. *Vayikra*, 23:1.
7. *Rosh HaShanah*, Perek 2.

Chapter

1

*A succession of
turbulent political
and military
events agitated
the Jewish
population in
Eretz Yisrael.*

Without any further hesitation, on the day which he had reckoned to be Yom Kippur, Rabbi Yehoshua took his staff and his money in his hand, and went to Yavneh to Rabban Gamliel.

When Rabban Gamliel saw Rabbi Yehoshua coming towards him, he stood up and kissed him on the head, saying, "Please come in, my Master and my Disciple; you are my Master in wisdom and my Disciple in that you accepted my words."

Rabban Gamliel was not trying to gain a personal victory over Rabbi Yehoshua; he was taking the opportunity to reinforce his role as Nasi. Despite his awe and respect for Rabbi Yehoshua, he did not shy away from the leadership that had been imposed on him.

Other stories related in the Talmud also serve to demonstrate the greatness of the Tannaim, both in character and in intellect.

The Bar Kochba Rebellion
(122-133 C.E.)

As time passed, the Romans realized that, with the revival of Jewish government in Eretz Yisrael under the leadership of the Sanhedrin, their assumption of the national demise of the Jews had been premature. The appointment of Rabban Gamliel, a member of the House of David, as Nasi, also served to strengthen their suspicions that the Jews might by trying to reestablish their kingdom. The Romans began to display overt hostility towards Yavneh and the Sanhedrin.

In an effort to divert Roman suspicions, the Sages periodically replaced the Nasi with other members of the Sanhedrin who were not of Davidic descent. Rabbi Elazar ben Azariah was Nasi for some time, as was Rabbi Akiva, who was a descendant of a convert.

The Sanhedrin was also constantly on the move, changing its location from Yavneh to other cities seven times in the first hundred years following the destruction of the Bais HaMikdash.

Unfortunately, their actions weren't enough to appease the Romans. The situation worsened as a succession of turbulent political and military events agitated the Jewish population in Eretz Yisrael.

One such event took place in the year 114. The Roman Emperor Trajan set out to invade Persia, a country in which the Jews had lived peacefully since the destruction of the First Bais HaMikdash. The Persian Jews sided with their hosts and fought with courage and valor against the Romans. When Persia fell to the Romans, the victors turned with fury against the Jews throughout the Roman Empire. Trajan ordered a special governor to treat the Jews in Eretz Yisrael severely, and the Greek population of Egypt used the opportunity to massacre the Jews in Alexandria and destroy its ancient synagogues.

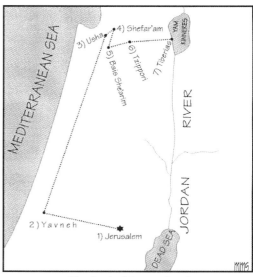

The Sanhedrin wandered

Rosh HaShanah 31a-b
"The Sanhedrin wandered... from Jerusalem to Yavneh, from Yavneh to Usha, to She'arim, from Shefar'am to Bais She'arim, from Bais She'arim to Tzippori, from Tzippori to Tiberias."

After Trajan died, Hadrian became Emperor. At that point, the Romans were ill-equipped to continue their long war with Persia. Hadrian needed to win the support of his subjects in order to pursue his ambitious plans for future conquests.

He enticed his Jewish subjects with various promises, including a commitment to allow them to rebuild the Temple in Yerushalayim if they pledged him their loyalty and support. As the wily Emperor had expected, the Jews eagerly accepted his proposal. But it did not take long for the Jews to discover that Hadrian never had any intention of keeping his promise. Their fury, humiliation and frustration were overwhelming, and the Jews rebelled.

At that critical moment, a man named Ben Kuziba stepped forward and presented the claim that he was *Mashiach,* the Messiah, sent to restore the Jewish kingdom and rebuild the Bais HaMikdash. Ben Kuziba was a brilliant, heroic man whose faithfulness to Torah and mitzvos is well-documented in the Gemara. When he was introduced to Rabbi Akiva, the Sage was so impressed by Ben Kuziba that he exclaimed, "*Darach kochav miYaakov*—A star has come out of Yaakov,"[8] a verse relating to *Mashiach.* From then on, Ben Kuziba was called Bar Kochba (meaning "star"), and he was accepted by many as the Redeemer sent by Hashem to bring about the redemption of the Jewish people.

Bar Kochba performed acts of enormous bravery and heroism over the next two years. But in the course of that time, he dropped his semblance of piety. He made arrogant public statements to the effect that he didn't need or want the help of Hashem; he just didn't want Hashem to "interfere" with his efforts. The support of the Sages and the faith they had placed in him faded quickly in the light of his newly revealed behavior.

The final proof that Bar Kochba was not *Mashiach* came when he heard unjustified rumors that his uncle, Rabbi Elazar HaModai, had committed treason. In a fit of anger, Bar Kochba had his uncle killed. Such a merciless act convinced the Sages that Bar Kochba was an impostor and that his revolt was doomed to failure.

Rome sent one of their ablest generals, Julius Severus, to crush the rebellion. Bar Kochba's final stand was in the city of Beitar, where he put up a brilliant defense against the Roman onslaught. In the year 133, the city was finally taken by the Romans, albeit with tremendous losses on both sides. Roman sources claimed that close to half a million Jews were killed; Severus, when reporting his final victory, left out the customary closing, "I and the army are well," which indicates how heavy the Roman casualties had been.

In order to punish the Jews even further, the Romans ordered that the slain Jewish bodies be piled up around the ruins of Beitar, refusing to allow the Jews to bury their dead. When this cruel decree was finally abolished on the fifteenth of Av several years later, the Sages gave thanks to Hashem by adding the blessing "*HaTov v'HaMaitiv*" to Grace After Meals.

The fall of Beitar is one of the events that occurred on Tishah B'Av. The Romans looked upon the victory at Beitar as their final assault against the Jewish people. They had begun with the spiritual destruction when they burned the Bais HaMikdash; with the fall of Beitar, they believed that they had begun to destroy the Jews physically as well. Now, the evil Hadrian planned to take even further measures in his plans to annihilate the Jewish people.

---

8. *Bamidbar* 24:17

"Darach kochav miYaakov—A star has come out of Yaakov."

Now, the evil Hadrian planned to take even further measures in his plans to annihilate the Jewish people.

Chapter

1

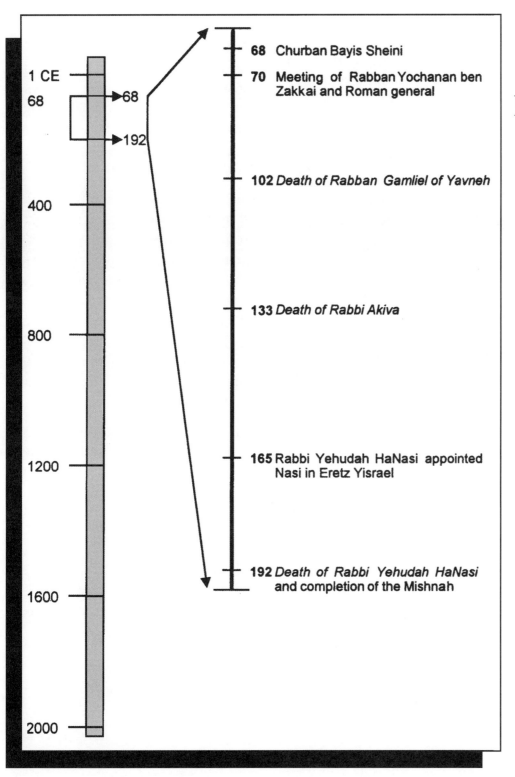

1 CE
68

400

800

1200

1600

2000

68
192

68 Churban Bayis Sheini

70 Meeting of Rabban Yochanan ben Zakkai and Roman general

102 *Death of Rabban Gamliel of Yavneh*

133 *Death of Rabbi Akiva*

165 Rabbi Yehudah HaNasi appointed Nasi in Eretz Yisrael

192 *Death of Rabbi Yehudah HaNasi and completion of the Mishnah*

Chapter
2

ar Kochba's final, desperate rebellion against the Roman Empire had been crushed. Rome's victory had not come easily, but Judea had been battered into submission. Emperor Hadrian was now ready to destroy completely the exasperating Jewish people who stubbornly refused to assimilate and blend together with the rest of Rome's conquered nations.

> *Four basic commandments of the Torah had been outlawed: circumcision, Shabbos observance, family purity, and the reading of Shema.*

Hadrian was a ruthless, evil man, but he was certainly no fool. Unlike Vespasian, who had magnanimously granted Rabban Yochanan ben Zakkai's three innocuous-seeming requests, he realized that it was a mistake to allow the Jews to continue to study Torah and to practice their religion. With the revival of the Sanhedrin, the Jews possessed a source of spiritual strength and inspiration which gave them the courage to defy Rome. Hadrian, like Antiochus of Syria before him, understood that he needed to strike at the very root of the Jewish nation. Without the Torah and mitzvos to sustain them, the Jews would surely wither away completely.

Hadrian's methods for achieving his goal were direct and unbelievably brutal. He decreed that learning Torah and doing mitzvos were illegal acts punishable by beatings or death. With this decree entered in the annals of Roman law, Hadrian ushered in the *Dor HaShmad*, the generation of systematic annihilation.

Hadrian had already begun to forbid Jewish practices before the battle at Beitar. Four basic commandments of the Torah had been outlawed: circumcision, Shabbos observance, family purity and the reading of *Shema*. After Bar Kochba's death and the end of the rebellion, Hadrian added many more mitzvos to the list of forbidden activities, among them wearing tefillin, reading the Megillah, building a sukkah, taking the lulav, and wearing tzitzis.

The wily Hadrian realized the necessity of "making an example." Accordingly, he focused his barbarous attentions on the Sages of the era, to whom the entire Jewish people turned for guidance and counsel. The Emperor felt sure that, with the death of the Sages, the very heart of the Jews would suffer a mortal blow; the last vestiges of the Jewish nation would simply dwindle into nothingness without their leaders to guide them.

The extent to which Hadrian tortured his victims can be inferred from the observation of Chiya bar Abba, an Amora who lived after the time of *Dor HaShmad*.

> *"Why are you going to be put to death?"*
>
> *"Because I circumcised my son."*
>
> *"Why are you going to be burned by fire?"*
>
> *"Because I read the Torah."*
>
> *"Why are you being nailed to the cross?"*
>
> *"Because I ate matzah on Pesach."*
>
> *"Why are you being beaten mercilessly?"*
>
> *"Because I took the lulav."*
>
> *And so said the Prophet Zechariah: "That I was beaten in the house of my beloved One." Those beatings cause me to be beloved by my Father in Heaven.*
>
> From the *Mechilta* (Shemos, 20:6)

> *Hadrian, like Antiochus of Syria before him, understood that he needed to strike at the very root of the Jewish nation.*

"If a person were to order me to give up my life to sanctify Hashem's Name, I would be ready to do so—provided that he kill me quickly. However, the tortures administered during the *Dor HaShmad* I could not endure."[1]

The malicious, sadistic tortures that Hadrian inflicted upon his victims, as well as the noble heroism of the Sages, are documented in the poignant narrative, *Aileh Ezkera,* which is recited during *Mussaf* on Yom Kippur.

The *Asara Harugai Malchus,* or Ten Martyrs, were not all murdered at the same time. There is some disagreement over whether they were all killed within the same generation, or over a longer period of time. Rabbi Akiva, the foremost scholar among them, was most likely murdered soon after the fall of Beitar. The account of his last moments is recorded in the Gemara.[2]

Rabbi Akiva was subjected to the most diabolic tortures imaginable. But even in the depths of his most extreme suffering, Rabbi Akiva continued to serve Hashem with joy. His students, amazed at his tenacity in the face of his torment and anguish, wondered, "Rebbe, to what extent must you fulfill Hashem's mitzvos?"

Rabbi Akiva explained, "All my life, I have been troubled by the *pasuk,* 'Love Hashem with all your soul.'[3] I questioned whether I would ever have the chance to fulfill this commandment. Now, the opportunity to fulfill this mitzvah has come to me. Shall I not fulfill it? Should I not rejoice?"

Rabbi Akiva, as witnessed by his weeping, grief-stricken students, gave up his pure soul while reciting "Shema Yisrael." His death has served as an inspiration to the Jewish martyrs of all generations who have given up their lives *al kiddush Hashem,* for the sanctification of Hashem's Name.

Meanwhile, Hadrian's drive to destroy the Jewish people appeared to be succeeding. With so many of the era's great Sages murdered, the Sanhedrin was left in tatters; there seemed to be no one left to carry the Torah's banner. Nevertheless, with the distinctive tenacity of the Jewish nation, the few remaining Sages ignored the danger and took steps to ensure that Torah would not be forgotten in Klal Yisrael.

Rabbi Yehudah ben Bava, an elderly member of the Sanhedrin, had the foresight to recognize the dangers inherent in the imminent loss of *semichah,* rabbinical ordination; without leaders qualified to answer halachic questions and guide the nation, the Jewish people would not be able to survive. Rabbi Yehudah was well aware that Hadrian had imposed the death penalty on anyone who gave or received *semichah.* Nevertheless, he took five of Rabbi Akiva's younger students into the Galilee mountains and gave them *semichah,* ignoring the threat to his life.

Rome discovered Rabbi Yehudah's "heinous crime" and sent soldiers to kill him and the students on whom he had bestowed *semichah.* With the enemy approaching, Rabbi Yehudah commanded the five students to flee for their lives.

"But, Rebbe, what will become of you?" they protested.

"Love Hashem with all your soul."

Rabbi Akiva's death has served as an inspiration to the Jewish martyrs of all generations who have given their lives al kiddush Hashem.

He took five of Rabbi Akiva's younger students into the Galilee mountains and gave them semichah.

---

1. *Midrash Shir HaShirim,* 2:7.
2. *Berachos,* 61b.
3. *Devarim,* 6:5.

Chapter
2

*Iron spears were
driven into Rabbi
Yehudah's body.*

*Rabbi Shimon bar
Yochai headed a
delegation to
Rome in an
attempt to
persuade the
Senate to remove
Hadrian's decrees
from Roman law.*

Rabbi Yehudah replied, "I remain here, blocking the Romans' path, like a rock that cannot be overturned."

Rabbi Yehudah did, indeed, block the Romans' path; it is said that the Romans did not leave until they had driven three hundred iron spears into his body.[4] But the five young students—Rabbi Meir, Rabbi Yehudah, Rabbi Shimon bar Yochai, Rabbi Yosei and Rabbi Elazar ben Shamua—managed to escape. These five men, with their vast knowledge of the Oral Torah, would eventually become the very pillars of the Torah's survival; their halachic teachings would become fundamental elements of the Talmud.

One of them, Rabbi Shimon bar Yochai, was to author one of the most influential works in our history during the *Dor HaShmad.* An informer overheard him speak disparagingly of Rome's achievements.[5] Judged *in absentia* and sentenced to death, Rabbi Shimon had to flee to escape execution. During the twelve years in which he and his son Rabbi Elazar remained in hiding, Rabbi Shimon brought into the world a masterpiece that would enlighten world Jewry with its most important work of mystical teaching, the *Zohar HaKadosh.*

Hadrian's brutal rule finally ended with his death in the year 138. Like every tyrant that has followed Hadrian's path throughout the centuries, he failed to annihilate the Jewish people. Indeed, he merely served to intensify the determination of the surviving Jews to remain steadfast in their learning and dissemination of Torah. Hadrian's error lay in his failure to account for the indomitable spirit of the Jews, the strength of their faith and their determination to live up to their commitment,

"Love Hashem, your G-d, with all your heart and with all your soul."[6]

From Ashes to Achievement

Hadrian was dead. His successor, Antoninus Pius, let Hadrian's hideous decrees fall into disuse; he seemed inclined towards allowing the Jews to regain their religious independence. However, the Sages were aware that Hadrian's cruel edicts still lurked in the background, an evil shadow over everything they hoped to accomplish. The Sanhedrin could not be reconvened; technically, the Jews were still forbidden to observe Shabbos. All it would take was a single anti-Semitic advisor to the Roman Emperor to bring Hadrian's laws back into full, horrifying force.

A general assembly of all the Sages living in Eretz Yisrael convened in Usha. Their intentions were to lay the foundations for the reestablishment of the Sanhedrin and to endeavor to discover some way to have Hadrian's decrees abolished. Rome's threat to crush the gathering as a potential rebellion forced the Sages to move to Shefar'am and underscored the urgent need to have Hadrian's anti-Jewish laws repealed.

Rabbi Shimon bar Yochai headed a delegation to Rome in an attempt to persuade the Senate to remove Hadrian's decrees from Roman law. The Talmud relates that when the delegation arrived in Rome, Rabbi Shimon bar Yochai cured the Emperor's daughter, who was suffering from severe depression. In gratitude, the Emperor led the Sages to his treasury.

"These are Rome's greatest treasures," Antoninus told them. He gestured expansively at the glittering array of jewels

---

4. *Sanhedrin,* 13b-14a.
5. *Shabbos,* 33b.

6. *Devarim,* 6:5.

and gold. "Examine them well. You may take whatever you desire."

The Sages did, in fact, find the treasure they desired. Searching through the archives, they found the official document containing Hadrian's decrees, which they took and promptly destroyed.

Matters were expedited further by the close friendship of Rabbi Yehudah HaNasi and the Roman Emperor, Marcus Aurelius Antoninus. The two of them shared a peculiar history, as related by the Gemara.[7] Rabbi Yehudah, born during the *Dor HaShmad,* was circumcised by his father, Rabban Shimon ben Gamliel, in defiance of the law. Rabban Shimon and his wife were ordered to present their child at the Roman court to verify the charges against them; should it be found that their child was truly circumcised, they would be executed.

On their way to Hadrian's palace, fully aware that they were going to their deaths, Rabbi Yehudah's parents stopped at an inn. There they met a young, noble Roman couple who had a newborn son of their own. The Roman couple felt sympathy for the innocent Jewish child and his anguished parents, and they offered to switch babies until after the Emperor's examination.

Rabban Shimon and his wife took the Roman baby to Hadrian's court, where the child was examined and found to be uncircumcised. The reprieved parents returned to the inn and recovered their circumcised Jewish son, thanking the Roman couple for saving both their lives and the life of their child.

As the years went by a friendship developed between Rabbi Yehudah and Marcus Aurelius Antoninus, the philosopher —the child that had been presented at his father's court as an uncircumcised Jewish boy. Even after Antoninus succeeded his father as Emperor of Rome, he maintained his deep friendship with and admiration of Rabbi Yehudah. They often met, albeit secretly, and Antoninus sought Rabbi Yehudah's advice on many important political decisions. Impressed and humbled by Rabbi Yehudah's greatness, Antoninus elicited a promise from his friend that he would have a place in the World to Come, if only "to serve as Rabbi Yehudah's footmat."

It is not surprising, then, that Antoninus allowed the Jews to establish a Sanhedrin led by Rabbi Yehudah HaNasi, about whom the Talmud states, "From Moshe until Rabbi Yehudah HaNasi, we do not find such Torah wisdom and worldly greatness combined in one person."

Makers of the Mishnah

Rabbi Yehudah HaNasi stood among the ruins of the *Dor HaShmad* and sought ways to nurture the fragile remnants of the Jewish people that still stubbornly clung to life. With Klal Yisrael demoralized and deprived of its greatest leaders by Hadrian's systematic persecution, drastic measures needed to be taken. Faced by the threat of the Torah being lost and forgotten in the wake of Hadrian's inhuman decrees, Rabbi Yehudah HaNasi, together with the Sanhedrin, made the momentous decision to write down[8] the Oral Law.

Rabbi Yehudah HaNasi, together with the Sanhedrin, made the momentous decision to write down the Oral Law.

7. Tosefos, *Avodah Zarah,* 10b.

8. According to some opinions, Rabbi Yehudah HaNasi only codified the Oral Law.

Matters were expedited further by the close friendship of Rabbi Yehudah HaNasi and the Roman Emperor, Marcus Aurelius Antoninus

Chapter 2

Torah must remain committed to memory, passed on from father to son, and taught from generation to generation.

When Moshe Rabbeinu stood at Mount Sinai and received the Torah, it was given to him in two distinct forms: *Torah Shebiksav,* the written Torah, composed of the five Chumashim; and the Oral Torah, *Torah Sheb'al Peh.* The names themselves are an indication of how the Torah must be studied. The Chumash explicitly states that Written Torah must be studied from a book, while the Oral Torah must remain committed to memory, passed on from father to son and taught from generation to generation.[9]

The two parts of the Torah, *Torah Shebiksav* and *Torah Sheb'al Peh,* are inextricably intertwined. While the Written Torah is accessible to all mankind—Moshe Rabbeinu wrote it on stone in seventy languages—the Oral Torah is the exclusive property of Yisrael. Without *Torah Sheb'al Peh,* the Chumash cannot be properly understood. We need the explanation of the Sages in order to fulfill the mitzvos properly. Without the Oral Torah, the Torah is incomplete, like a puzzle that is missing its most important piece.

For example, when the Chumash describes the law of tefillin, it merely states that one must "bind them as a sign on your hands."[10] But what are "them"? How are "they" made? What do "they" look like? How are "they" put on the hands as a sign? Where on the hands are "they" put? Is it written in ink on the skin, or perhaps inscribed on a bracelet? How are we to know exactly how to fulfill the mitzvah of tefillin properly? Only the Oral Torah supplies us with all the information we need.

Yet, the Ribono shel Olam decreed that the Oral Torah must not be written, but should remain oral. As a matter of fact, it

is a living, growing entity, never completely finished. Debates on points of law were woven into the mesh of the Oral Law as handed down by Moshe Rabbeinu. In addition, Chazal tell us that a student who, at any time in the future, might add novel thoughts that will help to clarify difficult passages in the Talmud—that, too is going to become part of the Oral Torah. By what right, then, could Rabbi Yehudah and his Bais Din violate Hashem's decree?

And yet, that is exactly what Rabbi Yehudah HaNasi and the Sanhedrin decided had to be done. The Rambam, in *Hilchos Mamrim* 2:4, compares Rabbi Yehudah's decision to a doctor who is treating a patient with a badly injured leg. The wound has become infected, and gangrene has developed. The doctor decides to amputate the leg in order to save the patient's life; if the leg is not removed, the gangrene will spread throughout the patient's body and kill him.

The application, or *nimshal,* is that the Sanhedrin was faced with an extremely ill patient: Klal Yisrael. Under the terrible weight of Hadrian's persecutions, the collective memory of the Jewish people had become impaired. Bits and pieces of the Oral Law were already lost. The ability to relay the *Torah Sheb'al Peh* accurately had waned, and there was a distinct possibility that it would be forgotten altogether; without the Oral Torah, the Written Torah would be lost as well. The Sanhedrin realized that, like a doctor who removes the leg to save the whole person, they must allow the Oral Law to be written down so that the whole Torah would not be forgotten.

---

9. *Shemos,* 34:27.
10. *Devarim,* 6:8.

Rabbi Yehudah was not interested in claiming any glory for himself; his sole intention was to facilitate Torah learning in Klal Yisrael. Throughout the Mishnah, Rabbi Yehudah HaNasi avoided the use of the first person. He never wrote "it is my opinion"; instead, he stated the opinions of Tannaim directly. Most anonymous statements are the opinions of Rabbi Meir, Rabbi Akiva's most outstanding pupil.

The Rambam, in the introduction to his *Mishneh Torah,* writes, "From the days of Moshe Rabbeinu until Rabbeinu HaKadosh (Rabbi Yehudah HaNasi), no one ever compiled a book with which to disseminate the Oral Torah to the public. Rabbeinu HaKadosh collected all the traditions, all the laws and all the explanations which had been heard from Moshe, plus those which had been taught by previous Sanhedrins, and from all of these, he created the Mishnah."

Title Page of the Mishnah

Rav Sherira Gaon, who lived in the tenth century, differs slightly from the opinion of the Rambam. Rav Sherira writes that Rabbi Yehudah HaNasi did not "create" the language of the Mishnah, as the Rambam believes, but that he compiled it from the many different versions taught in previous generations by sifting through the different versions and determining which was correct.

The Mishnah is written in a clear, easily understood Hebrew. Yet, the content of the Mishnah is so brief and concise that it is almost impossible to comprehend without the extensive comments of the Gemara, which was not recorded until approximately three hundred years later.

The cryptic style of the Mishnah was deliberate. Like a doctor who will remove as little of the patient's leg as possible, Rabbi Yehudah HaNasi limited the writing of the Oral Torah to a minimum. He wrote down only enough to serve as a crutch for the faltering memories of the students who had survived the *Dor HaShmad.*

Rabbi Yehudah HaNasi divided the entire body of material into six sections, known as *Sedarim.* The same order was used in the writing of the Gemara, generations later. Because of the six different sections, the Gemara became known by the abbreviation "Shass," denoting the *Shishah* [six] *Sedarim* it contains.

Together, the Mishnah and Gemara are known as the Talmud.

The *Sedarim* of the Talmud are: *Zeraim,* which pertains to the laws of the Land; *Moed,* which pertains to the Holidays; *Nashim,* which pertains to marital issues; *Nezikin,* which pertains to damages and civil laws; *Kodashim,* which pertains to the Bais HaMikdash and sacrifices; and *Taharos,* which pertains to the laws of ritual purity.

Yet, the content of the Mishnah is so brief and concise that it is almost impossible to comprehend without the extensive comments of the Gemara.

Chapter 2

*We eventually get
up again and
emerge stronger
than we ever were
before.*

Every *Seder* is subdivided into *masechtos* (tractates) bearing titles related to a subject associated with the *Seder.* Every *maseches* is divided into *perakim* (chapters), which in turn are divided into *mishnayos* (paragraphs).

The completion of the Mishnah was a monumental accomplishment, overshadowing the myriad political events, triumphs and sufferings that followed the destruction of the Bais HaMikdash. Indeed, the spiritual vitality of the era was the perfect demonstration of the *pasuk,* "They kneel and fall, and we stand up and are strong."[11] When the non-Jewish nations begin to fall, they go down forever. But we, although we are also brought down to our knees, eventually get up again and emerge stronger than we ever were before.

With the destruction of the Bais HaMikdash, the defeat at Beitar and the annihilation of so many of the great Sages of that time, it seemed as if the Jewish people were descending into miserable obscurity that would end with complete assimilation and ruin. Instead, less than one hundred and fifty years after the destruction of the Bais HaMikdash, because of the farsighted leadership of Rabbi Yehudah HaNasi, the Jewish nation arose from the ashes to achieve spiritual heights of almost unparalleled dimensions.

Chapter
2

---

11. *Tehillim, 20:9.*

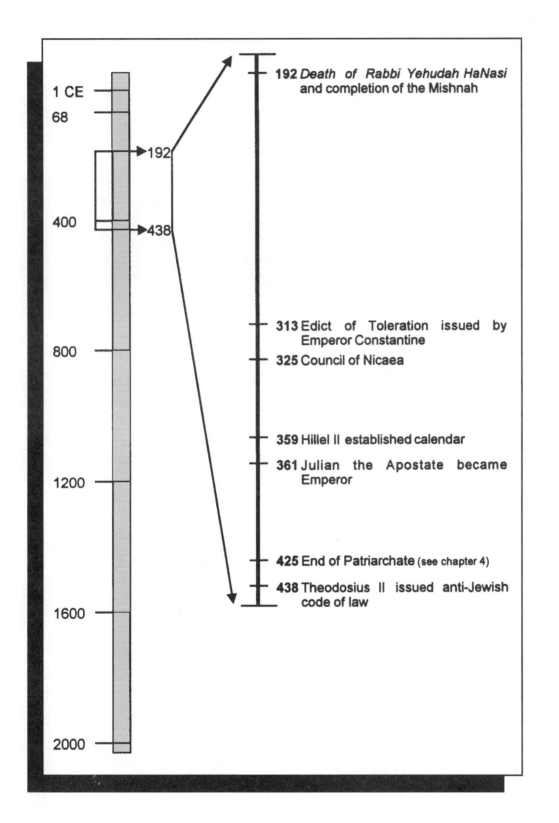

1 CE

68

192

400

438

800

1200

1600

2000

192 *Death of Rabbi Yehudah HaNasi* and completion of the Mishnah

313 Edict of Toleration issued by Emperor Constantine

325 Council of Nicaea

359 Hillel II established calendar

361 Julian the Apostate became Emperor

425 End of Patriarchate (see chapter 4)

438 Theodosius II issued anti-Jewish code of law

One Fades,
One Rises:

The Decline
of Jewish
Life in
Eretz Yisrael

The Talmud relates that when the time of Rabbi Yehudah HaNasi's death drew near, he summoned all the Sages of Israel to his home in the mountain town of Tzippori (Sepphoris). The Sages, concerned about the impending loss of the beloved "Rebbi," as Rabbi Yehudah is referred to by the Mishnah, were anxious to hear his sage advice and wise words. How were they to carry on their task as leaders of the Jewish people after Rabbi Yehudah HaNasi was gone?

"Although my son Shimon is the greater scholar," Rebbi told them, "my oldest son Gamliel shall be the Nasi; and Chanina bar Chama shall be head of the Yeshivah."[1]

With these words, Rebbi instituted the structure of Jewish leadership for the next two centuries, following a pattern that had been in existence much earlier when the rabbinical leadership was divided into Zuggos: The Nasi and the Av Bais Din (as the Mishnah in tractate *Chagigah* 2:2 enumerates). Rabban Gamliel, who was the first-born son and a man of fine character, performed the *administrative functions*; he was the political leader and chief legislator, convening the Sanhedrin whenever necessary. Chanina bar Chama, on the other hand, took over the *rabbinical functions* of the Yeshivah. With Rabbi Yehudah HaNasi's farsighted decision to separate the role of Nasi from the Torah leadership of the Yeshivah, he created a safeguard that would protect the Yeshivah during the turbulent years that lay ahead.

For two hundred years after Rebbi's death, the Jews in Eretz Yisrael suffered from the capricious predilections of the Roman Emperors. At times, Rome treated Judaism with benevolence; then, with a new ruler on the throne, the Jews would

1. *Kesubos*, 103 a-b.

be subjected to fierce persecutions. In addition, war between Rome and Persia remained constant, and the Roman Empire, in general, remained corrupt and unstable. During this turbulent period, the Nasi continued to hold his leadership, but the Nesius (Patriarchate) eventually diminished to the role of a figurehead, with mere political status and no real association with the great Yeshivos of Eretz Yisrael. Torah leadership rightfully went to the outstanding Amoraim, who authored the Talmud Yerushalmi.

Now, however, a new threat loomed on the horizon. Christianity, which had functioned as a relatively minor sect, suddenly bloomed into a widespread religion that went on to engulf the entire Roman Empire. With the growth of Christianity, the life of the Jews in Eretz Yisrael suffered a severe blow, from which it would never truly recover.

The Spreading Sect

Christianity began as a small, obscure sect that considered itself a branch of Judaism. The early Christians kept Shabbos as their day of rest, followed most of the Jewish calendar and kept many of the mitzvos of the Torah. In fact, to the outside world, they were virtually indistinguishable from religious Jews. However, they claimed that the Messiah had already arrived. Of course, there was a slight problem—their "Savior" had not fulfilled any of the prophecies concerning *Mashiach* before his death by crucifixion.

The Christians solved this nettlesome problem by the idea of a "Second Coming" when he would "complete his mission." They were vigorously denounced by the Sages of their day, but the Christian sect persisted in relative obscurity for some time.

All this changed when a Jew named Saul of Tarsus, later known as Paul, came upon the scene. Charismatic, energetic and dynamic, Paul felt dissatisfied with Christianity's obscurity. He and his faction felt that the pagans were repelled by the sect's similarity to Judaism. Eventually, Paul decided that it would be necessary to reshape the Christian religion to make it more palatable to others: once Christianity became more alluring and interesting, it would be much simpler to missionize and gain converts.

Paul set about modifying the Christian religion, altering various elements to make the new doctrine more attractive. He dropped the mitzvos, incorporated Greek philosophy, and added practices from the popular pagan rites of his day. Then he took to the road, preaching the revamped Christian religion throughout Asia Minor, Syria, Greece, and Italy.

Paul's efforts proved largely successful. His lively propaganda, as well as his magnetic personality, helped him attract hundreds of

Paul decided that it would be necessary to reshape the Christian religion to make it more palatable to others.

thousands of followers. However, his attempts to convert his fellow Jews to Christianity met, for the most part, with utter failure. Disgusted by his lack of success, Paul largely abandoned his attempts to missionize among the Jews and stopped using synagogues as his primary bases during his travel. Instead, embittered by the Jewish rejection of Christianity, he turned against the Jews with a vengeance. Paul's attitude gradually evolved into the typical enmity of the Christian for the Jew, as Christian leaders proclaimed that the Jews deserved endless persecution for killing their Messiah.

The Roman Empire was antagonistic to Christianity at first. Alarmed by the growing numbers of new Christians, Rome instituted various persecutions and abuses; for example, one of the more popular entertainments of the day was watching a Christian prisoner fight off a starving lion with his bare hands. As time passed, however, Christianity swelled in popularity, eventually becoming the official religion of the new Roman Empire.

Emperor Constantine played a major role in legalizing Christianity in Rome. He did not actually convert until shortly before his death in 337, but he helped establish Christianity throughout the Roman Empire. In 313, he issued the Edict of Toleration in Rome. Twelve years later, in the year 325, a Church Council was convened, with his approval, in the city of Nicaea. The Christian leaders, determined to cut the final, lingering ties with Judaism, decided to move the Christian day of rest to Sunday. They also separated the celebration of Easter from the Jewish Passover. In addition, laws were instituted that discouraged the intermingling of Jews and

Paul's efforts proved largely successful. His lively propaganda, as well as his magnetic personality, helped him attract hundreds of thousands of followers.

Rome instituted various persecutions and abuses; for example, one of the more popular entertainments of the day was watching a Christian prisoner fight off a starving lion with his bare hands.

Chapter
3

One Fades, One Rises:

The Decline of Jewish Life in Eretz Yisrael

> *They wanted to ensure that no Christian would want to have any association with Jews, much less become influenced by them and convert to Judaism.*

> *Judaism was officially branded as a detestable, sacrilegious way of life. Inciting the populace against Jews was the next step.*

Christians, especially through the limitations of Jewish rights.

The Christian leaders viewed Judaism as a dangerous rival. They wanted to ensure that no Christian would want to have any association with Jews, much less become influenced by them and convert to Judaism. With this purpose in mind, a series of demeaning, humiliating edicts were issued against the Jews. Jews could not hold government office; they were forbidden to interfere with Christians; they were not allowed to convert pagans to Judaism; they could not own Christian slaves; and intermarriage between Jews and Christians was forbidden and punishable by death.

With these decrees, Judaism was officially branded as a detestable, sacrilegious way of life. Inciting the populace against Jews was the next step. Emboldened by having the law on their side, Christian leaders encouraged their followers to attack and plunder the hapless Jews. Many prominent Yeshivos in Eretz Yisrael were forced to close their doors, and scholars departed in ever-increasing numbers for Babylonia (Bavel).

In spite of the increasing harassment and persecutions, the Sages of that time greeted Christianity's final split from Judaism with a sigh of relief. The wide gap ensured that innocent Jews could not be misled into thinking that the Christians were a Jewish sect. The Jew thanks Hashem for setting him apart from those who err; the Sages were relieved to know that the Christians were completely estranged from Judaism, setting the Jews apart from their Christian counterparts.

Unfortunately, life in Eretz Yisrael grew steadily worse. With Emperor Constantine's death, his son Constantius took the throne. During his rule, it was decreed that Jews could not own any slaves at all,

including pagans. The economic and social system of the time made slave labor an absolute necessity; by forbidding Jews to utilize slaves, Constantius sought to impoverish the Jewish population. This initial step to enforce economic legislation against the Jewish population is one with which the Jews have become all too familiar during the long years of exile. Through painful experience, the Jew knows that when Jews begin to be singled out, persecution is not far behind.

As Christianity increased in popularity, persecutions increased. A short respite occurred during the rule of Emperor Julianus (Julian the Apostate), who became Emperor in the year 361. He personally detested the Christian religion, and he not only restored citizenship rights to the Jews, but also offered to permit the Jews to rebuild the Bais HaMikdash. Unfortunately, Jewish hopes for a more peaceful life ended abruptly with Julianus' early death during a battle with Persian forces, and persecutions came back into full force.

The first massacre took place during the rule of Emperor Theodosius II, early in the fifth century. Mobs of Christians stormed synagogues, convinced that Jews were an inferior people "cursed by G-d" for stubbornly refusing to embrace Christianity as their religion. The anti-Jewish disease which had sprung up in Alexandria spread rapidly throughout the Roman Empire.

> *The Jew thanks Hashem for setting him apart from those who err; the Sages were relieved to know that the Christians were completely estranged from Judaism.*

With the legal code he ratified in the year 438, Theodosius II excluded Jews from holding any public office at all. The code also included a wide array of anti-Jewish regulations and biases. A pattern was forming that would become the basis of medieval European law. Governments would create two different sets of laws, one for the general population and one that applied to the Jews.

Another important change occurred in the fifth century that profoundly affected the Jews of Italy. In 455, Rome was sacked by the Vandals, and henceforth the Roman Empire ceased to exist. The center of the former Roman Empire gravitated to the East, to Constantinople, where Byzantine Roman Emperors continued to rule. They were gradually dominated by Moslems of that region, both of whom shared violent hatred of Jews. The authority of the Pope, who still ruled from Rome, over spiritual leaders of the Christians, continued to weaken for hundreds of years.

Despite the relief at the official separation between Christianity and Judaism, the increasingly difficult living conditions began to take their toll on the Jews. The suffering and persecutions played a major role in diminishing the office of Nasi, and Torah learning in Eretz Yisrael as a whole deteriorated as scholars fled to Babylonia to escape the harassment of

In 455, Rome was sacked by the Vandals, and henceforth the Roman Empire ceased to exist. The center of the former Roman Empire gravitated to the East, to Constantinople, where Byzantine Roman Emperors continued to rule.

the Roman Empire. Once again, the Sages showed the wisdom and fortitude necessary to take steps to preserve Torah life in the face of Jewish suffering. This time, it was Hillel II, one of the last Nesiim, who seized an opportune moment to maintain one of the basic requisites for the Jewish religion—the calendar.

Fixing Times

The angels asked Hashem, "When is Rosh HaShanah?"

"Why do you ask me?" Hashem replied. "Go and inquire of those who live below."

Midrash Yalkut, Shemos 191

The Torah grants the Sanhedrin the power to fix the times and months of the Jewish calendar. There were halachic considerations that sometimes caused a delay in declaring the new month, but generally, the exact date of Rosh Chodesh each month was dependent on three factors: the *molad*, the mathematical calculation of the exact moment of the reappearance of the moon; the testimony of two eyewitnesses before a court of three qualified judges; the subsequent proclamation of Rosh Chodesh by the Sanhedrin or, more precisely, by the Nasi.

With the destruction of Beitar and the increasing persecutions in Eretz Yisrael, the Sanhedrin was often unable to function officially. Still, despite the tremendous difficulties involved, the Sanhedrin managed to maintain the declaration of each new month. But as Christian persecution became more and more severe, it became increasingly difficult to continue proclaiming the New Month.

Hillel II, a thirteenth generation descendant of Hillel the Elder, was one of the last Nesiim. He had the foresight to realize that the end of the Sanhedrin and its ability to proclaim the new month

The authority of the Pope, who still ruled from Rome, over spiritual leaders of the Christians, continued to weaken for hundreds of years.

Generally, the exact date of Rosh Chodesh each month was dependent on three factors.

Chapter
3

*"On the basis of
the information
that we received, it
is as if the Bais
Din in Eretz
Yisrael established
for all time when
the new month
should begin and
on which day Yom
Tov should be."*

was imminent. In 359, during the brief respite of the benign rule of Emperor Julianus, Hillel II seized the opportunity to establish a permanent calendar.

The Mishnah in tractate *Rosh HaShanah* describes the method used to publicize the proclamation of the new month in distant locations, especially in Bavel where the majority of Jewish communities had been established after the *Churban Bayis Rishon.* In the age prior to telegraphy and wireless, it was nevertheless possible to send messages by lighting torches on the mountaintops connecting Eretz Yisrael with the lower levels of Bavel, as long as the Sanhedrin in Eretz Yisrael was able to function.

The concept of using mathematical calculations to determine the new month was not unknown. For generations, the spiritual leaders of Klal Yisrael had been using mathematical calculations prior to the summoning of witnesses to validate their testimony. In addition, Jews in distant countries, who could not rely on timely notification by the Sanhedrin, made widespread use of mathematics. The Talmud remarks that, even before Hillel II established the calendar, "we in Babylonia know exactly when the new month begins."[2]

Hillel II's contribution was not the concept of using mathematics to establish the calendar; this was already well-known. What Hillel II had the sagacity to do was to establish an official calendar for future generations. In addition, he actually sanctified the "Heads" of all future months, instead of depending on month-to month calculations and sanctifications.

The Rambam, in his *Mishneh Torah,* explains:

"The fact that we now calculate in each and every part of the world by mathematical rules when Rosh Chodesh should fall, and when the Yomim Tovim should come out, should not be considered as if we, by our own authority, establish the calendar...this being the exclusive right of those who live in Eretz Yisrael....By what right, then, do we rely on our own calculation? It is because we know that the original leaders of the Sanhedrin relied on those formulas. We share the knowledge of these principles with them. On the basis of the information that we received, it is as if the Bais Din in Eretz Yisrael established for all times when the new month should begin and on which day Yom Tov should be."[3]

In the year 359, Hillel II convened the Sanhedrin. Somberly, they discussed the situation and conceded that Hillel II was right: it would not be long before the Sanhedrin would be unable to declare the new months. Using the mathematical calculations that had been in use for generations, they declared that every Rosh Chodesh, Yom Tov, leap year, and regular year, from that year on, was officially proclaimed, provided the astronomical and halachic guidelines were met. The guideline, which has a nineteen year cycle, has served us well up to our time and, except for an abortive Karaite attempt in 921, has never been disputed.

Hillel II's sad prediction that the Sanhedrin was destined to be disbanded was all too true. With Julian's death, the persecutions resumed, quickly reaching intolerable levels. In the year 425, the Byzantine Empire officially abolished the office of Nasi. Most of the remaining Sages of the Talmud Yerushalmi fled to the Yeshivos of Babylonia to continue the holy work of producing the Talmud.

---

2. *Baitzah,* 4b.

3. *Hilchos Kiddush HaChodesh,* 5:13.

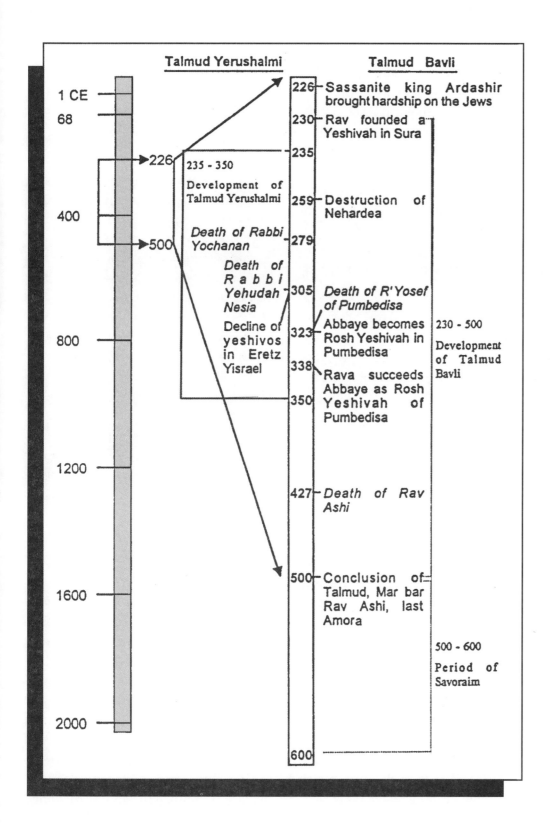

Talmud Yerushalmi

Talmud Bavli

1 CE

68

226

400

500

800

1200

1600

2000

226 — Sassanite king Ardashir brought hardship on the Jews

230 — Rav founded a Yeshivah in Sura

235

235 – 350

Development of Talmud Yerushalmi

259 — Destruction of Nehardea

Death of Rabbi Yochanan

279

Death of Rabbi Yehudah Nesia

305 — *Death of R'Yosef of Pumbedisa*

Decline of yeshivos in Eretz Yisrael

323 — Abbaye becomes Rosh Yeshivah in Pumbedisa

338 — Rava succeeds Abbaye as Rosh Yeshivah of Pumbedisa

350

230 – 500

Development of Talmud Bavli

427 — *Death of Rav Ashi*

500 — Conclusion of Talmud, Mar bar Rav Ashi, last Amora

500 – 600

Period of Savoraim

600

Chapter
4

The Mishnah, together with the recorded work of the Amoraim, known as the Gemara, comprises the entire Talmud.

The Jewish nation is not alone in recognizing the Talmud as a sacred work that lies at the very center of the Jewish religion. Throughout the ages, anti-Semites have crowned their acts of hatred with the destruction of the Talmud. From the public burning of thousands of handwritten volumes of the Talmud in Paris in 1242, to the ban against printing the Talmud that lasted for centuries in Europe, to the public burning of countless volumes of the Talmud by the Nazis in modern times, enemies have always sought to prevent the Jews from learning and growing through the study of the Talmud.

The Tannaim, teachers of the Mishnah, bequeathed a great treasure of teachings to Klal Yisrael. Our precious legacy includes not only the six orders of the Shass, compiled by Rabbi Yehudah HaNasi, but also the *Toseftos* and *Breisos* (a collection of teachings which were not included in the Mishnah) as well as three halachic books on the Torah: the *Mechilta* on *Shemos*, the *Sifra* (also known as *Toras Kohanim*) on *Vayikra,* and the *Sifrei* on *Bamidbar* and *Devarim.*

With the passing of the era of the Tannaim, the Amoraim, the teachers of the latter Talmudic era, took up the burden of guiding and teaching the Jewish people. The term "Amora" is derived from the word *amar,* "to speak," and is defined as "speaker." The Amoraim accepted the great task of assembling the teachings of the Tannaim and explaining them so that the Torah could continue to guide the daily lives of our people. In addition, the Amoraim recorded the rabbinic legislation and the customs which became binding upon world Jewry. This portion of the Talmud is commonly referred to as Halachah.

Another section of the Talmud deals with explanations of Tanach and stories with an underlying moral lesson. Collectively referred to as the Aggadah, these insights are interspersed with the halachic discussions and form a monumental lesson in proper living and a better understanding of our past.

The Mishnah, together with the recorded work of the Amoraim, known as the Gemara, comprise the entire Talmud. The Talmud remains the primary subject of Jewish learning to this day.

To the unpracticed eye, the Mishnah and the Gemara may seem to be outdated relics of the ancient past. In reality, nothing could be further from the truth. From the moment we open up the pages of the Gemara, we come to the realization that the teachings of the Tannaim and Amoraim are as amazingly relevant in modern times as they were almost fifteen hundred years ago. The compilers of the Gemara are not illustrious authors who wrote a book centuries before our time; they are our contemporary leaders and guides, the mentors to whom we turn for counsel in every aspect of our lives.

Talmud Yerushalmi

Immediately after Rabbi Yehudah HaNasi completed the formation of the Mishnah, the Amoraim began the monumental work of producing the Talmud. It started simultaneously in the two existing Torah centers, Eretz Yisrael and Babylonia. The edition of the Talmud that was produced by the Yeshivos in Eretz Yisrael is commonly known as Talmud Yerushalmi, "the Jerusalem Talmud," even though the Yeshivos had fled the devastation of Yerushalayim and were located in other cities such as Tiberias and Tzippori.

Newcomers to the Talmud are sometimes baffled by the seemingly random use of rabbinic titles. A terse statement of Chazal (quoted in the Aruch under Abbaye) clarifies this issue: "Greater than 'Rav' is 'Rabbi', greater than 'Rabbi' is 'Rabban', greater than 'Rabban' is his (own) name."

Those who were on the highest level of scholarship are simply called by their names (Hillel, Shammai, etc.). Because they were such great scholars, it was impossible to find a fitting title to honor them, just as no titles were given in Tanach to the prophets.

Rabban was given as the title to those who almost reached this degree of scholarship, such as the Nesiim of the Sanhedrin (Rabban Gamliel, etc.).

Rabbi was the title given to anyone who received *semichah* in Eretz Yisrael, while the Amoraim who lived in Babylonia were given the lowest title, *Rav.* On occasion, a visiting Amora from Babylonia would receive *semichah* in Eretz Yisrael and be honored with the title "Rabbi."

The foremost scholar of the second generation of Amoraim in Eretz Yisrael was Rabbi Yochanan ben Naphcha. Despite his young age—he was only seventeen at the time of the passing of Rabbi Yehudah HaNasi—his brilliance was such that he had been admitted to the Yeshivah at a very young age, and he had the privilege of spending a few years under Rebbi's tutelage. Rabbi Yochanan's teachings are found throughout the Talmud Bavli, but his main contribution was in the development of the Talmud Yerushalmi. He played such an important role in this project, that the Rambam (twelfth century) refers to Rabbi Yochanan as the author of the Talmud Yerushalmi.

Rabbi Yochanan's partner and colleague in the leadership of the Yeshivah of Tzippori was Rabbi Shimon ben Lakish (Resh Lakish). But when Rabbi Yochanan and Resh Lakish first met, Torah was the last thing on Resh Lakish's mind. On the contrary, Resh Lakish utilized his exceptional strength and athletic skill to pursue a highly successful career as a highway robber!

When Resh Lakish encountered Rabbi Yochanan, the Torah Sage turned to the thief and urged him to use his strength for Torah, offering to give Resh Lakish his sister's hand in marriage if he repented. Resh Lakish agreed to Rabbi Yochanan's proposal. Rabbi Yochanan taught him and helped Resh Lakish become a great scholar, and the promised marriage to Rabbi Yochanan's sister took place.

Rabbi Yochanan, said to be the only one left of the "beauty of Jerusalem,"[1] soon

Title Page of Talmud Yerushalmi

1. *Bava Metzia,* 84a.

The foremost scholar of the second generation of Amoraim in Eretz Yisrael was Rabbi Yochanan ben Naphcha.

Chapter

4

Only the central Yeshivah in Eretz Yisrael was given the honored title Mesifta, a place designated not only for Talmudic discussion but also for the institution of new laws.

became the leading Sage of all Jewry. Resh Lakish, the former highway robber whose potential Rabbi Yochanan had recognized and developed, was constantly at his side. The two engaged in spirited debates on every point. Ulla, one of the Amoraim, said of Resh Lakish that one who saw him in the Bais Midrash, taking apart every problem and expounding on it from every angle, would think that he was uprooting mountains and grinding them against each other.[2]

Although Rabbi Yochanan was at least ten years older than Resh Lakish, he outlived him by several years. However, Rabbi Yochanan never really recovered from the death of his beloved brother-in-law and study partner; he tore his clothes and wept constantly, crying out: "Where are you, ben Lakish? Where are you, ben Lakish?" The Chachamim feared for his mind and found no way to cure him—so they prayed for him to die.

For five generations, from approximately 200 to 350, the Sages of Eretz Yisrael and Babylonia developed the Talmud. It is assumed that the Yeshivos in Eretz Yisrael studied the same *masechtos* as their counterparts in Babylonia, but unfortunately, the Talmud Yerushalmi has not come down to us in its entirety. In our current editions, the *masechtos* of *Seder Kodashim* and *Seder Taharos* are missing. The work on the Talmud Yerushalmi was inhibited by the constant attacks against the Jews instigated by the Christian clergy, and the Yeshivos of Eretz Yisrael were eventually forced to close. With the flight of the remaining Chachamim to Babylonia, the Talmud Yerushalmi was left incomplete; the Sages of Eretz Yisrael, unlike the Amoraim in Babylonia, did not have the chance to render halachic decisions at the end of their debates.

2. *Sanhedrin*, 24a.

This decision would thus be left for future generations.

Even before the flight of the Sages of Eretz Yisrael to the refuge of Babylonia, the two Torah centers were not isolated from one another. We find frequent reference in the Talmud to Amoraim who traveled "up" from Babylonia to Eretz Yisrael to present problems to their colleagues, as well as Amoraim who went "down" to Babylonia to consult with the Babylonian Sages. The Sages of Babylonia yielded their authority to Eretz Yisrael, which was represented by its Sanhedrin and its Nasi. Only the central Yeshivah in Eretz Yisrael was given the honored title *Mesifta,* a place designated not only for Talmudic discussion but also for the institution of new laws. The Yeshivos in Babylonia were called *Sidrah,* to distinguish them from the *Mesifta* of Eretz Yisrael. There was no rivalry between the two Torah centers or between individuals. The arguments and debates that raged throughout the Yeshivos were *lishmah,* for the sake of Torah only. There was no animosity if two people disagreed, only respect, mutual appreciation, and the common search for the truth.

Talmud Bavli

The Sages of Eretz Yisrael who fled to Babylonia found a thriving community. Jews had been living there for over six centuries, since the first exile of Nebuchadnezzar. Unlike the Jews in Eretz Yisrael, who suffered the persecutions of the Christians and were forced to disband the Sanhedrin, the Jewish people in Babylonia were granted a great deal of independence by the Babylonian government. The political head of the Jewish community was given the title *Reish Galusa,* "Leader of the Exile." He was a descendant of Yechonya, and his royal lineage and authority were acknowledged by the Babylonian government.

However, things in Babylonia took a turn for the worse in the year 226. The Parthian Dynasty, which had ruled benevolently for over three hundred years, was overthrown. Ardashir, the new king from the family of the Sassanids (Neo-Persian), proved to be a harsh and intolerant ruler. Ardashir belonged to a sect of fire-worshipers, and the new regime passed laws which prohibited the Jews from lighting any fire for religious reasons, including the kindling of Chanukah candles. Ardashir also decreed that immersion in a *mikveh* was against the law; he ordered the destruction of synagogues; he forbade the eating of meat unless part of the animal was brought to the fire-worshipers' altars; he denied permission for burial in the ground and demanded that bodies already buried be exhumed.

Ardashir's cruel regime lasted for fifteen long years. Despite the suffering and intolerance, however, Torah learning thrived.

The religious leadership in Babylonia remained in the hands of the Roshei Yeshivah of the central institutions of learning in Babylonia, separate from the *Reish Galusa*. Until the death of Rabbi Yehudah Nesia, Rebbi's grandson and the last of the Nesiim to combine Torah and leadership in Eretz Yisrael, the Sages of Babylonia yielded to the authority of the Amoraim in Eretz Yisrael. But with Rabbi Yehudah Nesia's passing in 305, the prestige of leadership in Eretz Yisrael declined, and the Roshei Yeshivah of Babylonia no longer deferred to the Sages of Eretz Yisrael in

> *He was a descendant of Yechonya, and his royal lineage and authority were acknowledged by the Babylonian government.*

matters of Halachah. The Batai Din, the central courts of justice and legislation, were considered to be in Babylonia, and the term *Mesifta* was adopted for the main Bavli Yeshivah.

Seven generations of Amoraim, noted in pairs, contributed to the development of the Talmud Bavli. Those marked with an asterisk are discussed in greater depth.

*1) Rav and Shmuel
  2) Rav Huna and Rav Chisda
*3) Rabbah and Rav Yosef
*4) Abbaye and Rava
  5) Rav Nachman bar Yitzchak and Rav Pappa
*6) Ravina and Rav Ashi
  7) Mar bar Rav Ashi and Ravina II

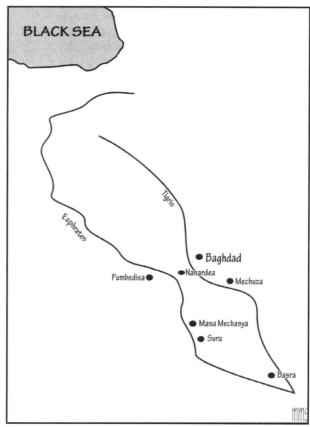

Major Jewish communities in Babylonia during the Talmudic Era

> *Ardashir belonged to a sect of fire-worshipers, and the new regime passed laws which prohibited the Jews from lighting any fire for religious reasons.*

Chapter 4

He was a skilled physician, mathematician and astronomer who could prepare the calendar by his own calculation; he once remarked: "I am as familiar with the paths in Heaven (the constellations) as with the streets of Nehardea."

Rav and Shmuel

In the year 230, an eminent scholar returned to the city of Nehardea near the Euphrates River, the home of the central Yeshivah in Babylonia. He had spent several years studying in Eretz Yisrael with his uncle Rabbi Chiya and Rabbi Yehudah HaNasi. His name was Rabbi Abba Aricha ("the Tall One"), but he was known affectionately and reverently simply as Rav.

Rav returned to Nehardea shortly before the death of its Rosh Yeshivah, Rabbi Shila. After Rabbi Shila's passing, Rav was offered the position. Out of respect for his close friend Shmuel, Rav declined the position. Instead, he founded a new Yeshivah in Sura, a city farther to the south.

The two Yeshivos remained in close contact with each other. Shmuel, who accepted the position of Rosh Yeshivah in

Title Page of Talmud Bavli

Nehardea, was younger than Rav, but he was not only a brilliant Torah scholar but also proficient in the field of science. He was a skilled physician, mathematician and astronomer who could prepare the calendar by his own calculation; he once remarked: "I am as familiar with the paths in Heaven (the constellations) as with the streets of Nehardea."[3] The two Roshei Yeshivah engaged in fierce Talmudical debate, and in most cases on record, they did not agree with each other. Students of the Talmud relish the few instances where the Talmud states "Both Rav and Shmuel agree in such a case."

As a rule, in cases that involve *issur* and *heter,* what is permitted or forbidden, the opinion of Rav is followed, as he is considered the greater authority in those cases. However, in financial matters, Shmuel's opinion prevails; as the foremost judge in Nehardea, a city bursting with business activities, Shmuel had more experience ruling on financial matters than Rav.

After Rav's death, Shmuel became the spiritual leader of all the Jews in Babylonia. Many of Rav's former students journeyed to Nehardea to study under Shmuel, although the Yeshivah in Sura continued to thrive for hundreds of years.

With King Ardashir's death in 241, the Jews breathed a sigh of relief. King Shapur I, Ardashir's successor, was on amiable terms with Shmuel and anxious to obtain Jewish money to help finance his war against Rome. In an effort to win the Jews to his cause, Shapur eased the restrictions and prevented the slaughter of Jews living in newly captured territories.

Unfortunately, the respite for the Yeshivah of Nehardea proved all too short. Just a few years after Shmuel's death, in the

3. *Berachos,* 58b.

year 259, the small Arab principality of Palmyra invaded the Persian Empire, and the Jews fought alongside the Persians in an effort to repel the invasion. At the battle's end, the Jews of Nehardea found themselves in occupied territory, and the Palmyran soldiers fell upon the inhabitants of the largely Jewish city with a vengeance. Nehardea was razed to the ground; the illustrious Yeshivah was utterly destroyed.

With the shining light of the Nehardea Yeshivah gone, a new star rose on the horizon. The Yeshivah of Pumbedisa, which had been founded by Rabbi Yehudah, an outstanding student of Shmuel, grew in importance to become a major center of Torah for over eight hundred years.

Rabbah and Rav Yosef

Rabbah and Rav Yosef emerged as the leaders of the next generation. Their Talmudic arguments are found throughout the Gemara. Rav Yosef had such a phenomenal memory that he was called *Sinai,* for all the Mishnayos and Breisos were as clear to him as when Moshe first taught them at Mount Sinai. Rabbah's memory was not the equal of Rav Yosef's, but he had a brilliant analytical mind with which he could reconstruct any *halachah* that might have been forgotten. His tremendous intellectual powers earned him the name *Oker Harim,* "Uprooter of Mountains."

With the death of Rabbi Yehudah, the founder and Rosh Yeshivah of Pumbedisa, the Amoraim found themselves in a quandary. Both Rabbah and Rav Yosef seemed equally qualified for the position. The Chachamim who were authorized to make the decision sent a message to the Sages in Eretz Yisrael,

who were still considered the highest authority at that time.

"Who is preferable?" they asked. *"Sinai or Oker Harim?"*

The Amoraim in Eretz Yisrael sent back their reply, short and to the point: *"Sinai is better."*

Deferring to the judgment of the *Mesifta,* the Babylonian Sages offered the position of Rosh Yeshivah to Rav Yosef. Rav Yosef, however, declined the position, and Rabbah became the leader of the Yeshivah in Pumbedisa. Rabbah held the position for twenty-two years. After his passing, Rav Yosef took over, serving for two-and-a-half years as undisputed leader of the famous academy.[4]

Abbaye and Rava

Rav Yosef died in the year 323. With his passing, Pumbedisa found itself without a Rosh Yeshivah for over two years. During that time, Pumbedisa saw a huge influx of scholars who were forced to flee the brutal persecutions perpetrated by the Christians in Eretz Yisrael. The Yeshivah could not help being changed by the new group of Sages that swelled its ranks. From that time on, the Amoraim in Babylonia are referred to as *Basrai,* "the later ones." The Shulchan Aruch states as a general rule, *hilchesa kebasrai,* "the final decision is the one determined by the later generations."[5]

Rabbeinu Yitzchak Alfasi, an eleventh century Rishon known as the Rif, suggested that with the Sages of Eretz Yisrael absorbed into the great Torah centers of Babylonia, their opinions should be incorporated into the Talmudic discussions. Thus, the Talmud Bavli has the advantage that its halachic conclusions were reached after the Amoraim

---

4. *Berachos,* 64a.
5. *Choshen Mishpat,* 25:2, Rama.

The Yeshivah of Pumbedisa, which had been founded by Rabbi Yehudah, an outstanding student of Shmuel, grew in importance to become a major center of Torah for over eight hundred years.

gave full consideration to all opinions, both of the Sages of Babylonia and the Sages of Eretz Yisrael. In Sura and Pumbedisa, the celebrated Torah centers of Babylonia, the Talmud Bavli and Talmud Yerushalmi came face to face.

With the growing numbers of Amoraim fleeing to the havens of Babylonia, a committee of four of the greatest Sages of Eretz Yisrael and Babylonia was asked to choose the leader of the central Yeshivah of Pumbedisa. Two outstanding students of Rav Yosef, Abbaye and Rava, were considered equal to the task. It was up to the committee to determine which one should serve as Rosh Yeshivah.

Abbaye and Rava made enormous contributions to the clarification of the Oral Torah. The discussions between Rava and Abbaye, known as *havayos,* were a blend of all the singular qualities contained in the study of Gemara. They can be compared to an intellectual battle, a *shakla vetaria,* a rapid give-and-take of question and answer, proof and refutation, which lasts until either one side yields or a stalemate is declared. Abbaye, who lived to the age of sixty, is cited by the Gemara some fourteen hundred times. Rava, who lived past the age of seventy, is cited over two thousand times! These staggering figures help illustrate the tremendous role Abbaye and Rava played in shaping the Talmud Bavli.

Abbaye was chosen to head the Yeshivah of Pumbedisa. Nevertheless, the Gemara explains that the final halachic outcome always follows Rava's rulings, except in six specific cases known as *ye'al kegam,* a mnemonic acronym for the cases.

They can be compared to an intellectual battle, a shakla vetaria, a rapid give-and-take of question and answer, proof and refutation.

Despite the enormous contributions of Abbaye and Rava, the task of finalizing the Talmud Bavli was not yet complete. It would take another generation of Amoraim under the outstanding leadership of Rav Ashi to accomplish this goal.

Ravina and Rav Ashi

Our Sages said of Rav Ashi, "From the days of Rabbi Yehudah HaNasi until Rav Ashi we have not found Torah and greatness combined in one person."[6]

"From the days of Rabbi Yehudah HaNasi until Rav Ashi we have not found Torah and greatness combined in one person."

In the fifty-six years that Rav Ashi served as the head of Masa Mechasia, the Yeshivah that was considered a continuation of the great Sura Academy, he assembled all the Sages of his generation under his guidance. With his firm, guiding hand, the Amoraim organized all the material of the Talmud Bavli in the order in which we have it today. Rav Ashi was regarded as the leader of all Jewry, and with the Sassanid persecutions in abeyance, the nation enjoyed a renewed sense of stability and direction.

Rav Ashi and his colleague Ravina reviewed the entire Talmud Bavli in their daily sessions, generally completing a *masechta* every six months. The Talmud, as it was put into writing later on, is a product of those daily sessions.

A typical session began with a *mishnah* introducing the *halachah.* Ravina and Rav Ashi would check the origin of the *halachah* and discuss the various conflicting interpretations of the Tannaim and the previous Amoraim. A lively debate of the pros and cons of each opinion flew back and forth across the study

6. *Gittin,* 59a.

hall. Occasionally, Rav Ashi or one of his colleagues rendered a specific decision; most often, however, there was no final conclusion. The task of resolving the issue was left for future generations. With no final ruling, a student learning Gemara must plunge into the recorded debate with an active mental participation in the discussions, as if he were personally involved in the *shakla vetaria* of the opinions presented.

The End of an Era

After Rav Ashi died in the year 427, his students continued the monumental task of compiling and editing the Talmud. As with the closing of the Mishnah, there was no official act of Bais Din declaring the work of the Talmud officially ended, but the year 500 was accepted as the end of the Talmudic era. This meant that no one could make amendments to the Talmud after that time. No later individual opinion could be incorporated into the Gemara, and no one had the right to disagree with the opinions voiced by the Amoraim.

The year 500 was accepted as the end of the Talmudic era.

The Rambam, in his introduction to his *Mishneh Torah,* explains why this line of demarcation was universally accepted: "Thus it turns out that Ravina and Rav Ashi, the last of the Sages of Israel who put together the Oral Torah, made decrees and ordinances and established customs that were generally accepted wherever Jewish settlements existed all over the world. But after the Bais Din of Rav Ashi, who edited the Gemara, and after the days of his son [Mar bar Rav Ashi], who finished this task, the Jews were scattered all over the world. They reached the very ends of the inhabited parts of the continents and the distant islands. Worldwide turmoil disrupted communication, and traveling was edangered by marauding bandits.

"The result was a decrease in the study of Torah. Jews were no longer able to gather by the thousands in the big centers of learning. Rather, they studied alone or in small groups, relying on the assistance of the few individuals who were knowledgeable in the writings of the Sages and the intricacies of the Halachah.

"Therefore, any Bais Din that arose after the era of the Gemara could have no more than a limited authority. The decrees or customs it established covered only its own countrymen, for it could not command universal recognition. Such a Bais Din, consisting of only a small number of judges, could not compel the Jews of another country to abide by its decrees and accept its customs, nor could it impose on another Bais Din in a different location to pass similar ordinances for Jews under its jurisdiction."

The Savoraim (500-600 C.E.)

With the death of Mar bar Rav Ashi, the mantle of leadership fell to the successors of the Amoraim, called the Rabbanan Savorai, or Savoraim. In a famous letter written in the tenth century, HaRav Sherira Gaon describes the task of the Savoraim:

"The number of teachings grew from generation to generation until Ravina. After Ravina, Talmudic teaching ceased. Thereafter, although there were no further teachings added, there were the Savoraim who provided explanations that were almost like new teachings, for they resolved what had been left undecided."

The Savoraim did not have the authority to contradict anything an Amora had

"Jews were no longer able to gather by the thousands in the big centers of learning."

HaRav Sherira Gaon describes the task of the Savoraim.

> *The task they accepted was to summarize, to count the numbers of opinions in a dispute and, consequently, to determine the final halachah.*

sanctioned. The task they accepted was to summarize, to count the numbers of opinions in a dispute and, consequently, to determine the final *halachah.* With the invention of the printing press still many centuries in the future, copies of the Gemara needed to be handwritten, and such copies were both rare and expensive. Much of the study had to be memorized. The Savoraim provided valuable aids for students trying to remember the names of the participants in a halachic debate as well as the sequence of arguments and the proofs presented. In our editions of the Talmud today, the visible contributions of the Savoraim are marked by brackets, often containing only abbreviations.

In addition to their summarizations of the Gemara, the Savoraim wrote a number of additions to the text of the Gemara, mainly for clarification of marginal issues.

> *The Savoraim wrote a number of additions to the text of the Gemara, mainly for clarification of marginal issues.*

While the additions of the Savoraim are not visibly distinguishable from the main text, there are perceptible stylistic divergences that enable the accomplished student to determine where those additions are. For example, it is known that the beginnings of *maseches Pesachim* and *maseches Kiddushin* were added by the Savoraim.

For the most part, however, the Shass of Ravina and Rav Ashi was left intact. After *Chasimas HaTalmud,* the Sealing of the Talmud, anyone who wanted to determine *halachah lemaaseh,* what the *halachah* is in an actual case, had to do an enormous amount of research from the entire Shass before arriving at a conclusion. The tremendous responsibility of presenting *halachah lemaaseh* was undertaken by the Geonim, intensified during the eras of the Rishonim and Acharonim, and still continues to this day.

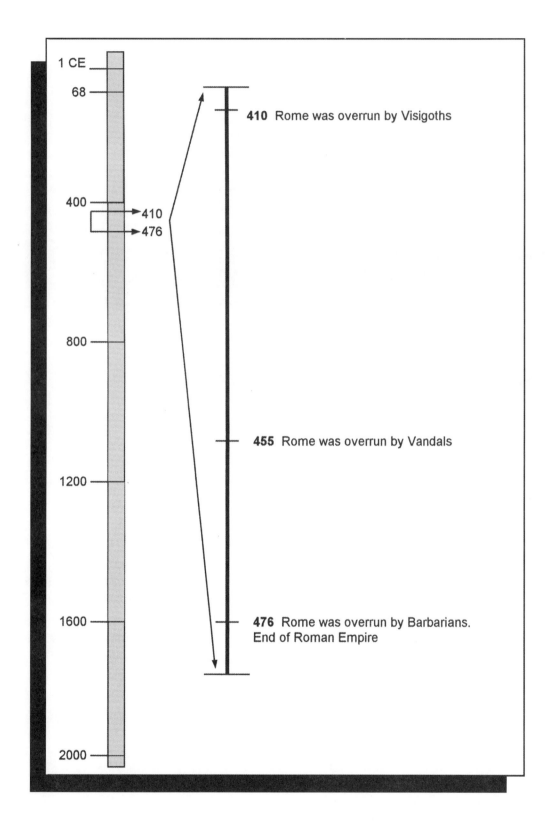

1 CE

68

400

410
476

800

1200

1600

2000

410 Rome was overrun by Visigoths

455 Rome was overrun by Vandals

476 Rome was overrun by Barbarians.
End of Roman Empire

Chapter

5

Dark Ages, Jewish Light

Books of European history often describe the thousand years following the completion of the Talmud as the "Dark Ages." The Roman Empire, which was already tottering under the weight of its own decadence and corruption, was sacked by the Visigoths in the year 410 and by the Vandals in the year 455. By the year 476, whatever was left of the Roman Empire had faded away. Without firm and enlightened leadership, the cultural advances that Europe had made in the past were forgotten and reversed. There were, of course, some few exceptions to this trend in isolated pockets of Europe, but on the whole, the Dark Ages were crude in comparison to the sophistication of earlier civilizations.

Under the rule of barbaric tribes, Europe entered a period of stagnation and ignorance.

Under the rule of barbaric tribes, Europe entered a period of stagnation and ignorance. The vast majority of the population labored beneath the harsh, medieval economic system of Feudalism. A small number of feudal lords spent their lives in an orgy of idle luxury, supported by the vassals who pledged their loyalty in return for land and protection. These vassals, in turn, ruled over the peasants, who were forced to pay enormous taxes to their despotic lords and eked out a miserable living barely above the starvation level. These peasants were known as serfs, and they were little more than slaves, tilling the land with no rights of ownership. Superstition and ignorance ran rampant. In time, the literacy of the general population dropped. Most peasants couldn't even write their own names. The standards of art, music and architecture declined: the serfs were not given the chance to achieve culture, while the nobles and feudal lords, with plenty of time and opportunity on their hands, chose instead to indulge in the savage pleasures of violence, hunting, and killing.

In stark contrast, during that selfsame period, the Jewish people enjoyed an era of enlightenment and knowledge. The Jews have been promised that "there would always be light in all their dwelling places."[1] The Dark Ages were no exception. While Europe wallowed in barbaric ignorance, the Jews experienced the uplifting period of the Geonim and achieved greatness in Torah and knowledge.

While Europe wallowed in barbaric ignorance, the Jews experienced the uplifting period of the Geonim and achieved greatness in Torah and knowledge.

During the time of the Geonim, the guidelines established by the Talmud Bavli were developed into specifics for the organization of communal life. For example, the Talmud instructed that *kehillos*, or communities, should be established, and the Geonim developed the structure of the *kehillah* as we know it. The Talmud gave specific directions for the order in which prayers should be said; the Geonim arranged the first complete siddur, containing the prayers that are still used by Jews all over the world today. A greater understanding of the era of the Geonim can be derived from the prayer *Yekum Purkan,* which is said every Shabbos in shul:

"May salvation arise from Heaven, grace, kindness, compassion, long life, abundant

---
1. *Shemos,* 10:23.

sustenance, heavenly assistance, physical health, lofty vision, living and surviving offspring, offspring who will neither interrupt nor cease from the words of the Torah, for our masters and Sages, the holy fellowship that are in Eretz Yisrael and that are in the Diaspora, *for the Leaders of the Exile, the Leaders of the Academies, the Leaders of the Torah Assemblies, the Judges at the Gateways,* and to all their students, and to all the students of their students, and to everyone who engages in Torah study."

This prayer was composed by the Babylonian Geonim in Aramaic, the spoken language of that country. It lists the revered authorities of the Jewish community at that time (italicized above). An explanation of the function of each office helps create an understanding of the Geonic Era.

The Leader of the Exile

The political head of the Jews in Babylonia was called the *Reish Galusa* ("Exilarch," or Leader of the Exile). In order to qualify for the office, he had to be a direct descendant of King Yechonya (thus a descendant of King David). His authority was recognized by the Babylonian government. The Babylonian Jews, who considered the *Reish Galusa* to be the fulfillment of the prophecy *"Lo yasur shevet miYehudah,* The scepter of the kingdom shall not be removed from [the tribe of] Yehudah,"[2] treated the Exilarch with great honor and respect.

On the Shabbos after a new *Reish Galusa* was appointed to office, a formal celebration took place:

"A high platform bedecked with colorful rugs was set up in the study hall. The *Rosh Haknesses,* the *Reish Galusa* and the

Roshei Yeshivah prayed in a separate room concealed from the public by heavy curtains. After the davening, the *Reish Galusa* ascended the platform and took his seat on a throne prepared for him there. The Roshei Yeshivah followed and bowed down before him.

"Afterwards, the two Geonim, Roshei Yeshivah of Sura and Pumbedisa, sat on both sides of the *Reish Galusa* and the chazzan stood in front of the platform to chant special blessings in honor of the *Reish Galusa.* At the end of each blessing a boys' choir sang 'Amen.' If the *Reish Galusa* was learned [occasionally he was not], he gave a lecture on the weekly portion. Otherwise, he would ask the Gaon to give the lecture on his behalf.

"During the Kaddish, an extra phrase was inserted which referred to the *Reish Galusa* with the words: *Uv'chayei n'siainu reish hagoloh.*

"Afterwards, the chazzan again blessed the *Reish Galusa* and the other spiritual leaders. He also mentioned by name all the communities which had given sizable donations to the Yeshivos of Bavel.

"At the reading of the Torah the *Reish Galusa* was given *shlishi,* but he did not go over to the bimah where the Torah was read. Instead, the Torah was brought over to him....At the conclusion of Mussaf, the entire congregation escorted the *Reish Galusa* to his home singing and dancing. The festivities lasted seven days, during which time members of the community alternately gave service to the Exilarch."[3]

Such honor and prestige was given to the *Reish Galusa* with the intention to uphold and carry on the image of the Kingdom of Israel, albeit in a dimin-

The Reish Galusa had to be a direct descendant of King Yechonya (thus a descendant of King David)

2. *Bereishis,* 49:10.

3. From *Toldos Am Yisrael,* by Harav Dr. M. Auerbach.

*The king promised
that he would
personally nurture
this plant and
guard it until it set
forth many roots
and was restored
to its former glory.*

ished form. Unfortunately, the person who held this high office was not necessarily worthy of it. There were occasional reports of corruption, misuse of power and displays of arrogance. By and large, however, the *Reish Galusa* bowed to the dictates of *daas Torah,* decisions based on a Torah view, and consulted with the Roshei Yeshivah in major decisions.

Among the duties of the *Reish Galusa* was the requirement to appoint a judge in every community and to remove them if they proved unfit. He also had to approve the Roshei Yeshivah of the great academies. Thus, the *Reish Galusa* exercised a great deal of spiritual influence on the Jewish population of Babylonia.

During the cruelest period of the Sassanid regime at the beginning of the seventh century, a king determined to permanently terminate the rule of the *Reish Galusa* by systematically killing every male descendant of David HaMelech. In this process of annihilation he rounded up the wives of the Davidic royal family who were with their children, to have them killed. At that moment, when it seemed that the House of David would be utterly destroyed, a remarkable, well-documented event took place:

Hashem took mercy on the seed of David, and a certain pregnant young woman whose husband had been murdered survived. One night, the king dreamt that he was in a palace garden filled with every delightful kind of fruit tree. Recognizing that this garden did not belong to him, the king became furious, and he began to destroy all the fruit trees. Upon inspecting the garden to make sure that he had utterly destroyed it, he came upon a root from which one

single branch was sprouting. He raised his axe to destroy the last remnant of the garden, but before he could strike the root, an old man of reddish complexion appeared. The man rebuked him sharply, snatched the axe from the king's hand and dealt him such a tremendous blow on the forehead that his whole face was covered with blood and he feared for his life.

The old man said, "You were not content to uproot the branches with their leaves still on them but you have returned to make sure that not one living branch survives. I mourn for this, my garden, which I have planted, tended, and raised for many years! And now there is only this single root left and you, in your wickedness, have raised your axe to destroy it? There is only one answer to your foul deeds, and that is to remove you from the Land of the Living and to eradicate your very memory."

The king began to plead for his life, "If only you will forgive me for what I have done!" Throwing himself at the feet of the old man, he promised that he would personally nurture this plant and guard it until it set forth many roots and was restored to its former glory.

When the king woke up, he found blood all over his face. He was disturbed and shaken by his experience, just as Pharaoh and Nebuchadnezzar had been when they awoke from their respective dreams, and he searched frantically for someone to interpret his dream. An old Jewish Sage, who had been imprisoned by the king in the course of his extermination campaign, was able to convince the king that the dream had been a Divine warning to save the last offspring of King David and to secure the future of the royal succession.

The king ordered that the expectant mother be brought to the palace together with her father and the rest of the family. When her term was complete, she bore a son who was named Bustenai, the Persian equivalent of "Fruit Garden," an obvious reference to the king's dream.

The boy grew up under the protection of the king. He displayed great brilliance of mind and outstanding personality traits. When he matured, he was appointed *Reish Galusa* with the backing of the king and he served in this capacity with great distinction.[4]

As the Persian Empire began to totter and collapse, the position of *Reish Galusa* also declined in power. While the loss of prestige served to injure Jewish pride, the *Reish Galusa's* decline proved to be of benefit to the Jews; the authority of Torah, as represented by the *Leaders of the Academies,* was increased to become the undisputed highest authority.

The Leaders of the Academies

While the *Reish Galusa* served as a source of pride and glory during the Geonic era, the true leaders of Babylonian Jewry were the heads of the two great Yeshivos of Sura and Pumbedisa. Young Jews from all parts of the country flocked to these institutions. They would study in the Yeshivos until they became mature rabbis, and then carry their Torah knowledge back to their places of origin.

With the decline of the *Reish Galusa,* the heads of the two Yeshivos served as the leaders of Babylonian Jewry. They appointed judges, local rabbis and

When her term was complete, she bore a son who was named Bustenai, the Persian equivalent of "Fruit Garden," an obvious reference to the king's dream.

teachers in various localities. In addition, they had the power of *cherem,* excommunication, a mechanism through which anyone willfully disobeying Torah law could be excluded from society. Eventually, each head of the two Yeshivos became known by the title "Gaon." All other rabbis were known simply by their names. The names of forty-two Geonim in Sura are recorded, but there is no list of the names of rabbis.

Leaders of Torah Assemblies

The Leaders of Torah Assemblies, known as *Roshei Kallah,* were chosen to teach during the *Yarchei Kallah.* The word *kallah* means "assembly"; the *Yarchei Kallah* were the two months of the year, Elul and Adar, when Jews from all corners of Babylonia gathered in the Yeshivos to learn, review and be tested on certain tractates of Gemara. At the end of the four-week session, questions of Jewish law sent to the Yeshivah were discussed, and the Roshei Yeshivah rendered a final decision. Before leaving for their homes, members of the assembly were assigned a new tractate of Gemara for home study during the next five months.

There is no record of the names of the *Roshei Kallah.* Like the *Judges at the Gateways,* no listing of their names has survived.

Judges at the Gateways

Among the offices appointed by the Geonim was that of *Dayanei di Bava,* Judges at the Gateways of the various localities, appointed to their position by the Roshei Yeshivah of Sura and Pumbedisa. These *dayanim* were supported by

The Yarchei Kallah were the two months of the year, Elul and Adar, when Jews from all corners of Babylonia gathered in the Yeshivos to learn, review, and be tested on certain tractates of Gemara.

---

4. From *Seder HaDoros,* by Rabbi Yechiel Halpern.

Chapter
5

a general tax levied on the community, but communal leaders could neither appoint nor dismiss them. It was customary for the leaders of the locale to write to the Roshei Yeshivah, expressing appreciation or voicing complaint about the appointees. If an appointment turned out badly, the Roshei Yeshivah would remove that *dayan* from his position.

For hundreds of years, the Jews of Babylonia reaped the benefits of Babylonian religious tolerance. But while the Jewish community was well-organized and thriving under the auspices of the Geonim, the world around them suffered from constant upheaval. Soon, the Jews found themselves struggling against a new force that would go on to change the entire world.

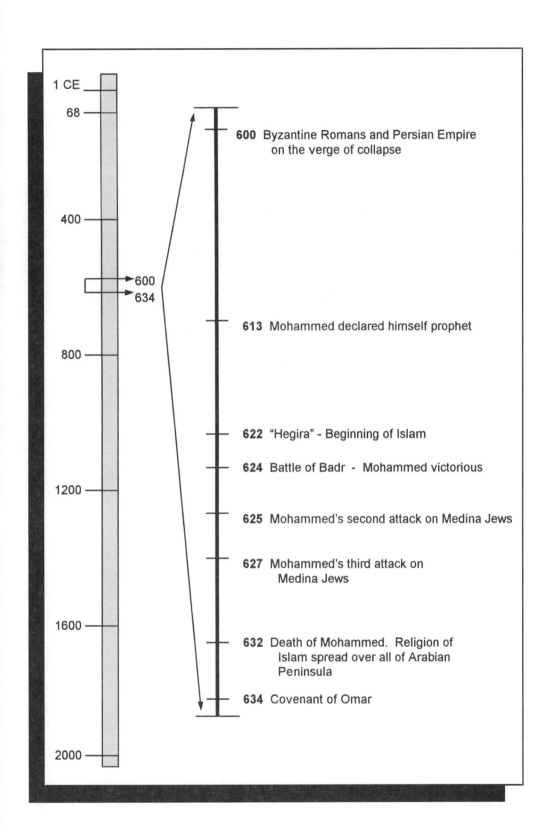

600 Byzantine Romans and Persian Empire
on the verge of collapse

613 Mohammed declared himself prophet

622 "Hegira" - Beginning of Islam

624 Battle of Badr - Mohammed victorious

625 Mohammed's second attack on Medina Jews

627 Mohammed's third attack on
Medina Jews

632 Death of Mohammed. Religion of
Islam spread over all of Arabian
Peninsula

634 Covenant of Omar

Chapter

6

The anti-Semitic trend that had begun with the Sassanid dynasty during the time of Rav and Shmuel continued, with the Jews persecuted by both the Byzantines and the Persians at the same time.

The years following the inexorable collapse of the Roman Empire were tumultuous, as Persia and Byzantium contended for supremacy. Beneath the shadow of constant warfare, life for the Jews of Babylonia took a steady turn for the worse. The anti-Semitic trend that had begun with the Sassanid dynasty during the time of Rav and Shmuel continued, with the Jews persecuted by both the Byzantines and the Persians at the same time.

Over the centuries of conflict, both empires were drastically weakened by the constant draining of resources. Thus, by the seventh century, Persia and Byzantium were helpless to contend with the new power that appeared on the horizon, ready to devour them both—the Muslims.

The Arabian Peninsula, which stretches over a vast territory of largely uninhabitable desert between Asia and Africa, had been largely ignored by the two rival powers of the Near East. After all, the Arab tribes who inhabited the peninsula were primitive nomads who never stayed long enough in one spot to establish a lasting, civilized community. Why pay any attention to them?

The most important city in the Arabian Peninsula was Mecca, situated on the western coast. Mecca had been considered a holy city from ancient times

Mecca had been considered a holy city from ancient times because of the existence of a black stone, called the Kaaba, which the Arab tribes believed came down to earth from G-d.

Persia and Byzantium were helpless to contend with the new power that appeared on the horizon, ready to devour them both—the Muslims.

because of the existence of a black stone, called the *Kaaba,* which the Arab tribes believed came down to earth from G-d. While each tribe had its own set of idols, they all worshiped the *Kaaba.* The Arab tribes were accustomed to making a six-week pilgrimage to Mecca each year. Each tribe would erect its own idols at the shrine, and, by mutual agreement, any warfare was temporarily suspended by truce during the period of the pilgrimage. The merchants of Mecca derived the bulk of their income from doing business with the pilgrims, living for the six-week period when pilgrims streamed into the city.

Some of the Arab tribes considered themselves to be descendants of Yishmael, and greeted the Jewish exiles from Eretz Yisrael warmly. Most Arabs admired the Jews for their love of learning and for the body of written laws that guided their lives. They were known to the illiterates of Arabia as the "People of the Book," although there was not a single Yeshivah on the entire peninsula. Through their contact with these Jewish immigrants, as well as with Christian soldiers, the Arabs were introduced to monotheism. The concept of an invisible G-d who communicates with man through prophets gradually sank into the Arab consciousness. It remained only for a charismatic, ambitious leader named Mohammed to step forward and galvanize the Arab population, leading them to abandon the polytheistic worship of wood and stone.

Mohammed

Mohammed came from a rich merchant family in Mecca. Having lost his father at an early age, he had great difficulties making ends meet until he met a widow who helped him start a business of his own in which he drove camels and sold dates, one of Arabia's most valuable products. He made considerable profits and traveled extensively, meeting Jews and Christians in many areas. Through his many contacts, he became acquainted with the basics of their religions, which made a deep impression on him. He felt troubled that the Jews and Christians had sophisticated religions and their own prophets, while his own tribesmen remained ignorant and backward.

Mohammed had dreams of grandeur, in which he imagined that the angel Gavriel came to him and ordered him to found a new religion, combining elements of both Jewish and Christian traditions. With his admiration for the "People of the Book," Mohammed adopted many practices from the Torah, including the belief in one G-d, the lunar calendar, turning towards Jerusalem during prayer, and a written legal code.

In the year 613, Mohammed formally declared himself a "prophet." His initial attempt to spread his beliefs in Mecca was rudely rebuffed. Nobody in Mecca wanted to change the *status quo;* the elders resisted any change in their pagan practices, and the merchants feared anything that might have an adverse effect on the pilgrimages to the *Kaaba* from which they derived such a satisfactory income. By 622, Mohammed had agitated the Meccans to the point that he and his followers were forced to flee the city. This flight, known as the Hegira, marks the formal beginning of the Islamic religion.

Mohammed went to Medina, a city with a large number of wealthy Jews. Naively, he thought he could attract the Jews of Arabia to his new faith because he had included so many practices from the Torah. In order to make his religion even more attractive to the Jews, he stressed that all prayers should be said facing the city of Jerusalem, and incorporated Yom Kippur as a day of fasting for his followers. To his dismay, however, his claim to be a prophet was summarily rejected by the Jews. In desperation, he charged that the Torah had predicted his ascendancy, but that the Jews and Christians had changed the text of the Torah to delete any reference to him. This absurd notion was greeted with ridicule and led only to further rejection.

Within two years, Mohammed was forced to give up the idea of luring the Jews to his new religion. Like Paul of Tarsus, inflamed by Jewish rejection, Mohammed turned into a rabid Jew-hater. He dropped the more Jewish characteristics of his religion; the direction of prayer was abruptly switched from Jerusalem to the *Kaaba* in Mecca, and Yom Kippur was reduced to a voluntary custom. Instead, the month of Ramadan was declared a fast period during which foods are either restricted or entirely forbidden from sunrise to sunset.

Islam's main concepts were later recorded in a book called the Koran, which calls

> *He felt troubled that the Jews and Christians had sophisticated religions and their own prophets, while his own tribesmen remained ignorant and backward.*

> *By 622, Mohammed had agitated the Meccans to the point that he and his followers were forced to flee the city. This flight, known as the Hegira, marked the formal beginning of the Islamic religion.*

Islam's main concepts were later recorded in a book called the Koran, which calls upon its Muslim believers to adhere to five basic requirements.

upon its Muslim believers to adhere to five basic requirements: to believe in one G-d, and Mohammed as his prophet; to pray five times a day facing Mecca; to give alms to the poor; to observe the fast of Ramadan; and to make an annual pilgrimage to Mecca.

Mohammed was not content merely to preach a new religion. He was determined to consolidate his supporters and gain military and political power. Aware that the Jews were unlikely to support him, he chose to make them his scapegoats.

His first true military conquest took place in 624, in the Battle of Badr. Although his men were heavily outnumbered, they managed to rout the enemy and secure Islam's position in Medina. Heady with victory, Mohammed declared that his holy cause could only be won by a *jihad,* a holy war against the non-Muslims, and he turned in fury upon the Jews.

Three large Jewish clans, each numbering in the hundreds, resided on the outskirts of Medina. After the battle of Badr, Mohammed attacked the first of these groups, the *Banu* (*Bnei*) *Kainuka,* on the thinnest of trumped-up charges. He laid siege to their stronghold for fifteen days before they finally surrendered to his army. Mohammed offered them a choice: they must accept him as a prophet or be exiled immediately. The *Banu Kainuka* refused to surrender their principles and chose exile. The family had been famous as goldsmiths and armorers, and when they abandoned their stronghold and left (probably to Eretz Yisrael), Mohammed eagerly seized the armor and tools they

Heady with victory, Mohammed declared that his holy cause could only be won by a jihad, a holy war against the non-Muslims.

had been forced to leave behind, strengthening his own military power at their expense.

A second victory a year later gave Mohammed his excuse to drive out the second Jewish family, *Banu Nadhir.* Claiming divinely disclosed information, he charged that the Jews had plotted his murder. Again, the Jews withdrew to their fortress and held out for two weeks. At the end, facing defeat, they agreed to surrender, on condition that they could take with them whatever they could load on their camels. Mohammed agreed, and the shocked Muslims watched the Jews depart amidst music and song. Cheerfully playing small pipes and beating upon drums, proud to have successfully overcome the temptation to convert to Islam, the Jews wended their way westward, as the exiles before them had done.

Mohammed's third and final blow to the remaining Jews of Medina occurred two years later, in 627. This time, 10,000 troops marched against the small Muslim army of 3,000 men. The people of Medina, in a desperate attempt to drive Mohammed out of the city, had joined forces with Bedouin tribes and had gained the monetary support of the previously exiled Medina Jews. They besieged the city, but Mohammed had dug a trench around Medina and was secure. The attackers negotiated with the Jews who lived at the edge of the city to help them gain access to the Muslim stronghold, but their efforts proved fruitless. After some time, the troops abandoned the attempt to oust Mohammed from Medina, and departed, leaving the Jews to Mohammed's vengeance.

This last family of Jews, *Banu Kuraiza* (reputed to be a family of Kohanim), insisted they had maintained neutrality throughout the campaign. Mohammed hotly asserted that they had betrayed him to the enemy. A fierce struggle took place, and the Jews withdrew to their fortress, where they managed to hold out for two weeks. At last, at the point of starvation, they surrendered to Mohammed.

The *Banu Kuraiza* were all too aware that Mohammed would most likely unleash his frenzied rage against them. At the last moment, however, he offered them life. All they had to do was say, "Mohammed is the Sent One and he is the one whom we find mentioned in our Scriptures."

The reply was instant and unanimous: "We will never abandon the Law of our Torah and will never change it for another!"

On the spot, six hundred Jewish men were butchered, and their wives and children taken to be sold into slavery. One particularly beautiful Jewish woman named Rihana, who had just witnessed the killing of her husband, was reserved to be added to Mohammed's harem.

With Medina firmly established as his power base, Mohammed expanded his efforts. Within a few months, his army, by now a swaggering, vengeful horde, swept through the Jewish settlements of the Arabian peninsula. In town after town, the Jews defended themselves bravely, only to fall to the Muslim sword. On one occasion, after a Jewish leader had been tortured and executed, his sister tried to avenge his death by poisoning Mohammed's food. While the poison did not kill him, Mohammed suffered from its effects until the end of his life, four years later. By the time Mohammed

died in 632, the Jews remaining in the peninsula were helpless.

Marching under the banner of Islam, the Arab troops spent the next ten years expanding throughout the Near East and northern Africa. Persia and Byzantium, unprepared for the onslaught, were conquered relatively easily. The Jews and Christians were permitted in these conquered countries as guests, grudgingly admitted into the "House of Islam." As Mohammed wrote in the Koran: "A person, on maintaining his Judaism...should not be forced to convert. He must, however, pay his head tax...in which case he is entitled to G-d's and the Prophet's protection." They were also required to wear distinctive clothing and adhere to other laws that sought to demean them and separate them from Muslim society.

With the passing of the years, the Muslims interpreted the above passage of the Koran to mean that the Jews are not actually heretics, who must be forced to convert or be destroyed. Instead, the "People of the Book" were considered an "inferior sect" that still deserved the protection of the law—as long as they paid their taxes, that is.

The "Covenant of Omar," in the years 634-644, formalized the conditions under which Christians and Jews could obtain security from persecution, including:

1) The building of additional churches and synagogues, which did not exist before Muslim occupation, was forbidden.
2) The Koran could not be taught to Jews or Christians.
3) It was forbidden to interfere with anyone who wished to convert to Islam.
4) Jews and Christians must honor Muslims and stand in their presence.
5) Jews and Christians were forbidden to resemble Muslims in their hairstyles or dress.

The reply was instant and unanimous: "We will never abandon the Law of our Torah and will never change it for another!"

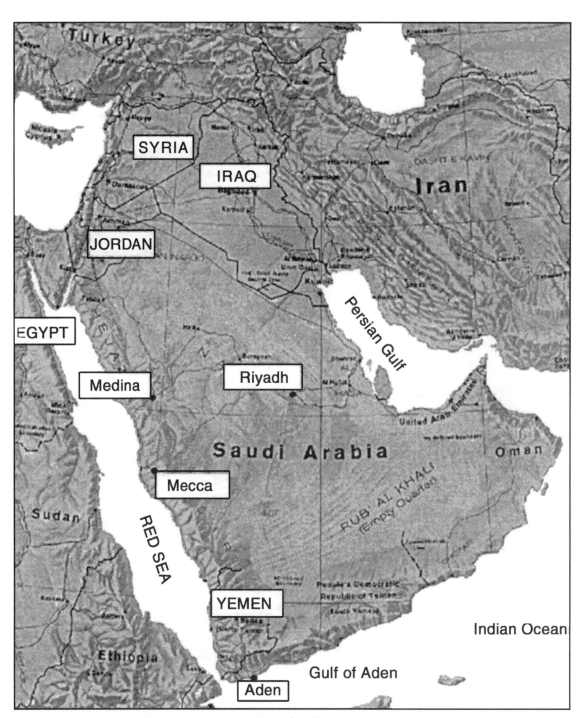

SYRIA

IRAQ

Iran

JORDAN

EGYPT

Persian Gulf

Medina

Riyadh

United Arab Emirates

Saudi Arabia

Oman

Mecca

RUB' AL KHALI
(Empty Quarter)

Sudan

RED SEA

People's Democratic
Republic of Yemen

YEMEN

Indian Ocean

Ethiopia

Gulf of Aden

Aden

Map of Arabia

6) Jews must wear yellow clothing and hats. The color of their shoes must differ from that of the Muslims.

7) Jewish and Christian houses could not be built higher than Muslim homes.

8) Jews and Christians could not be called by Muslim names.

The angel who predicted the birth of Yishmael to Hagar characterized him as a *perreh adam*, a combination of wildness and civility.[1] This seeming paradox serves as the perfect description of the behavior of the Arabs towards the Jews throughout history. The attitudes of the

---

1. *Bereishis*, 16:12.

Muslims were often erratic and inconsistent; the instruction to uphold the "Covenant of Omar" was reissued repeatedly through the years, a clear indication that there were frequent lapses when the conditions were not respected. The treatment the Jews received varied from ruler to ruler and from province to province.

In the seventh century, a conflict arose over the choice and qualifications of the successor to the Caliphate. A small group of Muslims, called the Shi'ites, asserted that only members of the family of Mohammed had a right to rule over Muslims, while the vast majority felt that any competent and knowledgeable Muslim could rule as Caliph. This latter group of Muslims, with a more open-minded attitude, vested authority in their most respected scholars, called "Sunna." Eventually, this large group of Muslims became known as Sunnites.

The Sunnites were generally tolerant to the Jews; when Maawiyah I, founder of the Omayyad dynasty, was selected as Caliph, the Shi'ites, who were rabid

fanatics, rebelled and formed their own sect. Those Jews living under their rule in Iran and Yemen were called "unclean," to the point where Jews were forbidden to venture outdoors in the rain, lest a drop of water that had touched a Jew would also touch a Muslim and render him unclean as well. The Jews of Yemen, under the rule of the Imamins, were subjected to constant persecutions, including forced conversion and threats of death. Nevertheless, Mohammed's basic rules did serve to alleviate some of the harsher decrees that threatened Jewish lives.

While the savage beginnings of Mohammed's sweeping massacres were often reflected by anti-Jewish legislation and vicious attacks against Jewish life and property, there were also long periods in which the Arabs accepted the Jews in their communities and valued them for their cultural and commercial abilities. Indeed, it was largely under the rule of the Mohammedan Caliphs that the entire Jewish nation enjoyed the "Golden Age of the Geonim."

Those Jews living under their rule in Iran and Yemen were called "unclean," to the point where Jews were forbidden to venture outdoors in the rain.

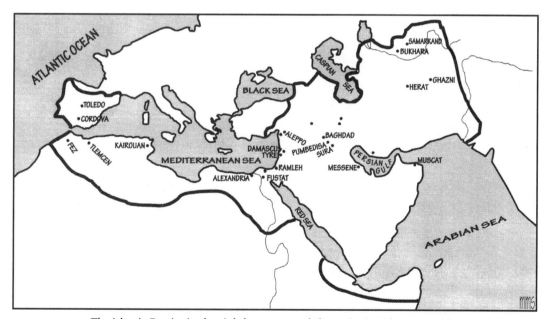

The Islamic Empire in the eighth century and the major Jewish communities

Chapter
6

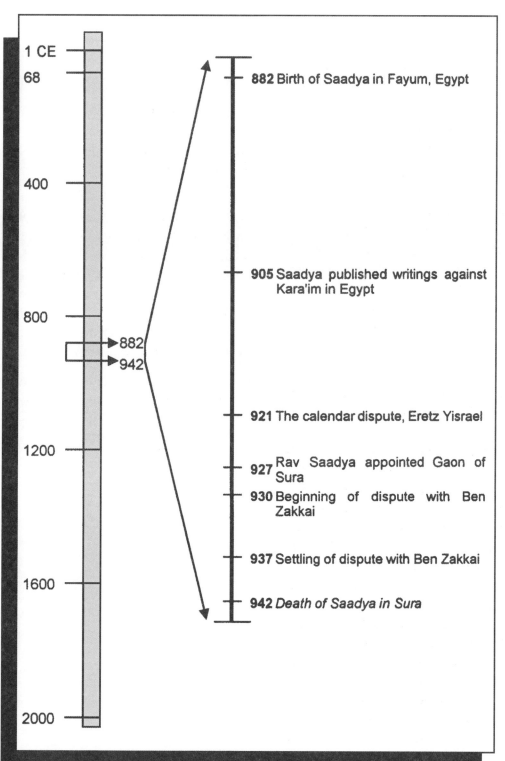

1 CE
68

400

800

882
942

1200

1600

2000

882 Birth of Saadya in Fayum, Egypt

905 Saadya published writings against Kara'im in Egypt

921 The calendar dispute, Eretz Yisrael

927 Rav Saadya appointed Gaon of Sura

930 Beginning of dispute with Ben Zakkai

937 Settling of dispute with Ben Zakkai

942 Death of Saadya in Sura

Chapter
7

*He intended to
open the holy
works of the Torah
to those who had
forgotten the
Hebrew language
under the Muslim
regime and thus
had no access to
Tanach.*

"Were it not for Saadya, the Torah would almost have disappeared from among Israel."
Iggeres Taiman, **Rambam**

uring the fourth generation of the Geonic Era (900-1000 C.E.), the Yeshivos in Babylonia went through a period of weakness. However, at the same time, Rav Saadya ben Yosef, one of the greatest personalities in Jewish history, became Gaon in Sura.

Rav Saadya was born in the year 882, in Fayum, Egypt, where he received his education. In his youth, he distinguished himself by his outstanding scholarship in Tanach and Gemara. He also excelled in other areas, including philosophy and Arabic literature. When he was only twenty years old, he published his *Sefer HaEgron* on Hebrew grammar, style, and poetics.

Rav Saadya never actually studied in the Yeshivos of Babylonia, but his reputation was well known among Jews throughout the continent, long before he was appointed Gaon. Like the other Sages of the time, he wrote responsa to the halachic questions addressed to him. Twenty-four of his works have weathered the passage of time. Among them is the first Arabic translation of the Tanach. Unlike the *Targum Shivim* (the coerced Greek translation) and, centuries later, Moses Mendelssohn's infamous *Biur* (in German), Rav Saadya's translation did not intend to introduce the Jews in Babylonia to the language and culture of other nations. On the contrary, he intended to open the holy works of the Torah to those who had forgotten the Hebrew language under the Muslim regime and thus had no access to Tanach.

Rav Saadya was also an outstanding Hebrew poet whose contributions have been incorporated into the prayers of

*Rav Saadya intended his work
to serve as an aid for those who
had already developed doubts
under the influence of Greek
and other foreign cultures.*

Rosh HaShanah and Yom Kippur. His work on Hebrew grammar, the *Sefer HaEgron,* is considered a classic contribution to the field.

His most outstanding *sefer* is a work originally written in Arabic, *HaEmunos VeHaDayos*—"Beliefs and Opinions." While he recognized that people of faith could be disturbed by the questions that his *sefer* raises, Rav Saadya intended his work to serve as an aid for those who had already developed doubts under the influence of Greek and other foreign cultures.

Rav Saadya's leadership qualities were put to the test in three crises which

*Sefer HaEmunos VeHaDayos—
"Beliefs and Opinions," 1653*

shook world Jewry to its very roots. In each case, Rav Saadya dealt with the crisis with decision, perception, and courage.

Crisis I: The Karaites

The Jewish nation is often referred to in the Torah as *am k'shei oref,* a "stiff-necked people."[1] While stubbornness is generally a negative trait, this national characteristic is one of the reasons Hashem selected the Jews to be His "Chosen People." Stubbornness results in a resistance to outside pressure; once a breakthrough had been achieved at Mount Sinai and the Jews accepted the Torah, their stubbornness became a tangible advantage: no force in the entire world could shake them from their commitment. The quality of *am k'shei oref* explains why the Jewish nation has survived throughout the annals of history, unlike all the other ancient civilizations of the world.

However, Judaism has had to cope with more than outside pressure; the Jewish religion has been threatened by dissension from within as well. From the initial emergence from slavery in Egypt, until the present time, the Jews have always been plagued by dissenting groups who have shaken the very foundations of Jewish faith.

An in-depth study of these various rebellions will show that their underlying causes were, for the most part, not truly ideological. Motivated by petty grudges and egotistical desires for power, the leaders of the various dissenting movements tried to justify their own base motives with ideological pretexts. When the precepts of the Torah interfered with someone's personal ambitions, he foolishly tried to change the Torah instead of modifying his goals.

A case in point is the rebellion of Korach against Moshe, which Rashi, in the name of our Sages, traces to a silent envious grudge.[2] Many of the other sects were the result of similar dissatisfactions: the *Misyavnim,* the Hellenized Jews, who accepted the Greek culture which elevates beauty, art, and the primacy of man's intellect over obedience to his Creator; the *Beisussim* (Boethusians) and the *Tzedukim* (Sadducees), two sects during the time of the second Bais Hamikdash, which damaged the unity of the Jewish people; and Christianity, which, until Paul of Tarsus branched off in radically different directions, also cast doubts on the doctrines of Judaism. But in the seventh century, the sect of the *Karaim,* the Karaites, arose, which threatened the survival of Judaism and nearly brought it to the brink of annihilation.

The founder of the Karaites was Anan ben David, one of the two nephews of the *Reish Galusa.* After the *Reish Galusa's* death, Anan, the elder of the two nephews, contended for the vacant position. Although he was a learned man, the Geonim chose his younger brother to act as *Reish Galusa.* Anan, infuriated at the rejection, took his case to the Muslim Caliph, who assumed that Anan was a rebel and had him imprisoned.

With the help of a fellow prisoner, a Muslim scholar, Anan devised a strategy that would enable him to realize his ambition. If he could not gain the recognition he craved from the Jews who believed in traditional Judaism, he could create a new religion that would gain him a following among Jews, as well as being more favorable to the Muslims.

Like his predecessors, the Sadducees, Anan preached that only the written Torah was binding upon the Jews and

---

1. *Shemos,* 32:9

2. *Bamidbar,* 16:1

An in-depth study of these various rebellions will show that their underlying causes were, for the most part, not truly ideological. Motivated by petty grudges and egotistical desires for power, the leaders of the various dissenting movements tried to justify their own base motives with ideological pretexts.

Chapter
7

Rav Saadya Gaon's rebuttals were so effective that he was actually physically assaulted by the Karaites, who recognized him as their most formidable opponent.

The Karaites, however, never died out completely.

Chapter
7

that the Oral Law was "man-made" and could be discarded. Like Korach, who claimed that every Jew was holy and that there was no need for the Kehunah, Anan argued that every Jew has the right to interpret the written Torah as he sees fit.

The "new religion" was dressed up in a disguise of piety. In many ways, the "Ananites," as they were called, were more strict in their observance of mitzvos than the Rabbanim, the traditional "Rabbanite" Jews. Because they did not accept the interpretations of our Sages and took the words of the Chumash literally, they often came to absurd conclusions. For example, when the Torah states *al yeitzei ish mimkomo bayom hashvi'i,* "No one should leave his place on the Seventh Day,"[3] the Ananites understood this to mean that one must stay glued to one's seat during the entire Shabbos. *Lo s'vaaru eish b'chol moshvoseichem b'yom haShabbos,* "Do not burn a fire in all your dwelling places on the day of Shabbos,"[4] was interpreted to mean that one must spend Shabbos in darkness and may eat only cold food.

Anan also designed his new religion to accommodate the Muslims; for example, he followed the lunar calendar without periodic adjustments to the solar year and accepted the concept of Mohammed's prophecy. When a new Caliph ascended the throne, Anan bribed him to confirm him as *Reish Galusa* over those Jews who followed his sect. The Caliph ruled that any ten Jews who deviated from the religious beliefs of the majority were entitled to their own *Reish Galusa.* With his personal ambition and cravings for power fulfilled, Anan proceeded to increase his following until his movement became

3. *Shemos,* 16:29.
4. *Shemos,* 35:3.

a strong challenge to the Oral Law and traditional Judaism.

Anan's movement was most successful outside of Babylonia, where the authority of the Roshei Yeshivah was not felt as strongly. By the ninth century, the Ananites were known as the *Karaim,* the Karaites, derived from their claim to be *Bnei Mikra,* adhering only to the written *Mikra* of the Torah. The sect became so widespread that, in an effort to rebut Karaite interpretations of Jewish law, the custom of eating hot food on Shabbos was instituted. If the Karaites had not posed such a major threat to traditional Judaism, the Geonim would not have deemed it necessary to make an official refutation of the sect's policies.

Rav Saadya Gaon took up the challenge of the Karaites. A brilliant scholar and a gifted writer, he issued a number of publications against them. His rebuttals were so effective that he was actually physically assaulted by the Karaites, who recognized him as their most formidable opponent. These violent attacks forced Rav Saadya to leave Egypt and emigrate to Eretz Yisrael, where he studied in the newly opened Yeshivos.

Rav Saadya spent a great deal of time in the Yeshivah of Tiberias. There he made contact with another leading personality, Rabbi Aharon ben Meir, who was of great help in his struggle against the Karaites. Through the combination of the superior intellects of these two great Sages, much of the threat of the Karaites was neutralized. The Karaites, however, never died out completely. Even today, isolated groups of Karaites still exist.

While the threat of the Karaites had largely dissipated, Rav Saadya soon found himself drawn into another crisis, with his friend and colleague as the focal point. This second crisis proved to be a more dangerous threat to Jewish unity than the Karaites, as it struck at the very heart of the Jewish religion.

Crisis II: The Calendar Dispute

With the erratic, sometime benevolence of the Muslim Caliphs, the Jews in Eretz Yisrael had experienced a gradual revival of Torah study. Rabbi Aharon ben Meir of Tiberias took over the leadership position that had been vacant since the abolition of the Sanhedrin, two hundred years before. As a direct descendant of Hillel, Rabbi Aharon asserted that he was entitled to assume the positions of both Nasi and Gaon. The latter title indicated that he was determined to cause Eretz Yisrael to regain its central position in spiritual matters, eventually challenging the Geonim of Babylonia.

Traditionally, the fixing of the calendar had been in the hands of the Sanhedrin and its leader, the Nasi. With the decline of the power of the Sanhedrin, Hillel II had seized the opportunity to preserve the Jewish Calendar by revealing the mathematical and halachic principles with which to calculate the new months and years. Now, however, Rabbi Aharon ben Meir challenged this system, which had been in practice in Babylonia for hundreds of years, by seeking to recover the Nasi's authority over the calendar.

A test case arose in the year 921, when Rabbi Aharon declared Rosh HaShanah to be on a Tuesday, whereas the Geonim in Babylonia had calculated that Rosh HaShanah would be two days later, on Thursday. As in all halachic disputes, the majority rules, but Rabbi Aharon refused to accept the decision of the Sages in Babylonia, saying that as Nasi in Eretz Yisrael, *his* decision should prevail. The result

was that in the year 921, some Jews kept Yom Kippur two days earlier than the others and ate *chametz* at a time when most others were still celebrating Pesach!

One can well imagine the catastrophic consequences a prolonged rift would have had on the future harmony of Klal Yisrael. Together with the schism caused by the Karaites, the calendar dispute could easily have resulted in total disunity. Here, too, Rav Saadya's genius saved the situation. By word and letter, he was able to convince the Jewish people all over the world that Rabbi Aharon ben Meir was in error. The authority of the Geonim of Babylonia was upheld, and the rift was eventually healed.

Crisis III: Rav Saadya and the Reish Galusa

With the Yeshivos of Babylonia passing through a period of weakness, there was great concern when the position of Rosh Yeshivah in Sura became vacant. While Pumbedisa still thrived, Sura had gone through a period of decline. The Yeshivah which had once been led by the greatest Amoraim, such as Rav and Rav Ashi, had to face the possibility of being forced to close its doors permanently.

In an unprecedented move, David ben Zakkai, the *Reish Galusa,* took steps to preserve the Yeshivah of Sura. He appointed Rav Saadya Gaon, who had never set foot in a Babylonian Yeshivah, as Gaon of Sura. David ben Zakkai was determined to restore Sura to its former glory, and he realized that Rav Saadya was capable of bringing fresh vigor to the declining Yeshivah. For two years, Rav Saadya led the Yeshivah of Sura with a firm hand and great foresight, but a personal crisis arose which threatened to bring Rav Saadya's career as Rosh Yeshivah to a premature end.

By word and letter, he was able to convince the Jewish people all over the world that Rabbi Aharon ben Meir was in error. The authority of the Geonim of Babylonia was upheld, and the rift was eventually healed.

Chapter
7

Rav Saadya Gaon (882-942 C.E.)

Rav Saadya's misfortune served to benefit the Jewish people; during his years of exile, Rav Saadya produced some of his most important Torah works.

David ben Zakkai had presided over a litigation in court and his verdict had been challenged. It was customary that when the *Reish Galusa's* decision was challenged, the two Geonim of Babylonia would be asked to co-sign the court document and thus endorse his decision. The Gaon of Pumbedisa signed willingly. David ben Zakkai then asked his son, Yehudah, to bring the document to Rav Saadya for his signature.

Rav Saadya refused to sign; he considered the verdict biased. However, he did not openly state his opinion, merely saying that his signature was not needed, since the other Gaon had already signed. Yehudah returned to his father, disturbed, and was immediately sent back to Rav Saadya with the demand that the Gaon comply with the *Reish Galusa's* order. Once again, Rav Saadya refused. At this point, Yehudah lost his temper and slapped Rav Saadya's face! Rav Saadya's students stormed into the room and threw Yehudah out.

Incensed, David ben Zakkai dismissed Rav Saadya from his post and appointed a minor scholar to serve as Rosh Yeshivah of Sura. Rav Saadya retaliated by deposing David ben Zakkai as *Reish Galusa.*

At this point, the Muslim Caliph died and a new Caliph took the throne, desperately in need of money. David ben Zakkai took advantage of the situation and bought the Caliph's favor; as a result, the Caliph confirmed Rav Saadya's dismissal and forced him to leave Sura.

Rav Saadya spent the next seven years exiled from his Yeshivah. While his absence was strongly felt in the academy of Sura, Rav Saadya's misfortune served to benefit the Jewish people; during his years of exile, Rav Saadya produced some of his most important Torah works.

After seven years, Rav Saadya and David ben Zakkai reconciled their dispute. Rav Saadya returned to his post as Gaon of Sura and remained a close friend of the *Reish Galusa.* After the death of David ben Zakkai and his son Yehudah, Rav Saadya brought the *Reish Galusa's* grandson into his home and raised him as his own child.

Rav Saadya was the first in the chain of great Jewish philosophers of the millennium. It is understandable that the Meiri, one of the great Rishonim, reverently refers to Rav Saadya Gaon as "*Rosh ham'dabrim b'chol makom,*" the first and foremost authority on all matters.

Chapter

7

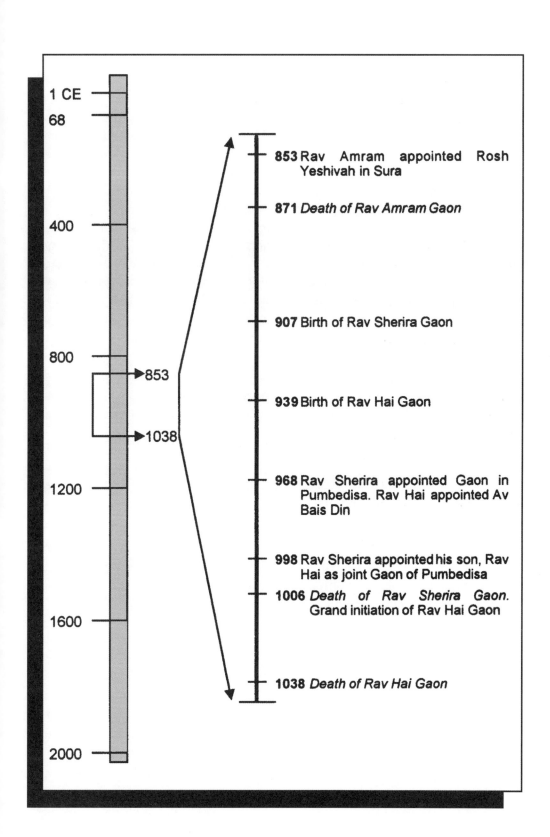

1 CE
68
400
800
853
1038
1200
1600
2000

853 Rav Amram appointed Rosh Yeshivah in Sura

871 *Death of Rav Amram Gaon*

907 Birth of Rav Sherira Gaon

939 Birth of Rav Hai Gaon

968 Rav Sherira appointed Gaon in Pumbedisa. Rav Hai appointed Av Bais Din

998 Rav Sherira appointed his son, Rav Hai as joint Gaon of Pumbedisa

1006 *Death of Rav Sherira Gaon.* Grand initiation of Rav Hai Gaon

1038 *Death of Rav Hai Gaon*

*These giants of
Jewry, a father and
his son, restored
the faltering
Yeshivah of
Pumbedisa to its
former eminence
at a time when,
due mainly to
political factors,
the academy
seemed doomed to
close its doors.*

ost of the responsa of the Geonim have been lost, but a great deal is known about two of the last Geonim, men of outstanding mental powers who were able to restore briefly the glory of the Era of the Geonim to its full height. These giants of Jewry, a father and his son, restored the faltering Yeshivah of Pumbedisa to its former eminence at a time when, due mainly to political factors, the academy seemed doomed to close its doors.

The situation in the Muslim Empire had changed. While Baghdad had originally served as its capital, the city had diminished in importance, with other cities vying for prominence. As a result, travel to Babylonia from other countries, as well as journeys within Babylonia itself, became highly dangerous and often impossible. Under the circumstances, the influx of students who came to study under the guidance of the Geonim dwindled, as did the monetary support upon which the Yeshivah relied.

In addition, internal political fighting had damaged the position of the Yeshivos and came close to destroying completely the existing structure. Bitter competition existed between candidates who wrangled for the position of Gaon, and a separate rivalry arose between the *Reish Galusa* and the *Rosh Yeshivah*. With little outside support and fighting from within, it seemed inevitable that the Yeshivah would have to close.

At that critical moment, a leader emerged who swiftly gained worldwide acclaim. In 968, at the relatively young age of sixty, Rav Sherira ben Chanina became Gaon of Pumbedisa.

With great courage and determination, he set out to repair the damage to the Yeshivah. He began by strengthening the inner life of the Yeshivah. His son, Rav Hai, taught in the Yeshivah, especially during the *Yarchei Kallah.* Once again, as they had in the days before Pumbedisa's decline, huge crowds gathered twice a year, this time to hear Rav Hai's insightful Torah lectures.

Rav Sherira also provided materially for the needy students of the Yeshivah. There is historical proof of this practice, as many of the letters Rav Sherira wrote have been preserved. In these letters, sent to distant communities, Rav Sherira also urged Jews to renew their ties with the Yeshivah, to tell him their problems and to await his reply, as had been the practice during the previous generations of the Geonic Era. Queries began pouring in, and Rav Sherira gave his answers in a clear and precise manner.

As a result of the halachic questions and correspondence directed to Pumbedisa, the Yeshivah's financial situation improved. The number of students multiplied, and a new period of prosperity ensued. Rav Sherira had, indeed, successfully met the challenge to revive Pumbedisa's former glory.

*The most famous
responsa of Rav
Sherira is the
Iggeres shel
Rav Sherira Gaon*

The most famous responsum of Rav Sherira is the *Iggeres shel Rav Sherira Gaon,* which is the main source for the history of the Talmud and the Geonim. This letter was written in reply to the leaders of the congregation of Kairouan (today known as Tunis, North Africa), thousands of miles away. Kairouan had been plagued by the Karaites' relentless attacks against the Oral Law, and the leaders of the community wrote to Rav Sherira, asking him to explain in detail how the Oral Law had been developed. Rav Sherira's detailed and clear response serves today as the major source of information about that period.

> *Rav Sherira's detailed and clear response serves today as the major source of information about that period.*

After Rav Sherira had been Gaon for seventeen years, he appointed his son, Rav Hai, as *Av Bais Din,* Head of the Rabbinical Court. Thirteen years later, after leading the Yeshivah with distinction for three decades, Rav Sherira resigned as Gaon in favor of his son. It was the first time in history that a son had been made Av Bais Din or succeeded his father as Gaon during his father's lifetime.

When Rav Sherira was in his nineties, he was falsely accused of disloyalty to the government. Rav Sherira and Rav Hai were imprisoned and subjected to brutal tortures. The Sages were released only after a massive bribe was paid on their behalf.

> *It was the first time in history that a son had been made Av Bais Din or succeeded his father as Gaon during his father's lifetime.*

Rav Sherira lived for eight more years after his abdication, and his mind remained clear until his death. Many of the responsa written by Rav Hai Gaon during this period contain the remark, "This is the correct *halachah,*" with the stamp and signature of Rav Sherira Gaon. With Rav Sherira's passing in the year 1006 at the age of ninety-nine, it

was a foregone conclusion that Rav Hai would be acknowledged as Gaon of Pumbedisa. There was no precedent, however, for the celebration of his initiation as Gaon, one week later. The weekly Torah portion was *Pinchas,* which includes the words of Moshe concerning the succession of Yehoshua: "May Hashem ...appoint a man to be over the congregation, one who will go out before them." Instead of the customary Haftorah for that week, they substituted the Haftorah for *Vayechi,* from *Melachim I,* which describes the death of King David and the coronation of his son, Solomon. When the reader reached the segment, "And Solomon sat upon the throne of his father David, and his kingdom was firmly established,"[1] the congregation interrupted spontaneously, "And then Hai sat on the throne of his father Sherira, and his kingdom was firmly established!"

> *"And then Hai sat on the throne of his father Sherira, and his kingdom was firmly established!"*

Rav Hai Gaon was fluent in five languages: Hebrew, Aramaic, Arabic, Greek, and Persian. He usually answered any queries directed to him in the same language in which they were written. The responsa that have been published bearing his signature, numbering in the thousands, comprise one-third of all the responsa of the entire Geonic Era.

A vast number of students from all over the world sat at his feet: Jews from Europe, Asia, and Africa. Even the head of the Yeshivah in Jerusalem sent his son to study with Rav Hai Gaon. Rav Hai served as Gaon of Pumbedisa for a total of forty years (just as King Solomon ruled ancient Israel for forty years), but he actually played a dominant role in the Yeshivah for at least

---

1. *Melachim I,* 2:12.

Rav Hai Gaon passed away at the age of one hundred, and with his death, an era of inspiration and central leadership came to an end.

seventy years. He stands out as the last of the Geonim to command the undisputed respect of world Jewry. In the year 1038, Rav Hai Gaon passed away at the age of one hundred, and with his death, an era of inspiration and central leadership came to an end.

After Rav Hai Gaon's passing, the outlying communities in the many countries of exile began to function independently. The Yeshivos of Babylonia, in their efforts to disseminate Torah worldwide, had actually contributed to their own decline; students who had sat at the feet of the Geonim in Babylonia returned to their home communities to take up leadership there and establish their own seats of scholarly learning. It was no longer necessary to turn to Sura and Pumbedisa for guidance. Nevertheless, these new Torah centers were the progeny of Sura and Pumbedisa, for their leaders were products of the Babylonian Yeshivos, all of them either directly or indirectly students of the last Geonim.

It is said that Hashem brings "the cure before the sickness." In this case, with the decline of the power of Sura and Pumbedisa imminent and inevitable, apparently coincidental events took place to ensure that new centers of Torah learning would take root in other parts of the world, ready to continue the chain of tradition and the high quality of learning that had prevailed in Babylonia.

A famous story, brought down by many authentic sources, is that of the *Arba'ah Shevuyim,* the Four Captives. Details of the story vary, but the essential truth of this miraculous transfer of Torah learning remains undisputed.

At Rav Hai Gaon's behest, four of the most prominent scholars of the Babylonian Yeshivos were sent overseas to collect funds: Rav Shmariah ben Elchanan, Rav Chushiel, Rav Nassan ben Yitzchak HaBavli (there is some doubt regarding his identity), and Rav Moshe ben Chanoch, accompanied by his wife and young son, Chanoch. Their ship embarked from the port of Bari, Italy, only to fall prey to a Muslim pirate ship. The pirate captain, well aware that the Jews would offer to redeem his rabbinical prisoners, offered his captives for ransom in various ports along the Mediterranean.

And so, by an apparent misfortune, these four great Torah Sages found themselves in four different parts of Europe. Rav Shmariah was redeemed in Alexandria, Egypt, where he ultimately started a Yeshivah of his own. Rav Chushiel landed in Kairouan, North Africa, where he became the Rosh Yeshivah, serving as a crucial link between East and West. Rav Nassan ben Yitzchak is believed to have been ransomed in Narbonne, France. Rav Moshe ben Chanoch was taken to Spain, where he was redeemed by the residents of Cordova.

Each of these places eventually became a great Torah center, educating some of the best-known scholars in Jewish history. Thus, the cure came before the sickness, for the seeds of Torah were well-planted on foreign soil before Sura and Pumbedisa were forced to close their doors.

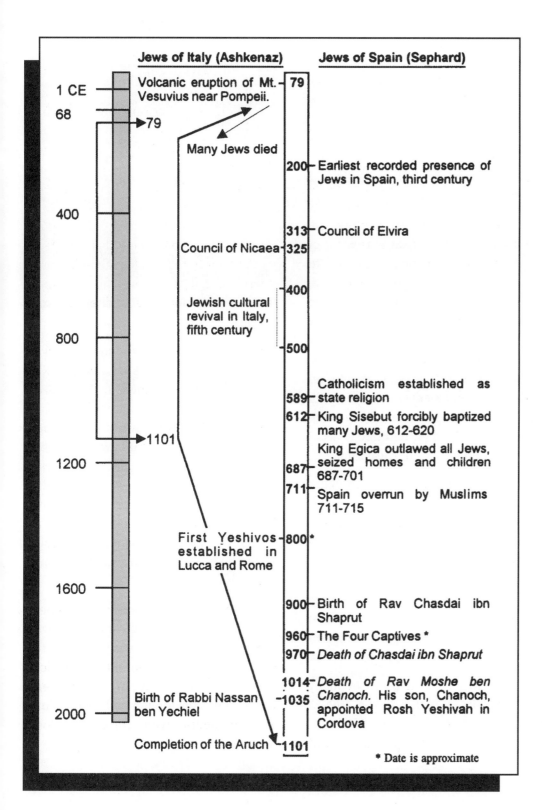

Jews of Italy (Ashkenaz)

- 1 CE — Volcanic eruption of Mt. Vesuvius near Pompeii.
- 68
- 79 → Many Jews died
- 400
- Council of Nicaea — 325
- Jewish cultural revival in Italy, fifth century
- 800
- 1101
- 1200
- First Yeshivos established in Lucca and Rome
- 1600
- Birth of Rabbi Nassan ben Yechiel
- 2000
- Completion of the Aruch

Jews of Spain (Sephard)

- 79
- 200 — Earliest recorded presence of Jews in Spain, third century
- 313 — Council of Elvira
- 325
- 400
- 500
- 589 — Catholicism established as state religion
- 612 — King Sisebut forcibly baptized many Jews, 612-620
- 687 — King Egica outlawed all Jews, seized homes and children 687-701
- 711 — Spain overrun by Muslims 711-715
- 800 *
- 900 — Birth of Rav Chasdai ibn Shaprut
- 960 — The Four Captives *
- 970 — *Death of Chasdai ibn Shaprut*
- 1014 — *Death of Rav Moshe ben Chanoch.* His son, Chanoch, appointed Rosh Yeshivah in Cordova
- 1035
- 1101

* Date is approximate

Chapter
9

*On the streets of
Rome, it was
whispered that the
eruption [of Mt.
Vesuvius] and
destruction were
signs of Divine
displeasure with
the new Emperor
who had once
dared to assault
the Temple in
Jerusalem.*

The first Jewish migration to Italy began before the destruction of the Bais HaMikdash, when Rome first extended its rule over Judea. Attracted by the glamor and economic opportunities of the Roman capital, many Jews settled in Italy and prospered. While based primarily in Rome, Jews eventually settled in other areas, particularly near ports of trade, including the city of Pompeii. It is assumed that the Italian Jews practiced the traditions they brought with them from Eretz Yisrael.

With Jerusalem destroyed and the Bais HaMikdash gone up in flames, Jewish captives were led in chains through the streets of Rome, forced to take part in the triumphal procession celebrating the victory over the Jews. These captives, destined to be sold into slavery, were redeemed by their Jewish brethren that had already settled in the city. Before long, the former slaves were freemen, Roman citizens, and part of the Jewish community, well-treated and able to practice their religion without interference.

Ironically, the obstinacy of the Jews in adhering to the Torah, which had caused the Romans a prolonged, costly war in Judea, was admired on Italian soil. Once the ecstasy of victory had worn off, the Romans were left with a gnawing conscience due to the destruction of Jewish holy places. With Emperor Vespasian's death in 79 C.E., Titus, who had taken Vespasian's place as general in the war against Judea and actually destroyed the Bais HaMikdash, ascended to the throne; in that same year, Mount Vesuvius erupted, burying five cities, including Pompeii, under layers of volcanic ash and lava. On the streets of Rome, it was whispered that the eruption and destruction were signs of Divine displeasure with the new Emperor who had once dared to assault the Temple in Jerusalem.

The citizens of Rome could not help but recognize the stark contrast between the simple purity of Jewish life and the luxurious, degenerate decadence of the Romans. Many Italians found themselves attracted to the fulfilling lifestyle of the Jew. Some Romans ultimately became outright converts, joining the fold of Judaism with much devotion. Others renounced idol worship and adopted some Jewish practices, but never became full Jews. The trend towards Judaism reached the point where it was actually common for Romans to kindle Shabbos lights. Seneca, a Roman leader, wrote bitterly, "Thus the vanquished imposed their laws upon the victors."

With the advent of Christianity's popularity in Rome, Judaism suddenly became unfashionable. In the fourth century,

*The trend toward Judaism
reached the point where it was
actually common for Romans to
kindle Shabbos lights. Seneca, a
Roman leader, wrote bitterly,
"Thus the vanquished imposed
their laws upon the victors."*

Emperor Constantine officially established Christianity as the state religion. Christians were instructed not to patronize Jewish peddlers and craftsmen, Jews were restrained in their religious practices, and their rights were curbed, economically, politically, and socially. Because of the new limitations, the Jews of Rome abandoned their earlier trades and turned to international finance as a means of support.

Despite new economic hardships, Jewish communal life continued much as before.

Elders were entrusted with the administration of synagogues and charity. Scribes were held in high esteem, with the skills often being transmitted from father to son. Synagogues, *mikvaos* and cemeteries were built and meticulously maintained.

While Jewish life prospered, it also became evident that, with the passage of years, the Jewish upper classes prided themselves on their mastery of secular culture. Early tombstones in Roman Jewish cemeteries were inscribed in Greek or Latin, not Hebrew, and the date of death frequently used the Roman calendar instead of the Jewish one. By the fifth century, however, a Jewish cultural revival apparently took place, as the tombstones dating from that period show a predominant use of Hebrew lettering, with the date of death counted either from Creation or from the destruction of the Bais HaMikdash. Acknowledgment and credit must go to the Torah scholarship emanating from Eretz Yisrael and Babylonia, which had a healthy impact on the Jews of Italy during this period and the succeeding centuries.

With the passage of time, Yeshivos were established in several Italian cities, including Lucca in northern Italy, Rome, and Otranto in southern Italy. Lucca was the birthplace of the famous Kalonymos family; centuries later, Emperor Charlemagne is reputed to have invited Rabbi Kalonymos to settle in Mayence, Germany, where he founded a Torah academy of lasting significance.

Italy also produced the outstanding leader and Rosh Yeshivah, Rabbi Nassan ben Yechiel, who authored the *Aruch,* the first known Hebrew dictionary. Completed in the year 1101, the *Aruch* not only defines words but gives the meaning, background, interpretation, and usage for

Credit must go to the Torah scholarship emanating from Eretz Yisrael and Babylonia, which had a healthy impact on the Jews of Italy during this period and the succeeding centuries.

each entry. Rabbi Nassan, who learned from the students of Rav Hai Gaon and is considered one of the early Rishonim, drew from numerous sources to complete the *Aruch,* including the Geonim in Babylonia, the scholars of Kairouan, North Africa, and works from Mayence, Germany. The *Aruch* serves as an important commentary on the Talmud; Rashi, a contemporary of Rabbi Nassan, quotes it in his commentary on the Gemara.

When Jews arrived in Italy from Eretz Yisrael, it is assumed that they brought

Map of Italy, 1000 C.E.

When Jews arrived in Italy from Eretz Yisrael, it is assumed that they brought their traditions, or minhagim, along with them. These minhagim became known as Minhag Ashkenaz.

their traditions, or *minhagim,* along with them. These *minhagim,* practiced in Italy and later, with further migrations to the north, in mid-Europe, became known as *Minhag Ashkenaz.* With time, the settlers of Italy and mid-Europe became known as Ashkenazim, while those Jews that settled in Spain and Portugal were called Sephardim. (It should be noted, however, that the term "Sephardim" refers only to Jews of Spanish descent and should not be confused with those who follow *Minhag Chassidim,* which is also commonly called *Nussach "Sephard."*)

Christian Spain

The name "Sepharad," referring to the Iberian Peninsula of Spain and Portugal, is first mentioned by the prophet Ovadiah. According to tradition, Jews lived in Spain as early as the time of King Solomon, whose tax collector, Adoniram, reportedly died there. Ships sailed regularly between Eretz Yisrael and Spain, doing brisk trade, and importing merchandise from one country to another.

The original Jewish settlers conducted themselves with great pride in their ancestry. It is known with certainty that the third century Jews enjoyed the freedom to practice their religion and pursue profitable careers. In some communities in Spain, Jews constituted the majority of the population. Jewish life was easy and prosperous, resulting in a unique personality type: while the Spanish Jew remained loyal to Torah and mitzvos, he was also fiercely patriotic and deeply rooted in the lifestyle of his adopted country.

Inevitably, such dualism led to unfortunate results. To the dismay of both Jewish leaders and Christian clergy, mixed marriages began to occur with increasing frequency.

While the Spanish Jew remained loyal to Torah and mitzvos, he was also fiercely patriotic and deeply rooted in the lifestyle of his adopted country.

The oldest record of Spanish Christianity, the canons of the Council of Elvira in 313, indicate that the Church attempted to solve the problem by setting up numerous barriers to the continuation of peaceful coexistence between Jews and Christians. While these canons served as the beginnings of persecutions in Spain in the fourth and fifth centuries, the Jews still led a profitable life in their adopted country. The Visigothic and Gothic rulers appreciated their Jewish subjects; the Jews held key economic positions in the country, and their settlements at the northern border of Spain provided valuable defense against invasion by the hated Franks.

This relatively tranquil period for Spanish Jewry came to an abrupt end in 589. King Reccared I announced his conversion to Catholicism and established it as the state religion. Henceforth, intermarriage was strictly forbidden, and the offspring of marriages between Christians and Jews were to be forcibly baptized. Jews were excluded from all public office and could no longer own Christian slaves, effectively impoverishing the Jewish farmers. Negotiations and offers of a hefty bribe proved useless; Reccared stood firm, and the edicts went into effect.

This relatively tranquil period for Spanish Jewry came to an abrupt end in 589.

The Spanish nobles, more pragmatic and less zealous than their kings, were inclined to treat the Jews decently, but the royal edicts of

Reccared's successors imposed harsh measures. Most infamous was the eight-year rule of King Sisebut (612-620), who forcibly baptized many Jews. His brutality manifested itself in an ultimatum: either accept baptism or leave Spain. Thousands of Jews fled to France and Africa at this point, but many lacked the strength to oppose the pressure. These Jews became Christians, at least outwardly. Even at that early date, the stresses and conflicting loyalties confronting Spain's Jewry spawned the split personality of the Jew who appeared to be a faithful Christian, but in the privacy of his own home adhered faithfully to the religion of his forefathers. The term *marrano* was not yet in use, but the concept was already born.

The remainder of the seventh century saw Spanish Jewry seesawing between Judaism and Catholicism, depending upon the extent of the fanaticism of the current reigning monarch. Instead of concentrated Jewish communities, the Jewish population became the minority, scattered sparsely throughout all the provinces of Spain. The situation could not help but have a damaging, corrosive effect on the education of the children and on the quality of Jewish life.

The most vicious attack occurred under King Egica (687-702). All Jews were declared slaves, their religion was outlawed, and their goods and homes were confiscated. Children, from the age of seven and up, were seized from their parents and placed in Christian homes. Mourning their children and embittered by their countless losses, the downtrodden Jews no longer felt any loyalty toward Christian Spain; when the Muslims invaded the country in 711, the Jews welcomed them with open arms. They did not know what Muslim rule would mean to them, but what did they have to lose?

The Early Middle Ages:

Jews in Italy and Spain

Mourning their children and embittered by their countless losses, the downtrodden Jews no longer felt any loyalty toward Christian Spain; when the Muslims invaded the country in 711, the Jews welcomed them with open arms.

Chapter

9

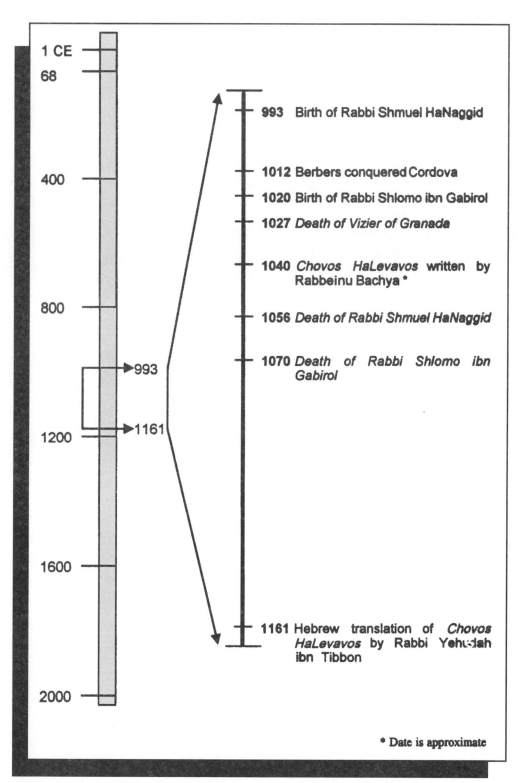

993	Birth of Rabbi Shmuel HaNaggid
1012	Berbers conquered Cordova
1020	Birth of Rabbi Shlomo ibn Gabirol
1027	*Death of Vizier of Granada*
1040	*Chovos HaLevavos* written by Rabbeinu Bachya *
1056	*Death of Rabbi Shmuel HaNaggid*
1070	*Death of Rabbi Shlomo ibn Gabirol*
1161	Hebrew translation of *Chovos HaLevavos* by Rabbi Yehudah ibn Tibbon

* Date is approximate

Chapter

10

The Jews living in the early "Golden Age" were blessed with a towering personality: Chasdai ibn Shaprut, a man whose leadership qualities went hand in hand with his unadulterated faith and dedication to Torah and mitzvos.

In July, 711, Berber and Arab invaders crossed the Straits of Gibraltar into Spain. In the course of four years, they overran the entire Iberian Peninsula, bringing it under Muslim rule. Cordova, a city in the southern part of Spain, became the new capital of the country.

Cordova was more than the seat of the Caliphate, which eventually declared its independence from Baghdad; it was a world center of culture, a magnificent metropolis bejewelled with palaces, mosques, parks, and fountains. Its tremendous library contained 400,000 manuscripts at a time well before the invention of the printing press. With the onset of such enlightenment and culture, a "Golden Age" began in Spain. The greatest philosophers, poets, and scientists of the world came to Spain, attracted to the city of Cordova.

The Jews, who now enjoyed considerable freedom, were drawn into the bustling cultural activity. Some had accompanied the Muslim invaders along their military route all the way from Persia, across the African coast and into Spain. Others gravitated to the Muslim capital from other parts of the country. Academic research flourished in Cordova; the Jews stood in the forefront of exploration in medical science, philosophy, poetry, and grammar. The new-found intellectualism carried over into Jewish studies as well, and a fervor of study created a revival in many Jewish endeavors, such as poetry and grammar.

At any point in history when Jews are exposed to a close association with secular wisdom, the seeds of potential disaster threaten to grow. Intimacy between the Gentile mind and the Jew opens the dangerous door to assimilation and the ultimate doom of Jewish identity. The notable success of the Jews in resisting assimilation was due largely to the quality of leadership of that generation. The Jews living in the early "Golden Age" were blessed with a towering personality: Chasdai ibn Shaprut, a man whose leadership qualities went hand in hand with his unadulterated faith and dedication to Torah and mitzvos. His efforts were reinforced by the unexpected, "coincidental" arrival in Cordova of Rav Moshe ben Chanoch, an exceptional Torah sage from the Yeshivah of Sura and a student of the last Geonim in Babylonia.

Chasdai ibn Shaprut
(900-970 C.E.)

Chasdai, the son of Isaac Shaprut, officially served as physician and statesman under two successive rulers in Cordova during the tenth century. He was a valued diplomatic advisor, appreciated by the Caliphs for his skill in settling border disputes with Christian kingdoms in the north.

Chasdai was fluent in many languages, including Hebrew, Arabic, and Latin. When a messenger from the Byzantine Emperor presented the Caliph of Cordova with a rare medical work written in Greek, the Caliph sent for a monk to translate the document from Greek into Latin. As the monk read off the Latin, Chasdai simultaneously translated the complicated text aloud into Arabic, amazing the court.

On one famous occasion, he used his medical skills to achieve a diplomatic triumph. The unfortunate King Sancho of Leon had nearly lost his kingdom to rebels who criticized and mocked his overweight bulk as much as they scorned his ineptness at ruling the country. Under the protection of his grandmother, the Queen-Regent of neighboring Navarre, Sancho tried in vain to shed the pounds which had made him a laughing-stock and almost cost him his kingdom. In desperation, his grandmother appealed to the Caliph for assistance. Chasdai, the physician *cum* ambassador, was quickly dispatched to Navarre, where he was able to cure Sancho's obesity and win his admiration. Through clever negotiation, Chasdai arranged for the Queen of Navarre and her grandson to appear before the Caliph in Cordova. The royal trio devised a pact, giving the Caliph favorable terms in Navarre in return for armed forces to help quell the rebels in Leon. The pact proved successful, and Chasdai, the Jewish statesman who had initiated the negotiations in the first place, became even more beloved by Muslim and Jew alike.

Chasdai was able to utilize his many contacts in court to better the lives of his fellow Jews in Cordova. He was also in a position to bring notable Torah scholars into the city. For example, the academic stress on philosophy and language arts in Cordova had stimulated a renewed interest in the study of Hebrew grammar and Hebrew poetry. Chasdai invited two outstanding Hebrew scholars to come to Cordova: Dunash ibn Labrat and Menachem ben Saruk, both of whom are frequently mentioned in Rashi's commentary. Indeed, the role of precise grammatical understanding of the Torah had its strongest foundations in the academies of Spain.

In addition to his efforts to improve Jewish conditions in his own country, Chasdai

Chasdai was able to utilize his many contacts in court to better the lives of his fellow Jews in Cordova. He was also in a position to bring notable Torah scholars into the city.

Dunash ibn Labrat and Menachem ben Saruk differed in the basic approach to the etymology of Hebrew words. Ben Saruk believed that the explanation of words should be derived exclusively from the Hebrew language itself, while Dunash felt that it was legitimate to investigate other languages for possible explanations of Hebrew roots. Rashi utilized Dunash's approach in his explanation of the word "totafos," used in reference to the tefillin. Rashi, pointing out that "totafos" is derived from the word for "two" in the African and Caspian languages, explains that the repetition of "two" refers to the division of the tefillin into four compartments.

shared the intense yearning of many other Jews in his era, and that of religious Jews throughout the ages: to see the Jewish nation become reunited on its own land, and with its own rulers. A popular theme of that time was the attempt to locate the "Ten Lost Tribes of Israel," and numerous stories abounded of Jews living in remote lands.

Prior to Chasdai's birth, a traveler called Eldad Hadani appeared in Kairouan, claiming to be a descendant of the tribe of Dan. He recounted his journey from his homeland in Ethiopia, which, he said, was also the homeland of three other tribes, Gad, Asher, and Naftali. Across from their settlement, he reported, lived the Children of Moses, descended from the Levites, but separated from the other tribes by the rushing torrent of the River Sambatyon. The river was made up of rocks and rubble, not water, and moved with such crashing force that no one could cross it. The river rested only on Shabbos, when it was covered by a thick mist. This nation of four tribes had its own king and kept the laws of the Torah, including a nucleus of the Oral Torah as handed down to them from the time of Yehoshua bin Nun.

This nation of four tribes had its own king and kept the laws of the Torah, including a nucleus of the Oral Torah as handed down to them from the time of Yehoshua bin Nun.

Chapter
10

Approximately two hundred years before Chasdai's time, King Bulan of the Khazars had converted to Judaism. In time, the Khazar nation became Jewish, and none but Jews were permitted to ascend to the throne.

Eldad Hadani's accounts had been accepted, albeit somewhat cautiously, in a letter from the Gaon of Sura, although the Gaon had instructed the leaders of North African Jewry not to change any of their religious practices in order to conform to those of Eldad. The fantastic story spread around the Jewish world, bringing ambivalent reactions. While most Jews *wanted* to believe it, the issue was hotly debated, and was still unresolved during Chasdai's lifetime.

Chasdai, fascinated by the tale, would have liked to use his high position to research Eldad Hadani's story and perhaps find other lost or forgotten Jewish groups. His opportunity arose when news reached him that a Jewish kingdom existed across the continent in southern Russia in the region of the Crimean peninsula.

Approximately two hundred years before Chasdai's time, King Bulan of the Khazars had converted to Judaism. In time, the Khazar nation became Jewish, and none but Jews were permitted to ascend to the throne. Chasdai, excited and enthralled to learn of this independent Jewish nation, went to great lengths to communicate with the Khazars. Correspondence between Chasdai and King Joseph, the last Jewish king of the Khazars, has been preserved.[1]

The Khazar Jewish Kingdom

1. The Khazar kingdom was defeated by invaders shortly afterward.

These letters, many years later, served as the inspiration and basis for the famous poet and philosopher, Yehudah HaLevi, to write his book, *The Kuzari.*

A Yeshivah in Cordova

Chasdai was known as an accomplished Torah scholar. He recognized the importance of Torah and encouraged its development in Cordova. Until his time, it had been the custom for parents to send their sons to Sura or Pumbedisa to study Torah, a hazardous journey of thousands of miles. Chasdai also recognized that the Caliph resented the influence and attraction the Babylonian academies had over his Jewish subjects. The solution was obviously to create a Torah academy in Cordova, but who in Spain could match the caliber and wisdom of the Geonim in Babylonia?

Nobody paid attention to the inconspicuous *shamash* of the small, local Yeshivah, a man who had been redeemed for a relatively small ransom from a pirate captain. The *shamash* was, in fact, Rav Moshe ben Chanoch, who had been rescued together with his son by the Jews of Cordova. In his modesty, Rav Moshe did not tell anyone who he was, and was content to remain in the back of the Yeshivah, doing the menial chores of a *shamash.*

One day, however, he overheard a Talmudical discussion in which Rabbi Nassan, the local Rosh Yeshivah, revealed an ignorance of a topic in *maseches Yoma.* Rav Moshe could not restrain himself and spoke up, clarifying the issue and surprising everyone with his Talmudic expertise. Rav Nassan, a man of extraordinarily refined character, immediately resigned his position as Rosh Yeshivah and offered it to Rav Moshe. Within a short time, the Yeshivah of Cordova grew and flourished into a famous academy that would produce some of the greatest Torah scholars of the Golden Age of Spain.

When the pirate captain discovered that he had completely underestimated the value of his former captive, he re-abducted Rav Moshe and demanded a much higher ransom. Chasdai, however, convinced the Caliph to intervene and rescue Rav Moshe by persuading the Muslim ruler that it would be to his advantage to have a world-renowned scholar heading the Cordova academy of Torah. Rav Moshe was released and resumed his position as Rosh Yeshivah. Chasdai's fondest wish had come true: those who wished to study the Talmud no longer needed to make an arduous trip to Babylonia, for Cordova now boasted a Rosh Yeshivah of the same caliber as those in Sura and Pumbedisa.

Coupled with the prevalent preoccupation with Hebrew grammar and poetry in Cordova, it is unsurprising that the scholars that emerged from the academy in Cordova prided themselves not only on their deep understanding of Torah, but also in their ability to compose *piyutim,* poems that flowed in the language of the Torah. Some of the most artful poetic prayers and haunting *zemiros* still enjoyed in modern times were composed during Spain's Golden Age.

With Rav Moshe's passing, his son, Rav Chanoch ben Moshe, became Rosh Yeshivah in Cordova. One of his prize pupils was destined to become the next generation's leader, a man who would rise to a position of extreme importance in Muslim Spain: Rabbeinu Shmuel HaNaggid.

Rabbeinu Shmuel HaNaggid
(993-1056 C.E.)

The tranquil, prosperous life in Cordova came to an abrupt end in the year 1012. The Berbers, a fierce Muslim sect of African descent, conquered the city, killing Muslims and Jews alike. Those who managed to escape with their lives fled the city, and the Caliphate of Cordova splintered into a number of small principalities.

Rabbi Shmuel HaLevi, who became known as Rabbi Shmuel HaNaggid, was among the refugees from Cordova. A former member of Rav Chanoch ben Moshe's Yeshivah, he had acquired a vast knowledge in both Torah and secular subjects, speaking Hebrew, Arabic and five other languages fluently. Like so many others living in Spain at that time, he had also mastered philosophy and poetry. His Arabic was especially poetic, and he had a great talent in calligraphy.

Rabbeinu Shmuel settled in Malaga and opened up a small spice shop near the palace of the Vizier, who served the king of Granada. While he was content to sit in his little shop and devote himself to the study of Torah, the illiterate workers in the Vizier's palace often asked him to write letters on their behalf. Eventually, the Vizier discovered that the man with such exquisite linguistic skill and elegant handwriting was none other than the Jew in the spice shop outside his palace. Captivated and impressed by Rabbeinu Shmuel's abilities, the Vizier appointed him as his personal secretary and brought him to Granada. When the Vizier realized that his private secretary was also an astute and highly gifted statesman, he followed Rabbeinu Shmuel's advice in all matters of state.

In 1027, the Vizier fell ill. While on his deathbed, he confessed to his master the king that his successes and diplomatic triumphs had been largely due to his wise Jewish secretary, Rabbeinu Shmuel. The king, pleased with Rabbeinu

Within a short time, the Yeshivah of Cordova grew and flourished into a famous academy that would produce some of the greatest Torah scholars of the Golden Age of Spain.

Rabbeinu Shmuel became well known for his strong ethical standards and fair treatment of rich and poor alike in a country that was almost incapable of operating without bribery.

Shmuel's sharp judgment and impeccable demeanor, appointed him as Vizier in his master's place and entrusted him with diplomatic and military affairs.

Rabbeinu Shmuel was now in a highly influential and powerful position. His sense of humility, however, remained intact, and he never lost touch with his Jewish brethren. He acted not only as rabbi of his community, but also as a benefactor to Jews everywhere. Olive oil from his plantations was sent on a yearly basis to the synagogues in Jerusalem. He used his great wealth to support Torah scholars and distributed many *sefarim* and copies of the Talmud, not only in Spain but throughout the Jewish world. Maintaining a cordial correspondence with Rav Hai Gaon and the *Reish Galusa,* he imported and preserved manuscripts from the closed Torah academies of Sura and Pumbedisa.

In his capacity as commander of the army, he directed military campaigns personally, often endangering his own life when he could have stayed safely behind the battle lines. But such behavior was not in Rabbeinu Shmuel's nature; his integrity was impeccable. Rabbeinu Shmuel became well known for his strong ethical standards and fair treatment of rich and poor alike in a country that was almost incapable of operating without bribery.

It was inevitable that Rabbeinu Shmuel's influential position and incorruptible standards would create numerous enemies among those who sought to buy the favors of the king. Nevertheless, his generosity disarmed even his opponents. Once, a jealous Muslim competitor in the spice business had the audacity to insult Rabbeinu Shmuel in the presence of the king. Infuriated, the king ordered

Rabbeinu Shmuel to cut out the man's poisonous tongue. Instead of obeying the king's orders, Rabbeinu Shmuel chose to act upon the advice in *Melachim:* the best way to defeat an enemy is to treat him as a friend.[2] He sent a present to the Muslim and assured him that he bore no grudge against him. When the Muslim spice merchant found himself once more in the king's presence, he could not find enough good words to say about the Jewish Vizier. The king, pleased at the Muslim's words but surprised that he was still able to talk, asked his Vizier why he had not carried out his orders to cut out the man's tongue.

"I did, your Majesty," Rabbeinu Shmuel swiftly replied. "I cut out his bad tongue and replaced it with a good one!"

Under the circumstances, it is unsurprising that Rabbeinu Shmuel was loved and revered by Jews and Muslims alike. Early in his thirty-year career as Vizier, he acquired the title *Naggid,* Prince, and the title remained with him for the rest of his life.

Despite the many secular demands on his time, Rabbeinu Shmuel authored a number of *sefarim.* The most famous is the *Mevo HaTalmud,* an introduction to the study of the Talmud which clarifies the language and structure which can be so confusing to beginners. In addition, the *Mevo HaTalmud* describes the development of the Mishnah and the Gemara and lists the Tannaim and Amoraim who were instrumental in preparing the Talmud. Today, the *Mevo HaTalmud* can be found as an appendix at the end of *maseches Berachos* in larger editions of Shass.

Rabbeinu Shmuel HaNaggid served his nation as a teacher, a philanthropist, a statesman, a philosopher, and a poet. It

2. *Melachim II,* 6:22. Also *Mishlei,* 25:21.

is rightfully said of him that he wore four crowns: the Crown of Torah, the Crown of Royalty, the Crown of *Avodah* (he was a Levi), and the Crown of Good Deeds.[3]

Shlomo ibn Gabirol
(1020-1070 C.E.)

During the lifetimes of Rabbeinu Shmuel HaNaggid and his son Yosef, Jewish poetry flourished to heights un-equaled at any time in history since the days of King David. Most outstanding among the Jewish poets was Shlomo ibn Gabirol, whose soaring talent might have otherwise remained dormant if he had not lived in an environment that ap-preciated and nurtured fine poetry. In-stead of using his talents for honor or monetary gain, Shlomo ibn Gabirol used his poetry to ex-press his love for Hashem and his yearning to come close to his Creator, composing some of the most inspiring and beautiful *piyutim* of the prayers of Rosh HaShanah and Yom Kippur. He was able to express his feelings in sim-ple words with masterful me-ter and rhyme, incorporating fitting phrases from Tanach into his poetry with exquisite precision.

Originally from Saragossa, Shlomo ibn Gabirol lost his father at an early age. He found a friend and benefactor in Yekusiel, the advisor to the king of Saragossa. Yekusiel encouraged the young poet and supported him, freeing him from finan-cial worries and allowing him to develop his great talent. After Yekusiel's death, ibn Gabirol felt slighted and rejected by the Jews of Saragossa, and he expressed his bitterness in sharply worded poetry.

The ensuing anger and resentment forced him to leave Saragossa, and he wandered through Spain until he arrived in Granada, where he was supported and protected by Rabbeinu Shmuel.

Many of ibn Gabirol's works have endured to become major parts of Jewish litera-ture. *Kesser Malchus* is read in some con-gregations after Maariv on Yom Kippur night. In this composition, ibn Gabirol speaks about the Oneness of Hashem and the beauty of creation, calling on the hu-man being to acknowledge Hashem's kingdom and completely submit himself to His rule. *Mekor Chaim* is largely philo-sophical, describing the relationship of created matter to the spiritual Creator and Master of the universe. One of his earlier efforts, a poem on the six hundred and thirteen mitzvos, is still recited by Sephardic congregations on Shavuos. He is also the author of the famous *Shofet Kol HaAretz* said on Erev Rosh HaShanah and Yom Kippur, as well as *Sh'ai Ne'esar,* which is recited on the 17th of Tamuz. Ibn Gabirol was even able to use his poetry to enhance the very mundane subject of grammar, writing some four hundred verses about its basic rules.

One of his earlier efforts, a poem on the six hundred and thirteen mitzvos, is still recited by Sephardic congregations on Shavuos.

A widely-believed legend alleges that Shlomo ibn Gabirol was murdered by an Arab who envied his talent and fame as a poet. His *piyutim,* however, serve as a liv-ing legacy in Jewish communities all over the world.

The *Chovos HaLevavos*

Another contemporary of Rabbeinu Shmuel HaNaggid, Rabbeinu Bachya ibn Pakudah, was an outstanding student of

Rabbeinu Shmuel HaNaggid served his nation as a teacher, a philanthropist, a statesman, a philosopher, and a poet. It is rightfully said of him that he wore four crowns: the Crown of Torah, the Crown of Royalty, the Crown of Avodah (he was a Levi), and the Crown of Good Deeds.

Chapter

10

---

3. See *Pirkei Avos,* 4:13.

Rav Moshe ben Chanoch and a renowned author and philosopher. His most famous work is the classic mussar *sefer Chovos HaLevavos,* "Duties of the Heart."

As with most works authored at that time, *Chovos HaLevavos* was originally written in Arabic. The great Jewish teachers and authors of the early Middle Ages addressed their readers in the vernacular so that language would not prove to be an obstacle towards understanding. Many of the *sefarim* of that period have been lost, but *Chovos HaLevavos* was preserved by Rabbi Yehudah ibn Tibbon, who lived in southern France during the twelfth century. Rabbi Yehudah and his family, who committed themselves to the tremendous undertaking of making the great Arabic works accessible to those Jews who did not understand the language, translated *Chovos HaLevavos* into Hebrew. The translation is often clumsy, as the Tibbonim sacrificed clarity in order to stay as close to a literal translation as possible.

Today, *Chovos HaLevavos* can be found in many Jewish homes all over the world. One of the most commonly used mussar *sefarim* in almost every Yeshivah, *Chovos HaLevavos* deals with the need to fear Hashem and love Him, as well as the need to be humble and love our fellow man. Despite its somewhat awkward rendition, *Chovos HaLevavos* has become a classic work, a link with the great thinkers and philosophers of Spain's Golden Age.

"Sh'ai Ne'esar" by R' Shlomo ibn Gabirol

Adapted from the Hebrew Text by Peninah Soloveitchik

Captured, all, by enemy hands
We long for You in foreign lands.
As children, begging for so long—
Our pain so great, our foes so strong.
    And on this day—the enemy won,
    The city's walls were overcome.

שְׁעָה נֶאֱסַר, אֲשֶׁר נִמְסַר, בְּיַד בָּבֶל וְגַם שֵׂעִיר,
לְךָ יֶהֱמֶה, זֶה כַּמֶּה, וְיִתְחַנֵּן כְּבֶן צָעִיר,
יוֹם גָּבַר הָאוֹיֵב וַתִּבָּקַע הָעִיר.

The tragedies that number five:
Mistaken death, a god contrived.
The shattered luchos in the dust.
The tomid stopped—the broken trust.
An idol placed within Your walls,
Charred ashes from Your Torah falls.
    And on this day—the enemy won,
    The city's walls were overcome.

לְזֹאת אֶכַּף, וְאֶסְפּוֹק כַּף, בְּיוֹם חָמֵשׁ פְּזָרוֹנִי,
וְעַל רֶגֶל, הָעֵגֶל, הַלּוּחוֹת יְצָאוּנִי,
וְגַם הֻשְׁמַד, הַתָּמִיד, וּבַסּוּגַּר הֱבִיאָנִי,
וְהוּשַׂם אֱלִיל, בְּהֵיכַל כְּלִיל, וּמֵעֲצָתוֹ, כְּלָאָנִי,
וְהַמִּנְחָה הֻנַּחָה, וְדָתְךָ, צָר בָּאֵשׁ הִבְעִיר.
יוֹם גָּבַר הָאוֹיֵב וַתִּבָּקַע הָעִיר.

Sick with fear as all sighs failed
Pushed aside while THEY prevailed.
Lost to Greece, to Roman laws!
Caught in Bovel's grasping claws.
    And on this day—the enemy won,
    The city's walls were overcome.

מְאֹד אֶתְחַל, וָאֶתְחַלְחַל, בְּיוֹם שַׁדַּי דְּחָפָנִי,
מְאוֹר חָשַׁךְ, וְגַם שֻׁשַּׁךְ, כְּמוֹ כַדּוּר צְנָפָנִי,
וְהַשְּׁפִיפוֹן מִצָּפוֹן, כְּשִׁבֹּלֶת שְׁטָפָנִי,
וְהַצַּיָּד, שָׁלַח יָד, וְהַצָּפִיר וְהַשָּׂעִיר.
יוֹם גָּבַר הָאוֹיֵב וַתִּבָּקַע הָעִיר.

Won't You please let wrath subside?
Our burns, our death, the tears we've cried.
We're blind, mute, lost in the night.
Come judge Your helpless nation's plight—
Mend the fence so cruelly torn—
Avenge the deaths the darkness caused.
Rebuild YOUR house the way it was!
    And on this day—the enemy won,
    The city's walls were overcome.

הוֹד לִבִּי, וּמִשְׂגַּבִּי, הֲלָעַד אַפְּךָ יֶעְשַׁן,
הֲלֹא תִרְאֶה, עַם נִלְאָה, אֲשֶׁר הָשְׁחַר כְּמוֹ כִבְשָׁן,
גְּדוֹר פִּרְצִי, בְּבֶן פַּרְצִי, וּמֶחֱדַק לְקוֹט שׁוֹשָׁן,
בְּנֵה בֵית זְבוּל, לְהָשִׁיב גְּבוּל, הַכַּרְמֶל וְהַבָּשָׁן.
וְעַיִן פְּקַח, וְנָקָם קַח, מֵאֶצֶר וּמִדִּישָׁן,
שְׁפוֹט אֵלֶם, וְאָז יְשֻׁלַּם, הַמַּבְעֶה וְהַמַּבְעִיר,
יוֹם גָּבַר הָאוֹיֵב וַתִּבָּקַע הָעִיר.

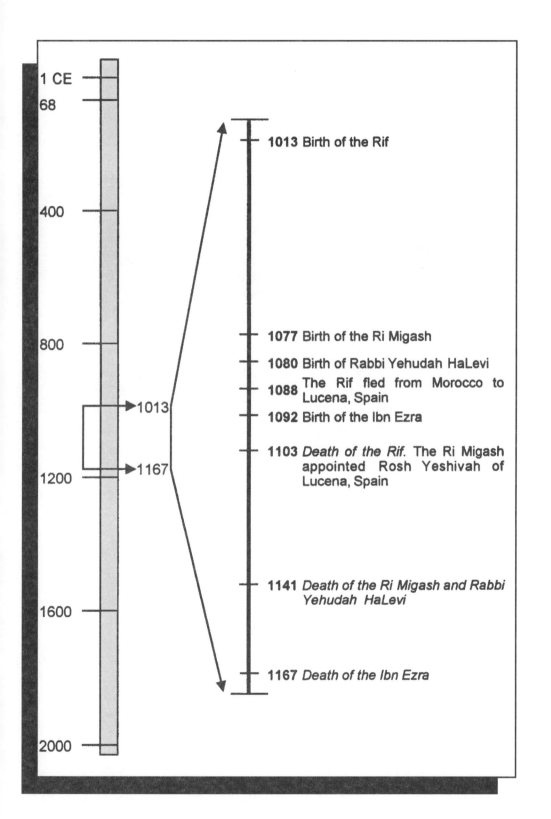

1 CE
68
400
800
1013
1167
1200
1600
2000

1013 Birth of the Rif

1077 Birth of the Ri Migash

1080 Birth of Rabbi Yehudah HaLevi

1088 The Rif fled from Morocco to Lucena, Spain

1092 Birth of the Ibn Ezra

1103 *Death of the Rif*. The Ri Migash appointed Rosh Yeshivah of Lucena, Spain

1141 *Death of the Ri Migash and Rabbi Yehudah HaLevi*

1167 *Death of the Ibn Ezra*

Chapter
11

*"No human being
could have put
together such a
work unless the
Shechinah rested
on him."*

Chapter

11

The great chain of tradition of the Spanish Yeshivos thrived and progressed under the tutelage of the Rif, Rabbeinu Yitzchak ben Yaakov Alfasi (1013-1103). Although he first arrived in Spain at the advanced age of seventy-five, he nevertheless became the spiritual leader of the city of Lucena, and his clear-eyed guidance as Rosh Yeshivah is reflected by the high caliber of the spiritual giants who were his students.

The Rif was born in the vicinity of Fez, Morocco. He received his outstanding Talmudic education in Kairouan, under Rabbeinu Chananel and Rabbeinu Nissim. Political intrigue and the threat of false arrest forced him to flee Morocco and come to Spain, where he had already acquired fame as the author of *Hilchos HaRif,* the halachic *sefer* that was his life's work.

> At times, Chazal compare Torah study to the planting of a tree: "Etz chaim hi," *it is a tree of life. Elsewhere, Torah study is compared to the building of a structure: "Do not call them your sons but your builders." These two comparisons explain the different approaches to learning that were inherent in the Franco-German centers of Torah and the academies of Spain. In France and Germany, the Torah leaders used the "etz chaim" approach, teaching their students to see Torah concepts as growing from the lines of the page of the Gemara, just as the boughs of a tree branch out from its trunk. In Spain, the Yeshivos were builders; their purpose was to construct a spiritual edifice without flaws and with no extra parts, a solidly constructed building with every brick laid in the proper place, with the ultimate objective of revealing the halachah, the final decision that would be clear and uncontested.*

Hilchos HaRif demonstrates how *halachos* are derived from the Gemara, excluding those *halachos* that pertain to life in Eretz Yisrael. The Rif rewrote the entire Babylonian Talmud; he omitted the discussions and deviating opinions, stating only the *halachah,* the final outcome, in clear terms. With this great work, the Rif began the monumental process of codification of the Talmud, a process that would be refined and reworked for generations before reaching its climax in the sixteenth century with Rabbi Yosef Karo's edition of the *Shulchan Aruch*; there were departures in style and format, but all the great scholars who furthered the codification of the Talmud relied heavily on the great trailblazing work of the Rif. The Rambam, one of the Rishonim who followed in the Rif's footsteps, wrote that in the entire work of the Rif, he found fewer than ten *halachos* that were questionable.[1] Another Rishon, one of the Baalei Tosafos, wrote that "no human being could have put together such a work unless the *Shechinah* rested on him."[2]

A typical page of the *Hilchos HaRif* looks very much like a page in the Shass itself. The large print in the center of the page is the work of the Rif, and commentaries of the Rishonim flank it on three sides, just as Rashi and *Tosafos* surround the main text of the Gemara in a page of Shass.

When the Rif died, two of the most outstanding scholars and poets who had taught in his Yeshivah, Rabbi Moshe ibn Ezra and Rabbi Yehudah HaLevi, competed to commemorate and celebrate his memory in verse. Rabbi Yehudah HaLevi's poem was chosen as a fitting inscription over the Rif's grave, to give future

---

1. Introduction to *Perush HaMishnayos* on *Zeraim.*
2. Ri Baal Tosafos, as brought down in the *Seder HaDoros,* 193.

generations a fleeting glimpse into the Rif's greatness:

> *"It was for thee that the mountains shook on the day of Sinai;*
> *For the angels of Hashem met thee,*
> *And wrote the Torah on the tablets of thy heart.*
> *They set the finest of its crowns on thy head."*

The Ri Migash (1077-1141)

After the Rif's passing, the position of Rosh Yeshivah in Lucena fell to Rabbeinu Yosef HaLevi ibn Migash, who guided the Yeshivah for nearly forty years. Rabbeinu Yosef, known as the Ri Migash, was only twenty-six at the time of his appointment; nevertheless, the Rif had specifically chosen his most outstanding pupil to succeed him as Rosh Yeshivah, even though his own son was fully qualified for the task.

The Ri Migash easily outshone all his contemporaries; the Rif wrote about him, "Even in the time of Moshe Rabbeinu there was no one like him."[3] One of his students, Rabbi Maimon, described his rebbe to his son, the Rambam: "The Talmudic knowledge of the man amazes everyone who understands his words and the depth of his speculative mind. It almost may be said that his equal has never existed."

Rabbi Yehudah HaLevi (1080-1141)

Rabbi Yehudah HaLevi, the great Torah Sage, philosopher, and poet, was another prodigious student of the Rif's Yeshivah. He became famous for his poetic work,

"Even in the time of Moshe Rabbeinu there was no one like him."

Tzionim, which exalts the Jew's love and yearning for Zion. He also authored a great classic of Jewish philosophy, the *Kuzari,* which takes the form of a dialogue between a non-Jewish king and a Jewish Sage.[4] Many classify Rabbi Yehudah HaLevi as the greatest Hebrew poet after the era of the Tanach; he was unquestionably the greatest of the Spanish era.

Yehudah ben Shmuel HaLevi was born in Toledo, one of the oldest Jewish communities in Spain. He joined the Yeshivah of Lucena at an early age, continuing his studies under the Ri Migash after the Rif's passing. At the same time, Rabbi Yehudah enriched his knowledge in the fields of philosophy, science, medicine, and Arabic literature. His main interest, however, remained poetry.

Sefer HaKuzari

In Rabbi Yehudah's day, poetry was considered the highest of all written art forms, combining precision, cleverness, beauty, and power.[5] The poets of the Jewish and Muslim worlds sought to achieve total perfection, and those who were successful were greatly revered by their contemporaries. Rabbi Yehudah's talents as a poet were outstanding even in his youth, when he wrote poetry as a source of income; eventually, however, Rabbi Yehudah

---

3. The Raavad explains that the Rif was referring to Moshe Rabbeinu's fruitless search for qualified judges who were both wise and understanding (*Devarim,* 1:12); the Ri Migash apparently possessed both attributes.

4. See Chapter 10, "Chasdai ibn Shaprut."
5. See Chapter 10, "Shlomo ibn Gabirol."

stopped writing poetry for any reason other than the glorification of Hashem's Name, utilizing his great talent only for holy purposes.

Rabbi Yehudah's masterful poetic works appear in many *machzorim,* both Sephard and Ashkenaz, and *Tzionim* is the climax of the *kinnos* recited on Tishah B'Av. His haunting songs reflect the author's love for Hashem and for Yisrael, as well as his constant yearning to live in the holy atmosphere and on the holy soil of Eretz Yisrael.

צִיּוֹן הֲלֹא תִשְׁאֲלִי לִשְׁלוֹם אֲסִירַיִךְ,
דּוֹרְשֵׁי שְׁלוֹמֵךְ וְהֵם יֶתֶר עֲדָרָיִךְ.
מִיָּם וּמִזְרָח וּמִצָּפוֹן וְתֵימָן,
שְׁלוֹם רָחוֹק וְקָרוֹב, שְׂאִי מִכֹּל עֲבָרָיִךְ.
וּשְׁלוֹם אֲסִיר תִּקְוָה, נוֹתֵן דְּמָעָיו כְּטַל חֶרְמוֹן,
וְנִכְסַף לְרִדְתָּם עַל הֲרָרָיִךְ.
לִבְכּוֹת עֱנוּתֵךְ אֲנִי תַנִּים,
וְעֵת אֶחֱלֹם שִׁיבַת שְׁבוּתֵךְ, אֲנִי כִנּוֹר לְשִׁירָיִךְ.
לִבִּי לְבֵית אֵל, וְלִפְנַי אֵל מְאֹד יֶהֱמֶה,
וּלְמַחֲנַיִם וְכָל נִגְעֵי טְהוֹרָיִךְ.
שָׁם הַשְּׁכִינָה שְׁכֵנָה לָךְ,
וְיוֹצְרֵךְ פָּתַח לְמוּל שַׁעֲרֵי שַׁחַק שְׁעָרָיִךְ.
וּכְבוֹד יְהוָה לְבַד הָיָה מְאוֹרֵךְ,
וְאֵין סַהַר וְשֶׁמֶשׁ וְכוֹכָבִים מְאוֹרָיִךְ.
אֶבְחַר לְנַפְשִׁי לְהִשְׁתַּפֵּךְ,
בִּמְקוֹם אֲשֶׁר רוּחַ אֱלֹהִים שְׁפוּכָה עַל בְּחִירָיִךְ.
אַתְּ בֵּית מְלוּכָה, וְאַתְּ כִּסֵּא כְבוֹד אֵל,
וְאֵיךְ יָשְׁבוּ עֲבָדִים עֲלֵי כִסְאוֹת גְּבִירָיִךְ.
מִי יִתְּנֵנִי מְשׁוֹטֵט,
בִּמְקוֹמוֹת אֲשֶׁר נִגְלוּ אֱלֹהִים לְחוֹזַיִךְ וְצִירָיִךְ.

*Part of Rabbi Yehudah
HaLevi's Tzionim*

Contemporary Jewish nationalists often refer to Rabbi Yehudah as one of the earliest and most outstanding "Zionists," pointing to his masterful *Tzionim* as proof of his longing for Eretz Yisrael. Such people miss the point completely. Rabbi Yehudah did not view Zion as a national homeland for the Jews like all other nations, void of Torah; Rabbi Yehudah longed for the holy Eretz Yisrael of Torah and the messianic dream of the Bais HaMikdash rebuilt.

Rabbi Yehudah HaLevi considered the Jews to be the crucial heart of all mankind, just as Eretz Yisrael is the vital, spiritual center of the entire world. Rabbi Yehudah used the *Kuzari* to expound his philosophy. Unlike Rav Saadya Gaon, who tried to create a bridge between philosophy and Judaism in his *HaEmunos VeHaDayos,* Rabbi Yehudah did not believe that reason and logic are necessary to prove the truth of Judaism; the foundation of Judaism rests, instead, on the revelation of the Torah at Mount

*Rabbi Yehudah
longed for the holy
Eretz Yisrael of
Torah and the
messianic dream of
the Bais
HaMikdash rebuilt.*

Sinai and the transmission of that knowledge from ancestor to descendant throughout the ages.

Like many of the Torah Sages of that era, Rabbi Yehudah wrote in Arabic. The *Kuzari* was later translated into Hebrew by Rabbi Yehudah ibn Tibbon.[6] The dramatic style of dialogue served as a model to later authors, including Rabbi Yitzchak Breuer, grandson of the famous Rabbi Samson Raphael Hirsch, who in modern times wrote *The New Kuzari.*

Against the advice of his family, Rabbi Yehudah finally set out in about 1141 to fulfill his greatest wish: to stand on the holy soil of Eretz Yisrael. The long, hazardous journey from Spain led him to Egypt, where many of his friends urged him to remain. Rabbi Yehudah, however, insisted on continuing the journey. Legend has it that when he arrived at the gates of Jerusalem, he fell on the ground and poured out his love for Zion in the most stirring of all the *Tzionim:* "*Tzion,* do you not ask about the well-being of your inhabitants in captivity?" Overcome with emotion, he was oblivious to the rapid approach of an armed, mounted Muslim, who contemptuously trampled

*Rabbi Yehudah did not believe
that reason and logic are
necessary to prove the truth of
Judaism; the foundation of
Judaism rests, instead, on the
revelation of the Torah at
Mount Sinai and the
transmission of that knowledge
from ancestor to descendant
throughout the ages.*

6. See Chapter 10.

the elderly Jew beneath the hooves of his horse. Even as he died, Rabbi Yehudah HaLevi sang his last verse in praise and thanks to Hashem.

Rabbi Avraham ibn Ezra
(1092-1167)

In today's modern era, it is difficult to comprehend that the greatest Rishonim of the eleventh century rarely had direct personal contact with one another. The extreme difficulties of travel, coupled with the great hazards on the road, left the sages of that time completely unknown to each other. The Rif presided over his Yeshivah, raising a generation of distinguished Torah sages in North Africa and Spain, and never met Rashi, who was imparting his unique way of learning and publishing his commentaries at the same time in France. There was, however, one lonely traveler named Rabbi Avraham ibn Ezra, who left his homeland of Spain and journeyed throughout the world, sharing the Torah of Spain with the wisdom of other countries.

No explanation has been given as to why the Ibn Ezra, when he was approximately fifty years old, began to travel the world over. Eventually known as "The Wandering Sage," the Ibn Ezra visited the great Torah scholars of each country, exchanging words of Torah and wisdom with the greatest minds of the early Middle Ages.

His most famous literary contribution is his commentary on Tanach, in which he stresses the role of grammar as the key to understanding. Although he is often independent in his approach, the Ibn Ezra yields to the explanations of Chazal with the greatest respect, even when they differ with what he believes to be

the proper approach to the text. When he feels justified in offering his own comments, his remarks reveal his incisive mind and clear thinking.

In his introduction to the Chumash, the Ibn Ezra explains his theory: "The rational approach to the understanding of Torah is the very foundation of learning. The Torah was not given to one who cannot think for himself, and the angel who serves as messenger between man and Hashem is his mind." The Rambam, who is said to have met the Ibn Ezra in Cairo, wrote a letter to his son, Avraham, in which he advises him to learn Chumash only with the commentary of the Ibn Ezra.

In addition to his Talmudic greatness, the Ibn Ezra was a poet of great skill. Although the Ibn Ezra family was extremely wealthy, he himself remained poor, despite his many efforts to earn a living. With his sharp mind and gifted pen, the Ibn Ezra expressed his wry frustration in a two-line poem:[7]

> "If candles were my business, the sun would never set;
>
> If I were dealing in shrouds, no one would ever die."

One of his inspired works is the composition "Tzamah Nafshi L'Eilokim," "My Soul Thirsts for Hashem," sung on Shabbos. His poetic genius is evident in the beauty of rhyme and meter as well as the easy flow of the words.

The Ibn Ezra was a close friend of Rabbi Yehudah HaLevi and, according to legend, his son-in-law as well.[8] The story is told that Rabbi Yehudah, who was extremely wealthy, had a beautiful daughter who was born to him in his old age. When she reached marriageable age, her

---

7. Some attribute this poem to the brother of the Ibn Ezra.
8. *Seder HaDoros.*

"The rational approach to the understanding of Torah is the very foundation of learning. The Torah was not given to one who cannot think for himself, and the angel who serves as messenger between man and Hashem is his mind."

Chapter

11

mother constantly pressured Rabbi Yehudah to find a proper husband for their daughter while both parents were still alive. Rabbi Yehudah swore in exasperation that he would marry off his daughter to the first Jewish man to enter their house.

Rabbi Yehudah's wife nearly fainted when the Ibn Ezra showed up at their doorstep the following morning, dressed in shabby clothing and appearing to be nothing more than a wandering beggar. Investigation into the stranger's background seemed to prove that he was completely ignorant, as the Ibn Ezra concealed his genius. With Rabbi Yehudah's vow, they would have no choice but to marry off their daughter to an ignorant pauper! Crying bitterly, she went to the study hall, where Rabbi Yehudah comforted her by saying, "Don't worry. I will teach him Torah and he will yet become a great man in Yisrael."

The Ibn Ezra and Rabbi Yehudah began studying Torah together, and the apparent "ignoramus" made astonishingly rapid progress. One evening, Rabbi Yehudah found himself unable to complete a stanza that he was composing; he could not find the proper words to complete a line beginning with the letter *resh*.[9] His "ignorant" study partner secretly filled in the missing line, and Rabbi Yehudah soon realized that the stranger was none other than the famous Rabbi Avraham ibn Ezra! The wedding was soon celebrated with great joy, and the two poets and scholars shared many years of scholarship and camaraderie together.

---

9. Most medieval poetry was based on acrostics, requiring the author to start his lines with predetermined letters.

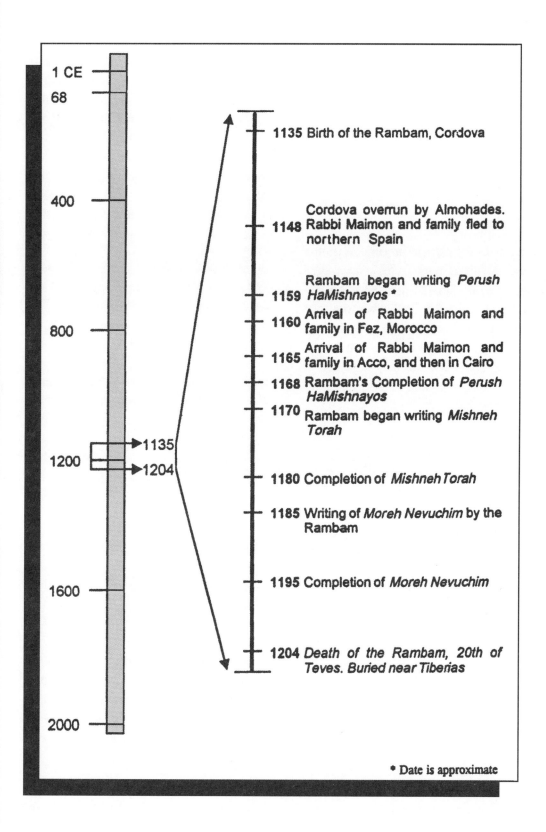

1 CE
68
400
800
1200
1600
2000

1135
1204

1135 Birth of the Rambam, Cordova

1148 Cordova overrun by Almohades. Rabbi Maimon and family fled to northern Spain

1159 Rambam began writing *Perush HaMishnayos* *

1160 Arrival of Rabbi Maimon and family in Fez, Morocco

1165 Arrival of Rabbi Maimon and family in Acco, and then in Cairo

1168 Rambam's Completion of *Perush HaMishnayos*

1170 Rambam began writing *Mishneh Torah*

1180 Completion of *Mishneh Torah*

1185 Writing of *Moreh Nevuchim* by the Rambam

1195 Completion of *Moreh Nevuchim*

1204 *Death of the Rambam, 20th of Teves. Buried near Tiberias*

* Date is approximate

Chapter
12

Rabbi Maimon's extensive library was lost, burned by the Almohades, but the precious contents of the Gemara and the other works in Rabbi Maimon's library remained indelibly imprinted in Moshe's memory.

The Golden Age of Spain reached its highest pinnacle in the twelfth century with Rabbi Moshe ben Maimon, better known as the Rambam (Maimonides). It is difficult to point to anyone else in history who was as revered by Jew and non-Jew alike. His unique stature is indicated by the words engraved in bold letters over the portals of his grave in Tiberias: "*MiMoshe ad Moshe lo kom k'Moshe.*" "From the time of Moshe Rabbeinu until Moshe ben Maimon there was no one like Moshe."

During the Rambam's lifetime and for many years after, many of his *sefarim* provoked violent, fiery controversy, to the point where the *Moreh Nevuchim* was put in *cherem,* or excommunication.[1] Such opposition, however, has long since abated; today, the world is unanimous in its praise of the Rambam and his awesome contribution to Torah.

The Rambam was born on Erev Pesach of the year 4895 (1135) at 1:20 p.m. His father, Rabbi Maimon ben Yosef, served as the Dayan of Cordova at a time when the city had lost its distinction as the world center of Torah it had been in the past. Still, Cordova remained a city steeped in learning, and young Moshe received an excellent education in Talmud from his father, a talmid of the great Ri Migash.[2] In addition, Moshe studied all the academic subjects popular in his day, leading a quiet, idyllic life of Torah until his thirteenth year.

In 4908 (1148), the splendor and beauty of Cordova was destroyed in a vicious invasion of a fierce, uncompromising Muslim sect, the Almohades. They gave the Jews of Cordova an ultimatum: accept Islam or die. Many Jews were savagely killed; others, who did not have the courage to resist, subsequently converted. Only a handful managed to escape.

Among the survivors were the Maimon family, who fled in haste, empty-handed and nearly penniless, to find temporary refuge to the north in Catholic Spain. Rabbi Maimon's extensive library was lost, burned by the Almohades, but the precious contents of the Gemara and the other works in Rabbi Maimon's library remained indelibly imprinted in Moshe's memory.

The Maimons did not stay in Spain for long. In approximately 4920 (1160), Rabbi Maimon and his family moved to Fez, Morocco, where they stayed for a short time. Once again, they found themselves faced with the hatred of the fanatic Almohades who ruled there. Scores of local Jews were forced ostensibly to convert to Islam, retaining their loyalty to the Jewish faith in fearful secrecy. Decree followed harsh decree, and the rabbi of Fez, who had taught both Rabbi Maimon and his son, died a martyr's death.

Rabbi Maimon's encouragement to the local populace and his public stand against conversions made his family a primary target. The pressure became too much to bear, and Rabbi Maimon was once again forced to abandon his home. Together with his family, he began the long, perilous journey to Eretz Yisrael. Their ship cast anchor in Acco in 4925 (1165), and Rabbi Maimon and his family gratefully kissed the ground of the Holy Land.

It is unknown why Rabbi Maimon was unable to remain in Eretz Yisrael, but

1. See Chapter 16.
2. See Chapter 11.

the family eventually migrated to Egypt, where the Rambam and his brother, David, finally established permanent residence in the city of Fostat.[3] The two brothers set up a partnership, modeled after that of Yissachar and Zevulun.[4] This made it possible for the Rambam to devote all his time to the study of Torah, earning the title of *Naggid* in Fostat, while David conducted a lucrative diamond business and supported their families.

Unfortunately, this ideal arrangement did not last for very long. David converted all the family's assets to precious stones for a business trip, set sail for India, and was never heard from again. Rabbeinu Moshe and his family lost not only their beloved relative, but also their sole financial support.

For an entire year, the Rambam was bedridden from grief and shock over this tragedy. Faced with the responsibility of providing a livelihood for both David's family and his own, Rabbeinu Moshe turned to the profession of medicine, which he had studied during the brief period he had lived in Spain. Within a short time, he was famed as one of the most outstanding physicians in the world. His reputation led to his appointment as the Royal Physician to the Sultan Saladin and his court.

From that time on, Rabbeinu Moshe had to divide his precious time between three major occupations: earning a livelihood for two families, serving as rabbi of the Jewish community of Fostat, and devoting himself to the writing of his *sefarim*. In a letter to a close friend, the Rambam describes his daily schedule. After an arduous day at the Sultan's palace he would come home, hungry and exhausted, only to find his home crowded with patients seeking his medical expertise. Instead of relaxing after a grueling day, he saw these patients while eating his evening meal, continuing in this fashion until well into the night.

It is incredible that despite the strain of such a grueling schedule, the Rambam managed to author his many *sefarim*. Most other great scholars would have needed to devote an entire lifetime just for the requisite research, not inclusive of the actual writing and revising of such major works; the Rambam's hectic schedule was interrupted only by Shabbos, when he gave *shiurim* and devoted his time to the needs of his congregation. Nevertheless, the Rambam somehow found time to produce three major works, besides writing many letters and halachic responsa.

Early Success: The *Perush HaMishnayos*

The Rambam began writing his first major work, a commentary on the Six Orders of the Mishnah, while he was still in his twenties. The manuscript accompanied him on his travels for nearly ten years, from Muslim Spain to Fez, to Eretz Yisrael, to Egypt, where he was finally able to complete it. In this ambitious work, the Rambam sought to make the Mishnah comprehensible to all Jews, even those who had not studied the Gemara associated with each particular Mishnah. The sheer volume of Talmudic debate in connection with each Mishnah made this a truly gigantic undertaking.

In addition to tracing the background and structure of the Mishnah, the Rambam

Within a short time, he was famed as one of the most outstanding physicians in the world. His reputation led to his appointment as the Royal Physician to the Sultan Saladin and his court.

---

3. Rabbi Maimon died either in Eretz Yisrael or in Egypt soon after their arrival.
4. *Devarim*, 33:18.

Chapter

12

The Perush HaMishnayos of the Rambam

Of special significance is the section known as the Shemonah Perakim, an introduction to Pirkei Avos, in which the Rambam writes about matters of faith in Hashem, proper understanding of prophecy, and explanations relating to mussar and middos.

offers guidelines to its proper understanding. At the beginning of every *masechta,* he explains its connection with the preceding one; at the conclusion of each *mishnah,* he notes the final outcome of the discussion among the Tannaim.[5] Quite often, he uses his vast scientific knowledge to clarify technical matters, enabling the average person to understand the discussion more clearly.

Of special significance is the section known as the *Shemonah Perakim,* an introduction to *Pirkei Avos,* in which the Rambam writes about matters of faith in Hashem, proper understanding of prophecy, and explanations relating to mussar and *middos.*

The *Thirteen Principles of Faith* was written as his introduction to the section of

_____

5. See Chapter 2 for clarification of terms.

Perek Chailek of *Sanhedrin.* According to the Rambam, it is mandatory for each Jew to believe in all these thirteen principles, and a Jew who lacks belief in any one of them is a *kofer,* a heretic. The *Ani Maamin* listing found in today's siddur is significantly changed from the Rambam's original version. A version of these principles is also found in the song *Yigdal,* at the beginning of *Shacharis.*

The Rambam wrote his commentary in Arabic, the most common language among Jews of his day. The commentary became so popular that a translation of the *Perush HaMishnayos* into Hebrew was begun during the Rambam's lifetime and was completed less than one hundred years after his death. Today, the Rambam's *Perush HaMishnayos* is included in most editions of the Talmud Bavli.

The *Mishneh Torah*

Two years after the completion of *Perush HaMishnayos,* the Rambam started his next monumental work, the *Mishneh Torah.* He devoted the next decade to this sefer, systematically collecting all laws from the Talmud Bavli and Yerushalmi, as well as the *minhagim* of the Geonic era. In his introduction, the Rambam writes:

"It was my intention that all the laws should become clear to everyone, from the smallest to the greatest scholar... a person should not need to study any other book on Jewish law, as this work contains a complete collection of the entire Oral Torah, including additional decrees and customs that were established from the days of Moshe Rabbeinu until the completion of the Talmud. That is why I named this book *Mishneh Torah* [literally, 'Review of the Torah'], because after a person learns the Written Torah, he can turn directly to this book and know everything there is to know about the Oral Torah, with no other book in between."

The concept of codifying the Talmud was not a new one; the Rambam was following in the Rif's footsteps.[6] However, unlike the Rif, the Rambam included *halachos* which apply only in Eretz Yisrael, as well as those that apply only at the time of the Bais HaMikdash. In addition, the Rambam was the first to deviate from the order of the Mishnah. A systematic thinker, he preferred a topical order to the one used in the Shass. For example, he arranged all the laws concerning Shabbos in one book, even though they are actually scattered among many *masechtos* of the Gemara. This arrangement makes research or study on any particular topic much simpler. Because the *Mishneh Torah* is divided into fourteen sections and the alphabetic equivalent of 14 is *yad*, the Rambam subtitled his work *HaYad HaChazakah*.

Unlike the Rambam's other literary works, the *Mishneh Torah* is written in classical Hebrew, imitating the style and the language of Rabbi Yehudah HaNasi.[7] The Rambam often introduces a new segment with a brief historical essay; one of the most famous of these is his explanation of the origin of idol worship. Other sections end with incisive remarks about the significance of the particular mitzvah discussed, and its purpose of bringing the Jew closer to Hashem. In addition, the Rambam often uses his broad education to enhance his work. For example, in dealing with the laws of *Kiddush HaChodesh,* the Rambam demonstrates his vast knowledge of astronomy and mathematics. In other parts of the *Mishneh Torah,* he dispenses

medical advice and recommends the practice of preventive medicine; he even guarantees a long, healthy life, with the help of Hashem, to those who follow his directions.[8]

Opposition to the *Mishneh Torah*

Given its radically novel approach, it is unsurprising that the Rambam's *Mishneh Torah* became engulfed in controversy both during and after his lifetime. The Rambam's premise in his introduction that his *sefer* would virtually eliminate the need for learning Gemara created a storm of protest among many *Gedolim*. They feared that even Jews who were capable of learning the Gemara and Rishonim might take advantage of the shortcut and neglect the study of the original sources.

The Rambam's omission of the sources for his halachic decisions also drew serious criticism as being highly presumptuous. How could the Rambam be so sure that his rulings were correct? And even if he was certain of his decisions, why did he not make it possible for others to examine his reasoning and then draw their own conclusions? The Rambam later admitted that he could not always remember the sources for his rulings. His intention had been to keep his book clear and uncomplicated, to make it accessible to those who had difficulties in mastering the language and style of Talmudic presentation.

Today, it is evident that history has completely vindicated the Rambam's approach. Fears that the *Mishneh Torah* would tempt scholars to neglect the Gemara have proven false; on the contrary, the *Mishneh Torah* has stimulated Talmud study and helped broaden and

"*After a person learns the Written Torah, he can turn directly to this book and know everything there is to know about the Oral Torah, with no other book in between.*"

6. See Chapter 11.
7. See Chapter 2.

8. *Hilchos Dayos,* 4:20.

> *Many contemporary scholars use the text of the Mishneh Torah to cast new light on difficult passages in the Gemara that would have otherwise remained enigmas.*

deepen its scope. Many contemporary scholars use the text of the *Mishneh Torah* to cast new light on difficult passages in the Gemara that would have otherwise remained enigmas.

The *Moreh Nevuchim*

The third major work of the Rambam is the *Moreh Nevuchim,* "Guide for the Perplexed." Like his *Perush HaMishnayos,* the *Moreh Nevuchim* was later translated from the original Arabic into Hebrew by the Ibn Tibbon family. The *sefer* deals with philosophy, a crucial subject that had raised many troubling questions in that era.

In the Rambam's day, many Jews studied Greek and Arabic philosophy, with its emphasis on logic and rational thinking. As a result, many questions arose which might have led to an undermining of belief in Hashem and His Torah. In response to a request for guidance from one of his students, Yosef ben Aknin, the Rambam wrote the *Moreh Nevuchim,* which explains to those exposed to the influence of Greek philosophy that there is no contradiction whatsoever between philosophy and *emunah.* He proves the truth of the fundamental principles of the Jewish faith and gives explanations for the 613 mitzvos.[9]

This work has since served as a valuable philosophical guide to many thousands of Jews. At the time, however, it aroused tempestuous opposition from others who preferred a pure, uncomplicated belief in Hashem and His Torah. These critics considered it wrong to introduce philosophical rationale to the general

Jewish population, who may have never questioned their faith in the first place. They also objected to many of his explanations of the mitzvos. Although the work was clearly intended for those who were already trained in philosophical thought, it was feared that others could stumble over the questions raised. The controversy raged, even long after the Rambam's death; but today, debate on the *Moreh Nevuchim* has long since vanished, and it has assumed a place of honor within the legacy of the Rambam.

Iggeres Taiman

One of the Rambam's most famous responsa is *Iggeres Taiman,* a letter written to the Jews of Yemen. At the time, the Yemenite Jews had been brutally harassed by their Muslim rulers, who forced many Jews to convert to Islam. Many of these Jews converted outwardly with the intention of reverting to Judaism as soon an possible, and they were condemned as outcasts who should no longer be considered Jews. At the same time, an impostor proclaimed himself to be the Messiah and attempted to attract the few remaining faithful Jews. The Jews of Yemen, unable to defend themselves against these challenges that threatened them on all sides, desperately turned to the Rambam for guidance.

In his elaborate epistle, the Rambam proves that although Islam is *kefirah,* heresy, it does not fall within the realm of *avodah zarah,* idol worship. Therefore, asserts the Rambam, Jews who lacked the inner strength to withstand forced conversion should not be treated as idol worshipers. Instead, they deserve the

---

9. The Rambam himself stresses very strongly at the end of *Hilchos Me'ilah* 8:8 that keeping the mitzvos of the Torah is not based on our understanding or philosophic rationalization of the mitzvos. We are obligated to follow the laws of the Torah, despite our lack of understanding.

compassion and concern of fellow Jews; they should be encouraged to repent and be assured that Hashem would welcome them with "open arms." The letter also completely demolishes the messianic claims of the impostor and implores the Yemenite Jews to ignore him.

The Rambam, with his incisive leadership, was not satisfied with merely addressing these urgent crises in his letter to Yemen. He used his personal influence with Sultan Saladin of Egypt to change the hostile attitude of the Islamic ruler of Yemen and persuade him to rescind his anti-Jewish decrees. The Yemenite Jews were so thankful for the Rambam's help that they incorporated blessings for him into the text of their daily Kaddish by adding the phrase: *Uv'Chayai Rabbeinu Moshe.*

A Shining Legacy

The Rambam passed away on the twentieth of Teves, 4965 (1204), just three months before reaching the age of seventy. His son, Avraham, an erudite scholar and able communal leader,

Grave of the Rambam

served as his successor. Following in his father's footsteps, he penned insightful Torah analyses and served with great skill as physician of the Sultan's court. The Rambam had asked that he be buried in Eretz Yisrael, where he had yearned to be all his life. As the entire Jewish world mourned, he was laid to rest near Tiberias in a grave overlooking Yam Kinneret. A noble leader, a profound thinker, a skilled spokesman, and above all, a towering Torah Sage, the Rambam lives in Jewish hearts and minds forever.

Chapter
12

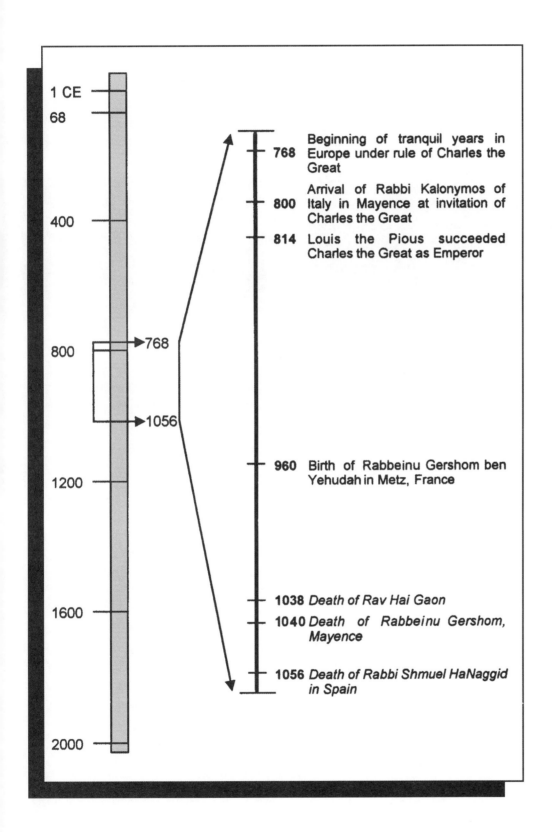

768	Beginning of tranquil years in Europe under rule of Charles the Great	
800	Arrival of Rabbi Kalonymos of Italy in Mayence at invitation of Charles the Great	
814	Louis the Pious succeeded Charles the Great as Emperor	
960	Birth of Rabbeinu Gershom ben Yehudah in Metz, France	
1038	*Death of Rav Hai Gaon*	
1040	*Death of Rabbeinu Gershom, Mayence*	
1056	*Death of Rabbi Shmuel HaNaggid in Spain*	

Chapter
13

*The well-being of
the Jews in
Germany and
France seesawed
according to the
balance of power
between the
temporal
authorities and the
Christian clergy.*

Chapter

13

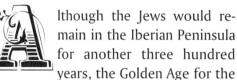lthough the Jews would remain in the Iberian Peninsula for another three hundred years, the Golden Age for the Jews in Spain essentially came to an end during the twelfth century. Increasingly larger tracts of territory in Spain and Portugal were conquered by Christian forces, which brought to an end the unique Spanish approach to Torah. While Torah Sages who later emerged on Spanish soil are ranked among the most prominent Rishonim, their outlook was not uniquely Spanish; the training of their homeland was tempered by a strong Middle European influence. A study of the history of the Franco–German Jewish centers aids in understanding the forces that shaped and tempered the Rishonim of that era.

Europe in the Early Middle Ages

In the Hebrew translation of Chovos HaLevavos, *Ibn Tibbon referred to the Jewish exile in the Franco-German countries as* Galus Edom *and the suffering of the Jews in Spain as* Galus Sepharad. *The distinction Ibn Tibbon made between Edom and Sepharad lay in the Gentile's attitude towards the Jews. In this case, Edom is represented by the Catholic Church, whose attitude towards the Jews was continuous, unmitigated hatred.*

The Jews had come to Europe at the heels of the Roman legionnaires as early as the first century C.E. At that time, Germany and France were not unified countries ruled by an absolute monarchy. Instead, they were inhabited by a number of tribes, split into many provinces and principalities which were constantly at war with one another. This left its savage mark on Europe, creating smoldering resentments and hatreds. Even when there were no actual battles taking place, mutual jealousy and rivalry between tribal

factions ruled out any possibility of peaceful, friendly relations.

In most European countries, the Jew was neither vassal nor serf, soldier nor citizen. He was an alien. As such, his rights and privileges were regulated by local authorities, varying drastically from place to place, and from time to time. His presence in a particular province could be legally banned altogether. Because the Jews were always considered outsiders, they were constantly suspected of collaborating with the enemies. Mob raids on Jews were not uncommon after a territory had been attacked by neighboring warriors.

The Franco-German tribes eventually accepted Christianity and came under the control of the Roman Catholic Church. Several of the tribes, slower to abandon paganism than others, resisted the interference of the clergy. The clergy's constant struggle for Christian supremacy soon became the basis for their treatment of the Jews.

The clergy was an independent social class, deemed to be equal to, or even higher than, the ruling class. These churchmen frequently enjoyed greater advantages than the lords, both economically and politically. The lords and the clergy maintained an uneasy balance of power, ruling their jurisdictions with joint, wary respect; at times, bitter struggles and deadly battles erupted between the two powerful and greedy factions. The well-being of the Jews in Germany and France seesawed according to the balance of power between the temporal authorities and the Christian clergy. When rulers had the strength to be more independent of the clergy, and it suited their economic purposes, or if the rulers wanted to exploit the economic strength of the Jews, they treated the Jews relatively well; if the balance of power tipped towards the clergy, the usual results were harsh decrees and pogroms.

Christianity's origins lay in an obscure Jewish sect, and the clergy feared that the Jews could somehow undermine their religion and undercut their power base. To prevent any such possibility, Church laws were framed with the intent of separating Jews from Christians and relegating the Jews to an inferior economic and social position. Even during the height of the Church's expansion in the twelfth and thirteenth centuries, the fear of Jewish influence led to vehement and often violent reactions. Jews were constantly suspected of instigating various heretical sects to challenge the Church. Any religious opponent of conventional Church doctrines was stigmatized as a "Jew," the term applying to anyone endangering the status quo, regardless of his nationality.

The Pope, the ruling head of the established Church, had his headquarters in Rome. Unlike their counterparts throughout Europe, the Roman Jews were able to establish a wary understanding with the clergy, to the point where some Jews were actually in direct service to the Pope. The Jewish community generally went out of its way to cultivate the good graces of the ruling Church head, steadfastly ignoring constant, pointed reminders that the Jews were a terrible, despicable race. As a result, the Pope tended to protect the Jews instead of encouraging assault, and Jews of other countries frequently looked to the Pope for defense against over-zealous local bishops.

According to Christian belief, their messiah was executed by the Romans following his betrayal to the heathens by a Jew named Judas. With time, the figure of Judas came to symbolize all Jews— and, of course, no "Judas" could ever be trusted. This traditional teaching was stressed by the Church in generation after generation, until the automatic distrust of any Jew became a deep-seated, absolute conviction in the mind of every Christian. The propaganda was spread throughout Europe via the written word, inflammatory sermons, and annual Easter plays, vividly depicting the betrayal and subsequent crucifixion of the Christian savior due to the evil actions of the villainous Jews.

As Easter is considered the date of his resurrection, the holiday lent itself to virulent attacks on the Jewish community. As early as the eighth century, it had become traditional for the Christians to mount a bloody pogrom against the "evil" Jews during the Easter season of spring. Each year, the Jews of Europe would brace themselves for the hysterical, bloodthirsty mobs which would come pouring out of the churches after being exhorted to destroy the enemies of their god. At times, Jewish communities could manage to raise significant sums of money to bribe the local clergy to prevent these attacks, but the Easter season was most often one of terror and death.

Even when the clergy had established a firm religious power base, the Jews still presented a problem for them—an economic one. It had become customary for the priests to collect considerable revenue from the "ecclesiastical tithe," a tax system based on the Biblical concept of *maaser*. Essentially a tax on land ownership, the giving of a tenth, or "tithe," applied only to Christians; because they were not subject to Church taxes, Jews were exempt from the tithe. Consequently, sharp opposition arose from the local church whenever land which

The fear of Jewish influence led to vehement and often violent reactions.

The typical Jew's faith remained pure and staunch; the constant threat of pogroms and other dangers caused the Jews of Ashkenaz (Germany) and Tzarfas (France) to acquire invincible belief in Hashem and an unquestioning readiness for mesiras nefesh.

had been owned by a Christian was transferred to a Jew. As more and more Jews bought land, the churches were gradually deprived of an extremely valuable source of wealth.

When Jewish land ownership expanded considerably in the tenth to twelfth centuries, the churches became alarmed and they agitated for permission to impose the tithe on Jewish landowners. In some areas, the tax was imposed, but it often proved unenforceable. When that ploy failed, the clergy reverted to the active encouragement of the expulsion of Jews from their territories; once the Jews were gone, the land reverted to Christian hands, and the tithes were once more resumed. With time, Jewish landowners became exceedingly rare; in Germany, Jewish land ownership was entirely impossible. With no other source of revenue, many Jews turned to commerce and money-lending. This was due to a ban on Christians lending money with interest; Jews thus became the middlemen between the Church and the borrower. The Torah forbids lending for interest only between Jews, but permits the taking of interest as legitimate profit in transactions between Jews and Gentiles.

The terms "Jew" and "merchant" soon became interchangeable in Europe. The Jews developed international trade routes, and later engaged in money-lending and banking. The prosperity and economic expansion of the largely illiterate German and French aristocracy depended on the Jews' superior education and experience. All too often, Jews were instrumental in building cities on sound financial bases, only to be dismissed from the province or relegated to inferior economic and social positions once they were no longer needed.

Because of the uneasy climate of alternating isolation and anti-Semitism in Europe, the Franco-German Jews, unlike their Spanish counterparts, were not culturally involved with non-Jews. Indeed, secular education could be found only in the monasteries. The typical Jew's faith remained pure and staunch; the constant threat of pogroms and other dangers caused the Jews of *Ashkenaz* (Germany) and *Tzarfas* (France) to acquire invincible belief in Hashem and an unquestioning readiness for *mesiras nefesh,* the willingness to completely dedicate one's life to Hashem. Hence, there were no Marranos in France and Germany. When faced with ultimatums of conversion or death, many thousands of men, women, and children died for the sanctification of Hashem's Name.

The reign of Charles the Great, also known as Charlemagne (768-814), and that of his son Louis the Pious (814-840) represented a relatively tranquil period for the Jews under the feudal system. One of the great Emperors to rule Germany during the Middle Ages, Charlemagne's kingdom stretched over the entire European continent from north to south and westward to the Atlantic Ocean. As a powerful and independent monarch, able to make decisions independent of the clergy's wishes, he attracted a number of Jews to his court.

It is largely believed that it was at Charlemagne's invitation that one of the leading scholars of Italy, the famous Rabbi Kalonymos, moved to the German city of Mayence and founded a Yeshivah there. The Emperor appointed a "Master of the Jews," a rabbi, in every locale throughout his kingdom to maintain their protection and welfare. Permission was granted for internal disputes between Jews to be judged by a *Din Torah.* New shuls were built and communities grew.

In some cities, especially in southern France, the Jews were treated well, enjoying numerous equal rights with the non-Jews; in Lyons, for example, the market day was changed to a weekday, because the Jews would not trade on Shabbos. This is not to say that the Jews lived in complete freedom; trade restrictions were still enforced and the penalties for crimes against a Christian were much more severe than those for crimes committed against a Jew. Still, the relative autonomy and tolerance granted the Jews by Charlemagne allowed Jewish life to flourish.

Rabbeinu Gershom
(960–1040 C.E.)[1]

After the fateful ransom of Rav Nassan ben Yitzchak, one of the four captives from Bavel, Rav Nassan founded a Yeshivah in Narbonne, France. It was there that Rabbeinu Gershom studied at the feet of Rabbi Meir Leontin, the man to whom Rabbeinu Gershom claimed he owed all his knowledge.

Rabbeinu Gershom and his brother, Machir, moved from Narbonne to Mayence, Germany, possibly at the invitation of the Kalonymos family. Rabbeinu Gershom, who was called *Meor HaGolah,* "The Light of the Diaspora," was quickly acknowledged as the leading Torah authority of three European countries, France, Germany, and Italy, who had the *mesorah* of the Geonim.

His innovative style of learning clarifies the apparent meaning of the Gemara. Recorded in the margin of the Gemara, his comments are always brief, clear, and pertinent. Rabbeinu Gershom's "footnotes" have become an indispensable key in understanding many difficult sections of the Talmud.

Rabbeinu Gershom also contributed to the liturgy of the *machzor* with compositions such as the beautiful and stirring *Zechor Bris.* In this poetic piece, he describes the suffering of the Jews in Germany during a time of upheaval and tragedy. At the beginning of the eleventh century, a Christian cleric converted to Judaism and later engaged in a bitter controversy with one of his former Christian students. This scandal shocked the Christian population of the city and caused Emperor Henry II to order the expulsion of the entire Jewish community of Mayence in the year 4772 (1012). Faced with the possible loss of their lives or properties, a number of Jews chose conversion instead, including Rabbeinu Gershom's own son. Shocked and grieved by his son's apostasy, Rabbeinu Gershom nevertheless sat *shivah* for him when he died shortly thereafter. With the rescinding of the expulsion decree some time later, many of the baptized Jews returned to Judaism. Rabbeinu Gershom decreed that no Jew should be so heartless as to remind these returned Jews of their prior conversions.

Rabbeinu Gershom is remembered chiefly for his *takanos,* special decrees binding upon all Jews under his jurisdiction. Rabbeinu Gershom's *takanos* were adopted by the leading rabbis, and he reinforced them by issuing a *cherem,* or excommunication, against transgressors. Despite the fact that there was no Sanhedrin in existence to support him, Rabbeinu Gershom commanded such universal respect and recognition that his *takanos* became accepted as law by the Ashkenazic Jews wherever they lived, and still remain in effect today.

His *takanos* are listed in the *Be'er HaGolah,* a commentary on the *Shulchan Aruch.*[2] Among them are:

In Southern France, the Jews were treated well, enjoying numerous equal rights with the non-Jews.

---

1. Some are of the opinion that he died in 1028.

2. *Yoreh Deah,* 334.

Rabbeinu Gershom serves as a crucial link in the chain of events that brought the scholarship of Babylonia to Europe, where the burning flame of Torah still brings light to the darkness of the Diaspora today.

Marriage

1) No man is permitted to be married to more than one wife under any circumstance. Polygamy is still practiced among some Oriental Jews, who did not fall under Rabbeinu Gershom's jurisdiction, but it was completely abolished in Europe. There are some halachic authorities who believe that this famous ban of Rabbeinu Gershom was temporary, slated to end by the year 5000 (1240), but the *takanah* still remains in force today.

2) A woman may not be forced to accept a *get,* a bill of Jewish divorce. Although the Torah gives a husband the right to divorce his wife, Rabbeinu Gershom decreed that the woman must agree to the divorce.[3]

Relationships among Jews

3) One may not violate the privacy of a letter which was entrusted to him for delivery to a fellow Jew. There was no postal service during the Middle Ages, and confidential correspondence was often carried by private couriers, making this *takanah* a necessity. The ban excluded open notes or any mail that had obviously been discarded.

4) One may not make derogatory comments to a Jew who had converted to Christianity and later repented his decision. In the light of the tragic events in Europe during Rabbeinu Gershom's lifetime, this decree was deemed a necessary humane gesture and was readily accepted.

Integrity of Learning and Prayer

5) A ban was decreed against cutting off the margin of paper on which *sefarim* are written, for the edges of each page were used by readers to record their own notes and comments. Indeed, Rashi wrote his famous commentary in the margins of his *sefarim,* and this technique is still employed by students of the Talmud.

6) One may not talk in shul during prayer. Rabbeinu Gershom wished to guarantee that every Jew would worship with awe and reverence, without engaging in idle conversation.

Rabbeinu Gershom's leadership in Europe during the eleventh century coincided with the decline of the Geonic authority in Bavel. Moreover, it may have actually been one of its causes, for the European Jews, who had previously relied upon the halachic decisions of the distant Babylonian leaders, now had their own Talmudic authorities nearby. Rabbeinu Gershom serves as a crucial link in the chain of events that brought the scholarship of Babylonia to Europe, where the burning flame of Torah still brings light to the darkness of the Diaspora today.

---

3. In cases of extreme hardship where the consent of the woman is impossible to obtain (for example, if the woman is mentally ill), there are halachic means to circumvent Rabbeinu Gershom's decree.

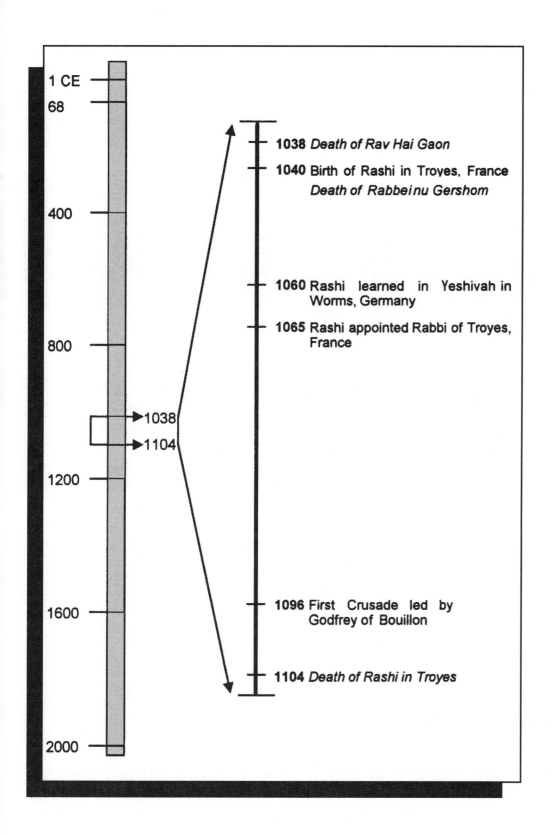

1038 *Death of Rav Hai Gaon*

1040 Birth of Rashi in Troyes, France
Death of Rabbeinu Gershom

1060 Rashi learned in Yeshivah in Worms, Germany

1065 Rashi appointed Rabbi of Troyes, France

1096 First Crusade led by Godfrey of Bouillon

1104 *Death of Rashi in Troyes*

Chapter
14

This child's Torah would indeed illuminate the world.

or sixty-four years, the Jews of Germany and France were blessed with the presence of a Torah sage about whom it is still said: "*Mipiv anu chayim,*" meaning that without him we could not be alive. His commentary lives and breathes on the lips of thousands of students of Torah, from the smallest child to the greatest Sage. This was Rashi, **R**abbi **Sh**lomo **Y**itzchaki (ben Yitzchak), a figure larger than life whose story cannot easily be reduced into a framework of time or space.

Rashi was born in Troyes, France, in the year 1040, in the same year as Rabbeinu Gershom's passing and not long after Rav Hai Gaon died in Bavel. In later years, this seeming "coincidence" was recognized as a fulfillment of the passage, "*Vezorach hashemesh uvo hashemesh,* "The sun sets and the sun rises,"[1] meaning that Hashem immediately compensates for the loss of the leading Sage of the generation with another great leader to take his place.

Before Rashi's birth, Rabbi Yitzchak made his living from selling precious stones. A famous story relates that he once possessed a very rare and precious diamond which the Christians in Troyes wanted for their church. When Rabbi Yitzchak refused to sell it for idolatrous purposes at any price, the priests set out to obtain it by force. Through false pretenses, they induced him to board a ship with them. Once on the high seas, they threatened him with death if he would refuse to sell them the coveted jewel. Realizing that he was trapped, Rabbi Yitzchak threw the jewel overboard, willing to suffer a tremendous loss rather than sell the diamond to the Church.

At that moment, a heavenly voice announced to Rabbi Yitzchak's students in the study hall, "Rabbi Yitzchak will be compensated for the loss of this brilliant jewel with the birth of a son, whose light will shine from one end of the world to the other."

When Rabbi Yitzchak returned to his study hall, a heavenly voice cried out again, "You have cast away a precious diamond, lest the name of the Creator become desecrated through you. You shall therefore be blessed with a son who will enlighten the eyes of Israel with Torah, and through whom the name of the Almighty will become exalted."[2]

The following year, Rashi was born. The succeeding years proved, without a doubt, that this child's Torah would indeed illuminate the world.

Rabbi Yitzchak, a renowned scholar, taught Rashi in his early youth. (According to the Taz, the words "Rabbi Yitzchak says" quoted in Rashi's commentary in the first *pasuk* of Chumash, refers to none other than Rashi's father.) It did not take long for all of France to recognize the young man as an outstanding scholar, surpassing his own teachers.

Rashi habitually recorded insights which he heard, and in some cases added his own. Rashi wrote his explanations or notes to himself in notebooks (in Hebrew: *kuntress*). Therefore his grandsons, the Baalei Tosafos, admiringly referred to his opinion as *Kuntress.*

Anyone who has ever studied Rashi is aware of the brevity and clarity of his explanations. It is said that Rashi wrote with "golden ink," meaning that he used it sparingly, only for what was absolutely

---

1. *Koheles,* 1:5.

2. From *Shalsheles HaKabbalah,* quoted in *Challenge of Sinai* by Zecharia Fendel, Hashkafah Publications, 1978.

necessary to write. In studying Rashi, the Torah student must examine the text closely, and constantly question why an extra word is used, or a seemingly necessary word is missing.

Rashi's *mesorah* of Rabbeinu Gershom gave him complete access to the tradition of all the Geonim and Rishonim before him, and his great diligence and intellect undoubtedly enabled him to master this vast material in solitary study. Nevertheless, he decided to leave his home to attend the Yeshivah in Worms, Germany, which had been founded by Rabbeinu Gershom. This Yeshivah, together with the Yeshivah of Mayence, Germany, had become the centers of learning in Europe. Rashi spent five years in Worms, learning under the tutelage of Rabbi Yaakov ben Yakar of Worms and Rabbi Yitzchak ben Yehudah of Mayence, both students of Rabbeinu Gershom. (One can still visit the Yeshivah of Worms today and see the bench on which Rashi sat as he learned and taught.) At the age of twenty-five, Rashi returned to Troyes and was named Rabbi of that city. In keeping with the prevalent practice of that era, he drew no salary for his position, but sustained himself and his family by cultivating a vineyard.

Rashi's Yeshivah in Troyes soon became the Talmudic center of Europe: with the passing of Rashi's former teachers in Germany, students from Worms and Mayence flocked to Troyes. Queries were addressed to Rashi from all over the world, just as they previously had been sent to the Yeshivos in Bavel. Rashi had no sons, but his three daughters became learned, righteous women. His sons-in-law were all outstanding Talmudic scholars. One of them, Rabbi Meir, was the father of three famous sons: Rabbi Yaakov ben Meir (Rabbeinu Tam),

Rabbi Shmuel ben Meir (Rashbam), and Rabbi Yitzchak ben Meir (Rivam). Together, these three formed the nucleus of the Baalei Tosafos.

Rashi's *Perush* on the Gemara

Rashi's commentary on the Gemara reflects the vast background of general and technical knowledge that he acquired through his foreign students and the merchants who streamed into Troyes, which was an important trade center at the time. His commentary includes clarifications of difficult Aramaic vocabulary. Quite often, Rashi uses the vernacular of his time, Old French, to translate Aramaic words and technical matters. Rashi prefaces these translations with the abbreviation: *belaaz,* which means, *belashon am zor,* "in the foreign language." Today, scholars use Rashi's translations as a primary source for French dialect spoken in the eleventh century.

In today's printed editions of the Gemara, Rashi's commentary is located on the inside margin of the main text. The commentary is indispensable for even a cursory comprehension of the Talmud. Although Rashi expresses himself with utmost simplicity, one must pay careful attention to every detail to grasp the incisiveness of his comment. Without exaggeration, millions of words have been written to explain the reason for Rashi's choice of words.

Rashi's illustrious grandsons and successors, the Baalei Tosafos, questioned many of his explanations and often disagreed with him. It is said that their objections led Rashi to rewrite his commentary on the Shass a number of times.

The first version is the one we use today. The second version includes changes instituted to answer the challenges of

The commentary is indispensable for even a cursory comprehension of the Talmud.

Rashi did not claim to be a mechadesh, one who originates an interpretation. Instead, he was a mekubal, one who receives the tradition and passes it on to future generations.

the Baalei Tosafos. The third version was written after Rashi reviewed and refuted all of their arguments and then concluded that his original version was the most correct one after all!

Six hundred years later, one of Rashi's descendants wrote a comprehensive defense of Rashi entitled *Meginai Shlomo*, "Shields of Shlomo ben Yitzchak." In this work, the author refutes every question posed by the Baalei Tosafos, thereby vindicating Rashi.

Rashi's third version of his commentary came to an abrupt end with his passing at the age of 65 in the year 1104. A stirring remark is inserted in Rashi's commentary on Gemara *Makkos* (19b) after the word *tahor*:

"Our Rebbe is *tahor* (pure), and his soul left in *taharah* (purity)."

At this point Rashi's commentary ends. The work continues in the language of his student and son-in-law, Rabbi Yehudah ben Nassan. In addition, most of the commentary on *Bava Basra* is the work of Rashi's grandson, the Rashbam. Although he tried to emulate his grandfather's simplicity of language, a student of Gemara can easily detect the differences between the authors.

"Chumash & Rashi"

Despite the immense importance of Rashi's commentary on the Gemara, the most popular and widely used of Rashi's works is his commentary on Chumash. Depending upon who is reading it, this amazing and versatile commentary can either be learned in its simplest sense, or can be understood on a deeper level. With each consecutive reading, the

Rashi's death as recorded in the Gemara

student gains a new and further insight into the Torah. There is a vast amount of scholarly material that discusses and comments on Rashi's commentary on Chumash, and there is an ongoing process of new works being created, even today.

Rashi often mixes *peshat,* the simple explanation, and *drash,* the midrashic explanation, but not at random. His rule is that every phrase has to be explained in such a way that every word fits into its context.[3] When the simple explanation satisfies these conditions, Rashi will look no further; indeed, he often explicitly states that it is not his habit to engage in homiletics. On the other hand, if the simple translation of the phrase is not satisfactory, he will paraphrase a *midrash* for better understanding. His commentary on the first word of the Torah, "*Bereishis,*" serves as an excellent example of this more complicated form of explanation.

Rashi's grandson, the Rashbam, disagreed with this method. In his own commentary on Chumash, he persistently adhered to the simple *peshat,* disregarding the midrashic version altogether. The Rashbam asserted that, while Chazal used the midrashic method as an independent approach to the understanding of Chumash, the simple meaning of the written word is valid by itself.

A remark that is frequently found in Rashi's commentaries on Chumash and Gemara sheds insight on Rashi's character: "This I do not understand," or, "Concerning this I have no tradition." By and large, Rashi did not claim to be

a *mechadesh,* one who originates an interpretation. Instead, he was a *mekubal,* one who receives the tradition and passes it on to future generations. With an authentic set of source material available, as well as oral communication with the greatest Sages of his time, Rashi was able to select what, in his opinion, was the true understanding of every passage of Torah.

Rashi's comment, "This I do not understand," should not be taken as a confession of ignorance. Many later commentators, among them notable Rishonim, have given plausible explanations of what Rashi left unanswered, although these commentators were certainly not superior to Rashi. Instead, it is necessary to understand that Rashi was fully aware of the range of possible answers and considered them carefully before commenting, "I do not know." One must learn to appreciate this straightforward statement, not only as a proof of humility and honesty, but also as evidence of Rashi's wisdom and painstaking scholarship.

In tribute to Rashi's role as the fundamental commentator on Tanach, he is often referred to as *Parshandassa,* the Commentator par excellence. When the printing press was invented, the first Hebrew book to be printed and distributed was the Chumash with Rashi's commentary; today, a "*Chumash & Rashi*" is often the first *sefer* a father presents to his child. It is a gift that he will be expected to use for the rest of his life.

> *One must learn to appreciate this straightforward statement, not only as a proof of humility and honesty, but also as evidence of Rashi's wisdom and painstaking scholarship.*

> *Today, a "Chumash & Rashi" is often the first sefer a father presents to his child.*

Chapter
14

---

3. See *Shemos,* 6:9 for an example.

Hearing of Rashi's wisdom, Godfrey went to seek his advice before setting out to reconquer Palestine.

Rashi and the First Crusade

Rashi lived through one of the darkest periods of the Middle Ages for the European Jews: the era of the First Crusade. The Crusades were military expeditions launched by Christians in order to regain Palestine from the Muslims. As rabid, bloodthirsty knights began their "holy" journey to the East, the Jews of France and Germany became their innocent, hapless victims, slaughtered en masse without mercy. The Crusader armies were followed by adventurers, paupers and criminals, who took advantage of the chaos to enrich themselves.

The leader of the First Crusade was a French nobleman, Godfrey of Bouillon, a man both famous for his heroism and infamous for his cruelty. A well-known story is told of the fateful meeting between Rashi and Godfrey.

Hearing of Rashi's wisdom, Godfrey went to seek his advice before setting out to reconquer Palestine. When his messenger came to Troyes seeking an audience with the scholar, Rashi refused him. Godfrey was furious at the rebuff and brought his army to the doors of Rashi's *bais hamedrash*. When he entered, he found the doors and the books open, but not a living soul in sight. He called out in a loud voice: "Shlomo, Shlomo!"

Rashi's voice replied, "What does His Highness want?" (This miraculous occurrence is referred to as *roeh v'eino nireh*, being able to see without being seen.) Godfrey was astounded and hastily left the *bais hamedrash*. Outside, he met one of Rashi's students and commanded him, "Tell your Rebbe that he should come to me, and I promise by my life that he will not be harmed."

At this, Rashi appeared and bowed down before Godfrey, who respectfully said, "Now I realize how wise you are. I beseech you to give me your advice on a great and important project that I plan. I have prepared 100,000 horsemen with which to wrest Jerusalem from the Muslims. I also have 200 ships and 7,000 horsemen placed in the port of Acco, in order to stop the local Arabs from intervening. Now tell me what you think of my plan. Do not be afraid to give me your honest opinion."

Rashi answered briefly:

> *"You will conquer Jerusalem, but will rule over the city for no more than three days. On the fourth day, the Ishmaelites will drive you out. You will flee and return to Troyes with exactly three horses."*

Godfrey was infuriated with this answer. He promised himself, "He may be right, but beware if he is wrong and I return with four horses instead of three! I will feed his flesh to the dogs and will kill all the Jews in France."

Rashi's prediction did come true. Four years after his arrogant promise, Godfrey returned to France, a beaten man with only three horses besides his own. The defeat, as well as Rashi's prediction of it, compounded his anger. He swore he would take revenge, thinking that Rashi had not been entirely right. After all, he was returning with a total of four horses, not three as Rashi had predicted. But as he and his men passed under the city gate, a stone broke loose from the lintel above, killing one of the riders and his horse. Now Godfrey was left with only three horses! Godfrey was shocked and humbled by the precision of Rashi's wisdom.

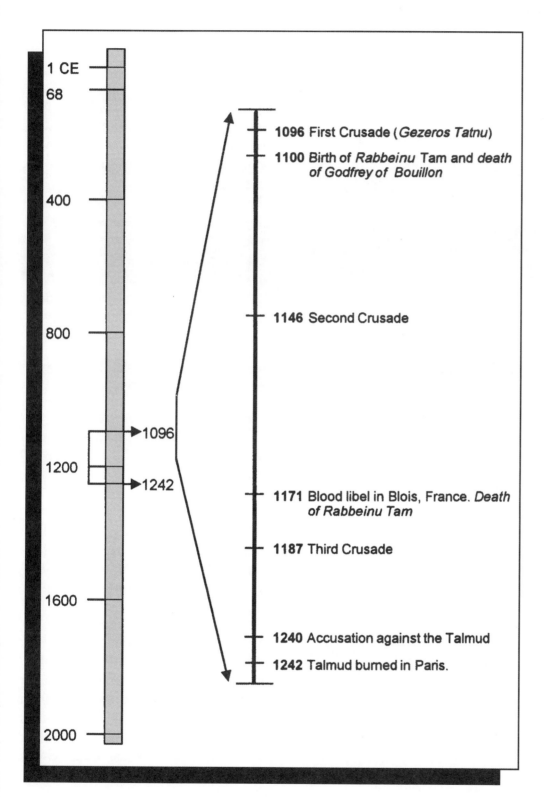

1 CE
68
400
800
1200
1600
2000

1096
1242

1096 First Crusade (*Gezeros Tatnu*)

1100 Birth of *Rabbeinu* Tam and *death
of Godfrey of Bouillon*

1146 Second Crusade

1171 Blood libel in Blois, France. *Death
of Rabbeinu Tam*

1187 Third Crusade

1240 Accusation against the Talmud

1242 Talmud burned in Paris.

Chapter
15

The Crusades and their Enduring Impact

The Jews did not realize at first that the religious hysteria was cause for alarm.

For centuries, the clergy and the secular rulers of France and Germany contended for sovereignty. One side would gain control for a short time, only to be supplanted by the opposing power a few years later. This struggle for supremacy finally came to a head in the eleventh century. Locked in battle against the powerful emperor Henry IV, Pope Urban II initiated a new strategy in his efforts to undermine the emperor's authority by calling for the unification of all Christians under the banner of a holy cause. In this manner, the secular emperor would be ignobly set aside as all his subjects rushed to obey the papal command.

When Christian inhabitants of the Holy Land sent an urgent appeal for help, complaining of their oppression at the hands of the Muslim rulers and the desecration of their sanctuaries, Pope Urban seized the opportunity. A French monk, Peter the Hermit, returned from Jerusalem with tales of horror and made an impassioned plea to the Pope to save the honor of the Church. The Pope, in imitation of the Muslim *jihad* (holy war), promptly declared a holy campaign for the recapture of Jerusalem from the Muslim infidels.

The Muslims who lived in Jerusalem at that time were called Saracens, and they had a well-deserved reputation as fierce warriors. To add incentive and to bolster flagging spirits, the Church promised that any Christians who fought in this holy war would be richly rewarded; not only would they obtain considerable booty, but they would also achieve salvation in the next world, as all sins would automatically be forgiven. Religious zeal was thus combined with natural greed, an unbeatable formula for raising a sizeable army. The Christians who volunteered to take up arms participated in the ceremony of "taking the cross," which led to the name "Crusader."

The Jews did not realize at first that the religious hysteria was cause for alarm. Although they knew that the march of the Crusaders would extend through France and Germany on its way to the Middle East, they assumed that the armies would merely require food and lodging as they moved through towns along the way. Moreover, they firmly believed that they could depend upon numerous princes and noblemen, who were understandably opposed to a call to arms by the Pope, to protect them should the armies get out of hand. Those who lived under the rule of Henry IV of Germany were particularly confident that his strength could withstand any invasion of the Christian forces.

Tragically, several crucial factors were left out of their calculation:

1) Both the regular Crusading armies and the mobs that accompanied them realized that before plodding all the way to Jerusalem to kill Muslim infidels, they had a golden opportunity to kill the infidels living in their midst—the Jews. After all, the Jewish nation had rejected their "messiah." Wouldn't it be more practical to eradicate the infidels living in Europe before continuing on to Jerusalem?

Moreover, it was their belief that their messiah had said that "there will come a day when my children will avenge my blood" on those guilty of the crucifixion. The Crusaders believed that the day had finally come, and now was the time to ensure that every last Jew would either convert to Christian belief or be killed.

The priests devoutly whipped the Crusaders into a frenzy, exhorting them to avenge their messiah, until the mobs streamed out of the churches and raged through the streets. A Crusader could piously butcher Jewish men, women, and children until he was virtually wading ankle-deep in blood. Then, after a day spent in merciless slaughter, he would kneel before the cross and sob for joy over his devout and chivalrous acts.

2) The savage frenzy of the mobs, bent on "holy work" and unholy wealth, surpassed all precedent. Widespread crop failure, starvation, and angry discontent added an estimated 300,000 of the desperate lower classes to the gathering horde of soldiers. Criminals and coarse thugs of every description also joined the Crusaders, seeing a ripe chance to loot and kill with impunity.

At times, the Crusading armies could be halted with a substantial bribe or by imperial order; even Godfrey of Bouillon's troops initially stopped short at the express order of Henry IV. The mobs, however, did not feel bound by any such agreements or threats, and they attacked regardless. Synagogues and houses were burned to the ground and entire populations were massacred. Everything belonging to the dead was taken, even their clothing. The princes, burghers and local peace-keeping authorities recognized that the mobs were perfectly capable of attacking non-Jewish towns in their wild greed, and some rulers tried to raise their own armies to fight the mobs, but the Jews were mostly left defenseless.

3) Henry IV had left Germany in 1090 to take up residence in Italy. His absence meant that the local authorities were left with the task of keeping public order. While they had been able to manage normal peace-time operation in their territories, they had no ability to quell the clamoring Crusader mobs. Some local church officials, subject to imperial order and also under vague instruction from the Church, went through the motions of hiding and saving some of the Jews; most did not. Forced conversion had been against the official policies of the Church, but Pope Urban II was perfectly content to do nothing when news reached him of the bloody massacres.

The First Crusade
(1096–1099)

Gezeros Tatnu

In the spring of the year 1096 (*Tatnu: 4856* after Creation), a bloodthirsty mass of thousands of Crusaders gathered in France, intent on killing and plundering. Havoc broke out as they fell upon the Jews of Rouen, slaughtering anyone who would not accept baptism. Jews in other parts of France, informed of the horrific disaster, tried to escape. Homes were abandoned and priceless possessions left behind as the Jews fled in panic, but the hordes caught up with them all too often.

At that point, the Jews of Germany still felt safe. When the French Jews appealed for help to the leaders of Mayence, Germany, a day of fasting was proclaimed and the German Jews prayed fervently for their French brethren, but they were not at all worried about their own safety. After all, they were under the imperial protection of Henry IV; surely, they had nothing to fear.

In less than ninety days, the army of the Crusaders reached German soil. As the Jews had hoped, Henry IV issued an express order (plus a generous gift of 500 silver marks raised by the communities of Mayence and Cologne) to Godfrey to halt his troops at the border. Godfrey did, indeed, obey the order; but the mobs accompanying the army felt no

After a day spent in merciless slaughter, he would kneel before the cross and sob for joy over his devout and chivalrous acts.

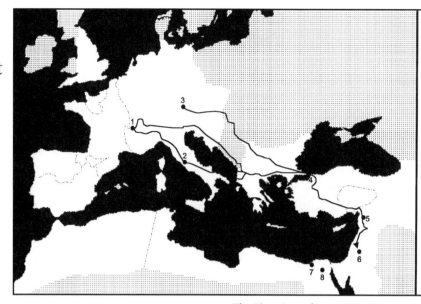

The First Crusade

In one quick moment this righteous woman inspired countless martyrs by spurning the offer of conversion and proudly choosing death.

obligation to honor this agreement and fell with unbridled atrocity upon the stunned Jewish communities.

Spires

For Jews living along the Rhine, the days of *Sefiras HaOmer* 4856 became days of horror and death. On the eighth day of Iyar, a Shabbos, the murdering Crusaders entered the town of Spires (also called Ashpiro or Speyer) and surrounded the synagogue. For a short while the congregation managed to fend off the attackers, but the mob succeeded in reaching ten individual Jews and killing them, one by one. One righteous woman took her own life rather than fall into the hands of the mob.

Just as it seemed that the Crusaders would break the Jews' defenses and enter the synagogue to indulge in an orgy of slaughter, help appeared in the unlikely form of John, the youthful Bishop of Spires. John, who was a loyal, ardent follower of Henry IV, appeared with a sizeable army to suppress the riot. The crowd dispersed, angry and disappointed, and the mob leaders were caught and punished by having their arms cut off. Later,

John secretly transported the Jews to fortified castles where they remained until the danger had passed.

Worms

On the 23rd of Iyar, the Crusaders reached the city of Worms on the Rhine. Many Jews had remained in their homes, counting on promises of protection from their Christian neighbors, and were now helpless to resist the ravaging hordes. The Crusaders rounded up the Jews and promised to spare them if they converted. A few did submit to conversion out of fear for their lives, but the story quickly circulated of a prominent Jewish woman named Minna, who was dragged from the cellar in which she had been hiding. In one quick moment this righteous woman inspired countless martyrs by spurning the offer of conversion and proudly choosing death. Like Minna, the majority of Jews died with the loud cry of *Shema Yisrael* on their lips.

For seven days, the Jews of Worms who had sought refuge in the palace of the bishop were well protected. But on Rosh Chodesh Sivan, the month of *matan Torah,* the bishop informed the frightened Jews that he could no longer guarantee their safety against the Crusaders and he advised them all to accept Christianity. The Jews asked for time to consider this proposal inside the great hall of the palace; the bishop agreed. After some time, when no reply was forthcoming, he gave orders to open the doors to the hall. A horrible scene was revealed: the men had slain their wives, their sons and daughters and then themselves *al kiddush Hashem,* for the sanctification of Hashem's Name, so that they would not violate the oath that their forefathers had sworn at Mount Sinai. The bloodthirsty Crusaders who invaded the palace fell upon the silent corpses and joyously robbed them.

Throughout the city of Worms, Jews of all ages met their deaths with courage and dignity. Because it was Rosh Chodesh, many were killed while singing *Hallel*; others were murdered as they bent over their open Gemaros, drinking in their last precious words of Torah before the Crusaders could find them. By the time the Crusaders departed from Worms, about eight hundred Jews had been slaughtered.

One boy named Simchah Cohen, who had witnessed the hideous murders of his father and seven brothers, agreed to accept Christianity. As he was brought into the church to be baptized, he suddenly pulled out a knife and stabbed the bishop's nephew! Within seconds the crowd was upon him, tearing him to pieces. For the Jews facing extermination in those bitter times, the very name of this bold child, like that of Minna, heightened their determination to die with true nobility *al kiddush Hashem.*

Mayence

A few days after leaving Worms, the Crusaders entered the city of Mayence. Supported by the Christian inhabitants, they stormed the hiding places of the Jews. A small group of Jews, led by Kalonymous bar Meshullam, fasted and prayed before taking up arms to defend themselves and their families. Three hundred men of the town came to their aid, but it soon became apparent that they would be defeated. Rather than let his son Yosef be dragged to the altar for forced conversion, Kalonymous slew the boy himself. Many others heroically followed his example; with knives carefully sharpened as though for proper *shechitah* of a sacrifice, parents slaughtered their children, then took their own lives. A chronicler of the time quotes these last words of the martyrs:

"Fortunate are we if we fulfill His [Hashem's] wish, and fortunate is he who is slain and slaughtered for the unity of His Name. Such a person will be prepared to enter the World to Come, to sit in the company of righteous men such as Rabbi Akiva and his peers, who are the foundations of the world and who have died for His Name. Moreover, he will have exchanged this world of darkness for a world of light, a world of suffering for a world of joy, the transitory world for a world enduring forever."

Part of the *kinnos* (Lamentations) read on Tishah B'Av are dedicated to these tragic events. In powerful poetry they describe the heartrending scene of a father addressing his son and Hashem:

"Since we did not merit to bring you up for learning Torah, we must now sacrifice you as [if you were] a burnt offering."

It is believed that Kalonymous was the author of the *kinnah* that describes the bloodbath in the three communities on the Rhine River: Spires, Worms and Mayence. He finds it no coincidence that

By the time the Crusaders departed from Worms, about eight hundred Jews had been slaughtered.

*The Crusades
caused a complete
upheaval of
European life,
economically,
socially, and
militarily.*

this supreme *kiddush Hashem* occurred at the time of Shavuos:

"On the day of the Torah's giving, so did the Torah return. It ascended on high to the place of its dwelling, together with its casing and covering, its interpreters and those who explored it, those who studied it both in the darkness of the night, and in the day."

The mutilated dead of Mayence, numbering in the thousands, were buried in nine ditches. The Crusaders moved on. The grim list of destroyed cities grew as the pillage and plunder continued: Treves, Cologne, Neuss, Mehr, Geldern, Ratisbon, to name just a few. It is estimated that approximately 10,000 Jews perished, though accurate statistics are difficult to ascertain. This, however, is only a count of the dead; an inestimable number of Jews were beaten, maimed, or exiled from their homes, forced to wander without money or possessions.

Worldwide Impact

The Crusades caused a complete upheaval of European life, economically, socially, and militarily. The decimation of the Jews and the economic chaos that followed took their toll on numerous towns and governments. Religiously, the Christian masses felt satisfied, strengthened, and emboldened by their bloody exploits against their Jewish victims.

There was further cause for feelings of religious triumph; the First Crusade had indeed been successful in wresting Jerusalem from the Muslims. Both the Jews and the Muslims had at last been eradicated from the holy city. The Christian world rejoiced at the news that churches were being erected all over Jerusalem and that pilgrims could visit there in safety.

Godfrey's brother, King Baldwin I, established a Crusader kingdom in Jerusalem

which lasted for 87 years. In the early decades of Crusader rule, no Jew or Muslim was allowed into the city. Later, a small group of Jews, impoverished by the heavy taxes they were forced to pay, were permitted to live in one corner of the city.

Even as Jewish communities began to recover from the horrors of the Crusades, the Jews found themselves faced with a new and frightening reality. Persecution could no longer be considered a sporadic and regional occurrence. Individual communities could not trust diplomacy and well-placed bribes to ensure their safety. The sweeping magnitude of the First Crusade made it clear to Jew and Christian alike that the Jews were vulnerable—any time, anywhere. Even local rulers who favored the Jewish population could not be counted upon for protection. The Jewish response was one of desperation and despair.

Yet the slaughter and mass suicides of the First Crusade gave rise to another legacy as well. Martyr after martyr, in town after town, had proven the triumphant spirit of the Jews. Their complete dedication and willingness to defend the eternity of the Jewish nation spread ripples of pride and commitment to Jewish communities worldwide. Looking back at the generation of the Crusades brings a sense of awe and inspiration for the bold actions of these people: the Sages and the simple folk; the men and women; the rich and the ragged—all of whom willingly sacrificed their lives rather than abandon Hashem and His Torah.

The Second and Third Crusades (1146 and 1187)

The Second and Third Crusades were a repeat performance of the atrocities of the first. But in the interim, life had changed drastically for the Jews of France and Germany. With the success of the First Crusaders, trade routes had opened to the East and Christian merchants rose in power, driving the Jews from numerous businesses and professions. In addition, the Church was undergoing a religious revitalization and began to abstain from its previous business of money-lending. The Christians abided by the Biblical law against "usury," the taking of interest on a loan. There was no objection however, from the Church's point of view, to a Jew lending money and collecting interest. (The Torah permits taking interest from a non-Jew.) Money-lending soon became a uniquely Jewish enterprise. The lending business was potentially profitable, but at the same time highly dangerous. Customers were always eager to borrow and to commit themselves to any rate of interest, but they were irate and often violent when the creditors came to collect.[1] In addition, rulers (who often maintained their extravagant lifestyles and financed military campaigns with funds provided by Jewish loans) would frequently call a moratorium on all payments, or suddenly cancel debts by imperial order. During the Crusades, many Gentiles who had gone into heavy debt took advantage of the unbridled chaos to kill their Jewish creditors.

Though the number of Crusaders in the armies of the Second and Third Crusades exceeded those of the First, a wholesale massacre did not result. Horrible scenes of martyrdom did indeed occur once again, but the total loss of life was not as great. This may have been due to a combination of several causes:

---

1. In fact, the Church benefited the most from this arrangement. The loans actually came from the Church; the Jewish moneylenders were allowed to keep a percentage of the interest. Yet since the Church's role was not well known, it was the Jew who became the focus of hatred of those who were unable to pay back their debts.

1) The armies of the Second and Third Crusades were generally made up of noblemen, who were military forces, not mobs of uncontrollable peasants. This is not to say that a "nobleman" was any less bloodthirsty or fanatic, but trained armies were more apt to obey their commanders. In addition, the knights were more interested in reaching the East than in slaughtering Jews along the way.

2) Having learned a painfully bitter lesson from the First Crusade, local princes prepared better protection for their Jewish subjects. The Jews sought refuge more quickly in the castles and fortresses of friendly noblemen because they no longer imagined themselves safe and impervious to harm.

3) There was a hesitation to do away with the Jewish population entirely, not because of any kindly feelings but rather due to financial and theological needs. The Jews now played an important economic role, albeit despised, as moneylenders. In addition, Christians were enjoined not to kill off the Jews completely, as they were to remain "living symbols of the crime of crucifixion" who must witness the "triumph" of Christianity.

This perspective was illustrated by a popular pictorial theme during this period (and for several centuries afterward) that contrasted the images of two queens, one named Ecclesia (Church) and the other, Synagoga. Often carved on the exterior of church entrances and depicted in numerous medieval illuminated manuscripts,

The Jews sought refuge more quickly in the castles and fortresses of friendly noblemen because they no longer imagined themselves safe.

Hashem, in His mercy, ensures that persecutions occur in cycles, making it possible for the Jewish nation to survive.

Ecclesia raises a cross and stands erect, a proud crown adorning her head. Defeated Synagoga is blindfolded, her head bowed as she clutches a broken staff. If the Jews had been completely wiped out in Europe, to whom would the clergy have pointed to prove the supremacy of Christianity?

Ongoing Persecution

In addition to the widespread slaughter that took place during the Crusades, the twelfth and thirteenth centuries were witness to many anti-Semitic persecutions. The concept of "blood libel" apparently emerged during this period: the widely believed notion that Jews killed Christians, particularly children, in order to use their blood in Passover matzos. This belief grew so pervasive that the murder of any Christian was immediately attributed to local Jews, and large groups would be massacred in retaliation.

One of the most famous of these cases involved the Jews of Blois, France. Accused of ritual murder, the Jews of Blois had little defense other than their own protestations. All attempts to reason or seek reconciliation with the ruler, Count Theobald, failed. Intervention from the spiritual leaders in other towns also failed. On the 20th of Sivan 1171, forty Jewish men and women were burned alive, loudly proclaiming *Shema,* and singing *Aleinu* until the flames engulfed them. Only a large gift of a thousand pounds prevented the similar destruction of every Jew in the province.

Of course, the concept that every Jew was vile, treacherous, and back-stabbing was not new. But the reality proved by the Crusades, that they were virtually defenseless, encouraged attacks by private individuals, as well as

on an official, governmental scale. The Jews of Europe tried to go about their daily business in a normal fashion, but the constant possibility of a sudden, drastic change for the worse cast a pall over their lives. Every time a new ruler came to the throne or a new religious leader held sway in the local church, the Jews held their breath, ready to flee for their lives at a moment's notice. Every time there was economic turmoil or political upheaval, Jews would pray for the safety of their families with greater intensity than ever before.

The Baalei Tosafos

When Yaakov Avinu sent his messengers to Esav, he commanded them, "Leave a space between one flock and the next one."[2] The Ramban comments that this spacing between the flocks symbolizes the Jewish suffering in exile. Hashem, in His mercy, ensures that persecutions occur in cycles, making it possible for the Jewish nation to survive. The chain of devastation has always been spread out over the centuries, with periods of relative respite in between, so that ruins could be rebuilt and life could return to a semblance of normalcy.

With this concept in mind, it is no wonder that those same centuries of tragedy were, at the same time, a most glorious period in the sphere of Torah learning: the era of the Baalei Tosafos.

It is remarkable that the Baalei Tosafos are not commonly known by their names, but just by abbreviations and appelations. The two most frequently mentioned are the Ri and Rabbeinu Tam. For the most part, these scholars wanted to remain anonymous Torah Sages, to be remembered for their contributions to the in-depth search of the Gemara and

2. *Bereishis,* 32:17.

not for the glorification of their names. The results of their efforts, the *Tosafos,* is printed on the outside margin of the Gemara page. To the serious student, the study of the Gemara is incomplete without *Tosafos.*

As the name "*tosafos,*" meaning "to add on," suggests, the aim of the Baalei Tosafos was to supply additional material, with Rashi's commentary as the base and starting point for understanding. Rashi had transcribed the tradition, the primary information as it was handed down from the Amoraim to the Geonim and the early Rishonim before his time. The Baalei Tosafos undertook the gigantic task of appending and clarifying Rashi's commentary on the Gemara. With their superior intellects and almost infinite collective memory, they could survey all of Shass in seconds and knew where any relevant statements were mentioned, even in a cursory fashion.

The Yeshivos of the Baalei Tosafos attracted students from Spain, who had received their early education in the Spanish approach to learning (oriented towards the gleaning of the final *halachah,* as opposed to explorations of *peshat,* which was the main concern of the French Yeshivos). Some of the greatest minds of Spanish descent were thus exposed to the method of the Baalei Tosafos. The merging of the two methods raised the standards of Torah study to unequaled heights.

Rabbeinu Tam (1100–1171)

One of the great scholars among the Baalei Tosafos was Rabbi Yaakov ben Meir, known as Rabbeinu Tam. He was one of Rashi's grandsons, one of four brothers who became eminent scholars. The name "Tam" was added reverently to his title because he emulated our forefather Yaakov in his lifestyle and his character. Yaakov Avinu was an *ish tam* and *yoshev ohalim,* a man perfect in his character traits and totally devoted to his studies.[3]

Rabbeinu Tam was revered in all of France, not only as a scholar, but also as a religious leader. He attracted many students to his Yeshivah in the French town of Ramerupt and replied to countless queries on *halachah* that were addressed to him.

Rabbeinu Tam was independently wealthy for most of his life. During the Second Crusade (1147), his possessions were seized and his Torah scroll desecrated. He was attacked by a wild mob which inflicted numerous stab wounds on his head. He was saved at the last minute by a passing knight, who intervened for the sake of the magnificent horse Rabbeinu Tam promised him as a reward.

Rabbeinu Tam was one of the leaders in France who desperately did anything he could to stop the massacre in Blois. Grieved by the news of the martyrs' execution, he proclaimed a day of mourning and fasting throughout France and Germany.[4] He passed away, at the age of approximately seventy, just a few days later.

Sha'ali Serufah Ba'esh

In addition to the fear of blood libels, another danger threatened the Jews of France. Monasteries had seized powerful influence in the Church and among the populace. Certain orders of the monks, generally much more fanatical than the regular clergy, called for stronger, more

---

3. *Bereishis,* 25:27.
4. Some people still observe the 20th of Sivan as a *taanis tzadikkim,* a voluntary fast day which is not binding on the general public.

They could survey all of Shass in seconds and knew where any relevant statements were mentioned, even in a cursory fashion.

The Crusades and their Enduring Impact

> *Thanks to the foresight of the Rivash, the Talmud had been memorized and taught by word of mouth to some three hundred scholars.*

zealous adherence to Church principles, often taking it upon themselves to force compliance, by violence if necessary. A campaign was building to outlaw the Talmud, which the monks continually attacked as a book defamatory to the Christian faith. A student of Rabbeinu Tam, the Rivash (Rabbi Yitzchak ben Shmuel), watching the growing religious frenzy with increasing alarm, anticipated the possible destruction of the few available (handwritten) copies of the Shass in France. To forestall the potential disaster, he assigned sixty scholars to memorize one *masechta* each.

His fears came true in the year 1240, when a malicious Jewish convert to Christianity brought to the Pope a formal accusation against the Talmud. The convert insisted that the Talmud contained blasphemy and inflammatory statements against Christianity and claimed that without the Talmud, the Jews would be ready and willing to convert. At the Pope's order (and with the hearty cooperation of King Louis IX of France), every synagogue was raided and every copy of the Talmud seized. A panel of Church officials then presided over a debate, a trial of the Talmud, between the convert and four delegates of the Jewish community, led by Rabbi Yechiel ben Yosef of Paris. The panel solemnly ruled that the accusation had been proven and ordered that the books be burned.

On a bleak Erev Shabbos in 1242, twenty-four cartloads of books, including every known copy of the Gemara, were dumped in front of a cathedral in Paris. The Gentile throng watched in ecstasy, and the assembled Jews mourned, as a huge pyre was lit and consumed the holy pages.

Jews all over the world heard of the conflagration and mourned in unity. The Maharam (Rabbi Meir) of Rothenburg witnessed the barbaric act and composed a stirring *kinnah* which begins, *Sha'ali serufah ba'esh*:

"How can food ever be sweet to my palate after I have seen what you plunderers have gathered?"

Despite the efforts of the monks and the clergy, the burning of the Talmud did not result in the spiritual destruction of the Jews. Thanks to the foresight of the Rivash, the Talmud had been memorized and taught by word of mouth to some three hundred scholars. The Jews of France continued to learn, renewed in their commitment. Once again, the Oral Tradition was faithfully handed down and continues to this very day.

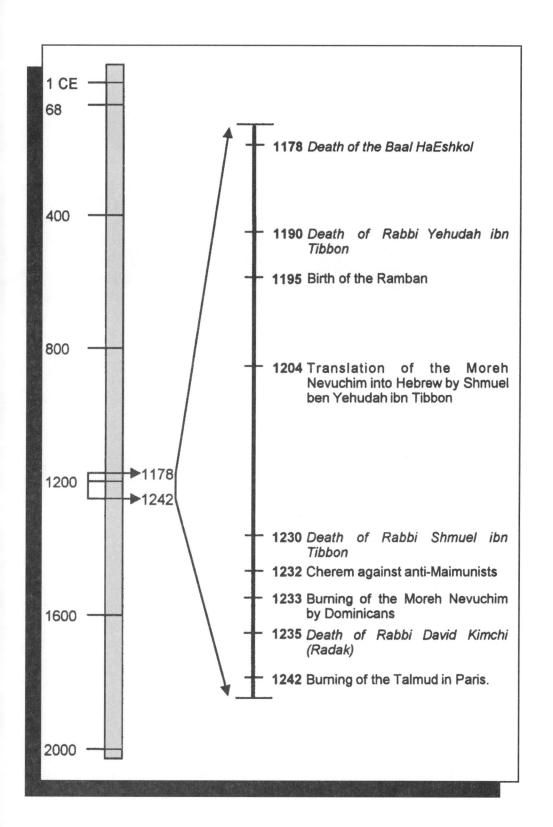

1178 *Death of the Baal HaEshkol*

1190 *Death of Rabbi Yehudah ibn Tibbon*

1195 Birth of the Ramban

1204 Translation of the Moreh Nevuchim into Hebrew by Shmuel ben Yehudah ibn Tibbon

1230 *Death of Rabbi Shmuel ibn Tibbon*

1232 Cherem against anti-Maimunists

1233 Burning of the Moreh Nevuchim by Dominicans

1235 *Death of Rabbi David Kimchi (Radak)*

1242 Burning of the Talmud in Paris.

Chapter
16

Many teachers at the noted school of medicine in Montpellier were Jewish.

uring the Middle Ages, France was divided into many provinces, many of which were ruled almost independently by various noblemen. The two southernmost provinces, Languedoc and Provence, made up an area bordered by the Mediterranean to the south and Italy to the east, one of the most fertile and prosperous regions in all France. With the French kings and German emperors living in large cities further to the north, the rabid anti-Semitism fostered by Christian influence did not lead to the typically warped perceptions of the Gentiles living in northern France and Germany. Instead, in direct contrast with the Jews of other parts of Europe, the Jews of this region were relatively secure.

The Jews of Provence enjoyed civic rights almost equal to those of non-Jewish citizens. They were permitted to own land and cultivate vineyards. They imported spices and sold them in the markets. In some cities, Jews were granted equal status to Christians and were permitted to engage freely in various professions and trades. The Gentiles admired the Jews for their superior skills as physicians; many teachers at the noted school of medicine in Montpellier were Jewish. In Narbonne, the Jews were responsible for collecting revenue and delivering it to the Viscount. In return, they were given the right to have their own community administered by a "king of the Jews" and their own police officers, who were supervised by the city police.

With Spain just across the border, the Provencal Jews became acquainted with the rich (Arab-)Jewish culture that had evolved during the Golden Era of Spain. Their method of learning Gemara became a blend of the Spanish system, with its emphasis on codification (as personified by the Rif and the Rambam), and the Franco-German method of delving into the depth of the *peshat*. Adopting the best of both methods, the Provencal Jews made considerable contributions to Talmudic literature.

Rabbi Avraham ben Yitzchak (died 1178), the Rosh Yeshivah in Narbonne, was known as the Baal HaEshkol after his sefer on *halachah* which he called *Eshkol*, cluster. Two of his most prominent students were Rabbi Avraham ben David, the famous Raavad, who enriched the *Yad HaChazakah* of the Rambam with his sharply worded critique, and Rabbi Zerachyah HaLevi, author of the classic *Baal HaMaor* on the *Hilchos HaRif.*

The Battle over the *Moreh Nevuchim* and the *Sefer HaMada*

It is unsurprising that the Rambam was deeply revered in the communities of southern France with their close ties to Spain. Ironically, it was in Provence that a fierce battle erupted between those who favored Rambam's approach of philosophic rationalism,[1] and those who upheld the traditional unquestioning belief in the doctrines of Judaism.

When the *Moreh Nevuchim,* "Guide to the Perplexed," first appeared, the rabbis of Lunel implored the Rambam to send them a copy of the *sefer* and to translate it from the original Arabic in order to make it accessible to more Jews. The book was received, but a translation was not forthcoming. The scholars of the city turned to Yehudah ibn Tibbon, a fugitive from the Muslim invasion of Granada, to translate the Rambam's monumental work.

A physician by profession, Yehudah ibn Tibbon owned a very extensive library.

---

1. See footnote 9, page 82.

He became known as the "father of the translators" for successfully rendering from Arabic into Hebrew the works of Bachya ibn Pakudah, Ibn Gabirol, Yehudah HaLevi, and Saadya Gaon. His son, Shmuel, was assigned the translation of the *Moreh Nevuchim* into Hebrew. He finished this translation in the year 1204, just fourteen days before the Rambam's passing.

The publication of the *Moreh Nevuchim* in Hebrew was received with great enthusiasm by many of the Jews of Provence. With political and civil liberties similar to the conditions enjoyed in Spain, the Jews of Provence were heavily involved in their country's philosophy and culture. The Rambam's *sefer* fulfilled a very important function in their lives, providing a rational approach for their confrontation with Gentiles. With his philosophical interpretation of basic Jewish belief in Hashem and the scrupulous practice of mitzvos, the Rambam enabled the Jews of Provence to "know what answer to give to the non-believer."[2]

At the same time, many Rabbanim in Provence saw great danger in the rationalistic approach of the Rambam's writings. They appealed to the *Gedolim* in northern France, whose spiritual environment was completely different from that of Provence. In northern France the hatred and persecution by the Gentiles had driven the Jews into isolation from the world around them. To escape this inhospitable environment, they sought shelter in the "four cubits of *halachah*." All Jewish cultural studies centered around Gemara and Tanach. Cultural contacts with the Gentiles were virtually unknown. From their perspective, introduction of philosophy into the sphere of Torah and mitzvos could undermine the

solid foundation of simple, unquestioning belief, and precipitate questions fraught with danger. Therefore they lent their support to the opponents.

The Jews of northern France were fearful of the possible influence of the Rambam's *Moreh Nevuchim* on their *kehillos*. Accounts of Jewish life in Spain revealed that many Jews had abandoned their allegiance to the Jewish heritage; too much emphasis on secularism had undermined the pillars of their loyalty to Torah. Rabbi Moshe, Prince of Coucy, one of the masters of *Tosafos,* visited Spain in 1235 and brought back a devastating report on the status of Jewish observance there. He found that in many Jewish communities hardly anyone still put on tefillin or fastened mezuzos to their doorposts.

With the support of the Rabbanim of northern France, the opponents of the Rambam's *Moreh Nevuchim* in Provence initiated a storm of protest. In the city of Montpellier, located in Provence, the great scholars Shlomo ben Avraham, Rabbeinu Yonah ben Avraham of Gerona, and Rabbi David ben Shaul urged that the study of the *Moreh Nevuchim* and the *Sefer HaMada* (a philosophical treatise which is in the first section of the *Yad HaChazakah*) be forbidden.

The followers of the Rambam, known as "Maimunists," considered this campaign an insult to their beloved teacher. A *cherem,* or excommunication, was declared against the three scholars. This meant that no Jew was permitted to have any dealings with them. In despair, the three rabbis turned for help to the leadership in northern France and presented them with the Rambam's writings in question. After reading the material, the rabbis there issued a *cherem* against the

2. *Pirkei Avos,* 2:19.

Southern France:

Problems in Provence

He found that in many Jewish communities hardly anyone still put on tefillin or fastened mezuzos to their doorposts.

Chapter

16

Because many Jews in Spain earned their livelihoods in the service of the government, it was necessary for them to have knowledge in secular studies.

study of the *Moreh Nevuchim* and the *Sefer HaMada.*

Now the communities of Provence rose in protest. The leaders of the Maimunists, headed by Rabbi David Kimchi (known as the Redak), urged a declaration of a counter-*cherem* against anyone who questioned the writings of the Rambam.

The battle lines had been drawn and no one could remain neutral. A fierce tug-of-war ensued that gradually took on an ugly form, despite the originally pure intentions of each side in fighting a *milchemes mitzvah,* a battle for the glorification of Hashem's Name. Ban was followed by counter-ban. The two factions

fought each other openly, even exchanging blows in the streets of Montpellier.

Efforts Toward Conciliation

Rabbeinu Moshe ben Nachman, known as the Ramban, was one of the towering personalities of the era. As he had studied under both Spanish and French teachers, he appreciated the merits of both viewpoints, making him ideally qualified to serve as mediator in the dispute. In a series of letters, he urged everyone involved in the controversy to withhold further action until the entire issue could be presented to a rabbinical court for a *Din Torah.* To the rabbis of northern France, he wrote:

The Ramban asserted that the Rambam deserves credit for wrestling with this evil by preparing books to serve as a shield against this danger.

"I have seen the clear decision of your holy gathering [the rabbis and leaders of all France] declaring the *cherem* upon every person who dares to study the words of the *Moreh Nevuchim* and *Sefer HaMada,* your intention being that these books be hidden forever. But why have you declared this ban on all communities, considering them all of one category, thus failing to give honor to the great rabbi [Moshe ben Maimon] who built a fortress around the Talmud, a mighty fortress for the glory of Hashem?"

With deep feeling, the letter went on to draw a sharp line between conditions in Spain and those in France. Because many Jews in Spain earned their livelihood in the service of the government, it was necessary for them to have knowledge in secular studies. While their interest in mathematics and science was not in itself a contradiction to the Torah, they gleaned their knowledge from the books of the Greeks, which unfortunately led many Jews to drift away

Sefer HaMada

from the path of the Torah. The Ramban asserted that the Rambam deserves credit for wrestling with this evil by preparing books to serve as a shield against this danger. He then contrasted these conditions with those of the French Jews:

"You, leaders of the French communities, in contrast, have been taught to rely upon tradition from early childhood; you have always been planted firmly in the House of Hashem. It is not for you that the Rambam has toiled. What he did was to prepare a haven of refuge from the storms of Greek philosophy, to save them [the Spanish Jews] from Aristotle and Galenus."

The Ramban insisted that if the rabbis of France desired to protect their people from the pitfalls of philosophical speculation, they should have limited their *cherem* to places where there was a need for it. Why did they make the ban all-inclusive by extending it to such countries as Spain?

The Ramban's proposal for compromise was quite clear. He appealed for annulment of the *cherem,* particularly with regard to the Jews of Spain, for whom the works of the Rambam had been a veritable lifeline. On the other hand, he preferred that individuals, especially those in France and Germany, who had never been exposed to the sciences, should not study the *Moreh Nevuchim.* Instead, they should devote themselves totally to the study of the Written and Oral Torah.

The words of the Ramban fell short of ending the controversy. The *Din Torah* that he proposed never materialized. Indeed, the immediate effect of his letters was somewhat counterproductive, for it gave ammunition to the Maimunists and encouraged them to attack the leaders of the anti-Maimunists even more violently than before.

A Drastic Step

In the month of Av, in 1232, the Maimunists declared a *cherem* against Rabbi Shlomo ben Avraham and his two talmidim, Rabbeinu Yonah and Rabbi David ben Shaul, for having spoken against the Rambam. With desperate hopes of crushing the controversy once and for all, Rabbi Shlomo resorted to reporting the

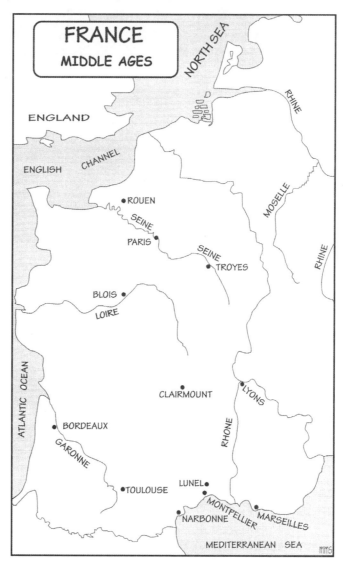

France in the Middle Ages

---

3. *Devarim,* 32:31.

Rambam's books to the Catholic Church as heretical works!

At that point, to suppress heresies within its own ranks, the Church had empowered its Dominican monks to seek and destroy all works which contradicted their theological concepts. This early inquisition was instituted originally to crush the Albigensian sect of Catholics, who had dared to oppose the Pope on various matters. The Dominicans carried out their mission against the heretics with zeal. They were thoroughly delighted when a Jew appeared in 1233 to denounce the works of the Rambam, and gladly authorized the public burning of these books in Paris, Montpellier, and other cities.

This shocking act of the anti-Maimunists was in direct contradiction to a warning in the Chumash, "Do not make our enemies judges."[3] Numerous attempts throughout history to appeal to non-Jews to settle arguments within the Jewish community have resulted in disaster. When the Talmud was publicly burned less than a decade later, the *Gedolim* who had fought the Rambam *LeShem Shamayim,* "for the glory of Hashem," were shocked into recognition of the terrible mistake they had made; this horrendous desecration was the direct consequence of their previous blindness. Rabbeinu Yonah, in particular, made a complete turnabout. He dedicated the rest of his life to traveling from community to community, going into each Yeshivah and declaring, "I have sinned against the great sage, Rabbeinu Moshe ben Maimon, and

Rabbeinu Yonah's Shaarei Teshuvah

I now confess, from the bottom of my heart and soul, that Moshe is true and his Torah is true." As a result of his soul-searing experience, Rabbeinu Yonah composed his famous sefer, revered as a classic work of mussar, *Shaarei Teshuvah,* "Gates of Repentance."

The ugly battle which had severely undermined the unity of the nation finally came to an end. Both the *Sefer HaMada* and the *Moreh Nevuchim* were restored to the same authority and sanctity as the other works of the Rambam. Since that time, these *sefarim* have been recognized as an integral part of sacred Jewish literature by Jews throughout the world.[4]

---

4. The Rogachover Rebbe stated that all of the Rambam's philosophical concepts had their origin in the Talmud and Midrash.

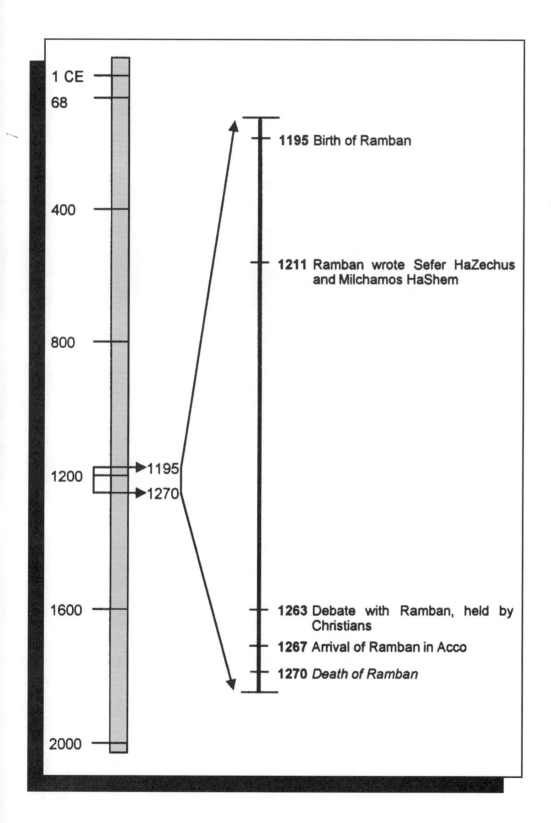

1 CE

68

400

800

1200 ►1195
     ►1270

1600

2000

1195 Birth of Ramban

1211 Ramban wrote Sefer HaZechus
and Milchamos HaShem

1263 Debate with Ramban, held by
Christians

1267 Arrival of Ramban in Acco

1270 *Death of Ramban*

The Galus and Geulah Calendar

The *Galus* and *Geulah* Calendar

According to the Talmud (*Avodah Zarah* 9a), the world in its present state is to last six thousand years which are divided into three periods of two thousand years,

each considered a separate era in itself.

The first two thousand years are called the era of *Tohu VaVohu*, "Chaos." This era began with the creation of the world and ended when Avraham Avinu, at the age of fifty-two, began his efforts to spread the concept of one G-d and the seven mitzvos of the sons of Noach.

The second era, "Torah," ended two thousand years later, in the year 4000, which coincides with the time that Rabbi Yehudah HaNasi completed the Mishnah in the year 3940.

The next era, from 4000 to 6000, is called the Era of *Geulah*, "Redemption." The first thousand years of this era were stained with the intense pain and suffering of the Jews in exile. At the end of the fifth millennium, the spiritual leaders of that generation made a number of calculations based on the Book of Daniel 12:12, and the apparent "deadline," the year 6000, as cited in the Gemara. They concluded that the dawn of redemption could not be far off.

It is no coincidence that the first of the Rishonim to write extensively and with precise detail about the eagerly awaited *Geulah* was Rabbeinu Moshe ben Nachman. Born in the year 1195 [4955 according to the Hebrew calendar], the Ramban was forty-five years old at the turn of the sixth millennium, in the year 1240. In his greatness, the Ramban had the merit to usher in the final thousand years of redemption.

Three centers of Torah study existed in Europe: Spain, northern France and southern France. While it is not entirely correct to overgeneralize the strengths of different Yeshivah systems, it would be fair to say that the scholars of Sepharad (Spain), under the magnetic influence of the Rif and the Rambam, concentrated on the final *halachah;* northern France, dominated by Rashi and the Baalei Tosafos, focused on finding the true meaning of every word and phrase in the Gemara;

and the Yeshivos of Provence in southern France, as personified by the Sages of Lunel, formed a unique blend of Torah and philosophy.

For many centuries, the Spanish and French schools had existed separately with little, if any, contact between them. The Rif and Rashi did not know each other, although they were contemporaries. Likewise, their talmidim, the Ri Migash and Rabbeinu Tam, were unacquainted with each other's activities.

The Ramban (**R**abbeinu **M**oshe **b**en **N**achman), however, had the benefit of all three schools. He received his early education from his cousin, Rabbeinu Yonah, who belonged to the Spanish school of thought; later, he studied under Rabbi Yehudah, a pupil of the Ritzba, one of the French Baalei Tosafos, as well as with Rabbi Meir of Provence. Thus, beginning with the Ramban, the three schools of wisdom were fused into one. This merging of the three approaches to Torah study within a single scholar brought great benefit to Klal Yisrael. It was as if "three springs had joined to form a mighty stream of knowledge, bringing a deep refreshing cascade of the waters of Torah."[1]

In addition to his Torah learning and attention to Kabbalah, the Ramban pursued the study of philosophy and science, and practiced medicine for a livelihood. He had two sons and a daughter. His daughter's son, Rabbi Levi ben Gershon, known as the Ralbag, became famous for his commentary on Tanach.

The Ramban's Talmudic Works

The Ramban's diverse background is reflected in his literary works. He began to write as a youth of sixteen, eventually

---

1. From Rabbi Chavel's biography of Ramban, *Rabbeinu Moses and Nachman,* 1967.

It is no coincidence that the first of the Rishonim to write extensively and with precise detail about the eagerly awaited Geulah was Rabbeinu Moshe ben Nachman, born in the year 1195.

Chapter
17

authoring an incredible number of *sefarim.* With his first publication, he defended the teachings of the Spanish masters against the attacks of contemporary Provencal scholars. One hundred years earlier, when Rabbeinu Alfasi had written his momentous work *Hilchos HaRif,* it had been universally acclaimed as a fundamental text of Jewish law which defied criticism. Then one of the Torah Sages of Provence, Rabbi Zerachyah HaLevi of Lunel, had taken issue with many decisions of the Rif in an exposition entitled *Baal HaMaor.* Another Sage of Provence, the Raavad, answered some of his objections, but he also differed with the Rif in a number of instances. The Ramban entered the fray, defending the Rif against both attackers. His rebuttal to the Raavad's disagreements was

called *Sefer HaZechus,* "Book of Defense," while his response to the *Baal HaMaor* was entitled *Milchamos Hashem.*

A recent biographer of the Ramban, Rabbi Dr. Chavel, who published a new edition of the Ramban's complete works, had this comment on *Milchamos Hashem:*

"At an age when knights fought with axe and spear to kill one another, Jewish scholars fought battles with the pen, to seek the truth in the words of Hashem.

"To this day, one of the greatest thrills that await the student of Jewish law is to enter into the midst of the arena and follow the Ramban as he proceeds to restore the positions of Alfasi."

In a further effort to complement the words of the Rif, the Ramban prepared a text for those *masechtos* of *halachah* that the Rif had omitted, *Nedarim* and *Bechoros.*

Another of the Ramban's great works concerns the mitzvos of the Torah. Although the Gemara states that Hashem gave the Jews a total of 613 (*taryag*) mitzvos,[2] the exact identity of these mitzvos is not explicitly stated. It is very difficult for the layman to determine whether a verse in the Chumash constitutes a commandment or is simply a statement of fact. As early as the ninth century, a listing of the mitzvos had been attempted by Rav Saadya Gaon and others. At approximately the same time, Rabbi Shimon of Kahira (Cairo), (known as the Bahag) wrote a *sefer, Halachos Gedolos,* in which he enumerates and comments on each one of the *taryag* mitzvos. His listing was held to be authoritative until the Rambam wrote his own *Sefer HaMitzvos,* often departing from the Bahag. In his quest to defend the position of the earliest Rishonim and to vindicate the Bahag, the Ramban wrote his

Ramban defending the Rif (From Rabbi Chavel's biography of Ramban)

2. *Makkos,* 23b.

own commentary on the *Sefer HaMitzvos*.

The Ramban showed both great courage in opposing the contemporary giants of *halachah*, and great reverence for the previous generations. He used his brilliance and vast knowledge to vindicate their authority, which had come under attack by later scholars, although he did concede that one might possibly disagree with some decisions of the earlier authorities.

Another valuable work is *Toras HaAdam*, "Torah of the Human Being," which deals with the subject of death, mainly about the *halachos* of burial and mourning. The last portion of this sefer is *Shaar HaGemul*, "Gates of Compensation," which deals with reward and punishment after death.

Later in his life, the Ramban turned his attention to the Baalei Tosafos, writing his classic commentary on the Gemara. Today, the student approaches this *sefer* with a particular sense of awe, often struck by its clarity and depth.

The most widely read of all the Ramban's writings, however, is his commentary on Chumash, which was described by the Chasam Sofer as "truly fundamental" to an understanding of our faith. Originally, the Ramban's intention was to create a simple commentary for laymen who wanted to devote time on Shabbos to study the *peshat* of the weekly Torah reading; ultimately, however, he created a work that is scholarly and profound. In his commentary, the Ramban often alludes to the *emes*, the true meaning of the Torah, which he found in the words of Kabbalah. Nevertheless, the Ramban cautions the reader that only someone who has received instruction in Kabbalah should expect to understand its deep meaning. In fact, to discourage self-instruction and faulty speculation, he often states at the end of a kabbalistic comment, *"ve'ha'meivin yavin"*: i.e., only one who possesses a working understanding of Torah mysticism can understand.

"Everyone is in this *Parshah*!"

A famous story concerning the Ramban was recorded by Rabbi Yechiel Halpern in his *Seder HaDoros*. It provides a glimpse of the wisdom, staunchness, and fearlessness of this towering leader.

The Ramban had a student named Avner who suddenly left the Yeshivah and converted to Catholicism. He quickly achieved distinction in the hierarchy of the Church and became a bishop who was greatly feared for his cruelty and overbearing manner.

Years later, Avner summoned the Ramban to his palace on Yom Kippur. As the Ramban watched, stony-faced, Avner killed a pig, cut it up, cooked it, and ate it. Afterwards, he brazenly asked the Ramban how many major sins (for which one suffers *karais*) he had committed by this foul deed.

"Four," the Ramban replied.

Avner argued, "No, five!"

Chiddushei HaRamban

The Ramban's intention was to create a simple commentary for laymen who wanted to devote time on Shabbos to study the peshat of the weekly Torah reading

Chapter
17

Whether they won or lost, following these public discussions the aftermath for the Jews was fraught with danger.

The Ramban glared at him angrily but did not say a word. His former student, who still harbored a vestige of reverence for his teacher, became silent.

After a time, the Ramban asked Avner what had made him decide to leave the Yeshivah and his religion. The Jew-turned-bishop explained that he had once attended a lecture on *Parshas Haazinu* in which the Ramban stated, "In this single portion of the Torah, one could find every one of the mitzvos and every event which befell the nation as a whole, as well as every single Jew, from the beginning of Creation until the end of time."

"And since this is clearly impossible," concluded the convert, "I decided to quit and to start a new life for myself."

"But I still maintain this claim," retorted the Ramban. "Ask me anything you want!"

Astounded, the bishop challenged his former Rebbe, "Show me where my name is in this *parshah.*"

The Ramban sighed. "Since you asked for it, I will tell you." He immediately went into a corner, prayed, and opened up a Chumash to *Devarim* 32:26, which states, "*Amarti afeihem ashbisa mei'enosh zichrom.*" "I said I will abandon them, obliterate their memory from humanity."

The Ramban showed this passage to his former student. "If you take the third letter of the last four words in this *pasuk,* you have the name *Avner* in an ominous context."

The bishop understood immediately and was horrified. Pale and distressed, he asked his former Rebbe whether there was any hope for him. The Ramban sadly replied, "You heard my words," and turned away.

It is said that Avner then set off in a boat without oars or provisions, never to be heard of again.

The Disputation

Every new publication of the Ramban's works increased his fame among Jews and non-Jews; he became recognized as the undisputed spiritual leader in Spain and well beyond its northern borders. Despite his acclaim, the great master was involved in a series of controversies which disrupted his peace of mind. His attempt to mediate the battle between the Maimunists and anti-Maimunists met with failure, causing him great grief. His role in a public disputation with Pablo Christiani, a Jew who converted to Christianity, was even more tragic.

In 1263, Christiani, who had been unsuccessful in converting other Jews to his adopted religion, sought to gain favor with his superiors in the Church by challenging the Ramban to a debate. Such debates, unfortunately, were not rare in the Middle Ages. Jewish leaders were forced to participate in philosophical and religious disputations under the most disadvantageous circumstances. Whether they won or lost, following these public discussions the aftermath for the Jews was fraught with danger. In this case, the disputation was to center upon whether *Mashiach* had already come (as the Christians believe) or not.

The outlook was gloomy. It was a foregone conclusion that the Jews could not be allowed to prevail on an issue so fundamental to the Christian faith, especially in the presence of the king and the leaders of the clergy. The Ramban had no choice but to accept the challenge, although he did manage to extract a promise that he was to have complete freedom of speech.

The debate dragged on for four days with no winner in sight. The Jews begged the Ramban to stop the proceedings, terrified that his victory would create danger for the community. A recess of several days was granted, but the king, James I of Aragon, fascinated by the eloquence and brilliance of the aged rabbi, commanded that the disputation continue. At last the king called an end to the debates.

"On that day," wrote the Ramban later, "I stood before my lord, the king, and he said to me, 'Let the disputation rest, for never did I see a man who was so wrong argue as well as you did.'"

The Ramban was awarded a large gift from the royal treasury, while Pablo Christiani was given permission to continue his debates with Jews in other areas of Spain. In addition, the Jews had to pay Christiani's expenses and supply him with books.

The Bishop of Gerona ordered the Ramban to record his arguments at the disputation. Humiliated by the account, Church officials maneuvered to have the Ramban punished. King James was ultimately swayed and agreed to have the book burned and the rabbi condemned to two years of exile from Spain. The Ramban decided to utilize the opportunity to fulfill a lifelong dream: he would journey to Eretz Yisrael.

The Last Years of the Ramban

Traveling to Eretz Yisrael from Spain was a hazardous undertaking. Not wishing to expose his family to those dangers, the Ramban decided to travel alone, leaving his wife and children behind. After an arduous journey, he reached the Holy Land and wrote a number of letters describing the conditions he found there. The Jews had been driven out of Yerushalayim and, to his dismay, there was not even a *minyan* of ten men left. He arranged to have a Sefer Torah brought from Shechem; soon, the Ramban was able to start a *minyan* in the first synagogue of the city after many years of devastation. Ever since then, shuls have been in existence in the Holy City without interruption.

The Ramban spent only three years in Eretz Yisrael, but they were fruitful ones. He laid the foundations upon which future generations were able to rebuild their spiritual lives in Yerushalayim. In addition to his shul, the Ramban established his own Yeshivah, attracting many students from neighboring countries. In one of his later sermons, he expressed, in moving words, his love of Eretz Yisrael and his wish to be buried in its holy soil.

No one knows exactly when or where the Ramban died, but there is an unusual story connected with his death. On the day of the Ramban's departure from Spain, his pupils asked him how they would know the time of his passing. He answered, "On the day of my demise, a crack will appear on the stone over my mother's grave. This will be a sign that I have passed away." Four years later, a student of the Ramban found that the stone had cracked.

The Ramban decided to utilize the opportunity to fulfill a lifelong dream: he would journey to Eretz Yisrael.

Chapter
17

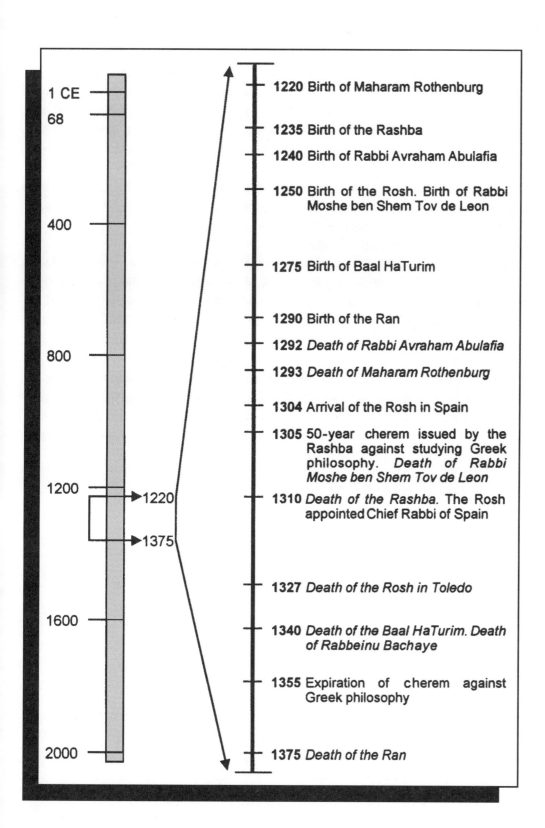

1220 Birth of Maharam Rothenburg

1235 Birth of the Rashba

1240 Birth of Rabbi Avraham Abulafia

1250 Birth of the Rosh. Birth of Rabbi Moshe ben Shem Tov de Leon

1275 Birth of Baal HaTurim

1290 Birth of the Ran

1292 *Death of Rabbi Avraham Abulafia*

1293 *Death of Maharam Rothenburg*

1304 Arrival of the Rosh in Spain

1305 50-year cherem issued by the Rashba against studying Greek philosophy. *Death of Rabbi Moshe ben Shem Tov de Leon*

1310 *Death of the Rashba.* The Rosh appointed Chief Rabbi of Spain

1327 *Death of the Rosh in Toledo*

1340 *Death of the Baal HaTurim. Death of Rabbeinu Bachaye*

1355 Expiration of cherem against Greek philosophy

1375 *Death of the Ran*

Chapter
18

While copies of the Talmud were being confiscated and publicly burned in France, while the Yeshivos of the Baalei Tosafos were being forced to close, and thousands of Jews were being slain in Germany, Rabbi Shlomo ben Aderes reigned in Spain as the spiritual leader of the exile.

The Crusades left northern France and Germany in a state of bloody turmoil, but Jewish life in Spain and Portugal developed relatively peacefully during the twelfth and thirteenth centuries. The foremost authority of the period was Rabbi Shlomo ben Aderes, also known as the Rashba (1235-1310). His rabbinate extended from his residence in Barcelona to the kingdom of Aragon, but his fame spread throughout Spain. Jews from as far away as Germany, France, and North Africa turned to the Rashba with questions of *halachah*. A record of some three thousand responsa that the Rashba penned during his lifetime has been preserved. While copies of the Talmud were being confiscated and publicly burned in France, while the Yeshivos of the Baalei Tosafos were being forced to close, and thousands of Jews were being slain in Germany, Rabbi Shlomo ben Aderes reigned in Spain as the spiritual leader of the exile.

A student of the Ramban and Rabbeinu Yonah, the Rashba perpetuated their approach to learning Torah. His analyses on Gemara, which earned him a place among the greatest Sages of all time, are still studied in depth. His responsa remain distinguished by their brevity and sharp logic. While the Rashba had the greatest respect for the wisdom of the Sages of previous generations, he did not hesitate to differ with their interpretations. In addition to the *Chiddushei Ha-Rashba,* he also wrote a *sefer* on *halachah, Toras HaBayis.*

As Chief Rabbi of Aragon, the Rashba was involved in the public affairs of the Jewish communities, especially with regard to court cases and tax collections. Occasionally he had to publish articles defending his people from anti-Jewish attacks. In particular, a certain Dominican monk attacked the Jews in his writings, accusing them of having caused the death of the Christian messiah. The Rashba refuted

Title Page of Chiddushei HaRashba

Title Page of Rashba's Toras HaBayis

the monk's claim in an article which defeated the accusations and avoided provoking the clergy to further attacks.

In the time of the Rashba, the dispute with the Maimunists had already ended in Spain; most rabbis conceded that the *Moreh Nevuchim* had brought more benefit to Jews beset by doubts than harm to Jews who had never questioned their faith. In general, the Rambam's writings had fostered new strength and devotion to Torah study in southern Europe. However, the Rashba was concerned about a different kind of study: Greek philosophy.

Many young Spanish Jews studied Greek philosophy in depth, causing a negative effect on their religious outlook. Greek philosophy questioned many fundamentals of Judaism; it also stripped away the spiritual core of the concept at hand and caused one to concentrate on its external values instead, almost like a body without a soul. Furthermore, the exclusive philosophical approach to religion causes conflicts that were bound to weaken the basic faith—*emunah peshutah*—which is the foundation of Judaism. The Rashba, who understood that this ideology posed a terrible threat to Spanish Jewry, issued a decree which forbade anyone under the age of twenty-five to study the works of the Greek philosophers in original or translated form. The only exception to this rule was the study of medicine. The Rashba, in his wisdom, limited this ban to fifty years, setting its expiration for the year 1355; this indicated that he did not object to the study of philosophy in principle, but to the threat it posed to the spiritual lives of Spanish Jews of his own era.

The Rosh (1250-1327)

In the year 1304, a German refugee by the name of Rabbi Asher ben Yechiel arrived in Spain. As a young man, he had been the most outstanding student of the most prominent rabbi in Germany, Rabbi Meir of Rothenburg, known as the Maharam (1220-1293). The Maharam had become a victim of an extortion scheme instigated by the German Emperor, who needed money for his military projects. The Emperor had the Maharam imprisoned for a fictitious crime, hoping that the Jews would pay any ransom to free their beloved rabbi. But the Maharam had given strict orders to his followers not to yield to this pressure because of the *mishnah* which states that one may not ransom Jewish captives for an excessive amount of money. The Jewish community, otherwise, would become vulnerable to ruin by encouraging escalated ransom demands.[1] The Jews, although desperate to redeem their beloved leader, reluctantly acceded to his decree, and the Maharam of Rothenburg spent the rest of his life in prison. Even after he died, the cruel Emperor refused to release the revered rabbi's body. It was only years later, after the death of the Emperor, that a new ruler arose who released the Maharam's remains for burial when a wealthy Jew paid a heavy ransom.

Before his death, the Maharam of Rothenburg had ordered his favorite pupil, Rabbi Asher, to leave Germany and find refuge in Spain. When he arrived in Barcelona, the Rashba received him with great honor. Soon after, he was appointed Chief Rabbi of Toledo, one of the foremost cities in Castile. Rabbeinu Asher, known as the Rosh, also served as Chief Judge to the Jews of Castile, by official authorization of

1. *Gittin*, 45a.

In general, the Rambam's writings had fostered new strength and devotion to Torah study in southern Europe. However, the Rashba was concerned about a different kind of study: Greek philosophy.

Chapter
18

the government. Consequently, he was empowered to administer capital punishment. While he was reluctant to sanction capital punishment (since according to Jewish law, only the Sanhedrin has the right to mete out the death penalty), he nevertheless gave his approval when circumstances demanded this drastic action. After the Rashba's passing in 1310, Rabbi Asher became the leading Rav of all Spain. Under his leadership, the Yeshivah of Toledo developed into a Torah center not only for Spain but for all of Europe, attracting students even from distant Russia.

The Rosh followed the Baalei Tosafos in his method of learning. His most famous legacy is the *Hilchos HaRosh*, a commentary printed in the more comprehensive editions of the Talmud Bavli at the end of the main text. In this work, the Rosh summarizes the Gemara and renders halachic decisions incorporating all the Rishonim before him, including the Bahag, Rif, Rambam, and Baalei Tosafos. Occasionally, the Rosh injected his own halachic opinion with the words *nireh li,* "It seems to me." As Rav Shlomo Heiman (1893-1944) explained to his students, this remark carried more weight than any other reference cited by the Rosh, for his mental faculties were so acute that he could survey the entire Shass instantaneously before arriving at a halachic conclusion. One can say that the Rosh's accomplishments in *halachah* are comparable to those of Rashi on the Gemara: the Rosh fused the traditions of both schools of learning, German and Spanish, and wove them into a single fabric.

The Rosh also wrote a small *sefer* containing his program for ethical living. *Orchos Chaim,* "Ways of Living," is an inspiring model for the Jew in his daily conduct toward Hashem and his fellow man. As it is divided into seven chapters, one

One can say that the Rosh's accomplishments in halachah are comparable to those of Rashi on the Gemara.

for each day of the week, it has become customary in many Yeshivos to recite a chapter daily during the month of Elul.

In his dealings with the Jewish communities of Provence, the Rosh became aware that Torah and Jewish ethics were being neglected by Jews over-exposed to Greek philosophy and science. Therefore, he joined in the prohibition issued by the Rashba and other leading rabbis against studying these books before the age of twenty-five. The Rosh died in Toledo in the year 1327.

This noble leader had been blessed with seven sons and daughters. The most famous among them was Rabbi Yaakov, the author of the *Tur,* known as the Baal HaTurim.

The Baal HaTurim (1275-1340)

The Baal HaTurim, who served as rabbi of Toledo, undertook the gigantic task of re-arranging halachic information systematically by subject, as opposed to the halachic discussions in every *masechta* which had been followed by the Rif and the Rosh. Rabbi Yaakov divided the material into four parts. In choosing a title for his work, he was inspired by the breastplate of the *Kohen Gadol,* which contained four rows of precious stones engraved with the names of the twelve Shevatim. The Hebrew word for row is *tur*; Rabbi Yaakov's work was titled *Arba'ah Turim,* "Four Rows." Into those four sections Rabbi Yaakov incorporated all the *halachos* and traditions of the Talmudic and Gaonic eras, plus any additional clarifications and customs of the early Rishonim that apply in all parts of the world. The four sections of the *Tur* are:

Orach Chaim—concerning the events of the Jewish year.

Yoreh Deah—concerning the laws of *issur v'heter,* what is permitted and what is forbidden.

Even HaEzer—concerning Jewish family life.

Choshen Mishpat—concerning justice between man and man.

This tremendous work was accepted and acclaimed in all parts of the world. In the course of time, however, Torah leaders realized that the *Tur* needed further clarification. Since Rabbi Yaakov was a very humble person, he often quoted the opinions of the great Sages without rendering a final decision concerning whose opinion one should follow. Furthermore, the *Tur* did not always quote the source of various opinions. Almost two hundred years later, another towering Torah Sage wrote a *sefer* in which he addressed these shortcomings.[2] The name of that *sefer* is the *Bais Yosef;* its author, Rabbi Yosef Karo.

The Ran (1290-1375)

Rabbeinu Nissim of Gerona, usually referred to as the Ran, was a student of the Rashba and a contemporary of the Rosh. He served as Rav in Barcelona after the Rashba's death. For some fifty years after the passing of the Rosh, he reigned as undisputed leader of his generation in Spain.

The initially idyllic period of Jewish life in Spain had since ended. Spanish Jews suffered from increasing religious persecution, leading to a decline of the Yeshivos as well as in the quality of Torah study. Nevertheless, the Ran's Yeshivah was attended by eager scholars from all over Europe and his opinion was sought on all matters of religious law.

The Ran is especially famous for his commentary on *maseches Nedarim;* his work is frequently studied in place of Rashi in this *masechta,* since Rashi's commentary on this section was not written by Rashi himself. The Ran also commented on the *halachos* of the Rif. In his commentary, he strove not only to clarify and explain, but also to arrive at a final decision. In addition, the Ran was acclaimed as a speaker and orator. A collection of his speeches, *Drashos HaRan,* gained wide popularity.

Revival of Kabbalah— Anshei HaChein

During the Spanish Era, exposure to academic life in the Muslim universities had stimulated an interest in philosophy that tended to undermine belief in Hashem.[3] In order to combat this negative influence, it was not enough to issue decrees and to announce threats of *cherem;* some stronger spiritual horizons had to be opened that would allow the thirst of the intellect to be quenched by gazing into the secrets and depth of Hashem's creation. This new horizon became the study of Kabbalah, and the people who specialized in this type of learning were called *Anshei Chochmas HaNistar,* "men of the hidden wisdom," commonly abbreviated as *Anshei HaChein.*

The study of Kabbalah was nothing new to the Sages of Israel; it is referred to in the Mishnah. Although the Tannaim did not teach it in public, they did study it in private. Outstanding individuals possessed writings on the "hidden wisdom" which they were careful not to publicize. One of these writings was *Sefer HaYetzirah,* "The Book of Creation"; those who mastered its contents claimed that they were able to perform supernatural feats, but they used their knowledge wisely.

---

2. See Chapter 22 for a discussion of the *Shulchan Aruch.*

3. See Chapter 19.

The Ran reigned as undisputed leader of his generation in Spain.

The Zohar, whose author was the illustrious Tanna, Rabbi Shimon bar Yochai, had been hidden from the world for almost one thousand years.

At the precise time that Spanish Jews were caught up in the inexplicable questions posed by Greek philosophy, the study of secret wisdom broke from its hiding place and gained new popularity. The spiritual answers it provided, and the revelation of the panorama of overwhelming perfection of Hashem's creations, attracted Jews who had been troubled by philosophical doubts.

The Ramban had been a *mekubal,* meaning that he had learned Kabbalah from the mouth of his Rebbe, who had received the secret wisdom orally from someone of a previous generation. The Ramban's talmid, the Rashba, also alluded to Kabbalah in many of his writings.

The study of Kabbalah was a hazardous one, which could only be attempted after much preparation and learning. One example of an overzealous student of Kabbalah was Avraham Abulafia of Saragossa, who immersed himself in the *Sefer HaYetzirah.* He then claimed that he was prompted by an inner voice to go to Rome and seek an audience with the Pope, in order to convert him to Judaism. Fortunately, the Pope died before Abulafia's mad plan could be put into effect. But upon reaching Sicily, he claimed to be a prophet and finally asserted that he was *Mashiach!* When the Jewish community there became alarmed by his growing number of followers, they turned to the Rashba for guidance. He quickly condemned Abulafia and warned the community not to tolerate this false messianic movement.

One student of the Rashba who used his understanding of this deeper wisdom properly was Rabbeinu Bachaye, author of an inspiring commentary on Chumash. In this *sefer,* the author attempted to express the kabbalistic concepts of the Ramban on a level suitable for the non-informed Talmudic student. His commentary enables the reader to feel—if not fully comprehend—the holiness and awesome depth contained in every word of the Chumash.

Most far reaching, however, was the influence of Rabbi Moshe ben Shem Tov de Leon (1250-1305), one of the greatest Sages of Kabbalah. He dedicated himself to the collection and reproduction of all written works of Kabbalah that had been in use among *mekubalim.* When Moshe de Leon passed away in the year 1305, a wealthy man bought a copy of the *Zohar* which had been found in his library. The *Zohar,* whose author was the illustrious Tanna, Rabbi Shimon bar Yochai, had been hidden from the world for almost one thousand years. With the acquisition of this handwritten copy, the ever-increasing number of

Title Page of Midrash Rabbeinu Bachaye

fourteenth-century *mekubalim* focused their attention on this *sefer*. The *Zohar* became the classic text of Kabbalah, treasured and revered among Torah scholars.

The study of the *Zohar* was like "the cure before the illness," fortifying Jewish faith in Hashem during times of intense suffering in the Middle Ages. It illuminated a world of darkness and pain with the brilliance of its light, and provided spiritual refuge and tranquility when the physical tortures became almost unbearable.

The Sages of Spain took the mysticism of the *Zohar* with them when they were expelled from Spain in 1492, establishing a new center of Kabbalah in the ancient city of Tzefas in the Holy Land. Today, the learning of mysticism is not encouraged in most Yeshivos; its accessibility is limited to those who have the maturity and guidance needed for its proper comprehension.

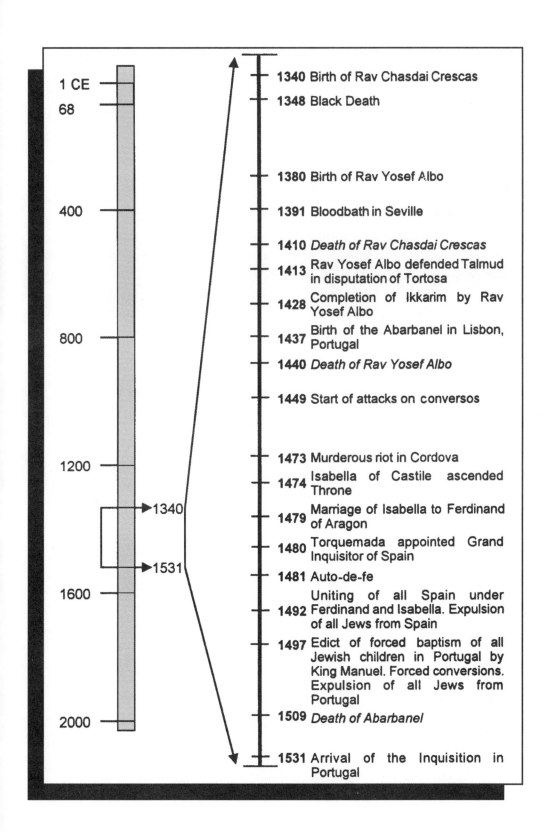

1 CE	
68	
400	
800	
1200	
1340	
1531	
1600	
2000	

1340 Birth of Rav Chasdai Crescas

1348 Black Death

1380 Birth of Rav Yosef Albo

1391 Bloodbath in Seville

1410 *Death of Rav Chasdai Crescas*

1413 Rav Yosef Albo defended Talmud in disputation of Tortosa

1428 Completion of Ikkarim by Rav Yosef Albo

1437 Birth of the Abarbanel in Lisbon, Portugal

1440 *Death of Rav Yosef Albo*

1449 Start of attacks on conversos

1473 Murderous riot in Cordova

1474 Isabella of Castile ascended Throne

1479 Marriage of Isabella to Ferdinand of Aragon

1480 Torquemada appointed Grand Inquisitor of Spain

1481 Auto-de-fe

1492 Uniting of all Spain under Ferdinand and Isabella. Expulsion of all Jews from Spain

1497 Edict of forced baptism of all Jewish children in Portugal by King Manuel. Forced conversions. Expulsion of all Jews from Portugal

1509 *Death of Abarbanel*

1531 Arrival of the Inquisition in Portugal

Chapter

19

Disaster struck the Jews of Spain in two powerful thrusts, one hundred years apart.

The relatively secure life of the Jews in Spain was in stark contrast to the sufferings of Jews in other parts of Europe during the Middle Ages. For over four hundred years, an impressive number of towering personalities led the Jewish population of Iberia (Spain) to a climax of spiritual achievement. At the same time, Spanish Jewry enjoyed unparalleled physical well-being. Many of the catastrophes occurring in other parts of Europe had little impact on them.

For example, in 1348, the Black Death, a fatal epidemic originating in India, ravaged most of the European mainland, killing more than one-third of the population. Frightened and hysterical, the survivors readily believed vicious rumors that the Jews had poisoned the drinking water in order to destroy the Christians. These rumors came about because Jews had been affected only slightly by the plague because of their cleanliness, especially their habit of washing their hands before eating, etc. In one uprising after another, surging mobs butchered thousands of Jews and plundered their possessions. Altogether, sixty large Jewish communities and one hundred fifty small ones were completely destroyed.[1]

The Jews in Spain were, for the most part, spared the worst of this ordeal, but their moment of disaster was not averted, merely delayed. Disaster struck the Jews of Spain in two powerful thrusts, one hundred years apart. Together, they completely wiped out the Jewish population in the Iberian Peninsula.

The Terrors of 1391

By the fourteenth century, constant warfare had seen large areas of southern Spain successfully wrested from the

Jewish Centers of Spain and Portugal in the 14th Century.

---

1. See Chapter 21 for further details.

Muslims by Catholic forces. With these battles finally over, the nobles found themselves drained of their resources. All of their energies and wealth had been devoted to the *Reconquista* (reconquest of Spain), and it was difficult for the new Christian rulers to build their kingdom from the ruins.

Out of necessity, rather than from kind feelings, they engaged the expertise and wisdom of some of their Jewish subjects for advice on financial and political matters. Jews occupied positions of prestige and power in the royal palaces. The Spanish common people began to look with envy on these Jewish men of influence. Over the years, their resentment grew; with time, the tolerance previously accorded the Jews became strained. The climate was ripe for a mass revolt of Spanish Catholic peasants against the polished and favored court Jews.

In the southern city of Seville, Archdeacon Ferrand Martinez declared a "Holy War against the Jews" and delivered fiery sermons inciting the Christian population against the Jews. On June 4, 1391, his impassioned sermons of hatred reached their height and ignited a mob which attacked the Jewish quarter of Seville. Ravaging crowds fell upon the Jews, plundering their homes and murdering those who did not submit to baptism. Of a congregation of 30,000 souls, 4,000 men were murdered, and their wives and children sold as slaves. Only a few Jews managed to escape. Many accepted conversion out of fear for their lives, with the secret hope that once the fury abated, they would return to Judaism.

After the bloodbath in Seville, brutal attacks broke out in eighty other communities. Synagogues were burned to the ground or turned into churches. Unlike the German Jews who died *al kiddush Hashem* during the Crusades, the vast majority of Spanish Jews submitted to baptism. To be sure, many suffered martyrdom rather than convert; yet it is reported that the number of converts reached close to 200,000.

Among the exceptions to this pattern of mass conversions was Rabbi Yehudah ben Asher, a son of the Rosh in the city of Toledo. He killed his family and then himself rather than submit to baptism. Another Sage, Rabbi Shimon ben Tzemach, was able to flee Spain and find refuge in Algiers, where he became famous as the Rashbatz. He was not only great in Torah, but also an expert on medicine and Catholicism. He used this expertise to write authoritative rebuttals to claims made by the Christian clergy against the Jewish religion.

The Jews who survived the holocaust of 1391 realized that their role in Spanish society had become an inferior one. The freedom and privileges they had enjoyed in the country that had been their home for centuries no longer existed.

It may seem astonishing that the "Golden Age of Spain," a glorious period distinguished by a parade of Torah Sages who left an indelible mark on Torah literature, could come to such an ignoble end. However, any interpretive approach to Jewish history can only speculate about the causes and ramifications of events. Even contemporary observations of the period by "eyewitnesses" are limited in knowledge and understanding. However, a few points can be suggested to explain the vast difference between Jewish reaction to persecution in Spain and the rest of Europe.

Rabbi Yosef Yaavetz, one of the spiritual leaders of the Spanish refugees, describes the Jews of Spain prior to 1492:

The Jews who survived the holocaust of 1391 realized that their role in Spanish society had become an inferior one. The freedom and privileges they had enjoyed in the country that had been their home for centuries no longer existed.

Chapter
19

> *The Spanish era
> can also be
> characterized as a
> nisayon shel osher,
> a test of the
> strength of faith in
> a time of material
> success and
> physical well-
> being. Wealth and
> security in exile
> have the potential
> to lead to spiritual
> inertia.*

"Never were there as many Yeshivos in Spain as in the generation before the expulsion. But the students who studied in those Yeshivos were split into numerous groups. Some of them had studied for six or seven years with the great Rabbanim, strengthening their minds in Talmudic debates, only to devote their mental agility eventually to other wisdom, and to become skeptical about their religious studies. Others turned away completely from their spiritual values and devoted themselves to the mundane vanities of this world. A third group, while retaining their interest in Torah, no longer studied Torah as a form of Divine service, but as a means of boosting their superior intellects. In this way they thwarted the purpose of Torah study, i.e., the ennoblement of human motivation and behavior."[2]

Rabbi Yaavetz was not referring to the absence of extreme piety but to simple adherence to the laws governing daily life, such as tzitzis and tefillin. This observation is not a reflection on the spiritual leaders of Spanish Jewry, nor on the founders of these great learning centers, but it does suggest a wide variety of attitudes on the part of the masses. It also suggests that the merit of such Torah study was too weak to avert the severity of the final punishment that fell upon all Spanish Jewry.

The Spanish era can also be characterized as a *nisayon shel osher,* a test of the strength of faith in a time of material success and physical well-being. Wealth and security in exile have the potential to lead to spiritual inertia. Once accepted among the Gentiles of his environment, a Jew may become reluctant to give up the comforts and privileges he

has gained, forgetting that the country in which he currently lives is only a temporary refuge. He begins to feel that no matter what happens, it will remain his home forever, and that the cruel persecutions are in the past.

The constant social and cultural contact which the Spanish Jews had with their Christian rulers, as well as their intellectual growth in mathematics and astronomy learned from the Muslims, put doubts in their minds about the validity of their own religion. Obviously, such a climate could not generate the powerful heroism and sacrifice shown by Ashkenazim who had been raised in a climate of isolation and poverty.

Jewish Philosophers During the Years of Decline

From the Jewish point of view, the study of philosophy had undergone a significant change in the final years of Jewish life in Spain. During the zenith of the Golden Era, the great Sages of those generations made use of the wisdom that they found in Greek philosophy; for example, the Rambam had utilized the philosophical methods of Aristotle to reinforce belief in Hashem for those who needed it. However, because of the repeated conflicts with the Church and ruthless attacks from Catholic leaders, the Jews were eventually forced into a position of self-defense. Jewish scholars realized that there were major weaknesses in the philosophical systems of the Greeks. Therefore, they emphasized to their students that the strength of faith in Hashem and His Torah does not depend merely on logic; one must accept the truth of the articles of Jewish faith as

---

2. From Rabbi Yaavetz's introduction to his *Ohr HaChaim.*

they have been handed down through the generations, extending to the revelation on Mount Sinai to the assembled masses of Klal Yisrael.

One of the first Jewish leaders to enunciate this concept was Rabbi Chasdai Crescas (died in 1410) in his philosophical work, *Ohr Hashem*. Rav Chasdai disputed the Rambam's thesis that religion and philosophy are compatible, listing many points of contradiction between Greek philosophy and the Torah. He explained that the purpose of the mitzvos is not to create logical proofs for the kingdom of Hashem, but to introduce a love for Hashem. The Torah appeals to the heart and soul to serve Hashem; thus faith is a product of emotions, rather than of impersonal logical calculation, as the Greeks believed.

Rav Yosef Albo (died 1440), a pupil of Rav Crescas, expounded this theory further in his *Ikkarim*. Rav Albo, a respected Jewish thinker, was the spokesman for the Jews in the famous disputation of Tortosa. This remarkable debate between Jews and Christians lasted almost two years, from February 1413 to November 1414. He based his theological system on the thirteen principles of the Rambam, which he defines as articles of faith to be accepted regardless of whether they can be supported by logic. Rav Albo himself, however, reduced these thirteen

One must accept the truth of the articles of Jewish faith as they have been handed down through the generations, extending to the revelation on Mount Sinai to the assembled masses of Klal Yisrael.

concepts to three basic principles: the existence of one G-d, the Divine origin of the Torah, and the concept of reward and punishment. Rav Albo believed that these three tenets incorporate all the thirteen principles of the Rambam; a close analysis would undoubtedly sustain this assertion.

Some accused Rav Albo of specifically omitting the belief in the future coming of *Mashiach* as an indisputable dogma of the Jewish faith. However, it is possible that Rav Albo specifically made the omission in a tactical move to avoid arousing the hostility of the Christians, who claim that the Messiah has already come.

One of the last of the Spanish Torah Sages was Don Yitzchak Abarbanel, a descendant of King David. His colorful life was punctuated with moments of great victory as well as disaster. Known as the Abarbanel (as well as *Maharia,* **M**orainu **H**arav **Y**itzchak **A**barbanel), he was born in 1437, in Lisbon, Portugal, where his father, Rav Yehudah, had been appointed Finance Minister at the royal court. After Rav Yehudah's death, Don Yitzchak inherited his father's position, which he held with distinction and dignity for sixteen years. From his writings, it is apparent that he regretted this period of his life, although it brought him material wealth and honor. He lamented that his preoccupation with the affairs of the state kept him from his main goal in life: to spread Torah to all Jews.

The opportunity to disseminate Torah arrived when King Alfonso V of Portugal died and his successor threatened the Maharia's life. Forewarned in secret, he quickly fled Portugal, leaving all his possessions behind. He found refuge across the Spanish border in Toledo, capital of

He explained that the purpose of the mitzvos is not to create logical proofs for the kingdom of Hashem, but to introduce a love for Hashem. The Torah appeals to the heart and soul to serve Hashem; thus faith is a product of emotions, rather than of impersonal logical calculation, as the Greeks believed.

Chapter
19

*Rav Abarbanel
used his position of
power and
influence to work
for the welfare of
his Jewish brothers
in Spain.*

Castile, where he lived in peace, albeit in poverty, for a short while.

During this time, he began his lifework, a gigantic commentary on Tanach. This famous commentary is distinguished by its incredible thoroughness. Every chapter of Tanach is introduced by a list of questions which arouse the reader's intellectual curiosity. The Abarbanel then presents a critical analysis of the classical commentaries before concluding with his own, resolving all the initial questions. Indeed, almost every major commentary written after his time quotes the Maharia.

During his sojourn in Spain, the Abarbanel was able to complete three books of the *Nevi'im Rishonim*: *Yehoshua, Shoftim,* and *Shmuel.* As he prepared to start his commentary on *Melachim,* King Ferdinand of Spain summoned him to the capital and appointed him Finance Minister of the Court. Ferdinand needed the Abarbanel's genius to plan and finance his ambitious policy of uniting all the Spanish provinces under his crown. Rav Abarbanel used his position of power and influence to work for the welfare of his Jewish brothers in Spain, as many other Sages in Spain had done before him. But a crisis soon arose that even Rav Abarbanel, with all his influence and power, could not prevent: the expulsion of the Jews from the entire Iberian Peninsula.

As part of his scheme to unite all of Spain under his rule, Ferdinand, royal successor to the throne of Aragon, married Isabella, who had inherited the throne of Castile in 1474. This nuptial united the largest Christian domains in Spain under two fanatic, cruel, and ambitious rulers. Ferdinand and Isabella determined to acquire all remaining areas of Spain which were still in Muslim hands, creating a unified kingdom under their power.

*Title Page of Rav Don Yitzchak Abarbanel
on the Book of Prophets*

At this point, the Jewish community of Spain consisted of three distinct groups:

1) Jews who had remained true to Judaism during the forced conversions and had managed to escape the persecutions. They lived normal Jewish lives, often with distinct privileges, but with the constant threat that the tide could turn against them. They maintained synagogues, performed mitzvos openly, and corresponded with the centers of learning in other parts of the world.

2) *Conversos,* or "New Christians," were Jews who had converted or were descended from converts to Christianity. Forced conversions had erupted periodically in Spain since the reign of the Visigothic King Sisebut in 613, but the vast bulk of converts were of more recent Jewish ancestry, descended from those who submitted to baptism in the raids during and after 1391. Many of these became devout Christians who not only turned their backs on their

Jewish brethren, but actually sought to impress the Christian clergy by joining them in persecuting the Jews with the utmost vigor. Often such converts were the backbone of Christian clergy in "disputations," public debates on theology in which Jewish Sages were forced to participate.

Over the years, *conversos* infiltrated every level of Spanish society, intermarried with the aristocratic Catholic population, and often attained highly eminent positions. While some ultimately blended into the Christian community, they were generally envied and hated by the "Old Christians." It was evident that the highly capable and energetic proselytes were pushing the original "Old Christians" out of the most prestigious roles in government, business, and the hierarchy of the Church.

3) *Marranos,* who formed a secret group within the *conversos,* were Jews who had outwardly renounced their faith and accepted Christianity. In their public conduct these Jews were indistinguishable from Gentiles. They dressed, spoke, and acted like devout Christians. Many of them studied in the Christian universities, excelling in scholastic achievement, and were appointed to the highest ranks of the ecclesiastic hierarchy. In their hearts, however, these Marranos remained Jews loyal to the Torah.

Because of their devotion to Torah, the medieval Spanish term "*marrano,*" meaning "swine," was applied to them by the Christian populace. It is unclear whether this was used simply as a general derogatory term or had emerged to ridicule the Marranos for going out of their way to eat pork in public, as if to confirm their Gentile status.

Marranos made it a point to marry only those from within their own community, in order to keep the purity and traditions of Judaism intact. In arranging such marriages, countless families endured the dangers of being discovered, as they attempted to ascertain the Jewish commitment of a potential spouse.

In the secrecy of their homes, in hidden caves dug deep under their cellars, Marranos practiced the mitzvos and prayed with secret, fervent devotion. Unknown to the outside world, even to their own domestic servants, they celebrated Jewish holidays and fasted on Yom Kippur. As time went on, it became nearly impossible for the Marranos to practice Jewish law correctly; all Jewish books were banned, and any Christian, be he *converso* or "Old Christian," could be sentenced to death for owning a book in Hebrew. After just a few generations, knowledge of Jewish law and customs grew painfully vague. Many Marranos knew nothing about Judaism except what they read in the Latin Old Testament Bibles. Nevertheless, they clung to their belief in Hashem with pride and determination.

The Marranos included some of the most prominent and wealthiest of Spanish citizens. Many of them longed to return to Judaism, but were hesitant to take the drastic, inevitable step of leaving their Spanish homeland and resettling in a foreign country where one could openly embrace Judaism again. Their ties to Spain, and perhaps to their comfortable, wealthy positions, were simply too strong. Many of these contented themselves with the hope that Christian hatred for Judaism would prove to be only temporary and their lives would eventually return to normal.

Such hopes were futile. As early as 1449, the anger and frustration of the Old

Marranos were Jews who had outwardly renounced their faith and accepted Christianity...In their hearts, however, these Marranos remained Jews loyal to the Torah.

Chapter
19

*Initially, Jews and
Muslims were not
subject to the
Inquisition; after
all, its aim was to
root out heretics of
the Christian faith.*

Christian populace, encouraged by impassioned sermons against the New Christians, reached an explosive height. Ruthless attacks on *conversos* began. In 1473, a rumor spread during a religious procession in Cordova about a Marrano girl who reputedly desecrated a holy image. A murderous riot broke out that lasted for three days, ending only when no more victims could be found. Massacres were sparked in town after town; the *conversos'* attempts to defend themselves and their families met with failure.

The question of what to do with the New Christians, many of whom were suspected of "Judaizing," or backsliding into Judaism, became the obsession of the Spanish clergy. Laws were passed to insure the separation between practicing Jewish communities and *conversos* in the hope that this would prevent the Jewish believers from influencing their former brethren. In some communities, Jews were banned from settlement entirely. In others, Jews were obligated to attend conversion sermons several times a year and to pay heavy taxes.

With the marriage of Ferdinand and Isabella in 1479, the position of the New Christians became even more vulnerable. In addition to the desire of Ferdinand and Isabella to unite Spain under their rule, they shared the religious goal of establishing the Catholic faith as the only religion of the state. This would only be achieved by the elimination of both Muslims and Jews, who would be forced either to convert or to leave the country. Isabella, who had ascended the throne five years earlier, was convinced that the only way to bring true unity to Spain was to rid it of the "heretics" who undermined its Catholic base. Indeed, the former confessor to Queen Isabella, Tomas de Torquemada, had made her promise, long before she ascended the throne,

that she would devote herself to the obliteration of heresy in her kingdom. All too aware that a good-sized segment of the New Christian population were Marranos, the Queen and her advisors sought to eliminate them through liberal use of the Inquisition, the infamous institution that struck terror into the hearts of Christians throughout Europe.

The Inquisition

For several hundred years, the Catholic Church had struggled against various Christian sects that threatened to break off from the Catholic religion. Each claiming to be the "true" Christianity, these groups posed a strong threat to the unity of the Church and to the authority of Rome, the headquarters of the papacy. One pope after another enacted laws with harsh penalties for heresy, but it was not until 1233 that Pope Gregory IX created the full-blown Inquisition in Germany.

This new system appointed Inquisitors, usually the most enthusiastic Dominican or Franciscan monks, to a tribunal, which would formally ferret out and put on trial any Christian suspected of heresy. At first, the Inquisition was confined to Germany; with time, its influence spread to France, Italy, and Lombardy. The Inquisition proved highly successful against Albigensians and other heretical groups, and was later employed to curb witchcraft. Initially, Jews and Muslims were not subject to the Inquisition; after all, its aim was to root out heretics of the Christian faith.

Whether spurred on by religious zeal or by downright cruelty and avarice, the Inquisition became known for its terrifying tactics and barbarous punishments. No one was safe. The accused, in attempting to prepare his defense, was never told what information had been gathered against him, or even who had informed on him. It could have been anyone: a servant, a neighbor, a business rival. All Christians were required to inform on anyone even mildly suspected of heresy. The withholding of information was considered heresy in itself, and made one answerable to the Inquisitors.

With such a free hand, the Church could accuse and punish anyone, provided confession could be obtained; and with the notorious cruelty and tortures inflicted upon the victim, such confessions were practically inevitable. A variety of punishments could be meted out, depending on the penitence of the accused. If one was not penitent enough, or was a "relapsed" heretic, he or she was "abandoned to the secular arm," i.e., given over to government authorities to be burned at the stake. The Church itself, of course, would never take a human life.

Both the Church and the government derived great benefit from this system; after condemnation, the entire wealth of the "sinner" was confiscated. At times, one already dead could be condemned, and his body would be disinterred to be publicly burned. This action was no mere theatrical event, for by branding the dead man a heretic, his entire fortune could be taken from his heirs, who would then bear the added disgrace of their parent's heresy. It was this terrifying organization that Isabella so eagerly instituted in her kingdom.

The Inquisition in Spain

With the marriage of Ferdinand and Isabella and the increasing stabilization, the next order of business was to "purify" the religious aspect of the country.

What better way to deal with heretics than to call in the Holy Tribunal of the Inquisition?

The request was made of Rome in 1478, but was not approved until 1480, primarily because Pope Sixtus IV wanted to keep the Inquisition under his own control. Patient negotiations ultimately brought the Inquisition to Spain in September of 1480. Its purpose was to root out the Marranos.

Much to his delight, Torquemada, the former confessor to Isabella, was appointed Grand Inquisitor. He quickly set the dreaded tribunal into motion. Notorious for his fanatical hatred of Jews, Torquemada used his considerable abilities with gusto, centralizing the authority of the Inquisition, and transforming it into a virtual state within the state of Spain. Despite protests from Rome, Torquemada declared the Spanish Inquisition almost completely autonomous, daring to initiate proceedings even against bishops and archbishops. In his zeal, Torquemada was determined to punish even those Marranos who had reached high positions in the Church itself.

The Christian population was recruited to gather incriminating evidence against suspected Marranos. Devout spies, in their efforts to discover secret Jews, scrutinized the shopping habits of housewives around Pesach time, watched for a lack of chimney smoke on Shabbos, and examined the types of meats purchased for their households. Even changing the linens on Friday was enough to create suspicion. Gentile domestic help were bribed and interrogated by the Inquisitors to reveal a family's habits and pastimes.

Both the Church and the government derived great benefit from this system; after condemnation, the entire wealth of the "sinner" was confiscated.

If one was not penitent enough, or was a "relapsed" heretic, he or she was "abandoned to the secular arm," i.e., given over to government authorities to be burned at the stake. The Church itself, of course, would never take a human life.

Gentile domestic help were bribed and interrogated by the Inquisitors to reveal a family's habits and pastimes.

Chapter
19

The Church shared in these confiscations as well; at the height of its power, the Inquisitors paid no taxes and gave no account of their substantial confiscations.

Often, the children of a Marrano family would not be trusted with the secret of the family's beliefs for many years; one slip of the tongue, a child's thoughtless prattle to a Christian neighbor, could bring death and ruin to the entire family.

In the year 1481, the first trial under the auspices of the Inquisition took place in Seville. It was a foregone conclusion that all the accused who had confessed under torture would be sentenced to death. Torquemada followed the clever arrangement used by the Inquisition in other countries; instead of actually carrying out the death sentences, the Inquisition handed the prisoners over to the secular authorities. In this way, the Inquisition not only avoided accountability, but actually made the government a partner in death.

On February 6, 1481, a group of six Marrano men and six Marrano women were burnt at the stake in the first of a series of pompous public ceremonies, called auto-de-fe, ("act of faith"). Magnificently garbed priests bearing huge crosses, led by a royal delegation and a parade of other dignitaries, marched to a specially built platform. At the end of the line were the hapless condemned Jews. The King and Queen, who bore responsibility for these murders, appropriated the victims' great wealth for their military and personal needs. The Church shared in these confiscations as well; at the height of its power, the Inquisitors paid no taxes and gave no account of their substantial confiscations.

The Marrano population was thrown into a panic. Their lives were in jeopardy every moment of the day, especially during the Jewish holidays. Many came forward voluntarily to confess and throw themselves on the mercy of the Inquisition, but the majority clung with tenacity to the faith of their fathers during this tragic period. From 1480 to 1492, the Marranos proved themselves to be heroic and admirable: nearly 30,000 Marranos were burned alive while hundreds of thousands more were tortured and given other harsh sentences.

It is shocking to note that the Inquisition stalked the Jews from country to country for hundreds of years. Emanating from Spain, Spanish territories in the Americas also fell under its jurisdiction. Though Jews had left Spain itself, the Inquisition was utilized and was not abolished in South America until as late as 1820!

The Expulsion

In 1487, Muslim-controlled Malaga fell into the hands of Ferdinand and Isabella. The last military hurdle that Ferdinand and Isabella had to overcome was the province of Granada, which was still under Muslim rule. With the help and advice of their able Finance Minister, Rabbi Yitzchak Abarbanel, the royal couple succeeded in wresting Granada from Muslim hands, leaving them as the supreme rulers of the Iberian Peninsula. On January 2, 1492, Ferdinand and Isabella made their triumphant entry into Granada as the undisputed leaders of united Spain.

Now that their rule was secure, they sought to fulfill their dream of a united Spain, governed solely by their authority and adhering solely to Catholicism. The Marranos were being rapidly expunged by the Inquisition, but they still had to get rid of the Jews. Now that the *Reconquista* was over, Jewish money, loyalty, and statesmanship, which had been so vital to Spain's success, was no longer necessary. Ferdinand and Isabella decided that they did not have to tolerate the hated presence of the Jews a moment longer in Catholic Spain.

On March 31, 1492, an edict was issued from Granada, giving the Jews four months to leave the provinces of Castile and Aragon unless they agreed to accept baptism. According to the decree, any Jew found living in these territories after this date would be put to death. Jews were permitted to take their movable goods into exile with them, excluding precious metals and jewelry. All land ownership had to be disposed of immediately. A potential buyer, knowing that the seller had no choice, could pay next to nothing for the most valuable piece of land.

Despite the long period of persecution which had culminated in this calamity, the Jews were stunned and horrified. Under the leadership of Rav Abarbanel, they sought to reverse the harsh decree by employing the method modeled by Yaakov Avinu in dealing with Esav: bribery. Rav Abarbanel, the royal Finance Minister, brought chests filled with gold into the king's palace. Ferdinand, whose greediness easily surpassed his religious fervor, was inclined to yield by overturning the expulsion order. But at this critical moment, the fanatical Torquemada burst into the room, threw his crucifix in front of the royal couple, and screamed, "Judas sold his master for thirty pieces of silver! Now you would sell him again. Here he is: take him and sell him!" The expulsion order remained in force.

The Jews prepared to leave Spain, led by Rav Abarbanel. Although Ferdinand and Isabella, reluctant to lose the talents of their Finance Minister, offered Abarbanel the opportunity to remain with his family at the Court of Spain, he chose to lead his people into exile. Eventually, Rabbi Abarbanel settled in Venice, Italy, where he completed his commentary on the Tanach. He also wrote extensively on the Rambam's *Moreh Nevuchim,* as well as many articles on the coming of *Mashiach.*

He died in Venice in the year 1509, an exile from his country, but a source of hope and faith to his people.

Most of the 600,000 Jews in Spain resisted the Church's final efforts to convert them, but others capitulated. Among the converts was Abraham Senior, Chief Rabbi and tax collector for the Spanish government.

On Tishah B'Av of 1492, 300,000 Jews trudged to the harbors of the Mediterranean Sea, ready to leave Spain forever. They sailed to many distant countries along the Mediterranean, but very few survived the harrowing journey. Ship masters extorted enormous sums for passage, and often tossed the passengers overboard before they could reach their destinations. A rumor had been spread that some Jews had swallowed precious jewels, and many fugitives were split open by the greedy knives of the ships' crews.

Those who were fortunate enough to reach the Ottoman dominions were received with open arms. The Sephardic schools of learning in Yerushalayim grew by leaps and bounds. Constantinople had come under the rule of the Ottoman Turks, who were ruled by a dynasty of Sultans, only forty years before; with the sudden influx of Jews, the Sultans were able to develop their new capital and the countries under their domain, both socially and culturally. The Sultan of Turkey gloated over the folly of the Spanish rulers, who had invited financial ruin for themselves by forcing the Jews to leave. Indeed, Sultan Bayazid II (1481-1512) issued an imperial edict in which he directed the governors of the Ottoman provinces to open their gates to all Jewish emigres:

"It is strictly forbidden for the rulers of any Ottoman community to refuse entry to any Jews, but they should be received with open arms and friendliness. Anyone

"It is strictly forbidden for the rulers of any Ottoman community to refuse entry to any Jews, but they should be received with open arms and friendliness."

Chapter
19

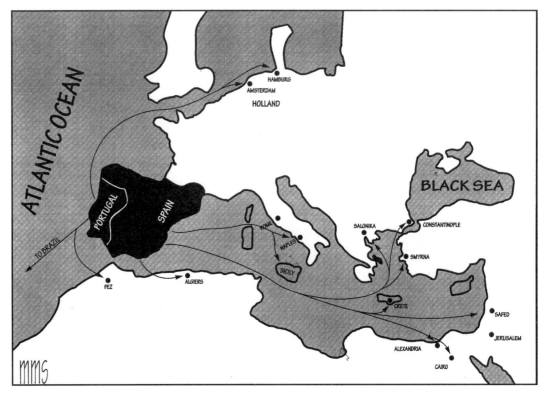

From Spain and Portugal to Holland and other distant countries

*Five years after the
initial expulsion
from Spain, the
Jews and Muslims
of Portugal were
given the
ultimatum: convert
or leave.*

Chapter

19

who disobeys this order will be subject to the death penalty."

Rabbi Eliyahu Kapsali, in his *sefer Eliyahu Zuta*, writes:

"...and his Royal Highness, the Sultan Selim I (1512-1520) liked the Jews very much because he realized that with their help he defeated nations and killed mighty kings. They built the mounds that helped break through the walls of enemy cities. They forged the weapons, shields, and armor, and they helped him in the battle of conquest..."

The other 300,000 Spanish Jews who did not march with the Abarbanel found temporary refuge in neighboring Portugal. This, however, proved to be an extremely short-lived haven. King Manoel of Portugal wanted to marry young Isabella, the daughter of Isabella of Spain. Ferdinand and Isabella agreed to the marriage only on the condition that Portugal rid itself of its entire Jewish

population. Though Manoel hesitated to take this step, preferring the lucrative tolerance of Jews in his realm, the matter was decided by the royal bride herself. She wrote to her prospective groom that she would not enter his country until it had been "cleansed" of infidels. Thus, five years after the initial expulsion from Spain, the Jews and Muslims of Portugal were given the ultimatum: convert or leave.

Manoel, however, was still reluctant to lose Jewish services and revenue. After a great deal of consideration, he decided that he could satisfy the Spanish monarchs and still keep Jewish talent within his borders if he simply converted the entire population to Christianity. As a result, a cruel edict was passed on Pesach of 1497, requiring all Jewish children between the ages of four and fourteen to come to the church for baptism on the following Sunday. When the appointed time came, officials were sent to Jewish homes to drag the children forth. As they were torn from their parents, scenes of indescribable horror took place. In many instances, while feigning a farewell embrace, parents smothered their children, then killed themselves. In some towns, officials thought a general baptism of all Jews had been ordered and drove every Jew they could find to the baptismal font, only to witness mass suicides when they got there.

The Jews had been technically granted the option of choosing baptism or leaving Portugal, but Manoel ordered that every Jew who wished to leave must first pass through the capital. When the Jews arrived, they were penned in a narrow stockade, without food or water, until they agreed to conversion. Those who still refused were denied access to the ships and were told that for their disobedience they were now the king's slaves, further breaking down their resistance to conversion.

In some cases, large groups of Jews would be penned in a corral and, over their loud protests, have holy water sprinkled on them and be declared henceforth Christians. In this fashion, the entire Jewish population, from children to the aged, the rich and the poor, the ignorant and the learned, became unwilling "Christians" in Portugal. Then, in 1531, the Inquisition came to Portugal, ready and eager to "cleanse" the country of those who were not fully devoted to Christianity.

Although they were forbidden to leave, a steady trickle of Spanish/Portuguese *conversos* managed to escape Portugal. Many secret Jews surreptitiously left the country, bound for the Netherlands, Italy, or the Ottoman Empire. Once free, they immediately threw off the mask of Christian piety and resumed their Jewish lives once again.

It is interesting to note that the diary of Christopher Columbus, who was attempting to discover a new sea route to India and ended up discovering America, begins with the words: "In the same month in which their Majesties issued the edict that all Jews should be driven out of the Kingdom and its territories; in the same month, they gave me the orders to undertake with sufficient men my expedition of discovery to the Indies."

Columbus's entire expedition was largely financed by Marranos. It is also likely that some of the sailors who agreed to this hazardous trip were Marranos, men to whom the terrors of "falling off the end of the earth" were considerably less than those of staying in Spain. It is certainly known that at least one, the interpreter Luis de Torres, was a Jew who was forcibly baptized the day before the expedition sailed. It was he who was the first European to set foot on land in the New World. Just as the door was shut in a major country of exile in the Old World, the gates to the New World were opened; in the coming years, the Jews would find a new temporary haven in a land which no one had ever dreamed existed.

"In the same month in which their Majesties issued the edict that all Jews should be driven out of the Kingdom and its territories; in the same month, they gave me the orders to undertake with sufficient men my expedition of discovery to the Indies."

Chapter
19

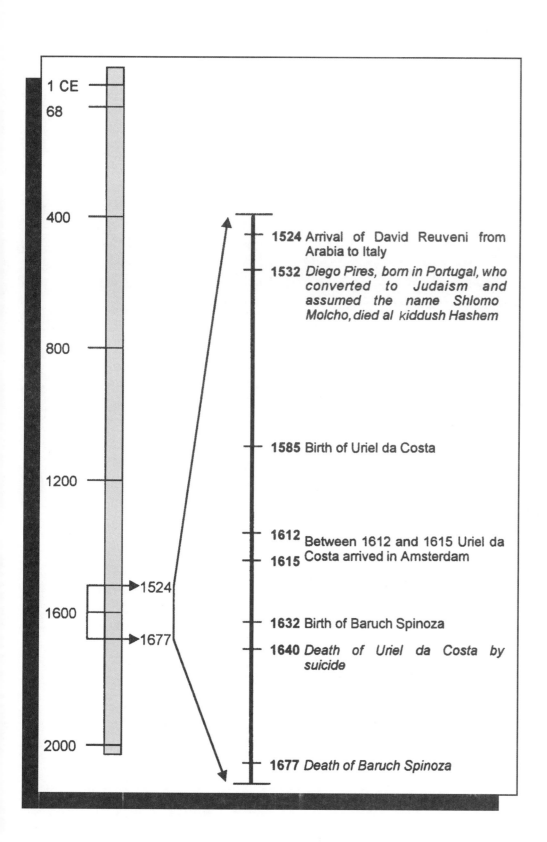

1 CE

68

400

800

1200

1600

2000

1524

1677

1524 Arrival of David Reuveni from Arabia to Italy

1532 *Diego Pires, born in Portugal, who converted to Judaism and assumed the name Shlomo Molcho, died al kiddush Hashem*

1585 Birth of Uriel da Costa

1612
1615 Between 1612 and 1615 Uriel da Costa arrived in Amsterdam

1632 Birth of Baruch Spinoza

1640 *Death of Uriel da Costa by suicide*

1677 *Death of Baruch Spinoza*

Chapter
20

*Shlomo Molcho
made his way to
Salonika and
Tzefas, where he
took on messianic
airs and gained
many followers.*

David Reuveni and Shlomo Molcho

The intense suffering during the fifteenth century created an urgent longing for *Mashiach* and the final redemption. At this critical point, two personalities made their dramatic appearance in Western Europe. At first, it seemed certain that David Reuveni and Shlomo Molcho would have a tremendous impact upon world Jewry, but the final analysis shows that they came and went without leaving any lasting mark on history.

David Reuveni was a Jewish adventurer from Arabia who claimed that he was the ambassador of his brother, Joseph, who reigned over the descendants of the tribe of Reuven somewhere in the East. While his "mission" is generally regarded today as a hoax, there has been some speculation that he may have been sent by the beleaguered Jews of India.

Reuveni arrived in Italy in 1524. The Italian Jews, highly impressed, paid honors to this exotic "ambassador" from his far-off Jewish kingdom. Reuveni visited Pope Clement VII, who was known for his benevolent attitude towards the Jews, and promised that he would raise an army of Jews to fight the Turks. He claimed that he was commissioned to buy ammunition; all he needed was the Pope's introduction to European kings in order to accomplish his mission. Although small of stature, Reuveni's dark Eastern complexion and outwardly pious behavior proved so convincing, that the Pope willingly gave him credentials to the kings of Portugal and Abyssinia.

King John III of Portugal received him with high honors, but became apprehensive when he saw the magnetic influence of the mysterious envoy; the Marranos flocked to him, convinced that he was *Mashiach.* John III suspected that the Marranos of Portugal might seize the opportunity to rise up against the crown. Aware of the danger, Reuveni quietly slipped out of the country.

Although Reuveni was gone, his appearance in Portugal had stirred a young Marrano named Diego Pires. Diego gave up his government post, converted to Judaism, and secretly left his native country. He reverted to his ancient family name and called himself Shlomo Molcho. He made his way to Salonika and Tzefas, where he took on messianic airs and gained many followers.

Molcho eventually made his way to Rome and gained access to the Pope. Molcho fascinated the leader of the Roman Catholic Church with a prediction of three catastrophic events that would take place in the near future: the overflow of the Tiber River in Rome, an earthquake in Portugal, and the appearance of comets. When the predicted overflow of the Tiber actually happened, Pope Clement invited Molcho to reside in the papal palace.

Bolstered by an increasing following, Molcho sought out Reuveni in Venice; but his association with the man who had originally inspired him to convert to Judaism soon began to falter as Molcho realized that Reuveni's tale was highly doubtful. Still, his own reputation had been boosted by the realization of his prophecy, and many Jews were convinced that Molcho was, indeed, *Mashiach.*

Other Jews were not so impressed by Molcho's story. One such Jew was Jacob Mantino, a prominent physician. In his effort to expose the former Marrano to the Church authorities, he found disparaging references to Christianity in one of Molcho's writings, translated it into Latin, and forwarded it to the clergy. The Inquisition tried Molcho, and sentenced him to death.

Pope Clement, who had taken a liking to this strange seer, interceded. He facilitated Molcho's escape by sending him a warning, and arranging for a man who resembled the condemned Molcho to be turned over to the authorities and burned at the stake. Molcho escaped and rejoined Reuveni in northern Italy.

Molcho had apparently made a miraculous escape from death. His predictions of an earthquake in Portugal and the advent of comets actually came true. His popularity soared as never before. Together, Reuveni and Molcho presented themselves to Emperor Charles V of Germany, flying a banner which bore the initials of the Maccabees. They intended to persuade the Emperor to call the Jews to arms against the Turks, but Charles immediately had them put in chains and taken to Italy for retrial by the Inquisition. Molcho was once again condemned as a traitor to the Catholic faith, but he stubbornly maintained his belief that he was the Jewish Messiah, dying a martyr's death at the stake. Reuveni was transported to Portugal where he, too, was burned alive.

It is a testimony to this strange Marrano that Rabbi Yosef Karo, a contemporary Torah Sage, remarked with regret that he wished to have the merit to die *al kiddush Hashem* like Shlomo Molcho.

A Parable To Remember

Rabbah bar bar Chanah related: "It happened that I was traveling on a boat when I saw a fish of tremendous size floating in the sea. Apparently, it had been floating in this position for a long time, because dust had settled on its surface and allowed a moss-like substance to cover it. The passengers thought this was an island. As they had been yearning for land during a seemingly endless journey, they left the boat and made themselves comfortable on this 'island.' They decided to start a fire to cook their meals. But when the fish felt the heat of the fire on its skin, it suddenly turned over and threw all the occupants into the sea. Were it not for the vicinity of the boat, we would all have drowned." [1]

The Maharsha explains that this story from the Gemara, one of the "exaggerations of Rabbah bar bar Chanah," is intended to symbolize the wanderings of the Jews in exile. Every so often, the Jews are provided with a temporary haven, a moment of respite from the endless wanderings. Jews begin to feel comfortable in the country that opens her doors to them. After a while, they forget that they are in exile—until they are rudely awakened from their illusions. The haven turns over and tosses its Jewish guests back into the wild waters of the Diaspora. It is only the ship, Hashem's guidance, that saves the Jewish nation from drowning and being utterly destroyed.

As refugees from the bloodthirsty Inquisition streamed into Amsterdam and Hamburg, they formed their own congregations. With time, two separate Jewish communities existed side by side: Sephardic, or Spanish-Portuguese, and Ashkenazic, which was German-Polish. Both communities strictly adhered to the *halachah* as it was finalized in the *Shulchan Aruch* during the sixteenth

1. *Bava Basra* 73b.

It is only the ship, Hashem's guidance, that saves the Jewish nation from drowning and being utterly destroyed.

In extreme cases, the community could resort to cherem, excommunication.

century, but they followed separate versions of prayer and maintained different customs. Indeed, the Sephardim, with their integration into Spanish culture and commerce, possessed a different way of thinking entirely. While the Ashkenazim retained an unquestioning simple faith in Hashem, the Sephardim were knowledgeable in philosophy and the disturbing questions that the Rambam so ably resolved in the *Moreh Nevuchim.*

Unlike the Ashkenaz title of *Rav* (rabbi), the spiritual leader of a Sephardic community is called *Chacham.* By the seventeenth century, the typical *Chacham* was a righteous person with a well-rounded education, both in religious and secular subjects; however, in many cases he was not as well informed in the Talmudic field as his Ashkenazic counterpart. Most parents of Marrano descent, while they certainly wanted their sons to have a Jewish education, were more interested in making sure that they were trained in a profession and were capable of intelligent, knowledgeable communication with the Gentile world. This attitude and the lack of organized Yeshivos may have resulted from the many years of Marrano conditioning, in which tradition was transmitted orally from father to son and mother to daughter, without teachers or books.

One particularly unique feature of Sephardic communal life was the zealousness with which they guarded the religious conduct of their membership, making sure there was no public deviation from *halachah.* It may have been a carryover from strict Church policies (still fresh in their memories!), or perhaps it sprang from their desire to ensure total acceptance and obedience to their newfound Judaism. Whatever the reason, the Sephardic community tolerated little deviation. With the Sephardic superior worldliness and strong inner organization,

the leaders were able to keep a tight rein on all members of the community. If a member was known to have expressed a heretical thought or departed from adherence to community rules, he was summoned for reprimand and could be required to pay various penalties. In extreme cases, the community could resort to *cherem,* excommunication.

Unfortunately, this system had its flaws. Two extreme examples, and their unhappy results, left a devastating mark on the morale of the Jewish communities around the globe. In the case of Spinoza, however, there was no other choice.

Uriel da Costa (1585–1640)

Uriel da Costa came from Portugal to Amsterdam some time between 1612 and 1615. He had been raised as a devout Catholic, receiving an education in canon law and becoming a minor Catholic official. In his autobiography, da Costa wrote that examining the Bible brought him back to Judaism. He came to Amsterdam with his brothers, reconverting to Judaism with the assumption that Jewish life would be just as he had read about it in the Bible.

Da Costa had no way of knowing that one cannot learn Judaism from the Written Torah alone. All too soon, he realized that his concept of Judaism was at variance with that of the Jewish community. He found himself unable to adjust to a life of adherence to all details of the *halachah,* and he could not accept many of the principles of the Jewish faith. In addition, he retained many of his Christian attitudes, and he came to regard adherence to the Oral Torah as a corruption of Judaism. When da Costa had the audacity to publish his heretical opinions, his book was burned and he was both fined and excommunicated from the community.

Da Costa's weak character left him incapable of admitting that he was wrong, but he could not properly defend his ideology either. He sought reconciliation with the Jews of Amsterdam, but soon after rejoining the synagogue, he expressed doubts about the Divine origin of the Torah, stating that any religion was no more than "human invention." A second excommunication was not long in coming. After several years, he applied again for readmission to the community. As a condition for pardon, he was severely punished in public. Da Costa found the shock of this humiliation too much to bear, and his confused, tragic life ended in suicide.

The communal leaders punished da Costa so harshly in order to set an example and to demonstrate that there was no room for heretics within the community. Their intentions backfired badly; many people, Jews and non-Jews, sympathized with the sinner and denounced the "intolerance" of the community leaders. Uriel da Costa became a martyr in the eyes of the Gentiles. Tragic accounts such as the episode of da Costa may have led to the Taz's recommendation that *cherem* should be used cautiously and with discretion, and, if there is a chance that it might drive the sinner away from Judaism altogether, it should not be used at all.[2]

Baruch Spinoza (1632-1677)

Baruch Spinoza, born in Amsterdam, was gifted with a dazzling intellect. He received his early training under Rabbi Menashe ben Israel and showed an early interest in the philosophy of the Rambam as well as that of other philosophical works. At the same time, however, Spinoza took instruction in Latin from a

physician of rebellious temperament. Under his influence, Spinoza developed an inclination towards independent and often contrary opinions.

Spinoza's knowledge of Latin led him to study the Gentile philosophers, particularly Descartes. With his unorthodox mind, he gradually grew lax in religious observance and formed strong friendships within Christian circles. The leaders of the community summoned him to give an account of himself, but he would not agree to comply with Jewish thought and practices in private, nor to curb his activities in public. The Elders of the synagogue warned him repeatedly, but when all admonitions and offers were spurned by Spinoza, they excommunicated him and forbade the reading of his heretical works. At that point, it was likely that he no longer cared.

Spinoza left the Jewish community, and took up a position of prominence among the great Gentile philosophers of his time. Taking up residence in the Hague, he lived a life of simplicity, earning his livelihood from grinding lenses. He rejected various prestigious offers to teach philosophy in major universities, devoting his time to the writing of his philosophical works instead. He developed a philosophical system which managed to utilize some of the deep-seated feelings of a Jewish soul while remaining entirely out of line with the fundamentals of the Jewish faith.

Spinoza believed in G-d with such a passionate fervor that he has been called the "G-d-intoxicated man," but his concept of G-d was radically opposed to the Torah view. To him, G-d and nature were the same thing. This concept is referred to as "pantheism" ("everything is God").

Marranos who Returned to Judaism

Spinoza developed a philosophical system which managed to utilize some of the deep-seated feelings of a Jewish soul while remaining entirely out of line with the fundamentals of the Jewish faith.

Chapter 20

---

2. *Yoreh Deah*, 334:48.

Spinoza rejected the concept of the revelation of Hashem's will to mankind; he did not accept the concept of prophetic communication or acknowledge the Divine origin of the Torah. His ideology denied the existence of Divine Providence, Hashem's control over man, and man's accountability to Him. To his way of thinking, Torah and mitzvos could be justified only as an expression of the people of Israel in the Land of Israel.

It is a great pity that Judaism lost such a brilliant mind. If Spinoza had found an inspiring teacher capable of properly channelling his superior intellectual capacity into greatness in Torah, he might have become one of the greatest Talmudic scholars. Instead, Spinoza became famous in the eyes of the Gentile world, where he was recognized and acknowledged as one of the greatest philosophers of all time.

Synagogue in Amsterdam, Netherlands

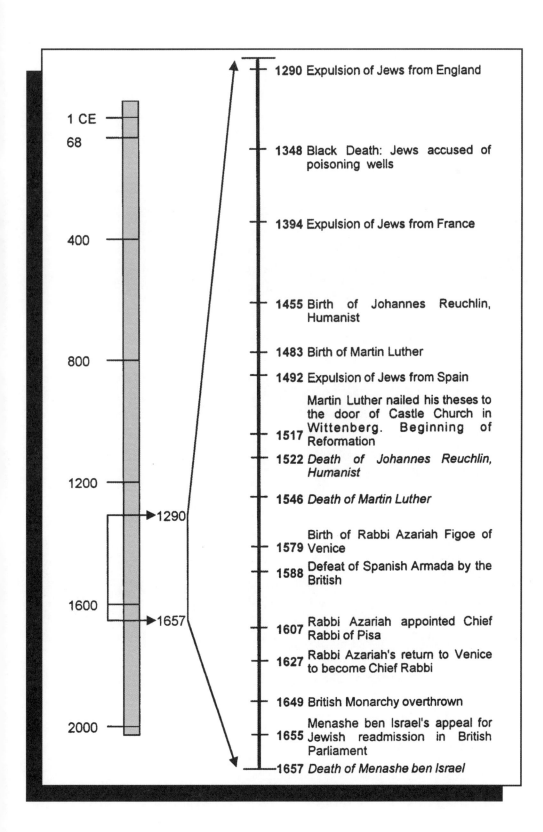

1 CE	
68	
400	
800	
1200	
	1290
1600	
	1657
2000	

1290 Expulsion of Jews from England

1348 Black Death: Jews accused of poisoning wells

1394 Expulsion of Jews from France

1455 Birth of Johannes Reuchlin, Humanist

1483 Birth of Martin Luther

1492 Expulsion of Jews from Spain

1517 Martin Luther nailed his theses to the door of Castle Church in Wittenberg. Beginning of Reformation

1522 *Death of Johannes Reuchlin, Humanist*

1546 *Death of Martin Luther*

1579 Birth of Rabbi Azariah Figoe of Venice

1588 Defeat of Spanish Armada by the British

1607 Rabbi Azariah appointed Chief Rabbi of Pisa

1627 Rabbi Azariah's return to Venice to become Chief Rabbi

1649 British Monarchy overthrown

1655 Menashe ben Israel's appeal for Jewish readmission in British Parliament

1657 *Death of Menashe ben Israel*

The economic system of feudalism, which had served the lords and their vassals so well for centuries, was beginning to change.

The era of the late Middle Ages is a clear example of Rabbah bar bar Chanah's parable. In the course of two hundred years (1290-1492), the Jews found themselves expelled from three European countries in which they had thought they had a permanent home. In the year 1290, England expelled her Jews; a century later, in 1394, France also closed her doors; and the expulsion from Spain took place in 1492.

The Jews in Germany had not suffered expulsion, but this was not due to the benevolence of their Gentile rulers. Germany did not yet exist as a united empire; instead, it was a conglomerate of loosely connected principalities. The Jews in each of the states were entirely subject to the whims of the local ruler. Each prince freely extorted as much money as possible from his Jewish residents. If he chose, the local prince could expel the Jews from his territory, but there was always another principality that was willing and eager to receive the refugees and begin the process of exploitation all over again.

While they did not live with the threat of complete expulsion, the Jews of Germany did not live in peace. Beginning with the time of the Crusades, periodic waves of massacres plagued their communities. Blood libel charges were common, with entire Jewish populations tortured to death in retaliation. At times, mobs attacked the Jews under no pretense at all.

In 1348 (as noted in Chapter 19), when the Black Death was sweeping through Europe and decimating entire populations, a Jew "confessed" under torture that the Jews had concocted an elaborate plot to kill all the Christians by poisoning the wells. This lie was strengthened by the Jews' apparent immunity; the Jews suffered less from the epidemic than their Christian neighbors. (It is likely that Jews were protected from this contagious plague by the laws of cleanliness and washing of hands before meals.) Scenes of incredible horror took place all over Europe, particularly in Germany. In Basle an entire congregation was taken to an island in the Rhine River, herded into a wooden shack, and burned alive. When the hysteria had died down, the surviving Jews of Nuremberg wrote down the names of 350 places in which the terrors had struck. Grieving, they recorded that over 60 large communities and 150 smaller ones had been totally demolished.

Even as the Jews braced themselves, over and over again, for sudden waves of howling mobs, new differences began to appear on the horizon. The economic system of feudalism, which had served the lords and their vassals so well for centuries, was beginning to change.

In the early Middle Ages, the ordinary person had a very narrow mental horizon. His entire life was wholly devoted to the cultivation of land and his efforts to produce a crop that would sustain him and his feudal lords. He did not travel or broaden his horizons with knowledge of other parts of the world; he did not even know very much about his own past. His book knowledge was restricted to the Bible as it was interpreted to him by the Catholic clergy.

With the tremendous impact of the Crusades, however, things began to change. The armies of Crusaders traveling through the European continent and the lands of the East were astonished by the various countries and civilizations which they encountered. Curiosity was aroused and a wider focus began to develop. The

Europeans began to recognize the common bond between all human beings, even though separated by national differences. The discovery that Latin was not the only language of the educated led to a questioning of the origins of the Bible and the doctrines of Catholicism.

The discoveries of new lands by European explorers opened up an entirely new dimension in economics as well. Desires for new and exotic products from foreign lands began to take hold. As a result, an unprecedented need arose for a change in the entire economic system, which had choked the majority of the population into a slavish existence. This new economic system, called "mercantilism" (see Chapter 32), impacted the relationship of the general European population with the Jews. Jews were no longer urgently needed for lending money. The influx of precious metals, and discoveries of new continents, manufacturing, and inventions, resulted in the rise of a middle class which produced more business and income possibilities. This, in turn, aggravated hatred of the Jews, who were less necessary than before. Despite the many changes in attitude, the Jews still found themselves confronted with senseless, rabid hatred.

On the other hand, there was an awakening of interest by the general populace in learning about themselves, their past, and their potential for the future. This awakening was called "Humanism." It was triggered in Italy in the sixteenth century as an upshot of the conquest of Constantinople by the Muslims in 1453. Many of the Roman and Greek scholars were forced to leave Ottoman territory and they went to Italy and other parts of Europe. Their culture, scholarship, and genius was deeply felt in those countries, especially in Italy.

Humanists and the Jews

Humanism brought a Renaissance to Italy, a renewed interest in classical antiquity. Christian scholars grew curious about Hebrew and Jewish literature. At the time, the Catholic Church considered the "Vulgate," the translation of the Bible into Latin from Hebrew by Jerome in the late fourth century, as the authentic Bible. With a new knowledge of Hebrew, and the opportunity to study original texts, the Church suddenly found itself under fire.

Foremost among the Humanists was Johannes Reuchlin (1455-1522), a Christian scholar who challenged the traditional view of the Dominicans. His independent research led him to a mastery of Hebrew language and literature, with a strong interest in Kabbalah. Reuchlin, taught by prominent rabbis of his day, was impressed by the Hebrew texts. He was a devout Catholic and as eager as any other Christian to convert Jews, but he believed that Jews should be won over to his religion by persuasion, not by brutal force.

Reuchlin's benevolent attitude proved instrumental in defeating the accusation brought by a Jewish convert to Christianity, Johannes Pfefferkorn. Pfefferkorn attacked the Talmud as a book full of defamation against the Christians, and obtained an imperial order to confiscate all editions of the Talmud and other Hebrew books. Rabbi Joselman of Rosheim, a famous advocate of German Jewry, helped persuade Reuchlin to intercede in the case. Despite denunciation by the Church, Reuchlin unmasked the shallow and groundless claims of Pfefferkorn, enabling the devastating edict against the Talmud to be suspended. Later, it was discovered that Pfefferkorn was motivated, not by belief in his new-found

An unprecedented need arose for a change in the entire economic system, which had choked the majority of the population into a slavish existence. This new economic system, called "mercantilism," impacted the relationship of the general European population with the Jews.

Once again, the Jews found themselves at the mercy of the frenzied believers of a new religion.

religion, but by a down-to-earth greed for money which he hoped to extort from the Jews as ransom for their cherished holy books.

As Reuchlin and other scholars developed their knowledge of Hebrew and Jewish works, many of the Catholic doctrines were called into question. Moreover, the pomp and richness of the Catholic Church seemed contradictory to the spirit of simplicity found in the Bible. The scholastic research of the Humanists forged the weapon with which the Reformation, led by the Augustinian monk Martin Luther (1483-1546), successfully rebelled against the Roman Catholic Church.

On October 31, 1517, Luther nailed his theses to the door of the Castle Church in Wittenberg, explaining his conviction that the dogma and rituals of the Roman Catholic Church, as personified by the pope in Rome, did not represent the true Christian faith, and asserting the need for reform. This act is generally regarded as the beginning of the Reformation.

Luther and his followers, who were known as the Protestants, believed in the New Testament. They declared that the Bible could be interpreted freely and that one was not bound by the unilateral interpretations of the Catholic Church. They also protested against many of the Catholic rites, and refused to recognize the dictatorial rights of the pope, who held almost absolute power over life, property, religious practice, and absolution from sin. The Catholic Church responded to the Reformation with the Counter-Reformation, in 1560. The Counter-Reformation brought about the needed reform of the Catholic Church, while at the same time battling the Protestant movement.

Luther envisioned himself as a redeemer of not only the Christians, but of the Jews as well. He theorized that the rejection of Christianity by the Jews was due mainly to the cruel behavior of the Church to Jews. He considered the Christian faith the legitimate heir of Judaism, and thus offered to receive the Jews with open arms into his new, benevolent Church. In his early writings, he expressed his compassion for the sufferings of Jews, and promised them happiness in both worlds if they would join him.

Luther, however, failed to understand the Jewish mind, and it did not take long for him to realize the futility of his offer. Protestant Christianity remained rejected by the Jews, despite his sugar-coated attempts to lure them to his side. Like Paul of Tarsus and Mohammed before him,[1] Luther's attitude took a complete turnabout. He became a rabid Jew-hater whose writings against the "blaspheming Jews" urged his followers to show no mercy in their destruction. Once again, the Jews found themselves at the mercy of the frenzied believers of a new religion.

New Horizons After the Expulsion from Spain

By the dawn of the sixteenth century, the Jews of Spain and Portugal had gradually moved eastwards, settling in Amsterdam, Holland; Hamburg, Germany; Naples and Venice in Italy; Salonika, Constantinople, and Smyrna in Turkey; Fez, Algiers, and Tunis in North Africa; Cairo and Alexandria in Egypt; Damascus, Syria; and Yerushalayim and Tzefas in Eretz Yisrael. Some immigrants from the Iberian Peninsula were faithful Jews affected by the expulsions from Spain

1. See Chapters 3 and 6 for further detail.

and Portugal in 1492 and 1496, while others were Marranos whose lives had been made unbearable by the Inquisition.

Many of the Marranos, despite the great wealth and honors they enjoyed in their beloved Spain, could not live with the hypocrisy and deceit of their precarious double life. The Inquisition remained intact, hovering over them as a constant, deadly threat. As time passed, families of Marranos quietly chose to transfer their funds to other countries and make their escape. Once in a free country, they frequently threw off their disguise as Christians and returned openly to the religion of their fathers. Others chose to retain their neo-Christian facade in order to help more Marranos escape, meeting clandestinely as Jews. With the Inquisition continuing to stalk them from country to country, extending even to Spanish possessions in the New World, many were still afraid to abandon the double life which had enabled them to survive.

A case in point is Chacham Azariah Figoe of Venice, Italy (1579-1647). Growing up in a city which had been exposed to the fanaticism of the Inquisition and which was permeated by Humanism and the Renaissance, he was not exposed to Torah and Judaism at all in his childhood. As he grew older, however, he willingly chose the path of Torah and made a meteoric rise in his studies. Within a short time, the Venetian Jews were seeking his advice in halachic decisions.

Rabbi Azariah was only twenty-eight years old when he was appointed Chief Rabbi of Pisa in 1607. During his twenty-year tenure in that city, he wrote his

sefer *Giddulei Terumah,* a commentary on *Sefer HaTerumos.* In 1627, he was invited to return to his hometown of Venice to serve as Chief Rabbi. The Jews of Venice were split into three groups—Ashkenazim, Italians, and Sephardim—but Rabbi Azariah was universally respected and admired. His oratory, combined with his great wisdom and charisma, succeeded in checking the rampant secularization of Italian Jewry. His sermons were printed in a sefer called *Binah L'Ittim.*

While the Marranos who had escaped Spain had managed to recover some measure of their Judaism, those still in Spain seemed to have little hope. At the close of the sixteenth century, however, world-shaking political and military events brought new anticipation to the Marranos still suffering under the Spanish regime. In 1588, the Spanish Armada, which hitherto had been considered invincible, was defeated by the British fleet. Out of 130 ships, only 67 returned to their Spanish homeland. The repercussions of this remarkable defeat served as a catalyst in changing the balance of power in Europe. Spain, once the wealthy and proud ruler of the seas, rapidly deteriorated, never to rise again as a major world power.

The Mendes Family

The house of Mendes was one of the richest and most respected Marrano families in Portugal. Its leading member, Francisco Mendes, owned a large banking house in Lisbon, with branches in other parts of Europe. After his death, the huge enterprise was inherited by his twenty-six-year-old widow, Dona Gracia, and his brother Diego, director of their Antwerp branch.

Spain, once the wealthy and proud ruler of the seas, rapidly deteriorated, never to rise again as a major world power.

In 1588, the Spanish Armada, which hitherto had been considered invincible, was defeated by the British fleet. Out of 130 ships, only 67 returned to their Spanish homeland.

*Praised as the
"heart of her
people" by a
contemporary
poet, Dona Gracia
did everything in
her power to help
her suffering fellow
Jews.*

Dona Gracia was a woman of noble spirit with a burning desire to live as a true Jew. Shortly after her husband's death, she fled Portugal with her only daughter, her sister, and her two nephews. Her first stop was Antwerp, where Diego married Dona Gracia's sister.

Dona Gracia spent many years in Antwerp, where she retained her Christian facade and set up an elaborate network to aid the escape of other Marranos and to encourage them to return openly to their true faith. She spent vast amounts of money to help Jews and support Yeshivos throughout the world. Praised as the "heart of her people" by a contemporary poet, Dona Gracia did everything in her power to help her suffering fellow Jews.

Her daughter married Yosef Nasi, Dona Gracia's nephew, who settled in Constantinople. When her brother-in-law Diego passed away, she moved to Venice, by now the sole administrator of the vast family fortunes. Diego had appointed her as guardian over his only daughter and as trustee for all her property. Dona Gracia's sister, who had been Diego's wife, was infuriated. In a fit of jealousy, she denounced Dona Gracia to the Church authorities as a secret Jew.

The Church acted swiftly. Dona Gracia was put into prison, her vast properties and wealth suddenly subject to confiscation. However, the clergy did not stop there; with bitter irony, Dona Gracia's sister found herself placed under arrest on the same charges! After all, if one sister was a Jew, why not the other one as well? Their daughters were also seized and placed in a nunnery to be brought up as dedicated Christians, paving the way for the entire Mendes fortune to be transferred to the Church and state treasuries.

At the last moment, the Ottoman Sultan brought strong political pressure to bear on the Church, forcing the clergy to release the two sisters. This intercession was not due to any humane feelings, but rather to the Sultan's common sense. Yosef Nasi, Dona Gracia's nephew, served as advisor to Prince Selim, the crown prince. Through his political connections, Yosef had cleverly suggested that if the two women would be free and able to move to Turkey, the family's entrepreneurial empire could bring vast economic benefit to the country. Eventually, Dona Gracia did move to the Ottoman Empire, although she still retained her Spanish customs. Once again, the Turks benefitted from Catholic rejection of Jewish aristocracy.

Yosef, as a refugee from Portugal and Antwerp, was able to advise Prince Selim on political matters concerning European governments. Like Chasdai ibn Shaprut, the Rambam, and Rabbeinu Shmuel HaNaggid before him, Yosef used his influence and position in court to benefit his Jewish brethren. As a case in point, he persuaded the Sultan to pressure the French court to compensate the Jews for all the property which had been confiscated at the time of their expulsion from France in 1390. Three years later, when the results had proved to be insufficient, as reparation for the Jews, Selim ordered the confiscation of one-third of every large cargo from France.

In recognition of Yosef's valuable service, the Sultan granted him the district around Tiberias as a perpetual gift to be used as a settlement for Jewish refugees. Together with his aunt, Dona Gracia, Yosef set out to create the ideal community in which learning, trade, and agriculture thrived.

The first step was to provide a livelihood for the prospective settlers. Yosef planted mulberry trees, intending to raise silkworms and turn Tiberias into a manufacturing city of highly priced silk garments. Once he had assured the future settlers a means of support, he invited Jews to settle in Tiberias, arranging for the pioneers to be transported on his own ships.

Unfortunately, Yosef's ambitious, well-planned project did not come to fruition. The majority of the ships were seized by pirates, and those few settlers who reached Tiberias did not prove successful in their attempts to manufacture garments. Despite the economic failure, Yosef's dream was fulfilled in one fashion: his vision of Eretz Yisrael as a renewed center of Torah learning did come true, as Tzefas, a city not far from Tiberias, became a thriving center of Torah in the sixteenth century.[2]

Menashe ben Israel
(1604-1657)

When the Marranos left the Iberian Peninsula, most of them made a genuine effort to mingle with their Jewish brothers and sisters. However, the Spanish immigrants had a certain aloofness and aristocratic bearing, the result of centuries of genteel life among the Spanish upper class. A good many of them led lives of privilege and affluence. The Sephardim established separate synagogues which maintained their customs and reflected their tastes. The Jews of "Ashkenaz," in comparison, tended to be much less cosmopolitan in their relationship with the Gentile environment.

The Marranos seemed different in other ways as well. Most had little training in Judaism, and it was sometimes difficult for them to separate Jewish and Christian practices and beliefs. For a long while, confusion reigned. Although they

respected the learning accomplishments of European scholars, they often looked down with arrogance upon the poor, unpretentious Ashkenazi Jews.

One of the many exceptions to this type of behavior was Rabbi Menashe ben Israel. As a small boy, Menashe ben Israel had left Portugal with his parents and settled in Amsterdam, where Portuguese Jews had founded three different congregations. Eventually, these three groups were consolidated into one large congregation named Neveh Shalom. Rabbi Menashe, who surpassed his colleagues in intellect, erudition, and creativity, was one of the most prominent of the four spiritual leaders of Neveh Shalom. He received a small salary, first as a teacher and later as a rabbi. He augmented his income by setting up a Hebrew printing press, the first in Holland. Both Jews and Christians respected him for his *sefarim* and writings, and he soon became a favorite of learned scholars and world leaders.

The world-shaking events in Spain and in other parts of the Jewish world had stimulated new interest in the anticipation of the forthcoming redemption from exile. The signs of extreme opposites in Spain—the long list of extraordinary spiritual giants alongside the devastation, sufferings, and pain of the Inquisition and expulsion—were interpreted as sure signs of the forthcoming redemption. The Jews were not the only ones convinced that momentous events were at hand; the Reformation had swayed Christians to believe that the world stood poised for a new period in history. It seemed universally agreed that a new era was about to begin.

Menashe ben Israel, too, longed to see the advent of the *Mashiach*. He undertook an ambitious search through Scripture,

2. See Chapter 22.

2000 YEARS OF JEWISH HISTORY ———— 155

The world-shaking events in Spain and in other parts of the Jewish world had stimulated new interest in the anticipation of the forthcoming redemption from exile.

Chapter
21

The silent stream of Jews into England, "through the back door," did lead to the establishment of a vibrant, thriving community.

particularly *Daniel,* to deduce the timing of the coming *geulah.*[3] He soon became convinced that the redemption was imminent. In his thesis, *Mikveh Yisrael* ("Hope of Israel"), he explained his theory that, before *Mashiach* could come, two preconditions must be met: the Ten Lost Tribes of Israel must be found, and the Jews must have extended their dispersion into all parts of the world. When that point would be reached, the ingathering of the exiles would take place.

The discovery of the location of the Lost Tribes seemed hopeless. In desperation, he theorized that the American Indians, newly reported by explorers to the wild shores of America, might be the Lost Tribes. Rabbi Menashe now focused his attention on the attainment of the other condition: Jews had to be scattered into all countries of the world. While Jews could certainly be found throughout the globe, there was one country right at the doorstep of the Netherlands that had expelled her Jews in the thirteenth century. Rabbi Menashe hoped that he might be able to use his Gentile connections to persuade the British government to rescind this edict, thus paving the way for the coming redemption.

In 1649, the British monarchy had been overthrown. Britain had become a republic under the leadership of Oliver Cromwell, who was apparently willing to consider the usefulness of the Jews in building up the commerce and colonial expansion of Great Britain. Rabbi Menashe received an invitation to plead the case for the Jews' readmission. With high hopes and accompanied by the fervent prayers of Jewish congregations throughout Europe, he left Holland and traveled to England.

In October 1655, Rabbi Menashe delivered his beautifully worded appeal. The messianic motive was certainly mentioned, but he gave weight to the more practical argument of the many benefits England could derive from the presence of Jews. Cromwell was sympathetic; no legal reason could be found barring Jews from settlement in England. However, heated opposition came from both religious leaders and merchants, who feared Jewish competition, and official readmission was ultimately denied.

Rabbi Menashe sadly left England, dejected by his failure, and stricken with the sorrow of the sudden passing of his only son. But his defeat was actually a blessing in disguise. Had the official recognition been granted, it undoubtedly would have been accompanied by amendments and conditions which would have placed the Jews at a disadvantage. With no formal grant, events took a completely different turn.

Marranos had actually been living in England for quite some time, officially registered as New Christians. As Cromwell's administration wore on, many of these Marranos professed Judaism openly. With time, a synagogue was built, a cemetery allotted, and the Jewish settlements began to attract those who sought refuge from mainland Europe. In this fashion, the Jews were allowed into England quietly, through no special legislation. They did not march in with banners flying as Menashe ben Israel had envisioned, but the silent stream of Jews into England, "through the back door," did lead to the establishment of a vibrant, thriving community.

---

3. See "The *Galus* and *Geulah* Calendar," Chapter 17.

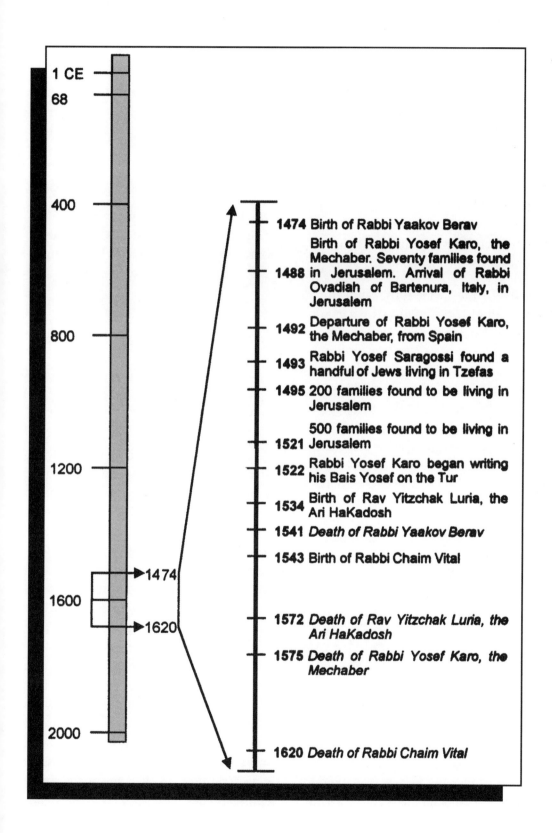

1474 Birth of Rabbi Yaakov Berav

1488 Birth of Rabbi Yosef Karo, the Mechaber. Seventy families found in Jerusalem. Arrival of Rabbi Ovadiah of Bartenura, Italy, in Jerusalem

1492 Departure of Rabbi Yosef Karo, the Mechaber, from Spain

1493 Rabbi Yosef Saragossi found a handful of Jews living in Tzefas

1495 200 families found to be living in Jerusalem

1521 500 families found to be living in Jerusalem

1522 Rabbi Yosef Karo began writing his Bais Yosef on the Tur

1534 Birth of Rav Yitzchak Luria, the Ari HaKadosh

1541 *Death of Rabbi Yaakov Berav*

1543 Birth of Rabbi Chaim Vital

1572 *Death of Rav Yitzchak Luria, the Ari HaKadosh*

1575 *Death of Rabbi Yosef Karo, the Mechaber*

1620 *Death of Rabbi Chaim Vital*

Chapter

22

Chapter

22

abbi Chaim Rabinowitz, author of *Daas Sofrim,* has pointed out that all major catastrophes in Jewish history are coupled with a positive aftermath, great spiritual rebounds that brought the Jewish people back on its feet and filled it with new strength and increased vigor. After the destruction of the first Bais HaMikdash, for example, Ezra HaSofer established houses of learning in Bavel and led the Anshei Knesses HaGedolah in Eretz Yisrael. The completion of the Mishnah and the development of the Talmud Bavli and Yerushalmi was a crowning achievement in the centuries after the *Churban Bayis Sheini.*

Contrary to the usual cause and effect throughout history, the disastrous expulsion from Spain was not countered by a general upsurge in spiritual greatness in the Jewish world. There was only one exception: the emergence of Tzefas in its glory. Despite its short duration as a center of Torah, Tzefas left an indelible mark on all future generations.

With the catastrophic expulsion in 1492, the Jewish population of Eretz Yisrael grew by leaps and bounds. In 1488, scarcely 70 families were to be found in Jerusalem; within seven years, the influx of refugees brought the number to two hundred, and there were five hundred families living in Jerusalem by the year 1521. With the arrival of Rabbi Ovadiah, of Bartenura, Italy, in 1488, the spiritual status rose to even greater heights. Rabbi Ovadiah, known throughout the world as the Ra'av, is the accepted commentator on the Mishnah, just as Rashi is on the Gemara.

In the north of Eretz Yisrael was Tzefas, where Rabbi Yosef Saragossi, after a long and exhausting trip in 1493, found a handful of Jews whose rabbi kept a small shop to make a meager living for himself.

One hundred years later, with the influx of Sephardic Jews into the city, Tzefas boasted 18 Yeshivos and 21 synagogues.

While Rabbi Yosef Saragossi certainly served as a primary catalyst in creating a flourishing Torah center in Tzefas, it was not the work of one man alone; several eminent personalities were drawn to the city and utilized Tzefas to develop their learning and rich inner lives. In addition, the climate and location of Tzefas were suitable for numerous agricultural efforts including planting olive orchards, raising sheep, and cultivating honey. The Jews of Tzefas used their talents, creativity, and money which they had managed to salvage from Spain, to turn the city into a successful business center. With quiet propriety, Tzefas quickly arose as a spiritual center of extraordinary proportions.

Rabbi Yaakov Berav (1474–1541)

At the age of eighteen, Yaakov Berav left Spain to accept the position of rabbi in Fez, Morocco. After the Spanish invasion of Morocco, he fled the country, passing through Cairo, Jerusalem, and Damascus in his travels. In 1534, at the age of sixty, he finally settled in Tzefas, where his vast knowledge, wealth, and strong personality led to his appointment as a leader of the community.

Soon after his arrival in Tzefas, Rav Berav conceived the idea of reinstituting the Sanhedrin. Like many other survivors of the tragic events of those times, Rav Berav longed for the redemption and sought for ways to hasten the coming of *Mashiach*.[1] He believed that one of the prerequisites for *Mashiach's* arrival was the establishment of the Sanhedrin, a central judicial court with authority to establish *halachah* throughout the world. In addition to his desire to expedite *Mashiach's* arrival, Rav Berav also felt that a Sanhedrin was actually necessary at that time. A central court was needed to solve the many problems that had arisen concerning Marranos returning to Judaism, including questions of intermarriage and other difficulties that needed urgent clarification.

Tzefas had become a haven for many distinguished scholars, Torah Sages who were eminently qualified to serve as judges in the Sanhedrin. This, however, was not sufficient. Rav Berav could not establish a Sanhedrin without *semichah,* the rabbinical ordination which had been discontinued during the era of the Amoraim.[2] *semichah* could be ordained only by someone whose own *semichah* could be traced back in an unbroken chain to Moshe Rabbeinu, who had received his *semichah* from Hashem Himself.

Rav Berav argued that the Sages of Eretz Yisrael could bestow *semichah* on one another. He based his belief that *semichah* could be reinstituted on an opinion stated by the Rambam:

"It seems to me that if all the scholars of Eretz Yisrael, without exception, were to agree to appoint judges who qualified for and did not receive *semichah,* they would be considered ordained and authorized

to pass sentences in all categories, and in addition, confer *semichah* on others."[3]

Rav Berav, assuming that the consensus of all the Sages in Eretz Yisrael was a foregone conclusion, proceeded to give *semichah* to ten candidates who passed all the required tests. Among them was the famous Rabbi Yosef Karo, author of the *Shulchan Aruch.* Only then did he send word to the renowned Chief Rabbi of Yerushalayim, Rabbi Levi ibn Yaakov Chaviv, requesting his approval after *semichah* had already taken place. To Rav Berav's shock, Rabbi Chaviv adamantly refused to approve the scheme.

Rabbi Chaviv contended that the Sanhedrin did not have to precede the coming of *Mashiach*; on the contrary, it was the reappearance of Eliyahu HaNavi which would make it possible for *semichah* to be reinstituted. The ongoing argument between the two scholars became very heated and led to the downfall of the whole undertaking. Rav Berav passed away in 1541, his attempt at recreating the Sanhedrin a failure.

Efforts to reorganize a Sanhedrin were repeated a number of times in the course of Jewish history. All such efforts have failed, and the Jewish nation still awaits the coming of Eliyahu HaNavi and *Mashiach*, when the Sanhedrin will once more serve as judges for the Jewish people.

Rabbi Yosef Karo, the *Mechaber* (1488–1575)

Rabbi Yosef Karo is lovingly called the *Mechaber,* the author par excellence, as well as the *Posek,* the one who gives the final ruling. He was only four years old when his family was forced to leave Spain in 1492. The family settled in

The Jewish nation still awaits the coming of Eliyahu HaNavi and Mashiach, when the Sanhedrin will once more serve as judges for the Jewish people.

---

1. See Chapter 20, "David Reuveni and Shlomo Molcho," and Chapter 21, "Menashe ben Israel."
2. See Chapter 4, "The End of an Era."

3. *Hilchos Sanhedrin,* 4:11

Turkey, where Yosef, under the tutelage of his learned father, became known as an accomplished Talmudist. He became close friends with the *mekubal,* Shlomo HaLevi Alkabetz, who is widely known as the author of the poem *Lecha Dodi.*[4] Rabbi Karo wrote that while the two of them were learning together on Shavuos night, Eliyahu HaNavi told them that they should move to Eretz Yisrael.[5]

At the age of 34, Rabbi Yosef began his gigantic work, a commentary on the *Arba'ah Turim* of Rabbi Yaakov ben Asher, the Baal HaTurim. Rabbi Yosef spent twenty years composing his commentary, called the *Bais Yosef,* and an additional twelve years revising it.

The Baal HaTurim often quoted the opinions of various Sages without giving the final *halachah.* In addition, Rabbi Yaakov sometimes omitted the source of the opinions and *halachos* he quoted. In response to these difficulties, the *Bais Yosef* cites all the sources for the rulings in the *Arba'ah Turim* and derives the final ruling from a careful analysis of all the pros and cons, following the rule of the majority.

No other sefer besides the Tanach, Mishnah, and Talmud has claimed such an important place in the library of the Torah-observant Jew.

Title page of Shulchan Aruch, Venice, 1565

Rabbi Yosef Karo realized that such a detailed work would be too difficult for the layman to use as a guideline for daily halachic decisions. With that in mind, Rabbi Karo composed an abbreviated edition containing only the "bottom line," the final outcome of *halachah.* He called this summary the *Shulchan Aruch,* the "Set Table." Since the *halachah* is presented in its final form and is ready to be used, Rabbi Yosef compared it to a set table where all the preparations have already been made. All that remains to be done is to eat.

Rabbi Karo had no way of knowing that the *Shulchan Aruch* would be received with universal acclaim by the entire Jewish world. No other *sefer* besides the Tanach, Mishnah, and Talmud has claimed such an important place in the library of the Torah-observant Jew.

In addition to these tremendous works, Rabbi Karo wrote a commentary on the Rambam's *Mishneh Torah* called the *Kesef*

From Spain to Constantinople to Tzefas

4. The acrostic of the poem indicates the author's name.

5. From *Maggid Meisharim,* by Rabbi Yosef Karo.

Mishneh. The *Posek* who laid down the final rulings in the *Shulchan Aruch* was also a *mekubal* who studied the secrets of the Torah. The Tzefas circle of *mekubalim* included Rav Yisrael Najara, author of *Kah Ribon Olam,* the poem sung on Friday night by religious Jews throughout the world. Such was the greatness of Tzefas: intense Talmudic learning coupled with a soaring, lofty spirit of Kabbalah.

It is told that Rabbi Yosef Karo, as the head of the rabbinical court in Tzefas, was asked to judge a young man who had arrived in the city and advocated various changes in the order of prayer. When the young man entered the court, Rabbi Karo arose, saying he could not judge this man who had come in accompanied by Eliyahu HaNavi and Rabbi Shimon bar Yochai. This young man was Rav Yitzchak Luria, the Ari HaKadosh, under whose auspices Tzefas was destined to reach the very zenith of its glory.

Rav Yitzchak Luria, the Ari HaKadosh (1534-1572)

The Tzefas school of Kabbalah flourished under the able guidance of Rav Yitzchak Luria and his talmid, Rav Chaim Vital (1543-1620). Rav Luria is often referred to as the Ari-zal, an abbreviation of **A**shkenazi **R**abbi **Y**itzchak, **z**ichrono **l**ivrachah. Some are of the opinion that the abbreviation stands for **A**mar **R**abbi **Y**itzchak, "Rabbi Yitzchak said," a strong suggestion of the Ari's powerful role as leader of Klal Yisrael; in addition, such personalities within a group of eminent people are frequently referred to as *Ari Shebechaburah,* "lion in the group." It is also noteworthy that the abbreviation *zal,* "of blessed memory," is added to the Ari's name, a highly uncommon usage in reference to historical personalities.

The Ari-zal was born in Yerushalayim in 1534. His father died when he was still a young child, and the Ari grew up in the home of his uncle, Mordechai Francis, a rich tax collector in Cairo, Egypt, who eventually became his father-in-law when the Ari, already famous as the greatest scholar in Egypt, married at the age of fifteen.

After his marriage, the Ari-zal spent seven years under the tutelage of the great scholar, Rabbi Bezalel Ashkenazi, author of the *Shittah Mekubetzes,* a comprehensive encyclopedia of all Talmudic commentaries known at that time. After seven years of intense study with Rabbi Ashkenazi, he spent six years learning on his own.

The Ari then immersed himself in the study of the Zohar for seven years. He isolated himself from the rest of the world during the week, visiting his home only on Shabbos. His father-in-law built him a hut on the Nile River, where he completely devoted himself to the study of Kabbalah, the *chochmas*

Shittah Mekubetzes

This man who had come in accompanied by Eliyahu HaNavi and Rabbi Shimon bar Yochai....was Rav Yitzchak Luria, the Ari HaKadosh, under whose auspices Tzefas was destined to reach the very zenith of its glory.

Chapter

22

Among the lasting contributions made by the Ari-zal during his short lifetime were changes in the version of the tefillah, based on his knowledge of Kabbalah.

hanistar.[6] It is said that when he reached an intense level of holiness, Eliyahu HaNavi appeared to him; from then on, he would not do anything without specific direction from his heavenly mentor.

In his mid-thirties, the Ari moved to Tzefas. A prominent group of disciples who recognized and acknowledged the superior spiritual qualities of their master quickly gathered around him. He encouraged his followers to pray with the most intense concentration and to sanctify their thoughts. His efforts were always directed toward serving Hashem in holiness and purity. He immersed himself in the *mikveh* with regularity, to maintain a status of absolute purity, especially at the time of prayer. Today, the Ari's *mikveh* in Tzefas is one of the special holy places in Eretz Yisrael, and is believed to be a source of blessing and health to all who enter it.

He emphasized the spiritual dimensions in man's relationship to Hashem in three different categories: *Kedushah,* sanctity of the mind and sanctity in action; *Kavanah,* intensive, concentrated attention to the wording and meaning of prayer; and *Perishus,* making the love of Hashem and closeness to Him the priority in life,

The Ari's Mikveh

6. See Chapter 18, "Revival of Kabbalah."

and looking on all physical activities and pleasures merely as a means of maintaining a healthy body in order to serve Hashem in the best possible manner.

Jewish prayers are not composed of merely superficial, poetic phrases. Behind every word and letter are deep secrets, combinations of the holy names of Hashem calculated by the Geonim to change Hashem's *midas ha'din,* or strict judgement, into *midas ha'rachamim,* mercy. Only the right combination can result in this breakthrough. The Ari, with his depth of understanding of the profound secrets of Kabbalah, analyzed these combinations and instructed his students as to the exact wording and syntax they should use. It is this version, the *Nussach HaAri,* that became the standard version of prayer for many Chassidim.

Among the lasting contributions made by the Ari-zal during his short lifetime were changes in the version of the *tefillah,* based on his knowledge of Kabbalah. Many of his customs have been preserved; for example, the Ari dressed entirely in white on Shabbos, a custom which is still followed today in Chassidic circles in Yerushalayim.

The Ari-zal succumbed to an epidemic disease and was taken from this world at the young age of thirty-eight. While he did not leave any *sefarim* behind, his great disciples recorded the Torah and great teachings of their master and teacher. Rav Chaim Vital, his most famous student and the author of *Etz Chaim,* studied under him for the two years before the Ari-zal's passing; the Ari-zal is quoted as saying that his tenure in this world was justified in order to teach Rav Chaim. Through Rav Chaim Vital and other great scholars, the Ari-zal's unique approach was preserved for posterity.

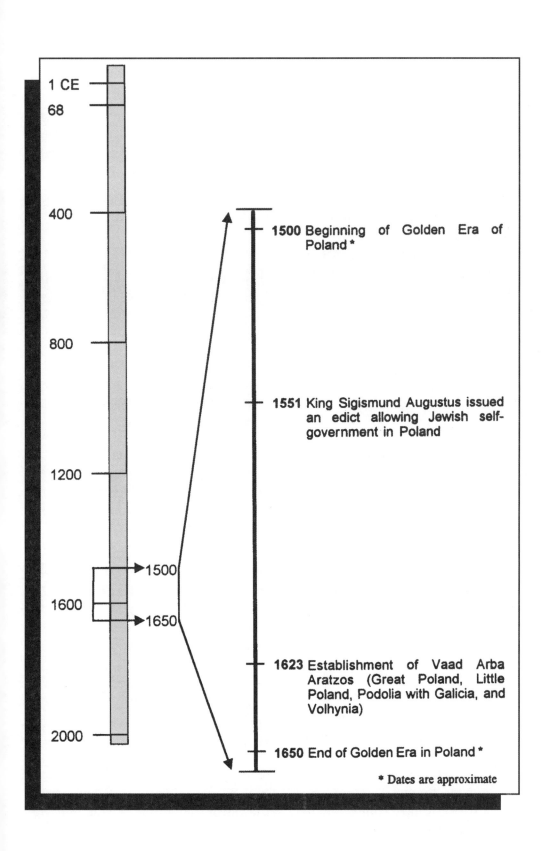

1 CE

68

400

800

1200

1500

1600

1650

2000

1500

1650

1500 Beginning of Golden Era of Poland *

1551 King Sigismund Augustus issued an edict allowing Jewish self-government in Poland

1623 Establishment of Vaad Arba Aratzos (Great Poland, Little Poland, Podolia with Galicia, and Volhynia)

1650 End of Golden Era in Poland *

* Dates are approximate

Chapter

23

With the vast majority of the peasantry completely illiterate, and most of the noblemen too ignorant to manage their own estates properly, there was ample opportunity for the Jews to find themselves a necessary niche in the local economy.

Pointing the Way

 popular legend of how the Jews came to migrate to Poland has been passed down for generations:

When the persecutions in Western Europe became unbearable, the Jews stood at the crossroads and asked themselves, "Where can we go?"

A note fluttered down to them, saying, "Go to Polen," the German word for "Poland." No one knew exactly where this country was located, but they knew it had to be somewhere in the East and set out. When they arrived, they heard the birds overhead singing, "*poh-lin, poh-lin,*" Hebrew for "sleep here," i.e., "this is where you should spend the next 'night,' the next stage of the exile." The Jews felt that Divine Providence had led them there, and there they remained.

For centuries, the Jews had been prosperous and culturally active in the countries of Western Europe, but the catastrophic events of the Crusades and the expulsions from England, France, and Spain, as well as the Black Death in Central Europe, drove home the realization that it was no longer possible to stay in that region. By the close of the fifteenth century, it was clear that the Jews would have to find somewhere else to live—but where?

Eastern Europe, the area which is now primarily Poland and Russia, seemed promising; the region was only partly cultivated, and sparsely inhabited by Slavic nationalities, most of whom were not rabid Roman Catholics. With the vast majority of the peasantry completely illiterate, and most of the noblemen too ignorant to manage their own estates properly, there was ample opportunity

for the Jews to find themselves a necessary niche in the local economy.

There were some Jews already living in the area, but a population explosion took place in the sixteenth century as the number of Jews living in Poland and Lithuania increased dramatically from fifty thousand to half a million within 150 years. In brief, the Jews emigrated to Poland for the following reasons:

1) Pressure to leave the persecution in their homelands.

2) Economic opportunity.

3) The dominance of the Greek Orthodox Church which, unlike Roman Catholicism, was not actively seeking to annihilate the Jews.

4) Government invitation by local noblemen as well as the monarchy, who welcomed the Jews' superior business expertise and literacy.

Most of the Jews who settled in Poland were not tempted to mingle socially and culturally with the non-Jews. Other than formal business relationships, they shared no common language or interests with the non-Jews; there were no institutes of higher education that could lure their youth intellectually or create any basis for cultural mingling between the Poles and the Jews. Instead, the Jews kept strictly to themselves. Jewish immigrants from Germany imported their German language, mixed it with Torah vocabulary and many Polish and Russian words, and thus created their own vernacular, known as Yiddish.

With time, Jews developed industries in lumber, salt-mines, and agriculture. They exported produce and imported goods. Contrary to the restrictions they had suffered in Western Europe, permission was granted to the Jews to deal in crafts, trades, farming, and other lines of work. For close to one hundred and fifty years (1500-1650), the Jews of Poland fulfilled the blessing of Bilam, "Behold this nation dwells by itself."[1] This period developed into one of the most productive eras in the history of the exile and is often referred to as the "Golden Era of Poland."

While Jewish life in Poland was apparently less perilous than the situation in Western Europe, the Jews were still faced with difficulties. The Jews were not the only ones to be attracted by the opportunities in the area; and when the non-Jews came eastwards, the anti-Semitic clergy came as well. In addition, Jewish success in business caused jealousy among the poorer Christian population. Most dangerous of all, the Jews found themselves squeezed between the nobility and the peasantry. The nobles appointed the Jews to administer their lands and collect taxes; soon, the Jewish tax collector became a hated middleman, caught between the avaricious nobility and the exploited common people, with both sides blaming and loathing the Jews.

As increasing numbers of Roman Catholic clergy settled in Poland and rose to positions of power, the Jews were once again faced with rabid hatred, against which they had little or no defense. The Jews in Poland became a toy, caught between the animosity of the Church and the toleration of the kings. Royal orders were issued permitting the Jews to engage in export trade, only to be revoked at the instigation of Christian traders. As in Western Europe, fanatical clergy incited the Christian population against the Jews by fabricating false accusations against them. Charges were made that the Jews stole sacred wafers from the churches and stabbed them until blood came out. Before the king could intervene to squelch such ridiculous charges, three Jews and their Christian "accomplice" were burned at the stake, although the Jewish martyrs had maintained their innocence even under torture. In Lithuania, a Jew was executed on the charge of having killed a Christian child. Cases of alleged ritual murder came up in Lublin, and charges of theft of church vessels were made against a Jew in Cracow. As a result, a mob invaded the Cracow ghetto with disastrous results. The king finally intervened and issued two decrees forbidding local courts to proceed against Jews on the charge of desecration of sacramental items or ritual murders.

While the Polish kings remained relatively tolerant, legislation concerning the Jews often reflected an anti-Semitic bias. In Posen, for example, the Jewish ghetto was strictly limited to only forty-nine houses. With the natural increase of the Jewish population, it became necessary to add extra stories to Jewish dwellings, even though the original foundations were not meant to uphold the extra weight. In Warsaw, additional Jewish settlers were not admitted; Jewish merchants visiting the city on business could not stay longer than three days.

It is against this background of animosity and bloody excess that one must view the phenomenal height of spiritual activity which Polish Jewry reached during this period. With the strain of dealing with the peasantry, the nobility, and the clergy, there was a compelling need to find some method of Jewish defense. The safeguards that developed were put into place in a unique way which had no equal in Jewish history.

1. *Bamidbar*, 23:9.

For close to one hundred and fifty years (1500-1650), the Jews of Poland fulfilled the blessing of Bilam, "Behold this nation dwells by itself." This period developed into one of the most productive eras in the history of the exile and is often referred to as the "Golden Era of Poland."

Chapter
23

*The appointed
Chief Rabbi was
answerable only to
the king, not to
the authority of
the royal officials
or courts.*

The Vaad Arba Aratzos, Council of Four Lands

On August 13, 1551, King Sigismund Augustus issued an edict allowing Jewish self-government in Poland. As the majority of the Jewish immigrants to Poland were deeply religious, this edict essentially ensured that the Polish Jews would be able to live a Torah life.

The edict empowered the Jews to elect their own Chief Rabbi and lawful judges who exercised jurisdiction in accordance with Jewish law. Jews who disobeyed the rulings of their spiritual leaders were given a month's time to repent, on pain of loss of property to the royal treasury. The appointed Chief Rabbi was answerable only to the king, not to the authority of the royal officials or courts.

By the middle of the sixteenth century, the Jews had formed a Council, or Vaad, as the overseeing administrative body of the entire country. At first, this Council had jurisdiction over three lands: Poland, Lithuania, and Polish Russia. In 1623, Lithuania formed a central organization of her own; for the next two hundred years, the common name used for the Polish administration was Vaad Arba Aratzos, the Council of the Four Lands, consisting of Great Poland, Little Poland, Podolia with Galicia, and Volhynia.

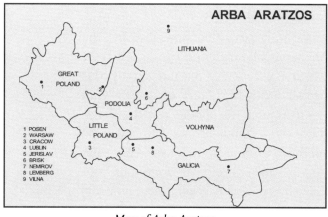

Map of Arba Aratzos

The Council held two meetings annually. One was held in Lublin during the spring fair before Pesach; the other took place in Elul in the Galician town of Jeroslav. In exceptional cases, sessions were held in other localities. The Council consisted of thirty delegates; six of these delegates were rabbis, and the remainder were prominent lay leaders. The Vaad's official task was to apportion the annual taxes which each district had to pay the government. In addition, there were common expenditures that came up regularly, such as the defense of innocent Jews charged with crimes, and efforts to ward off hostile legislation.

Obviously, the biannual meetings of the Vaad could not resolve all problems that would arise in the four regions. They established a general policy and set down guidelines, but the day-to-day enforcement of the rules was left to each community's council, or *kahal*. Disputes between individuals were settled by the local rabbis and their courts; cases involving communities came before a high court of justice, which met at the place and time of the semi-annual Vaad meetings.

The Council sent its representatives, called *shtadlanim,* to attend sessions of the Diet in Warsaw. Their role was especially imperative at the "Coronation Diet," when a new king ascended the throne and anti-Jewish forces might pressure the new government to curtail privileges previously granted to the Jews. The Council endeavored to maintain good relations between the Polish government and the Jewish population.

The Vaad did not confine itself to official relations with the Gentile government; it also used its prestige and authority to regulate the inner conditions of life within the Jewish communities. Laws were passed regarding proper attire. Council members made sure that businesses were conducted properly and that there would be no undue competition (*hasagas gevul*); it was against the law for an outsider to open a new business in a community without consent of the community leaders.

Special attention was paid to the education of boys. The Vaad determined a uniform curriculum for all schools under their jurisdiction. Rules were laid down for the proper supervision of schools and for periodic examinations. The *Cheder* school system was not based on large institutions of higher learning like the Yeshivos of modern times, but on small one-room schools called *Chadorim*. Children of poor families who could not afford the *Cheder* tuition were sent to the Talmud Torah, a school that was financed by the community; in this system, the boys learned the rudiments of Torah until they were ready to learn a trade or to enter business.

The aim of all elementary teaching was to inculcate the students with a desire to go on to a higher level of learning in the great Yeshivos that developed in the larger communities of Poland. At the head of the list was the Yeshivah in Cracow in southern Poland; other great Yeshivos existed in Lublin in central Poland and in Brisk, to the north.

At the higher levels of the Yeshivah, special emphasis was laid on *halachah* as a separate subject. With the invention of the printing press, the works of the Rishonim, as well as many new commentaries,

became widely available. Many scholars committed their halachic views to print; some of these commentaries adorned the pages of the *Shulchan Aruch*, while others were so voluminous that they were published in a *sefer* of their own.

Unlike today, the Yeshivos of Poland did not have dormitories; they functioned only because the entire community was involved in making them function. With Torah recognized as the lifeblood of Klal Yisrael, the members of the community dedicated themselves to making Torah learning possible. Occasionally, an extremely wealthy Rosh Yeshivah would provide for the needs of the Yeshivah students out of his own pocket, but it was usually up to the members of the community to care for the physical needs of the students. The *kest* system was established, in which a student coming to attend Yeshivah in a city far from his home would be assigned a schedule of private homes where he would get a free meal. The entire community committed itself to maintaining the Torah way of life.

A large number of eminent Torah scholars enriched the Golden Era of Poland. The Sages of Poland can be divided into two categories: those who concentrated on *halachah* and wrote commentaries on the *Shulchan Aruch*, and those who followed the method of the Franco-German Rishonim, dedicating themselves to the commentaries on Gemara. Within the framework of the Vaad, these Torah Sages helped raise the level of Jewish life in Poland to unparalleled heights.

Within the framework of the Vaad, these Torah Sages helped raise the level of Jewish life in Poland to unparalleled heights.

At the head of the list was the Yeshivah in Cracow in southern Poland; other great Yeshivos existed in Lublin in central Poland and in Brisk, to the north.

Chapter

23

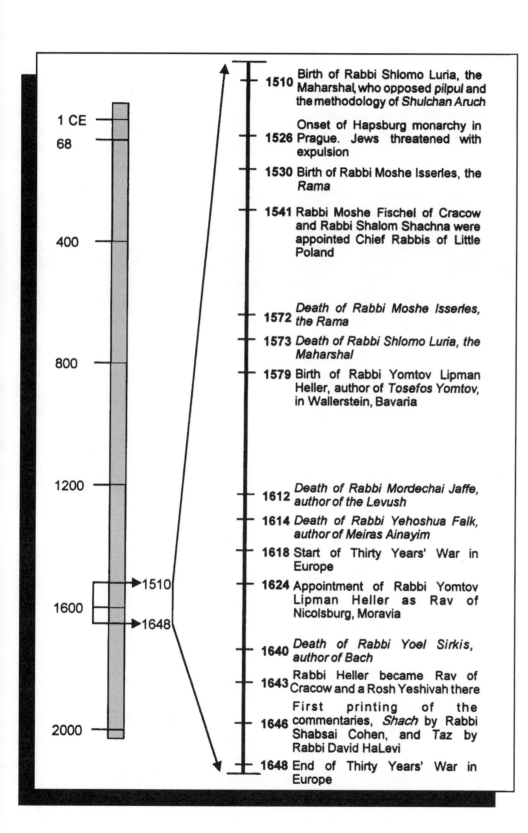

1510	Birth of Rabbi Shlomo Luria, the Maharshal, who opposed *pilpul* and the methodology of *Shulchan Aruch*
1526	Onset of Hapsburg monarchy in Prague. Jews threatened with expulsion
1530	Birth of Rabbi Moshe Isserles, the *Rama*
1541	Rabbi Moshe Fischel of Cracow and Rabbi Shalom Shachna were appointed Chief Rabbis of Little Poland
1572	*Death of Rabbi Moshe Isserles, the Rama*
1573	*Death of Rabbi Shlomo Luria, the Maharshal*
1579	Birth of Rabbi Yomtov Lipman Heller, author of *Tosefos Yomtov*, in Wallerstein, Bavaria
1612	*Death of Rabbi Mordechai Jaffe, author of the Levush*
1614	*Death of Rabbi Yehoshua Falk, author of Meiras Ainayim*
1618	Start of Thirty Years' War in Europe
1624	Appointment of Rabbi Yomtov Lipman Heller as Rav of Nicolsburg, Moravia
1640	*Death of Rabbi Yoel Sirkis, author of Bach*
1643	Rabbi Heller became Rav of Cracow and a Rosh Yeshivah there
1646	First printing of the commentaries, *Shach* by Rabbi Shabsai Cohen, and *Taz* by Rabbi David HaLevi
1648	End of Thirty Years' War in Europe

The word pilpul comes from the Hebrew word for "pepper"; its main purpose is to enliven the process of learning by stimulating debates, raising arguments and refuting them.

Rabbi Moshe Isserles, The Rama (1530–1572)

The Rama stemmed from a distinguished family; his father, Rabbi Israel Isserles, held the title of *Parnass,* head of the Cracow community. The Rama completed his early education in Lublin before settling in Cracow, where he maintained a Yeshivah at his own expense for twenty years. He was still a young man when he was chosen as assistant rabbi of the Cracow community, an honor which proved his excellence in all branches of Torah wisdom and law.

The Rama kept up a warm, close correspondence with the *Mechaber,* Rabbi Yosef Karo, whose *Shulchan Aruch* had just been printed.[1] Rabbi Isserles realized that the *Mechaber,* as a Sephardic Jew, had naturally given priority to the *minhagim,* or traditions, of the Sephardim; many of the Ashkenazic *minhagim,* which were binding on the Jewish population of Poland, had been omitted. The Rama proceeded to correct this imperfection by writing footnotes to the *Shulchan Aruch,* detailing customs, as well as halachic decisions, in which the *minhag Ashkenaz* differs from the *minhag Sepharad.* As his additions enhanced the "Set Table," the Rama called his work the *Mappah,* or "Tablecloth." All subsequent reprints of the *Shulchan Aruch* have these footnotes incorporated with Rabbi Karo's main text. With these amendments, both Sephardim and Ashkenazim have a concise code of Jewish law.

The Rama was also known to be a gifted *sofer,* or scribe; his writing style was highly valued not only for its beauty but also for the authenticity of his lettering. The

1. See Chapter 22.

Sefer Torah which the Rama wrote in his own hand was preserved in his shul in Cracow until the Second World War.

The broad range of the Rama's interests and written works was astonishing: *halachah,* Kabbalah, Jewish philosophy and history. With his passing, the Rama was honored with the same lavish praise that had been given to the Rambam: his tombstone reads, "From Moshe (Rabbeinu) to Moshe (Isserles) there was no one like Moshe."[2] Indeed, for a full three hundred years after his death on Lag B'Omer of 1572, it was customary for Jews to gather at his gravesite in Cracow to discuss his works.

The Introduction of *Pilpul*

In 1541, the king appointed Rabbi Moshe Fischel of Cracow and Rabbi Shalom Shachna of Lublin (1500-1559) as Chief Rabbis over the whole province of Little Poland. Rabbi Shalom introduced a new method of learning, *pilpul,* which he learned from his rebbe, Rav Yaakov Pollack. The word *pilpul* comes from the Hebrew word for "pepper"; its main purpose is to enliven the process of learning by stimulating debates, raising arguments and refuting them. In such debates, there is no such thing as the "last word." Argument is countered with argument in an effort to detect the weak points of the opponent and use them against him. This method enlivens the study hall, makes learning interesting, and sharpens the wits of the participants. While many scholars accepted this new method with great enthusiasm, it also aroused serious opposition. Rabbi Shlomo Luria, one of the great Torah Sages in Poland, became one of the most outspoken opponents of *pilpul.*

2. See Chapter 12.

It is significant that the names of the Acharonim are usually abbreviated with the first initials "Ma Ha" which means Morenu Ha-Rav, whereas the Rishonim were simply titled Rav, Rabbi, or Rabbeinu. The principle here is that the greater a person is, the less he is in need of titles. The Rishonim are recognized as being incomparably greater than the Acharonim; thus, the single title "Rabbi" is sufficient in front of their names.

Rabbi Shlomo Luria
The Maharshal (1510–1573)

The Maharshal was a brilliant Torah scholar with a sharp mind and tongue. He was known for his sharp criticism, expressed without hesitation; he was also known for his own humility, listening to a *baal mussar* on a daily basis. He had few intimate friends other than the Rama, with whom he disagreed on many points of Torah study, particularly philosophy and the concept of a *Shulchan Aruch;* nevertheless, he commanded tremendous respect.

The Maharshal opposed the *pilpul* method because it led away from what he believed was the main goal of learning: finding the truth. In *pilpul,* the fencing partners were out to refute one another; as a result, they could not come to a final conclusion. The Maharshal wrote against these wasted efforts of the "*pilpul* makers," also asserting that *pilpul* generated *gaavah* (conceitedness) and other negative traits of character which are contrary to the proper relationship between Torah scholars.

The Maharshal also raised objections to the *Shulchan Aruch* as a shortcut that discourages proper halachic research in the Gemara. While he conceded that the *Shulchan Aruch* was a great help for those unable to do the research themselves, he objected to the idea of scholars, capable of learning on their own, allowing their studies to deteriorate by taking the easy way out. His own sefer, *Yam Shel Shlomo,* is a profound work that is expressed with masterful clarity and without mincing words, much like its author.

The *Nossai Kailim*

The *Mechaber* called his work the *Shulchan Aruch,* or "Set Table." The Rama, in adding the Ashkenazic customs to the *Shulchan Aruch,* called his commentary *Mappah,* or "Tablecloth." In accordance with this analogy, the Torah scholars who wrote their commentaries on the *Shulchan Aruch* or the *Tur* are known as the *Nossai Kailim,* "Carriers of the dishes and silverware." Like the Baalei Tosafos, many of the Sages of this period did not as a rule want their names publicized; they wanted to be known only by their contribution to *halachah.*[3] Some of the most noteworthy of the *Nossai Kailim* are highlighted here.

Meiras Ainayim: Rabbi Yehoshua Falk (died 1614), Rav of Lublin and subsequently Rosh Yeshivah of Lemberg, wrote the *Meiras Ainayim,* "Enlightenment of the Eyes," on the *Choshen Mishpat,* which deals with civil law. This commentary is printed on the side margin of the *Shulchan Aruch.*

Bach: Rabbi Yoel Sirkis (died 1640), who occupied rabbinical positions in a number of communities and later headed the Yeshivah of Cracow, is chiefly known by the name of his commentary on the *Arba'ah Turim,* called *Bayis Chadash,* "A New House," abbreviated to *Bach.* He died before he was able to publish the fourth section of his commentary, but

The Maharshal opposed the pilpul method because it led away from what he believed was the main goal of learning: finding the truth.

---

3. See Chapter 15.

The Maharsha added a new dimension to his commentary by undertaking an explanation of the Aggadeta, the "stories" and the homiletics in the Gemara....With this commentary, the most puzzling statements of Chazal in these stories are explained in terms that are both logical and easy to understand.

he left a will directing his son that no money of his inheritance should be touched before all parts of his *sefer* had been completed.

Taz: The Bach's son-in-law was Rabbi David HaLevi, author of the *Turai Zahav,* or *Taz,* on the four parts of the *Shulchan Aruch.*

Shach: Rabbi Shabsai Cohen wrote his commentary on the *Yoreh Deah,* the second section of the *Shulchan Aruch,* and on *Choshen Mishpat*, the fourth section of the *Shulchan Aruch.* He named his commentary *Sifsai Cohen,* or *Shach.* His commentary and that of the *Taz* were first printed together in editions of the *Shulchan Aruch Yoreh Deah* in 1646. These two commentaries have become so important that anyone who studies for rabbinical ordination must master the *Shach* and *Taz.*[4]

Levush: Rav Mordechai Jaffe (died 1612) was a student of both the Rama and the Maharshal. He authored an independent digest of the Gemara, called *Levush,* "Robe." This *sefer* brings down the halachic ruling as well as the reasoning and background for it. The *Levush* has become an indispensable companion to the *Shulchan Aruch* for every serious student of *halachah.*

Mefarshai HaShass

The *Mefarshai HaShass,* an additional branch of scholars during this rich spiritual era of Torah in the sixteenth and seventeenth centuries, concentrated on an in-depth explanation of the *peshat* in the Gemara, following the method of Rashi, the Baalei Tosafos, and the Rishonim. These Acharonim, as well as subsequent generations, did not as a rule create new explanations; instead,

they explored and clarified the commentaries of the Rishonim. An Acharon could comment, explain, or prefer specific opinions among the Rishonim, but in general did not venture his own opinion. Acharonim have been quoted as avoiding open arguments between Rishonim with the remark, "How do I dare place my head between these mountains?"

The Maharsha: One of the better known *Mefarshai HaShass* was Rabbi Shmuel Adels, better known as the Maharsha (**M**orenu **HaR**av **S**hmuel Adels). The family name, Adels, is that of his mother-in-law, a righteous, wealthy businesswoman who supported from her income not only her son-in-law but also his entire Yeshivah. The Maharsha wrote a thorough analytical commentary on Gemara, Rashi, and Tosafos. His dialectic approach to Shass serves as a vital instrument for a deeper understanding of the *peshat.*

The Maharsha added a new dimension to his commentary by undertaking an explanation of the *Aggadeta,* the "stories" and the homiletics in the Gemara. Although the Maharal of Prague (born 1512) had preceded the Maharsha in a commentary on the *Aggadeta,* the Maharsha (born 1555) wrote the longest and most complete *perush* on this segment of the Shass. With this commentary, the most puzzling statements of *Chazal* in these stories are explained in terms that are both logical and easy to understand.

The Maharam: A commentator living in the same period was the Maharam Lublin (**M**orenu **HaR**av **M**eir Lublin). His simple, clear style seems to make the most difficult section of the Gemara easy to understand. His commentary

---

4. The Shach survived the holocaust of 1648. See Chapter 25.

seems almost to be the teaching style of a master educator, committed to paper to benefit all future generations of students.

The Jews of Prague

The Jewish community of Prague was one of the oldest communities in Central Europe; it had been in existence since the tenth century. However, with the onset of the rule of the Hapsburg monarchs in 1526, the Jews of Prague were frequently threatened with expulsion. They were actually expelled twice and then readmitted, thanks to the intervention of the famous *shtadlan,* Rabbi Joselman of Rosheim.[5]

Despite these interruptions, Prague Jewry had created a lofty spiritual climate, producing some of the most illustrious Jewish minds and Torah Sages of all times. Among them are the famous Maharal of Prague (Morenu HaRav Yehudah Loew), whose profound analytical treatises on Tanach and Midrash revolutionized the comprehension of Tanach; the Rav from Prague, Rabbi Yeshaya Horowitz, the Shaloh HaKadosh, author of the *Shnei Luchos HaBris;* and Rav Yomtov Lipman Heller, author of *Tosefos Yomtov, Maadanai Melech,* and *Lechem Chamudos,* who eventually left Prague and settled in Poland.

Rav Heller was born in Wallerstein, Bavaria, in 1579. He received his early education in Germany; later, he studied under the Maharal, who was Chief Rabbi of Prague and a Rosh Yeshivah there at the time, as well as with the Rama. When Rav Heller was only a boy of eighteen, the Maharal appointed his outstanding student as assistant Rav of the

city. In addition to their Torah studies, both master and pupil interested themselves in mathematics and astronomy.

In 1624, Rav Heller became Rabbi of Nicolsburg, Moravia. Three years later, he was called to Prague to serve as its Chief Rabbi, an extremely prestigious appointment. Unfortunately, the political climate of that time jeopardized his position and eventually forced him to leave Prague.

For eight years, Europe had been mired in the beginnings of the Thirty Years' War (1618-1648). With constant military campaigns, Emperor Ferdinand found himself badly in need of funds. To offset the considerable expenses of a decade spent in battle, the Emperor imposed a heavy tax on the Jews of Prague, and it became the Rav's unhappy task to raise the tax from among the rich members of his community. Such a responsibility often results in enmity, and it was not long before Rav Heller was denounced to the civil authorities and put in jail.

Rav Heller was brought before the Emperor to answer the charges made against him: he had made disparaging remarks about Christians in his recently published book, *Tosefos Yomtov.* Ferdinand pointed out sections of the *sefer* which were, indeed, contemptuous of the non-Jews. Rav Heller tried to explain that the term "non-Jew" referred only to idol-worshipers and was not intended as abuse against the Christians, but his reasoning fell on deaf ears. Rav Heller was held in custody until the Jewish community donated a substantial sum to the Emperor's treasury. Ferdinand released Rav Heller, but he would not allow the Torah Sage to function as the Rav of Prague. Rav Heller left the city

5. See Chapter 21, for additional efforts of Rabbi Joselman.

Prague Jewry had created a lofty spiritual climate, producing some of the most illustrious Jewish minds and Torah Sages of all times.

Chapter

24

and accepted a rabbinical position in Nemirov, Poland.

Grave of the Shaloh HaKadosh

Soon after his arrival in Poland, Rav Heller became active in the Vaad Arba Aratzos, where he was instrumental in renewing a decree that allowed the Jews to elect their own rabbinical leadership, thus strengthening Jewish power. In 1643, Rav Heller accepted the position of Rabbi of Cracow and Rosh Yeshivah there. Here, too, Rav Heller was unable to find peace; five short years later, a storm of hatred broke loose in Poland which brought a shocking and sudden end to the Golden Era.

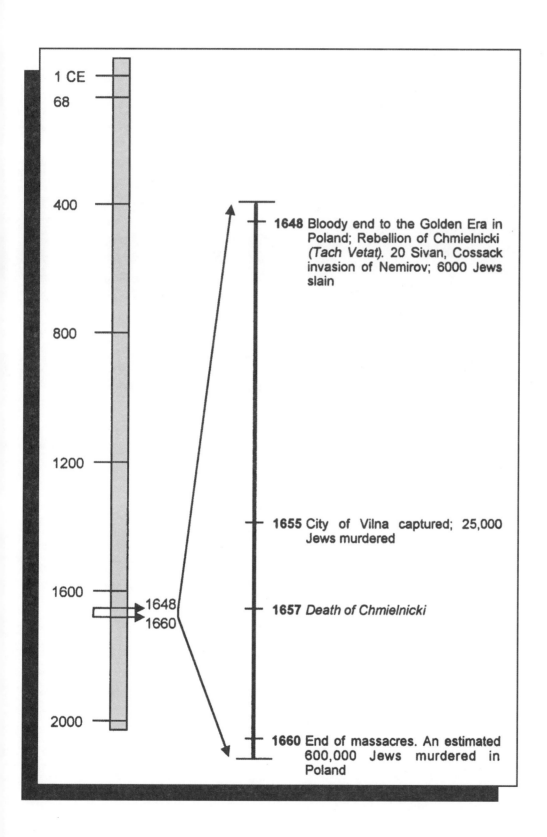

1 CE

68

400

800

1200

1600

1648
1660

2000

1648 Bloody end to the Golden Era in Poland; Rebellion of Chmielnicki *(Tach Vetat)*. 20 Sivan, Cossack invasion of Nemirov; 6000 Jews slain

1655 City of Vilna captured; 25,000 Jews murdered

1657 *Death of Chmielnicki*

1660 End of massacres. An estimated 600,000 Jews murdered in Poland

The Catastrophe of Tach Vetat

Chazal, as well as bitter experience, have taught the Jewish nation that if they do not repent their misdeeds, they will be stricken again and again with misfortune until comprehension finally dawns.

Understanding Why

he Talmud states that "when a person sees that sufferings befall him, he should search his actions" and try to find out what sinful conduct might have caused this calamity, with the understanding that "Hashem is the righteous one, and I am the one who defied His commands." This self-judgement is a basic requirement in the analysis of Jewish history; nothing happens that has not been caused by human behavior. Ultimately, "we must consciously search our past and draw the proper conclusion; we must return to Hashem." *Chazal,* as well as bitter experience, have taught the Jewish nation that if they do not repent their misdeeds, they will be stricken again and again with misfortune until comprehension finally dawns. Such self-analysis cannot always guarantee success in understanding, but the Jew is still compelled to search and to try to make the necessary amends.

The "Golden Era" in Poland, which had lasted approximately one hundred and forty years (1510–1648), came to an abrupt, bloody end in the year 1648. While a brutal, half-crazed savage was certainly to blame in leading such a violent revolt against the nobility and the Jews, Jewish history must look beyond the obvious factors to discover what shortcomings existed among the Jews of that time that could have caused the tragedy that swept across Poland, destroying a world of vibrant Torah life.

At first glance, it is difficult to assess Polish Jewry in this light. Poland had developed into a Jewish settlement that was full of Torah and mitzvos, as well as material well-being. Jewish family life was permeated with sanctity and purity. The shortcomings that were often rampant in other ill-fated Jewish societies seemed entirely missing. Why did Poland have such a short-lived era of peace? Jewish life in Spain lasted almost 400 years before the expulsion took place. In an atmosphere of such strong Torah learning and such great Torah scholars, why was Poland destroyed after only 140 years?

Such questions cannot be easily answered; often, they cannot be answered at all. However, the historian Rabbi Chaim Rabinowitz suggests in his sefer, *Daas Sofrim,* that life in Poland might not have been as idyllic as it appeared to be; friction, bickering, and arrogance undermined the foundations of peace, while affluence led to a weakening in moral values. Perhaps a close look at the weaknesses that existed in Jewish life at that time will serve to indicate the troubles lying underneath the surface.

The Authority of the Rav

The Rav was the central authority in every community. If another Rav, even one with a superior grasp of *halachah,* issued a contrary ruling, the members of the community still had to obey their local *Morah D'Asrah,* their "Master of the Area." For example, meat that was imported from slaughterhouses that were not under the local Rav's supervision was considered to be *shechitas chutz,* "outside meat," and was forbidden to the community.

This absolute authority was not easily acknowledged by all groups in the community, which could sometimes drive a rift into Jewish unity. Quite often, the citizenry was divided into different factions, each group bound together by a bond of common interests. In Warsaw, there were different shuls for different trades: a shul for tailors, carpenters, glassmakers, etc. The members of a certain group might raise objections to a particular ruling of the Rav; sometimes, such frictions reached the point of open rebellion, and the Rav, although he was not actually dismissed was compelled to leave the city and seek a position elsewhere.

Attitudes of the Torah Scholars

It was a source of pride to have sons who excelled in learning Gemara; parents boasted of children who became Torah scholars. At the same time, however, this pride manifested itself in an increasing arrogance on the part of some scholars, to the point where they considered themselves to be an aristocracy. Devoting a life to learning Torah was generally a vocation that could be afforded only by well-to-do families; even poorer *talmidei chachamim* would join this so-called aristocracy, by marrying into wealthy families. Generally, the sons of the poorer Jews, who could only be sent to the local Talmud Torah for their education,[1] were compelled to seek a livelihood and content themselves with a rudimentary knowledge of Gemara. These members of the working class were classified as *amei ha'aretz*, "people of the land," i.e., ordinary people; many Torah scholars treated these simple Jews with disdain, thus driving a painful gap between the common populace and the scholars of Torah.

Economic Conditions Leading to *Chilul Hashem*

The progressive rise of wealth within the Jewish community and the increasing challenge of individuals as entrepreneurs in the business world led to difficulties that created ill will. The prospect of a quick profit often tempted businessmen to enter into risky speculations, requiring the availability of ready cash to swing a fast deal. This cash was frequently obtained by taking loans on promissory notes. If the expected profit did not materialize and the borrower went into default, a chain of bankruptcies resulted.

In addition, enterprising Jews dealt in imports and exports, bringing products into the country and exporting salt mined on Polish soil. The hazards of travel, particularly during wartime, often made it impossible to deliver the promised merchandise, leading to a breakdown of financial commitments. This constant succession of broken promises created bad will among the Jews themselves, as well as between the Jews and Gentiles.

Luxuries

As always, an increase in affluence leads to a higher standard of living, sometimes to the point where materialism becomes the most important factor in life. In seventeenth century Poland, at a time when no formal Torah education for girls existed, it was incumbent on the parents to keep a watchful eye on their daughters and to raise them with proper Torah values. Unfortunately, many fathers were preoccupied with business and showed an increasing interest in materialism themselves, thus leaving little time to supervise their children; as a result, many of the Jewish women of that day were inclined to overindulge in jewelry, clothing, and the like.

Dispersion

The Jews living in large communities were strengthened by the vibrant community life, the Vaad, and other positive influences. However, many individuals, in search of a better livelihood, moved to small villages where they served the local *poritz,* or nobleman, as revenue

Devoting a life to learning Torah was essentially a vocation that could be afforded only by well-to-do families; poorer Jews, who could send their sons only to the local Talmud Torah, were compelled to seek a livelihood and content themselves with a rudimentary knowledge of Gemara.

1. See Chapter 23.

Still, while the wounds inflicted by the fiendish Cossacks took long to heal, the Jews of Eastern Europe emerged from the tragedy with renewed inner strength, enabling them to rebuild a Torah community which lasted well into the twentieth century.

collectors. Other Jews ran the local mill or the tavern, or cut lumber and shipped it to the builders. These Jews, isolated from the mainstream, had little defense in protecting their spiritual values.

Again, it must be stressed that the cause and effect of history is largely beyond human comprehension. Perhaps the shortcomings listed above were partially responsible for the terrible holocaust that brought Polish Jewry to the brink of extinction. Still, while the wounds inflicted by the fiendish Cossacks took long to heal, the Jews of Eastern Europe emerged from the tragedy with renewed inner strength, enabling them to rebuild a Torah community which lasted well into the twentieth century.

The Cossacks

The Cossacks were a Slavic tribe, originally living in the area of Lithuania, who had been forced to leave their homeland and settle east of the Dnieper River in the Ukraine. Their expertise as mounted warriors was matched only by their ruthlessness. While they were generally disliked by the Polish nobility, some Polish kings had engaged the Cossacks as mercenaries to help counter the Tatars, a fierce Mongolian tribe raiding Polish borders. In return, the kings granted the Cossacks a semi-autonomy in governing themselves, granting certain independent powers to the Cossack leader, who was called the "Hetman."

By the early seventeenth century, however, the power of the Polish kings had declined, leaving the Polish Diet with a great deal of authority. The nobles seized the opportunity to institute laws that restricted the autonomous privileges of the Cossacks, particularly those of the Hetman. In 1648, the Cossack Hetman Bogdan Chmielnicki (pronounced Chmel-NITZ-ky) attempted to regain the power revoked

by the Polish Diet. Enraged at his failure, Chmielnicki swore revenge.

While his ultimate objective was to crush the power of the Polish nobility, the Jews of Poland became the immediate target of Chmielnicki's fury. The Jews were despised by everyone: the Polish people who had to pay heavy taxes into the hands of the Jews; the noblemen who constantly accused the Jews of cheating them of their due revenues; and the Cossacks who hated the oppressiveness of the Polish nobility and considered the Jews the henchmen of the enemy.

Chmielnicki, realizing that his own forces could never win a battle against the overwhelming Polish armies, made an alliance with the Mongolian Tatars, the enemy the Cossacks originally had been hired to fight. Together, the two fierce, uncompromising tribes made their onslaught against Poland, directing their main attack against the Jews.

The Polish king, initially unaware of the magnitude of the danger, sent an army of only eight thousand men to crush the rebellion. The outnumbered Polish forces were annihilated and the king died before he could consolidate a larger contingent. The Polish nobles squabbled endlessly, delaying election of a new king and leaving Poland for several months without central leadership. With little or no resistance confronting them, Chmielnicki's Cossacks and their Tatar allies were free to overrun the Ukraine, slaughtering and burning at will.

Those Jews that were captured by the Tatars were relatively fortunate; although they lost their freedom and were sold as slaves to the Turks, most were ultimately ransomed by Turkish Jews. The victims of the Cossacks, however, suffered unbearable tortures before they were killed. Only those that agreed to baptism were allowed to live.

As the Cossack horde swept across Poland, many Jews tried to find shelter in the few remaining fortresses. All too often, however, such attempts met with failure; despite apparently impenetrable fortifications, the Cossacks were able to gain access even to some of the strongest fortresses.

On the 20th of Sivan, for example, the Cossacks approached the city of Nemirov, which was locked and barred. As they came within sight of the city, the Cossacks unfurled Polish flags. Its defenders thought that the Polish army was coming to their rescue and joyously opened the gates of the city. Rejoicing turned to horror as the Cossacks pounced upon the Polish and Jewish inhabitants and murdered them. 6,000 Jews were slain that day; later, the date was proclaimed as a fast day for the Jews of Eastern Europe, with appropriate *selichos* prayers composed by many of the Torah Sages who survived the Cossack invasion.[2]

Rav Yechiel Mechel, the Rosh Yeshivah in Nemirov, knew the entire Oral Torah by heart. On the Shabbos before the imminent battle, he spoke to his congregation, exhorting them to withstand the enticements of their enemies and sanctify the name of Hashem. The entire audience obeyed him, refusing all blandishments and demands to accept baptism in exchange for life. Rav Mechel himself fled the slaughter and jumped into the river. A Cossack pursued him, but Rav Mechel succeeded in persuading the greedy soldier to come with him to his house, where he was able to buy off his attacker with gold and silver that he had hidden away. Knowing that other Cossacks

would soon be at the door, Rav Mechel fled with his aged mother to the Jewish cemetery; but a Christian townsman, the local shoemaker, found the two Jews and beat Rav Mechel to death in front of his mother's horrified eyes, before murdering her as well.[3]

The city of Tulchin, like Nemirov, fell to the Cossacks through trickery. The invaders promised the Polish inhabitants that no harm would be done to them if they delivered the Jews into the hands of the Cossacks. When the Jews discovered the impending treachery, they were determined to fight the Poles. The Rav of the city, Rabbi Aharon ben Meir, dissuaded his congregation from undertaking this desperate course, fearing the revenge of the Poles on the rest of Poland's Jewry. Instead, he advised his congregants to surrender all their possessions as a ransom for the whole city. All efforts failed, and the Jews of Tulchin found themselves faced with the same dilemma as those of Nemirov: the Cossacks promised them their lives if they accepted Christianity. Fifteen hundred Jews stood their ground and died *al kiddush Hashem*.

על דבר התענית של כ' סיון

כוונת כ' סיון. כ' ני קנמו תפנית אחינו גני שולין ותיקך ויסוד תפנית זה של כ' סיון שהיה שם עדת ליהודים גזרות וקמדות גדולות בזמת (ת"ח ות"ט) לאלף הששי. ומסך דמן על אומה קדושה סיפוראלית כמה שם התמוגות לרגם וקבודולוס אשר סיו נגארך כזור כסוּל נגדי על זה תפנית וקנמו כנסס לזורוח יום ל'' כמס. וזורך התענית על פון כ' מסרכ בתורה הקדושה. במיתת מלך מסצדיקים כתיב ואחריכם כל בית ישראל יבכו את השרפה ש'. כרי למדרי מסתינו יגא מזה. שכל מיתת כנדיקים חיוב כיוים של כל איש מישראל'' לקינן ולכמות ולכמספר. לכן פיקר מסתפיס חיוב של כ' סיון לתת אל לג כמעם כל כנכ גב חרירנ נגדיקים ורחסגרים ומל בכל אומה מסיראלית הקדושה מסהרגנ במיתות מסרירות מסחונום ותקינו ולחספאר גלומ על קריעת גדי של מקום כ"ב. וכודלוי סיה מזה לכחרג יש'' נער גדול כמניגל. ומם כמאוי כחיים סיו למכדים מוראי הקדומה ומסתם מלונדי בן'' וסיך מניג להקג"ב נתח רוח גדול מזה ואזן מכתא לפי יתכדי נקר ג'' על כרנה גני מנמחדים. עוד מל ולהי רובומי וימוי כעומים מסתבו וום מספתים לפוריס קמסי ורדיס נתת ברינתם ג'' לנו לכנמפר כרבנה מלר. וכיוגה צ' לא תפתר מלאי כל יום התפגית. וכודלוי יתבו ג'' לעבודה גדולה לכאורל יש'' וכנזר ברננה מלר. חולת זה ספפר מוסנג לו לכלול סקריג ולנו ותוי מ"ב כמזוה אף גם כי מסל עלוי סקר גדול נגגר של מספקה מנמתו ומתקון על סעדך מ"ני מסתורלי יש'' כביבול ועל גמרני של בני הקדושים. (מתור כל מ).

ועל סנויוי של פמת ת"ח ות"ט ויפני מנאונים מנמבינו ריממתי פיו קרוב למן כל קמיות זום:ב) רמם מגולאו מסתי כמן (בכן מסי'ן) ג'ל ומדפו נפף סליות באמספרדם פת ת"מ ותקדפה מתב רבים הס"ך מאמר הנקרא כסם מכלה עפר מספר מחבר רעות מלמסו ברמית גנכרי נתרס נכארן אוקריימה ותלון ופלליה וליפל. רתב כמ"ע כסם מכלה הק"מ ות'ל ותם גנת ת"ח נמרם (מ') ג'ל ברבכן קהלות נדולות. בכ"ם מל חיום) צ"ל נכוח מקנה) כמ"ם נסלומוח סקבר גגל הק"ג. (נס) [של כן] מנכני להחמנוס כנכאלי ניסין נכל מלמו מלוך מל'ג. כ' רעו כפל תומי' י"ת מוגר כלוחות לג' מיון ומרוב תולחות נמסלצ. וברוב כ'אור הסבוך כמ' מ"ג ול'ל ומה מרבנתוו גל מיון לימ ונמ מם ליס סטוב זה ער גרס ליטרג מיום זה כמ"ם סים וקס ות"כ. לפי נבמים לממוניות תם תתכל'ת היתה ל'ג פת נרס לימרג מיום זה כנ''ם ים. בגלימות ומם כמף ל' פגם יומו כזמנויות פתך ותלמתו מתב רות מעירים סיותם לל כקבר מתב בס' תנמ בסל ספ'ד ה'ק'ך. ל'ל ומה מתוב מגוג סמתרי ניום זה מפני מאיו מל בכמנה פ'ח. מל'ל מסמ'ח. תתקולות נמרך בגלימיות מוסתר של נורת תומ'ל ור'' מלמם כתקן הקבגל מגגל כתכלו רם''ל נכיסודיו של נורת רכיננ גרמס ניר' כיחלוס ו'ק' כ' מ' מחר גרני תחס הוכיר ר'' כ' מיון מם מלטן. בגפרים נימון נוגר סירוח למכרת. ומתר'א. כ'תכיל'א לממנ נפמו נפם פום סרכלו'א מיתה כ'ל פת נרס לימרג כ' מיון ס'ז ת' כ' גמרי הקבל'ה נה יום כ' סיון והקלחות כ'ל:

Selichos for the 20th of Sivan

---

2. See *Otzar HaTefillos* for *selichos* commemorating *Gezeiros Tach Vetat*.

3. From the *sefer Ateres Tzvi*.

The 20th of Sivan was proclaimed as a fast day for the Jews of Eastern Europe, with appropriate selichos *prayers composed by many of the Torah Sages who survived the Cossack invasion.*

Chapter

25

As the Cossacks swept across Poland, their victories inspired a general uprising of the Polish serfs against their masters, including the hapless Jewish tax collectors who served as middlemen between the peasantry and nobility.

Even as the Jews lay dead in the streets, the Cossacks went in search of further victims, attacking and murdering the Poles of Tulchin. Frantically, the Poles reminded the Cossacks of their promise to spare them in return for handing over the Jews, but the Cossacks laughed and replied mockingly, "You showed no mercy to your Jewish allies, so why should we show mercy to you?" The Poles who had been so eager to abandon the Jews of their city were amply rewarded for their cruelty.

As the Cossacks swept across Poland, their victories inspired a general uprising of the Polish serfs against their masters, including the hapless Jewish tax collectors who served as middlemen between the peasantry and nobility. Estates were devastated and manor houses razed to the ground. The victims, both members of the nobility and the Jews, were flayed and burned alive, or mutilated and left to the agony of a lingering death. Infants were slit like fish or cast alive into wells. Thousands of Jews perished in the towns east of the Dnieper; only those who embraced the Christian faith escaped.

Chmielnicki's bloodbath continued during the following year. In the city of Kalish, the Cossacks killed most of its Jews. In Lublin, they slaughtered as many Jews as they could, before setting fire to the shul with its congregants still inside.

By the time the Polish lords buried their internal strife and agreed to elect John Cazimir as their king, the Polish army could not rally its strength to defeat the combined forces of the Cossacks and Tatars. With a huge sum of money, Cazimir, aware of his army's limitations, successfully bribed the Tatars to withdraw from fighting. Chmielnicki, realizing that he could not continue the war

successfully on his own, was forced to sign an armistice with the Poles, but the peace proved to be temporary. Shortly afterward, Chmielnicki persuaded the Czar of Russia to incorporate all of the Ukraine into his empire, thus providing an exemplary excuse to invade the eastern part of Poland.

Once again, the Jews were the first victims of the invading forces. This time, even the Jews of Lithuania were slain by the thousands. In Tammuz of the year 1655, the city of Vilna was captured. Rabbi Shabsai Cohen, known as the Shach, had come to Vilna after escaping the bloodshed in Nemirov. Once again, he fled for his life, one of the few who were able to evade disaster. 25,000 others were brutally killed.

Even as Poland floundered under the assault of Russia, King Charles X of Sweden invaded Poland and Lithuania. The Russians and Cossacks had barely left, when the Swedish armies penetrated deep into Polish territory, killing and burning whatever was left. In addition to these attacks by the Cossacks, Russians, Tatars, and Swedes, the Jews also fell prey to the general Polish population, who accused them of private dealings with the Swedes to save their lives. Rabbi Moshe Ravkash, one of the refugees from Vilna, wrote about those catastrophes, "We fulfilled the saying, 'Just like a person who runs away from the lion and is met by the bear.'"[4]

Chmielnicki finally died, not a moment too soon, in 1657. Three years later, the Poles and Swedes formally ended their war, bringing the merciless slaughter of Jewish men, women, and children to an end. It is estimated that between 1648 and 1660, 600,000 Jews, including many Rabbanim and *talmidei chachamim*, were

---

4. *Amos,* 5:19.

murdered. Three hundred Polish Jewish communities, and their Yeshivos, were destroyed. In addition, the upheaval and turmoil caused by twelve years of merciless slaughter left an enduring impact on the survivors. Refugees from Poland wandered across the continents of Europe and Asia, homeless and penniless.

One six-year-old girl lost her parents in the Cossack riots and was baptized by nuns in a Catholic monastery. Years later, she was found wandering in a semi-demented state in a Jewish cemetery, claiming that she had been transferred there by her dead father. She spoke as if in a trance, declaring that she was destined to become the wife of *Mashiach*. The local Jews took pity on the young woman and sent her to her brother in Amsterdam. There was no way of knowing that this half-crazed woman would subsequently play a major role in the story of one of Judaism's most infamous imposters, Shabsai Tzvi.

Some of the towns in which Jews were brutally killed during the Chmielnicki massacres (1648-1660).

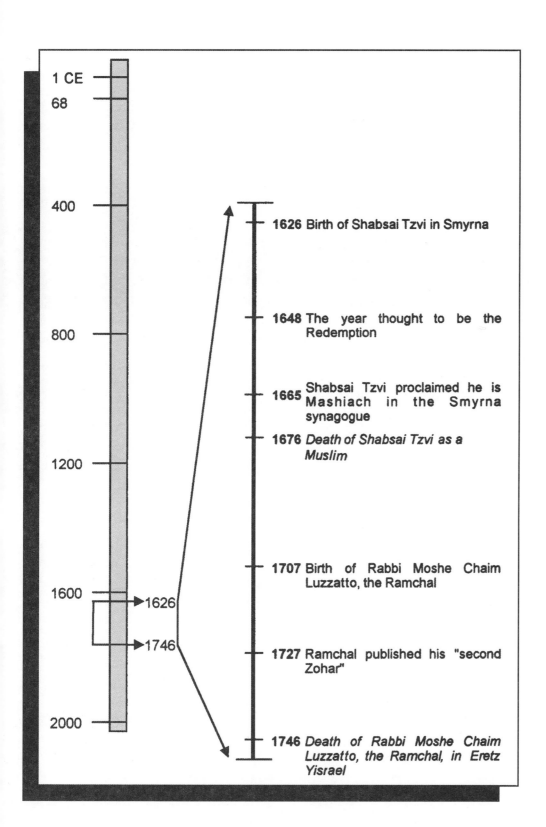

Desperation that Led to Disaster:

Shabsai Tzvi

1 CE
68
400
800
1200
1600
2000

1626
1746

1626 Birth of Shabsai Tzvi in Smyrna

1648 The year thought to be the Redemption

1665 Shabsai Tzvi proclaimed he is Mashiach in the Smyrna synagogue

1676 *Death of Shabsai Tzvi as a Muslim*

1707 Birth of Rabbi Moshe Chaim Luzzatto, the Ramchal

1727 Ramchal published his "second Zohar"

1746 *Death of Rabbi Moshe Chaim Luzzatto, the Ramchal, in Eretz Yisrael*

Chapter

26

Desperation that Led to Disaster:

Shabsai Tzvi

The catastrophic events that swept through Poland convinced them that while Mashiach had not yet arrived, these horrible massacres were surely the chevlei Mashiach (literally, "the birth pangs of Mashiach"), the tumultuous events that will precede the joyous arrival of the promised Redeemer.

Patterns in History

 fter each period of cruel punishment in Jewish history, there comes a tremendous outpouring of merciful kindness, far beyond the ordinary loving relationship between Yisrael and its Maker. After the destruction of the first Bais HaMikdash came the Anshei Knesses HaGedolah; after the destruction of the second Bais HaMikdash, the era of the Mishnah and Gemara brought light and hope to the Jews in exile. When the Chmielnicki massacres finally ended, the Jewish world looked desperately for a sign of Hashem's fatherly love to reveal itself. Surely these horrible disasters were a sign that the coming of *Mashiach* was imminent! Hope was raised, as it had been many times before, that the deep darkness of exile might herald the approach of dawn, and that the long-promised redemption was about to take place.

The desire for messianic fulfillment has been a recurring theme throughout Jewish exile. Many great men and scholars have attempted to determine the date of *Mashiach*'s arrival, and others have tried to expedite *Mashiach*'s coming.[1] Some scholars had calculated that the year 1648 was to become the year of redemption.[2] The catastrophic events that swept through Poland convinced them that while *Mashiach* had not yet arrived, these horrible massacres were surely the *chevlei Mashiach* (literally, "the birth pangs of *Mashiach*"), the tumultuous events that will precede the joyous arrival of the promised Redeemer.

To those seeking a hint of *Mashiach*'s arrival, Shabsai Tzvi, the son of a merchant of Spanish descent, seemed to be a strong possibility.

He was born in Smyrna in the year 1626, where his teachers marveled at his extraordinary mental ability and predicted a great future for him. When he was only fifteen years old, he occupied himself with Kabbalah. He attracted a circle of young men with whom he studied the subject of mysticism. He possessed a sweet voice, leading the singing of mystic texts that were filled with the anticipation of *Mashiach*'s arrival. His ascetic conduct (he fasted frequently and seemed very pious) and charismatic leadership generated a mood of ecstasy and enthusiasm that caught on like wildfire.

While Shabsai Tzvi's followers had only a vague idea of *Mashiach* at first, they soon began to believe that Shabsai was, indeed, *Mashiach*. The more they spoke about it and reinforced each other's fanaticism, the more they actually came to believe it.

Shabsai is Put in *Cherem*

Assuming that the backing of his ardent followers provided sufficient support, Shabsai committed his first blunder. He publicly pronounced the *Shem HaMeforash*, the ineffable Name of Hashem, in the synagogue of Smyrna, an act permitted only to Kohanim in the Bais HaMikdash. This incredible insolence shocked the rabbis of Smyrna; they put Shabsai in *cherem,* or excommunication. Nobody in Smyrna would have anything to do with him.

---

1. See "The *Galus* and *Geulah* Calendar," Chapter 17; "David Reuveni and Shlomo Molcho," Chapter 20; "Menashe ben Israel," Chapter 21; "Rabbi Yaakov Berav," Chapter 22.
2. The Jewish year was 5408; 408 is the *gematria,* or numerical value, of the word *zos,* a reference to *bizos*

yavo Aharon el HaKodesh, "with this will Aharon, [the Kohen Gadol], approach the Holy of Holies [on Yom Kippur]." They inferred that 5408 would prelude the rebuilding of the Bais HaMikdash, where the Kohen Gadol would once more perform the services on Yom Kippur.

Disgraced, the self-proclaimed Messiah left his birthplace in search of other, more credulous communities. He journeyed to Constantinople, where he made the acquaintance of Abraham Yocheni. Yocheni added to the deception by publicizing an allegedly ancient manuscript which predicted Shabsai Tzvi as the *Mashiach*. The parchment scroll read, "Behold a son had been born to Mordechai Tzvi in 5386 [1626]. He will subdue the Great Scorpion and take for himself the strength of a snake (that will destroy all our enemies) and be the true *Mashiach*."

Armed with Yocheni's "proof," Shabsai went out into the world, seeking public acclaim. He traveled to Salonika, hoping that the leaders of that community would accept his claim. Most of the rabbis, however, were not fooled; their personal meetings with Shabsai convinced them that this man did not meet the qualifications of the Redeemer of Israel. Unfortunately, Shabsai found many simple, pious Jews who were impressed by the magical charisma of his charming personality. Overwhelmed by their longing for a speedy redemption, these Jews clung fiercely to his pretenses and helped perpetuate the deception.

The imposter grew increasingly bold in his public conduct. He announced that he was celebrating his marriage soon, declaring a public holiday. Shabsai arrived at the wedding, resplendent and joyous. The *chuppah* was erected, all was in readiness—but where was the bride? As the ceremony began, it became obvious that the veiled *kallah* was actually a Sefer Torah! Affronted by the implications of this symbolic "marriage," the leaders of Salonika followed Smyrna's lead, putting Shabsai in *cherem*.

The imposter departed from Salonika in search of a better reception.

Shabsai made his way to Cairo, where he was received with great honor at the palatial estate of Refael Chalebi and his circle of *mekubalim*. With this backing, he went to Yerushalayim, but his efforts were largely unsuccessful. On his return to Cairo, Shabsai heard rumors of the strange, deranged girl who had undergone the catastrophe of *Tach Vetat* and claimed she was destined to become the wife of *Mashiach*.[3] Shabsai, determined to capitalize on the situation, had Sarah brought to Cairo, where he married her with great pomp and publicity. The Jewish public, desperate for Shabsai's claims to be true, ignored Sarah's doubtful reputation and unstable mind. Surely, Shabsai must be the *Mashiach*!

Autumn, 1665: Shabsai Proclaims He is the *Mashiach*

Shabsai returned to Eretz Yisrael on a wave of triumph, his previous ignoble reception forgotten. The considerable sums of money (supplied by Chalebi) that he distributed to the beleaguered Jewish community were as impressive as the public shows of piety that he carefully displayed whenever possible.

In order to enhance his image as *Mashiach,* Shabsai needed a "prophet" to establish his advent and to speak in the name of Eliyahu HaNavi. A young man named Nassan of Gaza rose admirably to the occasion. Claiming to be Eliyahu, Nassan made impassioned speeches publicizing his received "message" of the imminent arrival of *Mashiach*. In eloquent speeches and letters, he declared that Shabsai Tzvi's kingdom would be declared soon and that he would remove the crown from the head of the Turkish

3. See Chapter 25.

Unfortunately, Shabsai found many simple, pious Jews who were impressed by the magical charisma of his charming personality. Overwhelmed by their longing for a speedy redemption, these Jews clung fiercely to his pretenses and helped perpetuate the deception.

Chapter
26

Normal life came to a standstill as homes and businesses throughout Europe and the Middle East were sold in preparation to travel to Eretz Yisrael.

ruler (then ruler of Eretz Yisrael) and carry it on his own head.

In 1665, Shabsai left Eretz Yisrael and returned to his birthplace of Smyrna, where the original *cherem* was smothered under the vast number of followers he had gained due to tales of his sojourn in Yerushalayim. Here, he took the final, most audacious step. In the synagogue of Smyrna, amid great fanfare and the blowing of the shofar, Shabsai officially announced that he was *Mashiach*. Torah leaders watched helplessly as the congregation ecstatically burst out, "Long live our King, the *Mashiach!*"

Messianic Fever Rises Throughout Europe

Shabsai's official claim to be *Mashiach* proved to be only the beginning of disaster. Letters and messages were sent to all major Jewish communities, using generous exaggeration to relate the wonders and miracles that Shabsai had supposedly performed. The average Jew, even if he had doubted Shabsai's claims at first, became swept up in the frenzy. Normal life came to a standstill as homes and businesses throughout Europe and the Middle East were sold in preparation to travel to Eretz Yisrael. At once exultant and penitent, people did their best to merit the redemption: they sought to rectify their sins, learning Torah and giving charity as never before. The spirit of sincere repentance was so pervasive that, in later years, a potential witness in a Jewish court who had been an adult in 1665 was deemed valid even if he would have ordinarily been considered to be of questionable observance. If he had seen the events of 1665, it was presumed that he had undergone a thorough and genuine repentance.

The desire to fulfill all aspects of messianic preparation reached its height as children aged as young as ten or twelve were hurriedly married, since the Gemara relates that *Mashiach* will not come until all souls that Hashem intended to be brought into this world are actually born.[4]

Torah leaders were unable to put a halt to the hysteria. Most knowledgeable scholars and rabbis opposed the Shabsai Tzvi movement, but they were virtually helpless against it. They begged the exultant populace to use patience and caution instead of believing in miraculous signs and events, but nobody was willing to listen. Indeed, anyone who dared to cast doubt on the validity of Shabsai's claim was promptly silenced—by force, if necessary.

Shabsai, meanwhile, announced that shortly he would remove the Turkish Sultan from his throne and all the nations of the world would acknowledge him as their ruler. His followers issued a manifesto changing the fast of the Tenth of Teves into a holiday. The frenzied mood of the multitude, as well as his own urging towards the spectacular, prompted him to set sail for Constantinople, accompanied by his most enthusiastic followers. By now, Shabsai probably truly believed that he would be able to "remove the crown from the head of the Turkish ruler," as Nassan of Gaza had supposedly prophesied. He arrived in Turkey's capital, surrounded by his followers and confident of a royal welcome.

Instead of receiving the honors due to a king, however, Shabsai was immediately put under arrest and taken in chains to the palace. Confronted with charges of treason, Shabsai claimed that instead of coming to take over the rule of Turkey, he

---

4. *Yevamos,* 62a.

was merely a poor Jew from Yerushalayim who had come to collect funds for the impoverished. The Sultan's Grand Vizier, who had heard of this messianic pretender and his boast that he would soon rule the world, dismissed Shabsai's claims of innocence. The would-be Messiah was transferred to a fortress prison in Abydus, normally reserved for political prisoners.

Thanks to several well-placed bribes, Shabsai was treated with exceptional mildness and was allowed to receive visitors. This treatment may have resulted in his audacity in actually maintaining his messianic claims while in prison. First came his abolition of the Seventeenth of Tammuz as a fast day, allegedly because on that day he had first realized that he was *Mashiach*. Then he ordered a Great Sabbath, similar to the Shabbos before Pesach, to be kept on the following Monday. Next, he had the effrontery to proclaim Tishah B'Av, the day that mourns the destruction of the Bais HaMikdash, as a day of rejoicing!

The Deception Revealed

The leader of the Polish Sages, Rav David HaLevi, author of the *Taz,* sent his grandson and another relative to investigate the validity of Shabsai's claims. Shabsai's followers made every effort to influence this important committee in favor of their acclaimed *Mashiach,* telling amazing stories about the miraculous acts allegedly performed by the anointed prince. They had almost succeeded in convincing the two visitors that Shabsai was truly the *Mashiach* when a new circumstance arose, which, coupled with Shabsai's overwhelming arrogance, led to the eventual collapse of the deception.

The messengers told of an individual in Poland named Nechemiah Cohen, who

had independently predicted that *Mashiach* was about to come. With foolish confidence, Shabsai wrote to the Taz that he should send this "prophet" Nechemiah to him. Nechemiah arrived in Constantinople and was received at the prison with great honor and expectation. After many conversations with Shabsai, however, Nechemiah realized that Shabsai was nothing but a fraud who had managed to deceive the entire Jewish people. When Nechemiah announced his conclusions, Shabsai's followers tried to silence the Polish Jew permanently. However, he managed to escape to Adrianople, where he reported to the Turkish authorities that Shabsai did indeed seek to depose the Muslim government and replace it with his own.

Shabsai was confronted by the Sultan and accused of plotting against the Turkish government. Like Mohammed before him,[5] the Sultan offered Shabsai a choice: the Jew must either convert to Islam or be executed. Shabsai Tzvi, who

Shabsai Tzvi in prison

5. See Chapter 6.

They had almost succeeded in convincing the two visitors that Shabsai was truly the Mashiach when a new circumstance arose, which, coupled with Shabsai's overwhelming arrogance, led to the eventual collapse of the deception.

Chapter
26

*Decades later,
other impostors
appeared on the
horizon, all
claiming they were
the "incarnation"
of Shabsai's soul
and were
commissioned to
finish his work.*

had announced that he was *Mashiach* only one year before, swiftly removed his Jewish head-covering and donned the white turban of Islam. His followers watched, horror-struck at the hypocrisy of the man who had led them to believe that he was the destined redeemer of Bnei Yisrael. Shabsai died ten years later, a Muslim and forever disgraced.

One can imagine the traumatic impact this sudden, deliberate conversion had on the multitude of simple believers who had put their faith in this man. Some of his closest followers converted to Islam with their master, convinced that his action was still part of the Divine plan. They actually persisted in their claims that Shabsai was *Mashiach,* and that this step was merely Shabsai's way of converting all other nations to Judaism. But for most Jews, disillusion swept like shock waves through the cities of Europe, plunging the Jews into the depths of despair.

The Aftermath of Shabsai Tzvi

The horrific impact of Shabsai Tzvi, *yimach shemo,* did not end with the death of its founder. Decades later, other impostors appeared on the horizon, all claiming they were the "incarnation" of Shabsai's soul and were commissioned to finish his work.

One such group was led by Nechemiah Chayun. He expounded on Shabsai's ideas, winning a great deal of approval from the common Jews in Amsterdam. In one of his books, he developed a religious doctrine that came close to the Christian concept of trinity. He submitted this work to the Chacham Tzvi Ashkenazi of Amsterdam, one of the greatest Sages of his time. The Chacham Tzvi, who had spent his youth in Salonika and was intimately acquainted with the turbulent career of the false *Mashiach,* recognized

Nechemiah Chayun as a fraud and went to every extreme necessary to unmask this hoax. Unfortunately, the following that Chayun had won among the Jewish community of Amsterdam forced the Chacham Tzvi to leave city. At that juncture, the Torah leaders took up the battle and brought convincing proof of the fallacy of Chayun's philosophy. Nechemiah Chayun was driven from Amsterdam, wandering through the cities of Europe as a rejected fugitive who was unable to find acceptance anywhere. His son, continuing in his father's heretical footsteps, ultimately converted to Christianity. Nechemiah Chayun died, disgraced, in North Africa.

Another offshoot of the Shabsai movement were the depraved Frankists, named after Yaakov Frank, a German Jew who lived in Poland. His business connections brought him to Turkey, where he met Shabsai's adherents and grew intrigued by the messianic movement. When Frank returned to Poland, he claimed that he had been appointed to lead the Shabsai Tzvi movement in Poland. While he was unable to gain acceptance by most Jews, some of the less religious gave him credence; he interested them with a depraved, mystical "religion," in which all restraints of morality were removed. Eventually, when he realized that he would only be rejected and prosecuted by the religious leadership, he turned to the offensive. Enlisting the help of the Christian clergy, he denounced the Oral Torah and the Torah Sages who represented it. He staged a public trial, resulting in the public burning of many editions of the Talmud in the streets of the city of Kamenitz, Poland. Ultimately, the Frankist movement ended in shame with its leader converted to Christianity. Even the Christians suspected him of hypocrisy and treated him with contempt until his death in Offenbach near Frankfurt. Fortunately, his movement lost all traces of Jewish identity and was never heard of again.[6]

Rabbi Moshe Chaim Luzzatto, the Ramchal (1707–1746)

After the supreme disillusion of Shabsai Tzvi's apostasy, most leaders had a strong reaction against anything that had any trace of messianism. In Italy, where Shabsai's movement had been extremely powerful, the rabbis condemned the study of Kabbalah, seeing it as a smokescreen for Shabsai's sympathizers. Unfortunately, one truly righteous man, an extraordinary personality, suffered needlessly from these suspicions: Rabbi Moshe Chaim Luzzatto, author of the classic mussar work, *Mesilas Yesharim.*

Rabbi Moshe Chaim Luzzatto, lovingly and reverently called the Ramchal, was born to wealthy parents living in Padua, Italy. He learned Tanach, Talmud, and Kabbalah with the local Rav, Rabbi Yeshaya Bassau. In addition, he acquired extensive knowledge of Latin and several other languages, developing his natural talent as a poet. The Ramchal was particularly impressed with the style and thought of the *Zohar.* At the age of twenty, he wrote a work on mysticism which was so impressive that his admirers called it a "second *Zohar.*"

One of the young scholar's followers wrote to his friends with great enthusiasm about the *sefer,* and remarked that the Ramchal must have received instructions *min haShamayim* (from Heaven). Excerpts of this letter reached the Jewish spiritual leaders of Germany in Hamburg, Altona, and Wandsbeck. To the Torah Sages of Europe, this could mean

only one thing: the possibility of a revival of a messianic movement, with a young man acclaimed by his friends as *Mashiach.*

Rabbi Moshe Hagiz from Altona wrote an excited letter to the rabbis of Venice, urging that Rabbi Luzzatto's kabbalistic teachings be suppressed. The Ramchal, hurt by the accusation, defended himself passionately, showing that he had no connection with Shabsai Tzvi's deception. He stated that he was not a prophet, the son of a prophet, nor a miracle worker; by divine grace, he had been the recipient of revelation. Rabbi Hagiz did realize that the Ramchal was sincere and completely dissociated from the Shabsai group. Nevertheless, the rabbis insisted that he surrender all of his kabbalistic writings to the custody of his teacher and desist from engagement in kabbalistic teachings until he went to Eretz Yisrael.

The Ramchal accepted these demands and promised not to publish any *sefarim* without his rebbe's explicit permission. A few years later, the Ramchal did indeed receive permission to publish a

מסלת ישרים

Mesilas Yesharim

6. See Chapter 3, "The Spreading Sect."

Desperation that Led to Disaster:

Shabsai Tzvi

The Ramchal was particularly impressed with the style and thought of the Zohar. At the age of twenty, he wrote a work on mysticism which was so impressive that his admirers called it a "second Zohar."

Chapter 26

new *sefer* on this subject. Despite his adherence to the conditions that the rabbis had imposed, he was immediately accused of misconduct and breach of promise. The Torah leaders of Venice pronounced a *cherem* on Rabbi Luzzatto and burned his writings.

The Ramchal did not challenge the decision. Although he knew they had misinterpreted his intentions and did not understand his motives, he nevertheless acceded to the demands of the Torah leaders of his community. The

Grave of Rabbi Moshe Chaim Luzzatto

Ramchal left Italy and resettled in Amsterdam, where he found friends and recognition. It is there that he wrote his *Mesilas Yesharim,* which ever since has held a prominent place among all mussar *sefarim.*

At the age of thirty-six, the Ramchal determined to go to Eretz Yisrael and resume his study of Kabbalah, according to the terms of his agreement with the European rabbis. After living in Eretz Yisrael with his family for three years, they were stricken with pestilence and died. He was buried in Tiberias, next to the Rambam and the Shaloh HaKadosh.

The Ramchal left behind the legacy of a number of *sefarim* that reveal his profound mind, a deep understanding of Jewish thought, and a masterful command of the Hebrew language. During his lifetime, he was a victim of the aftereffects of a most tragic episode in Jewish history, suffering from groundless accusations in the wake of an understandable fear of new heresies. The famed Gaon of Vilna is known to have said that if the Ramchal were alive in his generation, he would go by foot from Vilna to Italy to sit at his feet and learn from him.

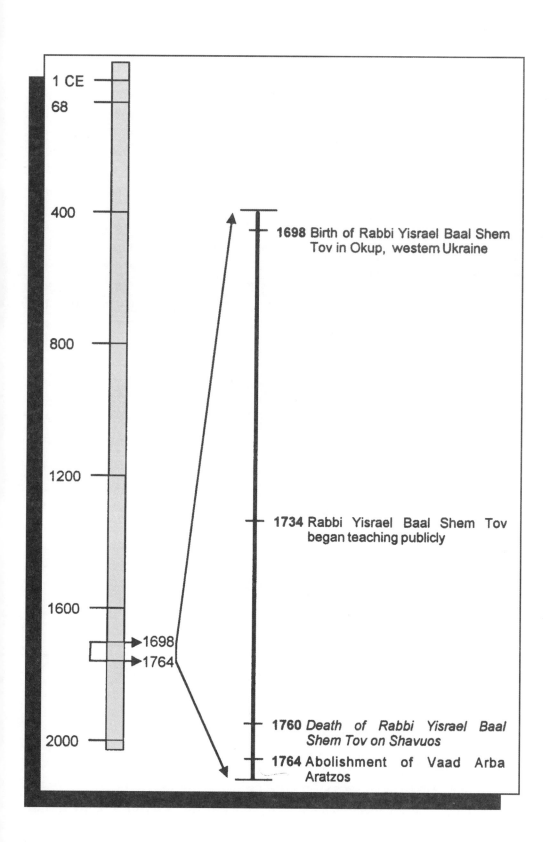

1 CE
68
400
800
1200
1600
1698
1764
2000

1698 Birth of Rabbi Yisrael Baal Shem Tov in Okup, western Ukraine

1734 Rabbi Yisrael Baal Shem Tov began teaching publicly

1760 *Death of Rabbi Yisrael Baal Shem Tov on Shavuos*

1764 Abolishment of Vaad Arba Aratzos

*With no one to
guide them in a
manner within the
bounds of their
comprehension,
these average Jews
found themselves
despised as amei
ha'aretz,
ignoramuses, by
the Torah scholars
of their day.*

In the aftermath of the Chmielnicki rebellion, the Jewish communities in Poland were devastated. Thousands of Jewish lives were lost. Homes were destroyed or ransacked and community life destroyed. Many of those who survived the terror were left homeless and wandering. The governing body of the Jews of Poland, the Vaad Arba Aratzos,[1] declined in power until it was officially abolished by royal decree in 1764. The Yeshivos and houses of learning, many of which had lost their teachers and leaders, were in shambles. The former concern of every member of the Jewish community, that no child should grow up without a thorough Jewish education, had surrendered to the mundane worry for daily bread.

The material poverty was matched by a spiritual crisis of unprecedented dimensions within the ranks of religious Jewry, caused by Shabsai Tzvi, *yemach shemo.* Armed with an arsenal of distorted Jewish mysticism and Kabbalah, Shabsai Tzvi had managed to conquer the hearts of large portions of world Jewry. The resulting disillusionment following his shameless conversion to Islam was so great that it threatened to crush the underlying foundations of Jewish belief completely.[2]

The Torah scholars of that era concluded that if the study of mysticism could have such disastrous results, that study must be discontinued, particularly by those who lacked the sophistication to temper their study with the necessary caution.[3] To prevent future disasters and perversions, Torah learning must be restricted to the area of *nigleh,* study that is within logical comprehension. Philosophy, one of the causes of the decline of Jewish observance in Spain, had long been dismissed by the

Sages of the Franco-German schools;[4] now, mysticism was rejected as a result of the Shabsai Tzvi debacle. The new generation of Torah scholars had to rely entirely on the study of the Talmud.

This approach, which seemed so necessary at the time, essentially reduced the average individual to spiritual poverty. Working desperately to provide his family with the bare necessities, the common Jew was unable to study Gemara; Torah study had become a luxury for the rich and fortunate. While ordinary Jews possessed faith and determination to keep the mitzvos, they lacked the inspiration and warmth of Torah study. With no one to guide them in a manner within the bounds of their comprehension, these average Jews found themselves despised as *amei ha'aretz,* ignoramuses, by the Torah scholars of their day.[5] This desperate, urgent need for warm and caring leadership was provided for by Rabbi Yisrael ben Eliezer, the Baal Shem Tov.

Rabbi Yisrael was born in Okup, a small village in western Ukraine, in 1698. He was orphaned at an early age; it is said that his father's last admonition was, "Fear nothing, my son, other than Hashem." As a destitute orphan, Yisrael grew up without a teacher; his immense knowledge, both in Talmud and in Kabbalah, was the result of rigorous self-study.

Yisrael concealed his superior intelligence and righteousness, preferring to remain a *nistar,* a hidden tzaddik. The members of his community accepted him as a good-natured young man, but it was assumed that nothing great could be expected from him. The only outward signs of Reb Yisrael's greatness were the intensity of his *tefillah*

---

1. See Chapter 23.
2. See Chapter 26 for more detail.
3. See Chapter 26.

4. See Chapter 13; Chapter 16.
5. See Chapter 25, "Attitudes of the Torah Scholars."

and the kindness he showed to the poor in the community.

Yisrael was given a job as assistant teacher in the local *Cheder*. His duties were to wake the children and escort them to shul in the morning, to see that they said their prayers properly and paid attention in class, and to escort them home again at the end of the day. The children's parents never discovered the almost magical influence Yisrael wielded over the children in his charge. He sang beautiful songs for them and kept them spellbound with his stories. Under his loving tutelage, the children grew to cherish their prayers and Torah studies, eager to please their rebbe's assistant. At night, while the children and adults slept, Reb Yisrael immersed himself in the study of Talmud and *Zohar*.

When he became too old for this job, he was given the position of *shamash* in the Bais HaMidrash. Essentially, his tasks were to keep the building heated in winter and to sweep the floor whenever needed. Even as he scrupulously performed his duties, Reb Yisrael maintained the image of a complete *am ha'aretz*. During the Torah lectures, he lay down on the bench near the stove and pretended that he was fast asleep; actually, he was wide awake and listening with rapt attention to every word that was said. At times, the rav was unable to answer questions that were asked of him; it is said that Reb Yisrael anonymously wrote down the answers and posted them on the wall of the Bais HaMidrash to be discovered the following morning. No one would have dreamed of tracing these answers to the simple *shamash* of their shul.

During the long nights in the Bais HaMidrash, Reb Yisrael mastered not only the Talmud and *Zohar*, but also the arts of healing. In time, he was able to cure

many diseases of the poor. Gradually, he acquired a name as a healer, or *Baal Shem*, Master of Hashem's Name, as such healers were called.

One scholar did recognize the greatness of the Baal Shem—the renowned Rabbi Chaim Kitover of the Chachmei Brod. He was so impressed by the Baal Shem's greatness that he chose to make him his son-in-law. When Rabbi Chaim died shortly before the wedding, his son Rabbi Gershon, one of the greatest scholars in Poland, rejected the shidduch on the grounds that the *chasan* was just a simple *am ha'aretz*. Despite this objection, the wedding took place. The young couple moved to a small village in the Carpathian mountains, where Reb Yisrael earned a meager living by digging lime in the mountains and loading it onto a cart, which his wife drove to the nearby city and sold for a small profit. Otherwise, Reb Yisrael spent most of his time in the solitude of the mountains, isolating himself from the tumult of the outside world in order to advance in holiness and purity. Having grown up as a poor orphan, he understood all too well the desperate need of the common people in Poland for someone who would lift them out of their spiritual stagnation. Seven years passed, however, before he understood that the time was ripe.

On Lag B'Omer, 1734, at the age of 36, he began teaching publicly, giving advice, healing troubled hearts, and gathering disciples—Chassidim. Eventually, he moved to Medzybozh in the western Ukraine, where he lived and taught for the rest of his life.

The term Chassid can be traced back to the Mishnah *Avos*, where it is mentioned as a degree of kindness that goes beyond the required measure, or *lifnim mishuras ha'din*. The term was adopted to describe

The Chassidic Movement:

The Baal Shem Tov

Even as he scrupulously performed his duties, Reb Yisrael maintained the image of a complete am ha'aretz.

The Baal Shem Tov offered the simple Jew... an avodah of intense prayer and devoted song, serving Hashem with dedication and joy.

Chapter
27

Twenty years after his death, a collection of his teachings, entitled Toldos Yaakov Yosef, was published by Rabbi Yaakov Yosef.

the Baal Shem Tov's attitude, based on an overflow of love and compassion for the common Jew, and the love of Hashem and love of man as the all-encompassing purpose of his actions. The Baal Shem Tov offered the simple Jew, who was unable to immerse himself in the Talmud, a different way of serving Hashem: an *avodah* of intense prayer and devoted song, serving Hashem with dedication and joy. Such a program, well within the grasp of the simple Jew, was tempered and guarded by a great leader—the Rebbe—who would ensure that joyousness did not degenerate into levity and that all intentions were holy and pure.

From Medzybozh, the Baal Shem Tov's fame spread all over Eastern Europe. Important scholars came to challenge him and his new, different methods of serving Hashem; many eventually became his most devoted disciples. His brother-in-law, Rabbi Kitover, who had been against Reb Yisrael's marriage, became one of his most ardent admirers.

On the first day of Shavuos, 1760, the Baal Shem Tov realized that his end was approaching. He gathered his closest disciples and spent the night reciting the *tikkun lail Shavuos* with them. In the morning, the Baal Shem Tov discussed with two members of the *Chevra Kaddisha,* or Burial Society, how his body should be laid to rest. He told everyone present to recite *Viy'hi Noam;* he trembled violently, and then his body suddenly quieted. Someone looked up and noticed that the clock had stopped.

The Baal Shem Tov did not leave any *sefarim* of his own. There are a few writings that are ascribed to the Baal Shem Tov's own hand, foremost among them a letter which he is said to have written to his brother-in-law who then lived in Eretz Yisrael. Twenty years after his death, however, a collection of his teachings, entitled *Toldos Yaakov Yosef,* was published by Rabbi Yaakov Yosef. Although Rabbi Yaakov Yosef had originally been an opponent of the Baal Shem Tov, he eventually became his prime pupil. Indeed, in page after page of *Toldos Yaakov Yosef,* the author respectfully states, "I heard from my master." It was Reb Dov Ber, however, who was designated as the next leader of the Chassidic movement.

Chapter
27

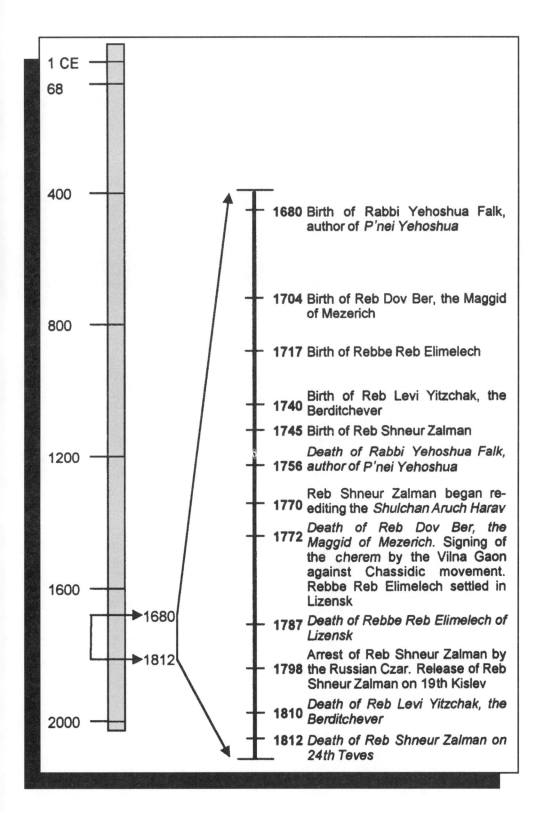

1 CE
68
400
800
1200
1600
2000

1680
1812

1680 Birth of Rabbi Yehoshua Falk, author of *P'nei Yehoshua*

1704 Birth of Reb Dov Ber, the Maggid of Mezerich

1717 Birth of Rebbe Reb Elimelech

1740 Birth of Reb Levi Yitzchak, the Berditchever

1745 Birth of Reb Shneur Zalman

1756 *Death of Rabbi Yehoshua Falk, author of P'nei Yehoshua*

1770 Reb Shneur Zalman began re-editing the *Shulchan Aruch Harav*

1772 *Death of Reb Dov Ber, the Maggid of Mezerich.* Signing of the cherem by the Vilna Gaon against Chassidic movement. Rebbe Reb Elimelech settled in Lizensk

1787 *Death of Rebbe Reb Elimelech of Lizensk*

1798 Arrest of Reb Shneur Zalman by the Russian Czar. Release of Reb Shneur Zalman on 19th Kislev

1810 *Death of Reb Levi Yitzchak, the Berditchever*

1812 *Death of Reb Shneur Zalman on 24th Teves*

The Disciples
of the Baal
Shem Tov

Chapter
28

The Maggid attracted many of the leading minds of his generation. These scholars, steeped in Torah and models of piety, were then trained to become regional "generals" of the various areas into which the Chassidic movement had spread.

Reb Dov Ber, the Maggid of Mezerich (1704–1772)

eb Dov Ber of Mezerich, who was born only six years after his mentor, the Baal Shem Tov, showed signs of brilliance in Torah in his early youth. All too quickly, he outgrew the educational facilities of his hometown, the village of Lukatch. He traveled to Lemberg, where he soon became one of the outstanding students of Rabbi Yehoshua Falk (1680–1756), the famous author of the *P'nei Yehoshua.*

At that time, the rabbi's role in the community was mainly to teach and to render halachic decisions; preaching was restricted to a *maggid,* one who enlightens the common man through stories, parables, rhetoric, and witticisms. Reb Dov Ber, who could have easily qualified for the highest rabbinical positions, chose to become a *maggid,* preaching in the cities of Turtzin, Dubno, Koretz, and Rovna. Due to the combination of his gift for oratory and his great scholarship, he quickly earned a reputation as one of the leading *maggidim* of his generation, called THE Maggid.

The Maggid suffered from lameness in his left foot and from general weakness. He visited the Baal Shem Tov to seek a cure, unaware that this meeting would prove to be a turning point in his life.

At first, Reb Dov Ber was disappointed; all he heard from the Baal Shem Tov were "stories about horses and coachmen." As he was about to leave, however, the Baal Shem Tov summoned him back. During a discussion about a difficult piece of the *Zohar,* the Baal Shem Tov offered a brilliant explanation. From then on, the Maggid became a disciple of the Baal Shem Tov and his eventual successor.

Unlike the Baal Shem Tov, who preached to the masses and was loved by the common Jew, the Maggid attracted many of the leading minds of his generation. These scholars, steeped in Torah and models of piety, were then trained to become regional "generals" of the various areas into which the Chassidic movement had spread. While these men became the bulwark of the movement, they also evoked strong opposition, creating a rift among the ranks of the religious Jews in Eastern Europe.

The Misnagdim

The Chassidic movement served as a lifeline for the common Jew who was unable to learn Torah. However, many Torah scholars of the day objected to the concept of *Chassidus.* The Chassidim called these men *Misnagdim,* or opponents. The antagonism between Chassidim and Misnagdim grew steadily over the years. Tempers flared, and sometimes the disrespectful and brazen attitude of Chassidim towards Torah scholars reinforced the opinions of their opponents. The objections to *Chassidus* were based on the following factors:

1) The adoration of the Rebbe, whom the common man evidently regarded as a sort of "superman," seemed to contain an element of heresy. The initiative demanded of every individual to elevate himself and make the most strenuous personal effort to come close to Hashem was reduced to a minor, subservient role as a person became subordinate to the Rebbe; all that seemed to be required by *Chassidus* was to attach oneself to the coattails of the Rebbe and be swept along to ultimate perfection. Moreover, since the position of leadership usually became hereditary, there was the danger of a subsequent successor to

the position of Rebbe who was not eminently qualified to lead his Chassidim as a role model.

2) The introduction of a substitute method of reaching closeness to Hashem, through prayer and joy instead of the intellectual study of Torah, seemed to be a potentially damaging and dangerous innovation. Although the original Rebbes were all great Torah scholars, it seemed apparently unnecessary for the common Chassidim to devote themselves to study. If it were possible to reach the elevated heights of closeness to Hashem in an effortless manner, why toil over a complex passage of the Gemara or spend sleepless nights over a difficult Rambam? After all, one could dance and sing or listen to a speech of the Rebbe to achieve the same spiritual heights.

The center of opposition to *Chassidus* lay in Lithuania, particularly in the community of Vilna. Often called the "Yerushalayim of Eastern Europe," Vilna had developed into an outstanding Talmudic center during the eighteenth century, with the Vilna Gaon, Reb Eliyahu, serving as the focal point for the community.[1] Known reverently and affectionately as the Gra (**G**aon **R**abbi **E**liyahu), the Vilna Gaon was at the forefront of the opposition to *Chassidus*. On Shabbos HaGadol in 1772, he signed a *cherem*, issued by the Rabbinical Court of Vilna, against the Chabad and Breslov branches of *Chassidus*, which was later expanded to include the entire Chassidic movement.

Just as the battle between Chassid and *Misnaged* reached its height, Reb Dov Ber's health failed. He passed away less than half a year after the *cherem* had been issued. With his death, there was no longer a universally accepted leader

---

of the Chassidic movement. The Chassidim were split into different branches, successfully led by the students of the Maggid of Mezerich.

In a whimsical analogy, it has been said that the disciples of Reb Dov Ber represented the different faculties of the human being:

> *The Baal HaTanya was the "brains" of Chassidus;*
>
> *The Chozeh of Lublin, Rabbi Yaakov Yitzchak Horowitz, who had the supernatural ability to see things that were distant and hidden from normal human beings, was the "eye" of Chassidus;*
>
> *The Maggid of Koznitz, Rabbi Yisrael Hopstein, was the "hand" of Chassidus;*
>
> *Reb Levi Yitzchak of Berditchev was the "heart" of Chassidus.*

Rabbi Elimelech of Lizensk (1717–1787)

The unusual title of *Rebbe Reb* was bestowed upon Rabbi Elimelech of Lizensk, known as the "Rebbe Reb Melech." It is possible that this unique title refers to Reb Elimelech's status as a general of generals, a Rebbe of Rebbeim. Like the Maggid of Mezerich, Rabbi Elimelech possessed a magnetic personality that attracted many of the Chassidic greats of his time, including the Chozeh of Lublin, the Koznitzer Maggid, and Reb Naftali Ropshitz. Together with his famous brother, Reb Zisha, the Rebbe Reb Melech helped the Chassidic movement reach greater heights.

Shortly after the Maggid's death in 1772, Reb Elimelech settled in Lizensk, which became a focal point for the spread of the Chassidic movement in Poland and

---

The introduction of a substitute method of reaching closeness to Hashem, through prayer and joy instead of the intellectual study of Torah, seemed to be a potentially damaging and dangerous innovation.

Rabbi Levi Yitzchak's love for the Jewish nation knew no bounds. He took it upon himself to become the defender of Klal Yisrael before the Throne of the Almighty, finding ways to declare their merits even when the record of their actions seemed to point in the opposite direction.

Galicia. Reb Elimelech maintained a court of Chassidim supported by *pidyonos*, contributions offered to the Rebbe in return for his praying for the welfare of the contributor. One who came to seek help or advice from the Rebbe would usually write a list of requests on a slip of paper, called a *tzettel*, accompanied by a *pidyon*. These *pidyonos*, however, did not remain in his home for very long; it is said that he gave all his money to the poor, not allowing even a single coin to remain in his house overnight.

Reb Elimelech developed the role of the Rebbe as the foundation stone of the Chassidic movement. In his view, the Rebbe should serve not only as the spiritual guide of the community, but also as the one who took care of its most mundane, physical needs. The Rebbe should be father and guide in both physical and spiritual matters.

Like his masters, the Baal Shem Tov and the Maggid, Reb Elimelech did not write his own *sefarim*, although a collection of his Shabbos lessons were compiled by his son, Rabbi Eliezer, and published the year after his death under the title *Noam Elimelech*. However, Reb Elimelech presented his followers with a program by which they would be able to achieve perfection through constant vigilance. This program is contained in the famous *Tzettel Katan*, or "Small List." The *Tzettel Katan* serves as a detailed pattern and guideline through which one can achieve holiness, and it is still used by Chassidim today.

Rabbi Levi Yitzchak, the Berditchever (1740–1810)

Another outstanding talmid of the Maggid was Rabbi Levi Yitzchak Berditchever.

The Tzettel Katan serves as a detailed pattern and guideline through which one can achieve holiness, and it is still used by Chassidim today.

He was an outstanding Torah scholar of eminent piety (his Torah thoughts were published in a *sefer* called *Kedushas Levi*), but he is best remembered for his *ahavas Yisrael,* the extreme love and compassion he possessed for his fellow Jews. Rabbi Levi Yitzchak's love for the Jewish nation knew no bounds. He took it upon himself to become the defender of Klal Yisrael before the Throne of the Almighty, finding ways to declare their merits even when the record of their actions seemed to point in the opposite direction.

One famous story relates that during the annual fair held in Berditchev, the Rebbe rose in the middle of the night and went to the marketplace with a package of meat in one hand and a bottle of liquor in the other. The revelry of the fair was apparent in the numerous visitors, Gentile and Jew alike, who lay snoring in the streets. Rabbi Levi Yitzchak approached one Jewish merchant, shook him awake, and offered him the meat and liquor, saying, "Get up, eat something, and have a drink."

The Jew mumbled, "I can't. I have no water for *negel vasser* (to wash my hands)."

Rabbi Levi Yitzchak stepped back, allowing the Jew to roll over and go back to sleep. He bent over a second Jew and made the same offer, receiving a similar reply. This was repeated many times before the Rebbe finally approached a non-Jewish drunkard, who grabbed the meat and the liquor and gulped them down eagerly. Rabbi Levi Yitzchak rushed to the shul, opened the holy Ark, and exclaimed, "G-d of the Universe, do You not see the difference between your sons and the Gentiles? How, then, could

You still have complaints about Your people of Israel?"

On another occasion, he is said to have argued, "Almighty G-d, why don't You deal with us as a simple Jew does when he drops his tefillin? If a Jew drops his tefillin, he immediately bends over, picks them up tenderly, and kisses them. But the people of Israel, who are Your tefillin that You wear as adornment on Your forehead,[2] have fallen from the heights of Heaven into a deep abyss, and this has lasted for almost two thousand years, and You have not lifted them to their former level!"

Rabbi Levi Yitzchak is the author of many impassioned songs that express, in moving verses, his deep love for Hashem and for Yisrael. The Chozeh of Lublin, his contemporary and a disciple of the Maggid, used to recite a special daily prayer, thanking Hashem for bringing a Jew like Rabbi Levi Yitzchak into this world. In 1810, with Rabbi Levi Yitzchak's passing, the community of Berditchev was so distraught that they refused to appoint a successor, declaring that it was impossible for anyone to fill the Rebbe's shoes. In deference to the great Rabbi Levi Yitzchak, it was decided that no one would ever again be honored with the title *Rav* in the city of Berditchev; instead, the Rabbi of Berditchev was called the *Dayan,* Judge, or *Moreh Tzeddek,* Torah authority for the community.

Reb Shneur Zalman of Liady, the Baal HaTanya

Reb Shneur Zalman was born on the 18th of Elul, 5505 (1745), in Liozna in central Russia. When Shneur Zalman was eight years old, his father, Reb Baruch, sent him to the city of Lubavitch to study under the Rav of the town. After three years, however, the Rav ad-

vised Reb Baruch to send the young boy elsewhere; he had taught him all he knew. The eleven-year-old boy had already mastered Shass; only the most outstanding Torah scholars could continue his education.

Reb Shneur Zalman spent some time in Vilna before going to Mezerich to learn from the Maggid. He said, "I have already been exposed to Talmudic discipline, but I have yet to learn the discipline of prayer." This decision became the turning point in his life.

On his arrival in Mezerich, the Maggid arranged for Reb Shneur Zalman to be introduced to the doctrines of *Chassidus* by his own son, Avraham, who is known as the *Malach,* or angel, because of his saintliness. By 1770, when Reb Shneur Zalman was barely 25 years old, the Maggid entrusted him with the task of re-editing the *Shulchan Aruch* of Rav Karo, which had been printed about two hundred years earlier; with the introduction of many new customs and the practices of the Ari HaKadosh into Chassidic lifestyle, such a revision was deemed necessary.[3] By assigning this tremendous work to Reb Shneur Zalman, the Maggid expressed the high esteem in which the young man was held within the circle of Chassidic leaders. This work eventually became known as the *Shulchan Aruch HaRav.*

When the Maggid died in 1772, the Chassidic movement was left without a central leader, and the central organization began to fracture into different branches. Reb Shneur Zalman and the Maggid's designated successor, Rabbi Menachem Mendel of Vitebsk, made an effort to achieve a reconciliation with the Misnagdim, specifically with the Vilna Gaon. They traveled to Vilna and

"The people of Israel, who are Your tefillin that You wear as adornment on Your forehead, have fallen from the heights of Heaven into a deep abyss, and this has lasted for almost two thousand years, and You have not lifted them to their former level!"

Chapter
28

2. See *Shir HaKavod* for Shabbos.

3. See Chapter 22 on both Rav Yosef Karo and the Ari.

*He named his
movement Chabad,
an acronym of
Chochmah, Binah,
and Daas:
Wisdom,
Understanding,
and Knowledge.*

tried to arrange a meeting with the Gaon. Reb Shneur Zalman, who was still well-known and respected for his years of study in that city, hoped they would be able to show the Gra that his opposition to *Chassidus* was based on a misconception. These hopes, however, were shattered; the Vilna Gaon did not see them, and the meeting never took place.

Reb Shneur Zalman became the founder of the Lubavitch branch of *Chassidus.* He named his movement *Chabad,* an acronym of **C**hochmah, **B**inah, and **D**aas: Wisdom, Understanding, and Knowledge. He explained his specific doctrine of *Chassidus* in his *sefer Likutai Amarim,* "Collected Sayings," a work on which he labored for twenty years. This sefer is popularly called the *Tanya,* "It is taught," after its first word. It is still the guidebook of Lubavitcher Chassidim today.

The *Tanya,* with its systemization of the teachings of *Chassidus* and its references to the doctrines of the earlier Kabbalists, made a deep impression on the Chassidic world. However, it also generated serious opposition from other Chassidic leaders. Such a *sefer,* which would popularize the study of Kabbalah among the rank and file of the masses, might lead to dangerous and frightening consequences, just as the study of Kabbalah had

Reb Shneur Zalman of Liady, the Baal HaTanya

With worldwide acclaim, the Baal HaTanya was accepted as a Torah genius who had brought Talmudic study back into Chassidus, giving it the prominence it deserved.

led to excesses under the leadership of Shabsai Tzvi.

With opposition and antagonism at its height, a man named Avigdor made the Baal HaTanya the victim of vicious slander, denouncing him to the Russian authorities for allegedly provoking the Jews to undermine the authority of the Czar. In the autumn of 1798, Reb Shneur Zalman was placed under arrest and taken from his home in Liozna to St. Petersburg. For months, he underwent a thorough interrogation by the highest Russian authorities. In the end, he was acquitted of all charges and released. The day when Reb Shneur Zalman regained his freedom was the 19th of Kislev, 1798. Today, the 19th of Kislev is a major day of celebration for Lubavitcher Chassidim.

In the wake of Reb Shneur Zalman's shocking incarceration and subsequent release, the fury of the antagonism between the Chassidim and Misnagdim abated somewhat. With worldwide acclaim, the Baal HaTanya was accepted as a Torah genius who had brought Talmudic study back into *Chassidus,* giving it the prominence it deserved.

After his acquittal, Reb Shneur Zalman became the rabbi of Liady, where he established his world headquarters and increased the number of his followers. Despite his failure to come to terms with the Vilna Gaon, he still made tremendous effort to come to a reconciliation with the Misnagdim.

All too soon, however, Reb Shneur Zalman found himself coping with a new danger. Napoleon Bonaparte of France, who possessed an overwhelming ambition to rule all of Europe, invaded Russia in 1812. While Napoleon tried to create an image for himself as the great liberator of the Jews, the Baal HaTanya was outspoken in his opposition to the French Emperor. Reb Shneur Zalman urged his followers to support the Czar. He commented, "If the Czar wins, it will be bad for the body of Klal Yisrael, but he won't touch its soul. But if Napoleon should win, it might be good for the body of Klal Yisrael, but its soul will suffer."

When the French invasion threatened to overrun Russia, the Baal HaTanya was forced to flee from Liady and seek refuge from Napoleon's wrath. He wandered from place to place until the fortunes of war turned and Napoleon, defeated by the fierce Russian doggedness and the harsh Russian winters, retreated from battle.

Reb Shneur Zalman passed away on the 24th of Teves, in the year 1812, at the age of sixty-eight. He was succeeded by his son, Rabbi Dov Ber Shneur, known as the Mittler Rebbe.

"If the Czar wins, it will be bad for the body of Klal Yisrael, but he won't touch its soul. But if Napoleon should win, it might be good for the body of Klal Yisrael, but its soul will suffer."

Map of Chassidic centers and Yeshivos throughout Eastern Europe

Chapter

28

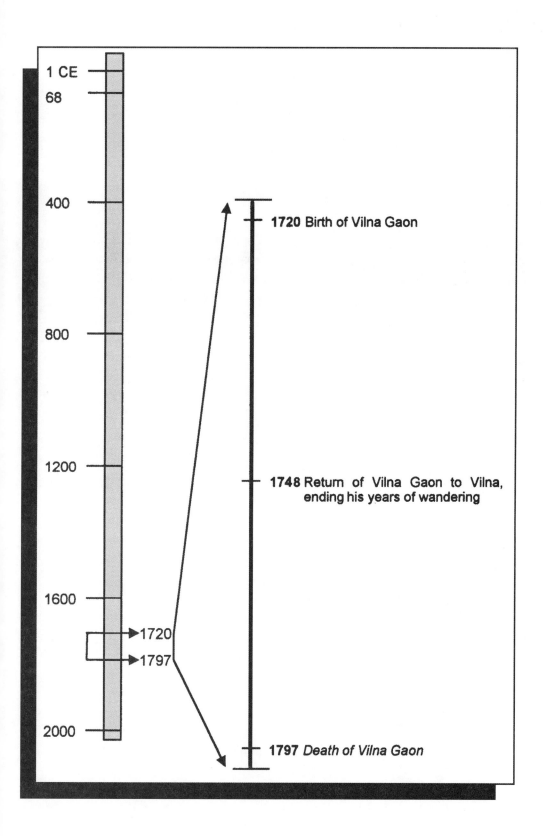

1 CE

68

400

1720 Birth of Vilna Gaon

800

1200

1748 Return of Vilna Gaon to Vilna,
ending his years of wandering

1600

1720

1797

2000

1797 *Death of Vilna Gaon*

"The Master of Destinies from the beginning of Creation knew that this child would bear a fruit destined to become a tzaddik and gaon of world-wide fame. In his merit was she kept alive."

Child of Destiny

On a cold winter day, an inhabitant of the village of Seltz, Poland, was crossing a bridge over the River Rom-nova near Slutzk, carrying her infant daughter on a pillow in her arms. Suddenly, she stumbled and lost her balance. The pillow with the sleeping baby slipped out of her hands and fell into the river below. The people around her were horror-stricken, certain that the baby would drown. To their amazement, however, the pillow re-emerged with the baby still on top of it. They pulled the child out and quickly brought her into a house, where they attempted to restore her frozen body to normal temperature. In their excitement, they brought the baby too close to the oven and almost burned her feet. Only through another miracle did she survive.

The author of *Aliyos Eliyahu* notes that "the Master of Destinies from the beginning of Creation knew that this child would bear a fruit destined to become a tzaddik and *gaon* of worldwide fame. In his merit was she kept alive."

The baby Trayne grew up to become the wife of Reb Shlomo Zalman and the mother of Eliyahu, the Gaon of Vilna.

The Gaon of Vilna, known as the Gra (**G**aon **R**abbi **E**liyahu), was born on the first day of Pesach, in 1720. He was named Eliyahu after his great-grandfather, Rabbi Eliyahu HaChassid, who distinguished himself not only by his scholarship, but by his extraordinary character traits (hence the title *HaChassid*, the pious one). Rabbi Eliyahu HaChassid descended from the famous author of the *Be'er HaGolah*, Rabbi Moshe Rivkes.

It was not until the Gra's time, however, that Vilna received the distinction of being known as the "Yerushalayim" of Lithuania.

Vilna, the capital of Lithuania, was a relatively young Jewish community; Brisk, Grodno and Minsk had preceded it by many years. Nevertheless, it was a city with a rich history of Torah Sages, including the Shach and the Gaon's own ancestors. It was not until the Gra's time, however, that Vilna received the distinction of being known as the "Yerushalayim" of Lithuania.

As a young boy, Eliyahu soon showed signs of extraordinary genius. He initially received standard tutoring at the local *Cheder*, but he outgrew his teachers rapidly. At the age of three, he was already deeply learned in all five books of the Chumash. When he finished all of Tanach, his father taught him Gemara, as well as trained him in *pilpul*, using debates and give-and-take as a method of learning.

At the tender age of six, Eliyahu repeated a Torah lecture in the big shul of Vilna in the presence of all the rabbinic leaders of the city. While the attending scholars marveled at this unprecedented feat by a young boy, one of the more prominent leaders suggested that this remarkable accomplishment only served to highlight Eliyahu's phenomenal memory. Could this small boy actually create a Torah discourse of his own? Eliyahu was sent into the next room with a new section of Gemara to study. An hour later, the six-year-old emerged from the room and delivered a brilliant lecture. Stunned, the eminent rabbis in the audience agreed that Eliyahu was, indeed, a genius.

Rabbi Avraham Katzenelenbogen, Rav of Brisk, was in Vilna at the time and heard Eliyahu's discourse. He approached Rabbi Shlomo Zalman and suggested that he allow him to undertake the further training of this amazing boy. With Rabbi Shlomo Zalman's approval, Rabbi Avraham took Eliyahu to Kaidan, where his father, Rabbi David Katzenelenbogen, and Rabbi Moshe Margalis, author of the *P'nei Moshe*, taught Eliyahu what they knew. All too quickly, however, Eliyahu outgrew his teachers. By the age of ten, Eliyahu had learned all of Shass with its commentaries, and had begun to learn the *Chochmas HaNistar*, the study of Kabbalah.

The Gaon's *Hasmadah*

His superior mental capacity was matched only by his enormous *hasmadah*, his diligence and concentration. One famous story relates that at the age of eleven, Eliyahu made a commitment to learn two *masechtos* by Simchas Torah. When the night of Simchas Torah arrived, Eliyahu realized that he had not even begun to fulfill his promise. After the *hakafos*, he retired to a room in the back and began to study.

One of the older rabbinic leaders of the community found the young boy studying. He watched Eliyahu for a moment, noting with displeasure that the boy turned through the pages of the Gemara as if he were casually reading them. Frowning, he stepped into the room and scolded Eliyahu for his lack of respect to the Gemara.

"This is not the way to study. You must examine and concentrate on every phrase, each word, every letter! How else can one properly learn?"

Calmly, Eliyahu suggested that the older man test him on the material he had already studied. Skeptically at first, then with increasing wonder, the scholar turned the pages back and forth, quizzing the boy on matters of increasing complexity. Eliyahu was able to answer them all. Well before dawn, Eliyahu completed the second *masechta* with a feeling of satisfaction. He had fulfilled his promise.

From the day Eliyahu reached the age of Bar Mitzvah, he kept his eyes glued to his *sefarim*. He kept the shutters of his windows closed, learning by candlelight all day long so he would not be tempted to look outside and turn his mind away from his learning. The room where he studied remained unheated in winter; often, he immersed his feet in cold water so he would not be overcome by drowsiness. All of his energy was devoted to one thing: learning Torah.

The Gaon's devotion to learning was such that he never slept more than a few hours a night. In his later years, he managed with only two hours sleep per night. His concerned relatives protested, citing the halachah brought in the Rambam's Mishneh Torah *that a person generally should sleep eight hours a night.*

Rabbi Eliyahu refuted this argument easily. He opened a copy of Iyov *and pointed out the passuk (3:13): "Yashanti az yanuach li." He interpreted this to mean that if he slept the numerical value of "az," eight, it would be sufficient for "li," which has the numerical value of forty. A total of eight hours of sleep would enable a person to function properly for forty hours which is a total of two days.*[1]

The Gaon kept a logbook within reach; whenever he felt he had wasted time from his Torah learning, he recorded those squandered minutes. On Yom Kippur, he would examine the logbook and add up the total number of minutes that he had wasted over the year. Reliable

---

1. The Gaon used this argument to refute the Rambam's *p'sak halachah*; as noted above, he himself slept only two hours per day.

By the age of ten, Eliyahu had learned all of Shass with its commentaries and had begun to learn the Chochmas HaNistar, the study of Kabbalah.

On Yom Kippur, he would examine the logbook and add up the total number of minutes that he had wasted over the year. Reliable sources affirm that during an entire year, the total amount of time lost never exceeded two hours.

Chapter
29

The author of the Chayei Adam, Rabbi Avraham Danzig, stated that if the Gaon had lived in the time of the Tannaim, he would have rated among the greatest of them.

sources affirm that during an entire year, the total amount of time lost never exceeded two hours. Even then, Rabbi Eliyahu was terribly upset. Eyewitnesses reported that he shed bitter tears of regret in his confession on Yom Kippur and solemnly resolved to do better in the future.

Every day, the Gaon reviewed one hundred pages of Gemara. Every month he completely went over all of Talmud Bavli. Before the holidays, he learned the *masechta* relevant to the occasion. Indeed, it is no wonder that the combination in Rabbi Eliyahu of extraordinary diligence and a prodigious mind produced a Torah Sage of such enormous dimensions. The author of the *Chayei Adam*, Rabbi Avraham Danzig, stated that if the Gaon had lived in the time of the Tannaim, he would have rated among the greatest of them.

The range of Rabbi Eliyahu's expertise went beyond the Talmud and commentaries, covering the branches of Kabbalah as well. It is known that he was capable of using his expertise in Kabbalah to perform supernatural acts, but he refused to do so. The one exception was when the famous *Ger Tzedek,* Count Potocki, languished in prison, awaiting death at the stake for his "heinous crime" of converting to Judaism. The Gra sent the *Ger Tzedek* a message, offering to free him from prison through the power of Kabbalah. Count Potocki declined the offer, preferring to make the supreme sacrifice of dying for the sanctification of Hashem's Name.

The Gaon's phenomenal erudition enabled him to make a unique contribution to the clarification of Talmudic problems that had arisen in the course of time. Almost inevitably, printing errors had crept into the text of the Talmud over the years, creating glaring contradictions that baffled many Torah scholars. These errors certainly needed to be corrected, but who would commit himself to such an awesome responsibility and dare to erase anything printed in the holy text of the Gemara?

The Gra undertook this gigantic task, sorting out the various discrepancies and deciding which version was the correct one. With access to a large number of different editions, he was able to compare the contradictions and determine which one was accurate. With his vast memory, he could track the wrong versions and find the reason that the mistake had been made in the first place. The caution and respect with which he treated this undertaking is evident in his requirement that a change could be approved only if it clarified a minimum of fifteen questions that had arisen over the other version that he rejected. In the field of Kabbalah, he was even stricter; a correction could be made only if it resolved at least 150 questions.

Years of Wandering

As the Gaon's fame grew in Vilna, he grew concerned that the constant praise and flattery would stain his character with self-glorification. In an effort to escape this danger to his integrity, the Gra followed the custom of many of the great Torah Sages of that time; he donned simple clothing and left his hometown to travel incognito.

The Gra's efforts to avoid honor were not particularly successful. As *Chazal* say, "if one flees from honor, honor will run after him."[2] Wherever the Gaon went, the Rav of the town would inevitably notice the quiet stranger sitting in a corner of the shul, immersed in Gemara. Rabbi Eliyahu

_____
2. *Eruvin,* 13b.

would be invited to the rabbi's home for a meal; all too soon, his great wisdom would become recognized and he would have no choice but to move on to a different destination.

When the Gaon reached Germany, he stopped in Berlin. One of the Gaon's friends, who knew that Rabbi Eliyahu had acquired an extensive knowledge of science and mathematics in his effort to study the more technical matters of the Gemara, told a professor at the Berlin University that a Jewish Sage had arrived in the city who was probably a greater expert at mathematics than the members of the university staff. Skeptical and contemptuous, the professor arranged for a meeting with the Gra. The professor had a mocking smile on his lips as he outlined a problem which had been puzzling the leading minds in the country. Calmly, the Gaon took a pencil and paper and immediately drew the solution to the problem. From then on, despite the pervasive contempt towards religious Jews, in the scientific circles of Berlin, the name of Rabbi Eliyahu was mentioned with the greatest respect and awe. (He wrote the sefer *Ayil Meshulash* about triangles.)

In the course of his travels, the Gaon seized the opportunity to examine many different editions of both the Talmud Bavli and Yerushalmi. In later years, this proved to be of tremendous assistance in his search for an accurate version of the Gemara.

In the year 1748, the Gaon returned to Vilna. He settled in his tiny study and learned. Despite his refusal to accept any title, he was the spiritual leader and authority in a city teeming with Torah scholars. He gave only one Torah discourse each week, but his word was accepted as law without question.

In his later years, Rabbi Eliyahu attempted to fulfill his innermost desire: to settle in Eretz Yisrael. He traveled through Prussia and reached as far as the city of Konigsberg before he abruptly returned to Vilna without explanation. Different explanations have been offered for the Gaon's inexplicable change of heart. One suggestion is that there were halachic difficulties involved in settling in Eretz Yisrael at that time. Another, more mystical theory is that the Gaon possessed the soul of Moshe Rabbeinu, who was forbidden to enter Eretz Yisrael. Whatever the reason, the Gra returned to Vilna and remained there for the rest of his life.

The Gaon in Vilna

In 1756, when the Gaon was only 35 years old, he received an urgent letter from Rabbi Yonasan Eibeschutz of the Hamburg community, requesting the Gra's help in mediating his dispute with Rabbi Yaakov Emden.[3] The Gaon refused to intervene, feeling unworthy of rendering a decision involving two of the great Torah leaders of that time. Still, this request addressed to him from a city hundreds of miles away is a measure of the international fame that this young master had gained.

Many years later, the Gaon was again approached and asked to intervene in public affairs, this time in the fight against the Haskalah movement, which threatened to undermine the religious stability of Jewish life in every city in Poland and Lithuania. The Gaon did not hesitate to join the battle. He devoted all his energy to fight the Haskalah movement, which threatened to leave a destructive influence on future generations. Since he was older and the effects of the conflict would have strong impact on coming generations, he could not refuse.

3. See Chapter 33.

The Gaon devoted all his energy to fight the Haskalah movement, which threatened to leave a destructive influence on future generations.

He personally supervised and participated in the public burning of Wessely's publication.

The doctor smiled and replied, "Er halt in maseches Kailim [he is holding by maseches Kailim]." When Rabbi Yaakov bent to listen to his patient's heart, he also heard him whispering the words of Maseches Kailim. Even in his very last moments, the Gaon never stopped learning.

Chapter
29

A new book had been published recommending a number of changes in the curriculum of the education of Jewish children. The author of the book was Naftali Hertz Wessely, a student of Moses Mendelssohn. Although the title of the book was innocent enough: *Divrei Shalom Ve'emes,* "Words of Peace and Truth," the Gra immediately recognized Wessely's work as nothing less than an attempt to destroy the time-honored system of Torah education. He personally supervised and participated in the public burning of this publication.

In another instance, the Gaon risked his reputation and safety to support the members of his community who were opposed to the appointment of Rabbi Shmuel ben Avigdor as Rav of Vilna. He felt that this man was unfit to hold such a responsible position. As a result, the Gaon suffered harassment and was imprisoned on trumped-up charges of receiving pay from community funds without performing services. He was arrested a second time when the authorities suspected that the Gaon had taken part in the rescue of the son of one of the community leaders from the clutches of Christian missionaries. Such setbacks could not stop Rabbi Eliyahu from accomplishing any task he set out to achieve. The same purity of heart and intentions which caused him to disagree with the Chassidic movement[4] also drove him to fight extensively against the Haskalah and to protect his people from any taint of corruption from the *Maskilim* as well as from the Christians.

The Gra was not particularly interested in publishing his responsa. His literary contributions were generally in the form of footnotes, containing references to other parts of the Talmud or *Zohar* that raise

questions or provide answers to some seemingly inexplicable contradiction. The various references serve as a guideline, opening new dimensions for an indepth comprehension of the subject.

Some of the Gra's publications are:
Hagahos HaGra (on the Gemara)
Beur HaGra (on the Shulchan Aruch)
Beur HaGra (on the Zohar)
Beur HaGra (on Mishlei)
Beur HaGra (on Nach)
Dikduk Eliyahu (on Hebrew grammar)

The Gaon's Last Days

Shortly before Rosh HaShanah, in the year 1797, the Gaon became sick with what was to be his final illness. The Gra had always refused medical aid, explaining that even if the Torah permits medical help by a trained physician, the preferred method is to seek help directly from Hashem through prayer and repentance. This time, however, seeing the agonized expressions of his family and students, the Gaon relented and agreed to have a physician summoned for an examination.

One of the foremost Jewish doctors, Rabbi Yaakov Lubashitz, came to Rabbi Eliyahu's tiny home. As was customary in this era before the invention of the stethoscope, the doctor bent over and pressed his ear against the Gaon's chest to listen to his heartbeat and other vital signs. As the doctor straightened, one of the men in the anxious crowd gathered around the bedside asked, "*Vu halt er?* [Where is he holding?]"

The doctor smiled and replied, "*Er halt in maseches Kailim* [he is holding by *maseches Kailim*]." When Rabbi Yaakov bent to listen to his patient's heart, he also

---

4. See Chapter 28.

heard him whispering the words of *maseches Kailim.* Even in his very last moments, the Gaon never stopped learning.

Before Sukkos, the Gaon examined the *esrog* that was brought to him and held it in his trembling hands before bursting into bitter tears. He insisted that his bed be moved into the sukkah, where he held tightly to the *arba'ah minim,* refusing to let go of this last, precious mitzvah until the moment of his passing.

Before his death on the fourth day of Sukkos, the Gaon gathered the strings of his *tzitzis* in his hand and whispered, "How difficult it is to part from this world, the world of deeds! For a few coins, one can fulfill such an easy mitzvah of *tzitzis* and reach the highest level of closeness to Hashem. Can I have such a chance in the world of *neshamos,* even for the highest price?"

It was the last thing he said.

> *"The Vilna Gaon? If you vil nor, if you truly have the will, you too can become a gaon."*

The Gaon's Legacy

The Gra helped create a climate of extraordinary Torah study in the Vilna community. His influence in this direction went far beyond the city boundaries and the Gaon's own lifetime. The Volozhin Yeshivah, known as the "Mother of Yeshivos," was established by the Gra's most prized student, Rabbi Chaim of Volozhin. It is no exaggeration to state that every Yeshivah that exists today is the spiritual heir of the Gaon, based on the model created by Rabbi Eliyahu's foremost pupil.

The Gra's life, his dedication to Torah, and his piety serve as a shining model to every Jew who aspires to achieve some degree of perfection in his lifetime. Rabbi Eliyahu's own quip in Yiddish still endures as a word of encouragement today: "The Vilna Gaon? If you *vil nor,* if you truly have the will, you too can become a *gaon.*"

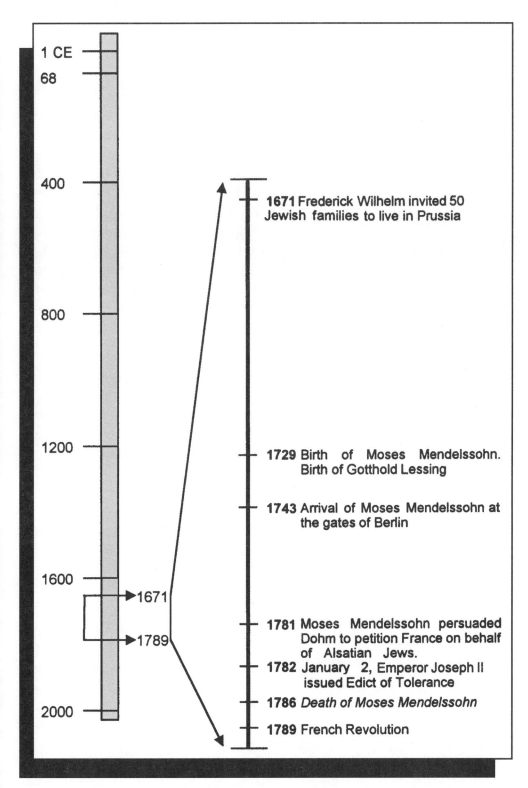

Moses Mendelssohn:

The Darkness of Enlightenment

1 CE	
68	
400	**1671** Frederick Wilhelm invited 50 Jewish families to live in Prussia
800	
1200	**1729** Birth of Moses Mendelssohn. Birth of Gotthold Lessing
	1743 Arrival of Moses Mendelssohn at the gates of Berlin
1600	
1671	
1789	**1781** Moses Mendelssohn persuaded Dohm to petition France on behalf of Alsatian Jews.
	1782 January 2, Emperor Joseph II issued Edict of Tolerance
	1786 *Death of Moses Mendelssohn*
2000	**1789** French Revolution

Moses Mendelssohn:

The Darkness of Enlightenment

The situation of the Jew in exile underwent tremendous changes. Materialism beckoned; at the same time, the walls of the ghettos, both figuratively and literally, began to develop cracks and finally fell, offering incredible new opportunities that had never even existed before in Jewish life.

Until the concept of equal rights and individual freedom sank into the general consciousness, most Europeans lived out their lives in squalor and poverty, comforted by the knowledge that Christianity promised them a wonderful afterlife. The Christian clergy, even as they lived in wealthy, comfortable homes, preached of the spirituality of man, emphasizing the need to disassociate oneself from the crass materialism of the mundane world in order to concentrate on the world to come. Education, science, and the liberal arts remained luxuries reserved exclusively for a few individuals.

As feudalism decayed and humanism and materialism began to develop, the general attitude began to change. The common man was no longer interested in a pious, simple life that would be rewarded in the world to come; instead, the new, vast frontiers beckoned towards a life of materialism and enjoyment. This new perspective towards wealth and expensive pursuits was in direct opposition to the frugal life encouraged by Christianity. Instead of abandoning the enticing opportunities suddenly available, many Europeans chose to abandon religion instead. The common man remained a devout Catholic, but there was a new and definite antagonism to religious discipline.

The Jew did not escape this new way of thinking. The situation of the Jew in exile underwent tremendous changes. Materialism beckoned; at the same time, the walls of the ghettos, both figuratively and literally, began to develop cracks and finally fell, offering incredible new opportunities that had never even existed before in Jewish life. The Gentile world found itself forced to come to terms with the Jews as fellow human beings. At the same time, however, the Jew, suddenly faced with equal rights and an open society, was tempted to adjust his eternal lifestyle to the so-called demands of the times. Indeed, many freedoms were offered for the specific purpose of enticing the Jew away from his religion.

As long as the Jews had remained locked in the tightly-woven life of their communities, they had remained largely impervious to outside influences. Now, however, the twin dangers of open horizons and sudden interest in material wealth led to a real danger of assimilation. With each new and different progression, the Jews found themselves coping with new crises and new problems, some of which are still begging for a solution today.

The crisis in Germany was sparked by Moses Mendelssohn (1729-1786), recognized as the forerunner of the Reform movement. In spite of a possibly promising beginning, Mendelssohn's influence on Jewish history was disastrous. An analysis of Jewish life in northern Germany during the eighteenth century, together with a close look at his unusual personality, helps explain the unhappy enigma of Mendelssohn.

Prussia

While Poland reeled under the onslaught of the Cossacks,[1] the German States were trying to recover from the devastation of the Thirty Years' War (1618-1648). This conflict, possibly one of the most destructive in European history, resulted from the antagonism between the Roman Catholics and the Lutheran Protestants. In the aftermath of the destruction and rampant brutalities of the warring

---

1. See Chapter 25 for further details.

armies, the German States slowly began to rebuild.

Prussia, one of the larger North German States, was ruled by the Hohenzollern Dynasty from the capital, Berlin. Like other neighboring states, Prussia had expelled all its Jews in the fourteenth century, when the Black Death had swept across Europe and the hapless Jews had served as a convenient scapegoat for the hideous disease.[2] In the year 1671, however, Frederick Wilhelm of Hohenzollern, one of the shrewdest kings of that dynasty, invited fifty exiled Jewish families to live in his kingdom. A limited number of Jews were actually given permission to settle in Berlin, where they were assigned a "Jews' street" at the eastern edge of the city and were given permission to build synagogues.

For the next 262 years, until the rise of Hitler, Jewish citizens lived in Prussia and contributed to the welfare of the state. Despite their relatively easy economic position, Jews in Prussia still suffered the uneasiness and dangers of exile. Only a small portion had the good fortune to be granted official status as "Protected Jews," with their right to live in Prussia protected by law; even these were restricted in their activities and were forced to pay special taxes. They were forbidden to have more than a certain number of children, and only one child could inherit the privileged status of his father. Their other children, as well as those Jews who had stolen into the city without permission, could best be categorized as "tolerated" Jews, living in constant fear of persecution and expulsion.

The low esteem in which the Jews were held can be gleaned from an entry made by the gatekeeper at the Rosenthaler Gate in his logbook one October morning in the year 1743: "Today six oxen, seven pigs, and one Jew passed through the Rosenthaler Gate." The lonely Jew whose entry was thus registered was a fourteen-year-old boy named Moses Mendelssohn, who had made the five-day journey on foot from the city of Dessau.

Mendelssohn's Early Life

Moses Mendelssohn was born in Dessau, the oldest son of Reb Mendel, who managed to earn a meager living from writing Sifrei Torah. The family boasted that its ancestors included the famous Rabbi Moshe Isserles, who wrote the *Mappah* on the *Shulchan Aruch* in the sixteenth century.[3] Moses, named after this illustrious ancestor, showed early signs of great potential. He had a prodigious mind and diligent study habits.

When Moses was still a young boy, his father sent him to the best teacher available: Rabbi David Hirsch Frankel, the author of the *Korban HaAidah,* a commentary on the Talmud Yerushalmi. This great scholar recognized the potential of his new pupil and took him under his wing, teaching him both the Talmud with its commentaries and the Rambam's *Moreh Nevuchim.*[4] Such a decision was in direct opposition to the long-standing

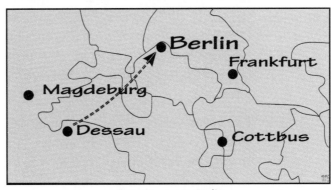

From Dessau to Berlin

The lonely Jew whose entry was thus registered was a fourteen-year-old boy named Moses Mendelssohn, who had made the five-day journey on foot from the city of Dessau.

2. See Chapter 21.

3. See Chapter 24.
4. See Chapter 12.

*The Jews made a
frenzied effort to
become socially
acceptable. In an
effort to become
"educated," they
studied German
language and
German culture,
spending less and
less time on the
study of Torah and
Judaism.*

rabbinic injunction against the study of philosophy by someone below the age of twenty-five.[5] Perhaps the study of the *Moreh Nevuchim* drove Mendelssohn to confront the dilemma between faith and doubt at an age far too young to understand and comprehend; troubled by unanswered questions, Mendelssohn began to seek answers outside the Yeshivah walls in places that would eventually corrupt his outlook on life.

Mendelssohn might have succeeded in squelching his doubts in the quiet city of Dessau, but when Rabbi Frankel accepted a position as Rav of Berlin, Mendelssohn was determined to follow his master to the capital city. His parents reluctantly gave their permission for their gifted son to leave home. With their blessings and prayers, and only one gulden in his pocket, he set out to walk to Berlin.

The Jews of Berlin had developed a unique relationship with the Gentiles of that city. It was a haven for intellectuals and entrepreneurs, invited by the Prussian rulers and accorded the status of "Protected Jews." With this backing and relative wealth, the Jews made a frenzied effort to become socially acceptable. In an effort to become "educated," they studied German language and German culture, spending less and less time on the study of Torah and Judaism. With Mendelssohn's arrival in Berlin and his subsequent impact on society, a new, unhappy chapter in Jewish history came into being.

For seven years, Mendelssohn struggled to eke out a meager living. As a student in Rabbi Frankel's Yeshivah, he was provided with a scant ration of bread which had to last him for an entire week; Rabbi Frankel found him a

5. See Chapter 18. Evidently, the Rashba's decree had been generally accepted for future generations.

part-time job to provide him with some additional money.

The common language among Jews in Germany at that time was Jewish-German, not German. Mendelssohn perceived this as a cultural barrier which separated him from the Gentile world. In an effort to surmount this obstacle, he provided himself with German books and began to teach himself the language. The small income he earned was spent to buy more books in German, French, and Latin.

The turning point came when a prosperous silk merchant, Isaac Bernhardt, offered him a position as tutor to his children. Mendelssohn moved into Bernhardt's house, developing a close and devoted relationship with the family. Bernhardt, who eventually discovered that his tutor had talents beyond Hebrew scholarship, offered Mendelssohn a position as bookkeeper, eventually making him a full partner in the firm.

For the first time in his life, Mendelssohn was in wealthy, comfortable circumstances. He was able to devote all his time to his studies, extending his horizon into the areas of philosophy and science of his German contemporaries. Ironically, despite his open leanings towards liberalism, he still spent time learning in Rabbi Frankel's Yeshivah. He was already one of the most learned men in his day, but he did not achieve recognition until he met a German poet, Gotthold Ephraim Lessing.

Lessing, the Liberal

Lessing, the same age as Mendelssohn, was the son of a Protestant vicar who had defied his parents' desire that he enter the ministry, and had become a dramatic poet. He maintained a liberal attitude; while he resented the church's stratified dogmas and religious formalism, he was not anti-religious. Lessing's liberalism and disgust with the inflexible Church prejudices led to a sympathetic attitude towards the Jews. Disturbed to see an entire nation cut off from European culture for narrow-minded religious reasons, he plunged into the fight to win human rights for the Jews.

Lessing became friendly with many of the rich Jews in Berlin. One of them, who customarily played chess with the German poet, grew annoyed at Lessing's constant wins over the chessboard. One evening, the wealthy Jew knocked over the pieces in disgust and exclaimed, "Come to my house tomorrow and I'll introduce you to an opponent who is worthy of you!" The next evening, Moses Mendelssohn was introduced to Lessing for the first time. It was the beginning of a lifelong friendship with far-reaching consequences for the two men as well as for German-Jewish coexistence.

Lessing believed that the three major religions of the world—Christianity, Islam, and Judaism—were equally valid and truthful. Adherents of each religion should learn to tolerate the others, no attempt should be made to force one's religion on one's fellow man, and no one should be penalized for adhering to the traditions of his ancestors. Mendelssohn embraced Lessing's theories, discarding the Torah of his youth for a new set of devastating values.

The Publication of *Biur*

By this point, Mendelssohn was associating with a group of Jewish intellectuals called *Maskilim*. The *Maskilim* (from the root *sechel,* i.e., logical thinking) claimed that truth is acceptable only if it

passes the test of logic. While this prerequisite did not necessarily mean a total rejection of Torah and mitzvos, it did result in a thorough, unnecessary analysis of the mitzvos and a selective commitment to keep only those that seemed consistent with logical thinking. Such thinking was, ironically enough, referred to as "enlightenment"; even while they turned their backs on the light of Torah, the *Maskilim* claimed to be more educated and informed than the religious Jews of their day.

Mendelssohn's first act of reform seemed to be little more than a minor infraction of halachic practice. The Prussian government had decreed that no one should be buried before waiting a period of three days after his death. Jews, on the other hand, follow the dictum of the Torah, which states, "For you should bury him on the same day." [6] Mendelssohn, in his efforts to avoid antagonizing the Prussian government, felt that the Jewish practice of burying the deceased without delay should be put aside; the Jews in Berlin ought to abide by government orders. In fact, "*dina d'malchusa dina,* the law of the government is law" as mentioned in the Gemara, only applies if it does not contradict the law of the Torah.

The matter was brought to the attention of the German rabbinic leaders, who obviously decided against Mendelssohn. In spite of a number of sharp letters of protest and reprimand, Mendelssohn stubbornly maintained his position, declaring that he was competent enough to disagree with the Torah Sages of his day. This rebellion against *daas Torah* may seem insignificant, but it was the beginning of a breakdown of halachic discipline which opened the door to more serious breaches, serving as an example

6. *Devarim,* 21:23.

The Enlightenment resulted in a thorough, unnecessary analysis of the mitzvos and a selective commitment to keep only those that seemed consistent with logical thinking.

Chapter
30

Despite his own piety and learning, he was convinced that the literary quality of the Bible was so sublime that it deserved worldwide acclaim as a masterpiece of literature.

to Mendelssohn's followers. With Mendelssohn's death, a campaign of systematic reform began.

While Mendelssohn personally disapproved of abandoning any of the mitzvos, he did believe that the Jewish people at large would continue to suffer from the strangulation of ghetto life as long as they did not break down the language barrier that separated them from the Gentiles. Jewish-German, which was essentially a medieval German dialect with a generous sprinkling of Hebrew, had become unintelligible to the educated German citizen. Mendelssohn devised a devious strategy to introduce the German language to traditional Jews without risking rejection as a formal language course. With an open line of communication, Mendelssohn was convinced that all Jews would follow Lessing's line of thinking and accept all religions and peoples as equal.

Mendelssohn's scheme was simple. He published a Chumash with a translation in classical German. Religious Jews would see nothing wrong in learning the language of the country as part of the process of learning Chumash, especially as he adopted the Yiddish custom of using Hebrew letters for the German translation. Such a *sefer* would be accepted as a religious textbook; once religious Jews realized that the language they had learned from his Chumash was the same one used in German literature, it would be a short step to reading German books and conversing with German intellectuals.

As a crowning touch, generous sponsors enabled Mendelssohn to offer free distribution of his work, called *Biur,*[7] or clarification. With his *sefer* on the market, Mendelssohn sat back and eagerly awaited results.

---

7. So called because of Mendelssohn's *perush* in Hebrew.

Reaction was not long in coming. The leading Torah scholars of the day recognized Mendelssohn's intentions and condemned *Biur,* putting the *sefer* in *cherem.* While the Chasam Sofer remarked that he was able to find only one passage in *Biur* that qualified as heresy, the book was designed as a vehicle to teach a foreign language and open the door to German culture. Mendelssohn's *sefer* could not be compared to the works of Torah Sages who had published in the vernacular of their day in an effort to make Jewish learning more accessible to those who did not understand Hebrew; Mendelssohn was using the Torah to further his own intentions.

Mendelssohn had an additional objective as well. Despite his own piety and learning, he was convinced that the literary quality of the Bible was so sublime that it deserved worldwide acclaim as a masterpiece of literature. By translating the Chumash into classical, poetic German, he could reveal the beauty of the Torah to the educated Gentiles of his generation. In essence, his translation stripped the Chumash of its holiness, leaving it as a mere triumph of literary mastery.

Mendelssohn's religious philosophy was hopelessly warped. He still studied Torah and remained highly observant, but his attitude towards Tanach was corrupted by his association with the liberal sophisticates of his day. In a letter to John Zimmerman, he remarked, "But in regard to a great many of the Psalms, I must admit that I simply do not understand them. The ones I find easiest to understand include many which I must classify as very mediocre pieces of poetry, incoherent verses, repetitions of the same idea *ad nauseam,* and abrupt transitions and modulations which no amount of inspiration could justify."

It is difficult to comprehend how a man whose religious piety was admired by Rabbi Yonasan Eibeschutz and Rabbi Yechezkel Landau, author of the *Noda B'Yehudah,* could possibly express dissatisfaction with Tehillim for its literary content. There is no doubt that he remained a strict observer of mitzvos until the end of his life. He defended his religion with great courage and persistence even in the face of open challenge by his intellectual Gentile friends, who did not understand why he would not take the "logical" step of conversion when so little separated the two religions. Yet this same man admired Tanach solely for its literary content!

His twisted outlook is painfully manifest in the way he brought up his six children. They were brought up in a glitter of social life, moving in upper-class circles and meeting their father's Gentile friends in lavish and prominent salons. The result? With only one exception, Mendelssohn's children converted to Christianity and married non-Jews. His grandson Felix, acclaimed as a famous composer, was the son of a Christian mother.

The Beginning of Emancipation

Mendelssohn's bleak record is relieved by one thing only: his work in promoting emancipation among European Jewry in his lifetime.[8] With the French Revolution only a few years in the future, the conscience of the world had been awakened to the injustice done to the underprivileged segments of society, including the Jews. Emancipation was in the air. With Mendelssohn's fame and mastery of the German language, his talents made him a pioneer in the effort to improve the legal status of Jews among the nations.

In 1781, Jewish leaders from Alsace approached Mendelssohn and asked him to write a petition to the French Government, requesting that the Jews be granted equal rights. Mendelssohn deferred the project to a Christian friend, a Prussian official named Christian Wilhelm Dohm, whose influence and penmanship would be most effective. The resulting work was entitled *Concerning the Improvement of the Jews' Civilian Status.*

In this book, Dohm concedes the "obvious faults" in the social behavior of the Jew, but blames these faults on the persecution to which they are subjected. Dohm is confident, though, that once the Jews are granted freedom by the authorities, all their faults will disappear. While the publication of this book did not have the desired effect on the French authorities, Joseph II of Germany was impressed by Dohm's proposals. He had already abolished the taxes levied against the Jews. Now, as a result of Dohm's publication, he went a step further.

On January 2, 1782, Joseph II issued his famous Edict of Tolerance, in which some of the worst restrictions imposed on the Jews during the Middle Ages were rescinded. Jews were given the right to earn a living as artisans, merchants, and manufacturers. They were entitled to lease land and cultivate it, although ownership of land was still denied to them unless they accepted baptism. Jews were admitted to colleges and universities, albeit with the purpose of encouraging them to forsake their

8. See Chapter 32 for a discussion on whether the emancipation of the Jews was truly beneficial.

Moses Mendelssohn:

The Darkness of Enlightenment

The conscience of the world had been awakened to the injustice done to the underprivileged segments of society, including the Jews. Emancipation was in the air. With Mendelssohn's fame and mastery of the German language, his talents made him a pioneer in the effort to improve the legal status of Jews among the nations.

Chapter

30

heritage and become integrated into the Gentile culture.

Many of Joseph II's other ordinances were also aimed at assimilation. Jews were liable for conscription into the army. They were required to use the German language exclusively in their bookkeeping and business correspondence and to adopt German family names. While the Jews were certainly aware of the ulterior motives of Joseph II's liberal edict, their gratitude and relief at the lifting of their overwhelming restrictions led to an outpouring of appreciation and a vast surge in the Emperor's popularity. The walls of the ghetto were weakening; with the French Revolution in 1789, many barriers were shattered completely.

Mendelssohn believed that all his actions were devoted to helping his fellow Jews. The Reform movement that arose after him, as well as the ignominious actions of his children, illustrate his error all too clearly. Rabbi Shimon Schwab writes, "We clearly see Torah and mundane knowledge were to Mendelssohn like two mountain ridges running parallel to each other, yet each totally independent of the other."[9] Mendelssohn failed to understand that the glittering charm of liberalism is no substitute for the eternal truth of Torah.

---

9. *The Jewish Observer,* Tammuz-Av, 1987.

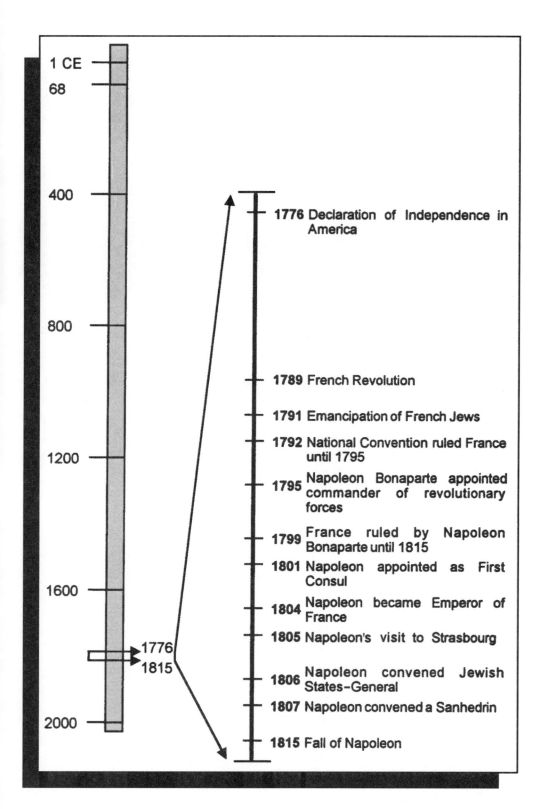

1 CE
68
400
800
1200
1600
2000

1776
1815

1776 Declaration of Independence in America

1789 French Revolution

1791 Emancipation of French Jews

1792 National Convention ruled France until 1795

1795 Napoleon Bonaparte appointed commander of revolutionary forces

1799 France ruled by Napoleon Bonaparte until 1815

1801 Napoleon appointed as First Consul

1804 Napoleon became Emperor of France

1805 Napoleon's visit to Strasbourg

1806 Napoleon convened Jewish States-General

1807 Napoleon convened a Sanhedrin

1815 Fall of Napoleon

Chapter
31

Napoleon and the Jews

(1799-1815)

There would no longer be Jews, merely "Frenchmen of Mosaic persuasion," Frenchmen who practiced the Jewish religion.

In the wake of the French Revolution in 1789, the French found themselves plunged into a series of wars against the leading monarchies of western Europe: Prussia, Austria and Great Britain.[1] Rival factions vying for power within the country only served to weaken them further. In their desperation, the embattled revolutionary Jacobins were temporarily willing to forego their dreams of democracy in order to alleviate the chaos which crippled the country. Napoleon Bonaparte, formerly little more than a lieutenant in the French artillery, became commander of the revolutionary forces in 1795. After a series of brilliant successes in battle, General Bonaparte was vested with dictatorial powers as First Consul. When a coalition against the French Revolutionary government was formed by Great Britain, Austria, Russia and Sweden in 1804, Napoleon declared himself Emperor of France.

Unlike many other would-be dictators who had arisen against the Jews in European history, Napoleon had no intention of eradicating the Jews of France. With his lifelong ambition to go down in history as the greatest conqueror since Alexander the Great of Macedonia and Julius Caesar of ancient Rome, Napoleon was too shrewd to discount the invaluable assistance of the Jews. Instead, he intended to assimilate this troublesome people to the point where Jews as a national entity no longer existed. In this manner, he would solve the problem of the Jews and at the same time retain his image as the great liberator and benefactor of a liberal French nation. There would no longer be Jews, merely "Frenchmen of Mosaic persuasion," Frenchmen who practiced the Jewish religion.

Napoleon's first encounter with Jews had not been, from his point of view, a pleasant one. In a military campaign, Napoleon crossed the Mediterranean with an armada of ships and laid siege to Acco, the heavily fortified gateway to the Holy Land and the East. In an effort to enlist the help of the Jews living in the Holy Land at that time, Napoleon promised them that if they would support him against the Turks and help him gain possession of the Holy Land, he would let them rebuild their Temple. Jews, however, traditionally support the governing authority of their host country, following the ruling of *dina d'malchusa dina,* the laws of one's resident kingdom must be obeyed.[2] Napoleon eventually had to give up his ambitious plans for the Middle East and could never forgive the Jews for what he considered their betrayal.

Napoleon's next encounter with the Jews did not take place until 1805, when he visited Strasbourg, capital of Alsace.[3] Gentile debtors had borrowed sizable amounts of money from the Jewish moneylenders without intending to repay these debts in the first place. Now, with their newly-won equal rights, the Jews were actually entitled to confiscate land as security against the many outstanding loans. The Gentile debtors were furious. How dare the Jews demand their money back! With indignation, these Gentiles approached Napoleon and demanded that he rescind the equal rights that would allow the Jews to confiscate the property they fully deserved.

Napoleon, however, did not immediately comply. If he could somehow win the Alsatian Jews to his side by apparently supporting them in this situation, his

---

1. See Chapter 32 for further details on the French Revolution.

2. *Nedarim,* 28a.
3. See Chapter 32 for more on the Jews of Alsace.

secret plot to cause their complete assimilation might gain credence. With this in mind, he prevailed on the courts to postpone any action on the monies owed to the Jews for one year, thus forcing the Jews to remain amenable as he raised hopes that he might rule in their favor.

The Jews of Alsace, however, remained stubbornly religious. As Napoleon realized that these Jews would not respond to his efforts toward assimilation, he struck back with vicious spite and dictatorial ruthlessness. With a scribbled stroke of his pen, Napoleon abrogated all privileges the Jews had gained during the Revolution. He canceled debts owed to the Jews in Alsace and imposed a series of restrictions on their daily lives: they could not move or engage in commerce. Disgusted with Jewish obstinacy, Napoleon determined to assimilate the Jews, no matter what!

The Notables' Assembly and the "Sanhedrin"

In 1806, Napoleon ordered that an assembly of Jewish notables, to be called a "Jewish States-General," be convened in Paris. One hundred-eleven representatives arrived from France and Italy; some were rabbinic leaders, but the majority were laymen. All the participants were uneasily aware that the government officials in charge of the meetings intended to make sure that any decision reached by the Jews would coincide with the Emperor's wishes.

The Notables' Assembly convened on Shabbos, July 29, 1806. Despite the desecration of the holiness of Shabbos, every single delegate appeared for the opening session. Such cowardice only served to strengthen the government's position in its efforts to countermand religious law in conformity with Napoleon's desires.

Napoleon presented a list of twelve questions to the Jewish delegates. The questions were obviously designed to force what the French considered to be the proper answers. If the Jews did not want to answer correctly, Napoleon had a number of threats in reserve to ensure that the Jewish delegates would be persuaded to change their minds.

None of the answers given by the Jewish delegates were based on Jewish law. Instead, under duress, they reluctantly gave Napoleon the answers he wanted to hear, all too aware that the Emperor's mind was closed to anything else.

Is it lawful to have more than one wife? The delegates replied that in France, the decree of Rabbeinu Gershom remained in force. No Jew could have two wives.[4]

Is divorce allowed by Jewish religion even in contradiction to French law? The assembly hassled over this delicate issue before they finally decided to answer that any *get,* or halachic divorce, would be dependent on governmental approval.

Are mixed marriages recognized by Jewish law? The representatives knew that Napoleon wanted a positive reply to this question, but how could they possibly agree? The conciliatory answer was that the Jews would consider such a marriage binding, but would not encourage such a union.

Would the Jews consider Frenchmen their brothers? The answer was a definite yes.

Would the Jews acknowledge France as their country? Again, a resounding yes.

4. See Chapter 13.

As Napoleon realized that these Jews would not respond to his efforts toward assimilation, he struck back with vicious spite and dictatorial ruthlessness. With a scribbled stroke of his pen, Napoleon abrogated all privileges the Jews had gained during the Revolution.

Chapter
31

The high point was reached when all seventy-one members declared unanimously that all Frenchmen were their brothers and that they were ready to defend their fatherland until death.

Would the Jews fight with France against her enemies, even if Jewish soldiers were on the other fronts? Helplessly, the representatives agreed to this as well.

Are there any dishonorable professions (such as money-lending, brokerage, commercial trading, etc.) which the Jews would be willing to give up? Should Jews take interest from Jewish debtors? What about non-Jewish ones? Under coercion, the delegates declared that Jews should not take interest even from non-Jews, despite the Torah ruling that allows a Jew to lend money with interest to a Gentile. This ruling effectively destroyed one of the few remaining livelihoods left to the Jews: money-lending.

Who elects the rabbis? What was the jurisdiction of the rabbis? Napoleon urged that the rabbis give up their status of autonomy in all administrative matters and confine their decisions to halachic questions. By destroying the *kehillah,* or Jewish community, the Jews would easily fall prey to assimilation.

While Napoleon was generally pleased with the results of the Assembly, he realized that outsiders would recognize that most of the answers had been given under coercion. Some grand gesture would be necessary to fire the imagination of Jews all over the world and give enthusiastic consent for his scheme of total assimilation. A chance remark by one of the notables about the ancient Sanhedrin caught Napoleon's fancy. Why not create a Sanhedrin of his own that would eventually serve as the final arbiter of Jewish law (according to Napoleon, of course) all over the world?

Napoleon invited seventy-one Jews to become part of his Sanhedrin. Invitations were sent to all countries, but responses came only from France and its satellite countries. The Sanhedrin was made up of forty-six rabbis and twenty-five laymen, both religious and non-religious. In order to grant an extra measure of legitimacy to his Sanhedrin, Napoleon appointed a prominent and scholarly Rav, Rabbi David Zinsheim of Strasbourg, to serve as its head. The venerable rabbi had no choice but to accept this appointment, but used his position of influence to dilute the significance of this event and secretly sabotage its decisions.

Napoleon's love for grandiose pomp and publicity asserted itself. He designed special robes for the members of the Sanhedrin and had them wear the triangular admiral's hat on their heads. As in the ancient Sanhedrin, the delegates sat in a semi-circle. Napoleon, pleased with his attempt to mimic the Sanhedrin of old, ordered the Jews to convene. They met in the winter of 1807.

The same twelve questions that had been imposed on the Assembly were asked again. Imperial commissioners supervised the Sanhedrin's meetings and made sure that all questions would be answered to Napoleon's satisfaction. The high point was reached when all seventy-one members declared unanimously that all Frenchmen were their brothers and that they were ready to defend their fatherland until death.

The Sanhedrin was still in session when news of the disastrous war in Russia first reached Napoleon's ears. Impatient and annoyed at the unfavorable reports from the Russian front, Napoleon had no time to complete his pet project of the Jews' assimilation. After only ten sessions, the Sanhedrin finally dissolved. Its only positive achievement was the establishment of "consistories" in every large Jewish community that were made responsible for the financial needs of religious institutions dependent on the control of the Consistory in Paris.

While the Sanhedrin failed to achieve Napoleon's purpose, it did catch the attention of European Jewry. When Napoleon conquered Poland, many Chassidic Jews flocked around the army and offered their help. Even more important, Napoleon's temporary position as an immensely powerful international figure, coupled with his evident fascination with the Jews, forced many monarchies in Europe, such as that in Russia, to refrain from their typical policies of oppression.

This breathing spell lasted for only a few short years. With Napoleon's ignominious death, many of the Jewish rights that had been granted in his lifetime were reversed. Nevertheless, the seeds of equal rights had been planted in European minds. With this beginning, eventual emancipation could not be far behind.

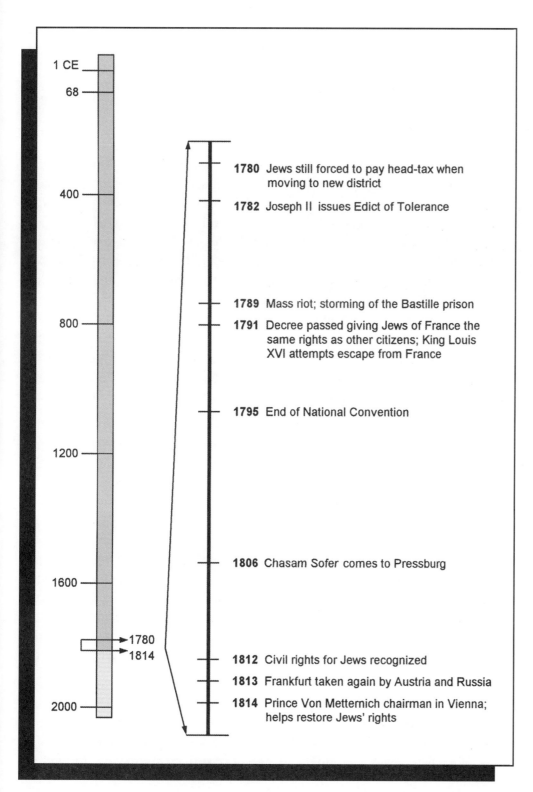

1 CE	
68	
400	
800	
1200	
1600	
2000	

1780 Jews still forced to pay head-tax when moving to new district

1782 Joseph II issues Edict of Tolerance

1789 Mass riot; storming of the Bastille prison

1791 Decree passed giving Jews of France the same rights as other citizens; King Louis XVI attempts escape from France

1795 End of National Convention

1806 Chasam Sofer comes to Pressburg

1812 Civil rights for Jews recognized

1813 Frankfurt taken again by Austria and Russia

1814 Prince Von Metternich chairman in Vienna; helps restore Jews' rights

Chapter 32

Emancipation: Really a Blessing?

The first European country that officially declared equality for all its inhabitants, including the Jews, was France in the aftermath of the French Revolution. Other countries were not far behind.

Over the centuries, rights for the Jews had usually been a direct result of hefty bribes and a reluctant, grudging admission that the Jews played a crucial, integral part in the economies of most countries. Concessions were usually little more than the right to be protected against mobs, and permission to deal in trade. In many locations, Jews had to pay a special "tolerance tax" for the very privilege of living in the land of the Gentiles. As late as 1780, they were still forced to pay a head-tax whenever they moved into a new district. Hard-won privileges often vanished with the crowning of a new ruler or even with a convenient "memory lapse" by the current leader. Many cities throughout Europe were completely off limits to the Jews, including Berlin, Paris, Vienna, and Strasbourg.[1] Exception was made only for rich Jews and those who had received special permits in return for a specific contribution to the common welfare.

In some places, Jews were denied permission to engage in trades and businesses except money-lending, tenant farming, and peddling wares. In many cities, such as Rome and Frankfurt, Jews still lived in ghettos. The ghetto gates were opened for a few hours during the day and locked tightly at night and on holidays. Other places still obligated Jews to wear humiliating badges of identification. They were frequently hampered in their rights to marry and establish new families.

With all these restrictions stretching back well into the Middle Ages, it is not surprising that actual equality for the Jews seemed beyond their reach, although

Mendelssohn had managed a small start in Germany with the Edict of Tolerance in 1782.[2] The first European country that officially declared equality for all its inhabitants, including the Jews, was France in the aftermath of the French Revolution. Other countries were not far behind.

"Liberty, Equality, and Fraternity"

The French Revolution was generated by the lowest of the three social classes, or "estates," into which the French population had been divided. While the nobility reveled in luxury under the feudal system and the clergy remained largely immune to the upper classes' rapaciousness, the common man, the third estate in France, suffered the same deprivations as the peasants of other European countries. With the onset of the Crusades and the opening of new horizons, the sullen acceptance of the common man's miserable life turned to a seething resentment that grew ever closer to the boiling point.

The French kings did nothing to defuse the tension. Instead of supporting the people, they used their power to live in luxury and decadence. Indeed, the name Louis XIV has become a synonym for unsurpassed greed. With the underlying philosophy of Humanism and the electrifying news of the Declaration of Independence in America—the astonishing new concept that "all men are created equal"—feelings of anger and rebellion surged until the third estate of France virtually exploded.

On July 14, 1789, a mass riot took place with the storming of the Bastille prison. The fledgling rebellion eventually resulted in the annulment of French royalty. The "Constituent Assembly," formed by

---

1. An exception to this rule occurred in Berlin in 1671. A limited number of Jews were given permission to settle in a restricted area called *Judengasse,* or "Jews' Street," and were allowed to build synagogues.

2. See Chapter 30.

the leaders of the Revolution, worked on a new French Constitution based on three principles that became the slogan of the new order: "Liberty, Equality, and Fraternity." Incredibly enough, some of the leaders suggested that the Jews should actually be included.

This proposal resulted in uproar. Emancipate the Jews? How was it possible? The Jews in southern France, with their pitiful eagerness to be fully accepted by their Gentile counterparts, might fit into the great scheme of a free France, but how could the Alsatian Jews possibly find a niche in the Revolution?

A brief glance at the background of the French Jews since the time of their expulsion in 1291 will help explain the controversy that surrounded their emancipation in France.

Quiet Renewal

The proud Torah dynasty of Rashi and the Baalei Tosafos[3] had been cut off by the French expulsion, but a small group of Jewish refugees from Spain trickled into the country after the onset of the Inquisition and the expulsion in 1492. They settled in southern France and soon became an integral part of the economy, albeit as inferior citizens. Hefty taxes allowed them to pursue their religion in peace. These Spanish Jews, with their own *mesorah* damaged by the persecution of the Inquisition, had little devotion to Torah and mitzvos.

The Jews of Alsace-Lorraine, however, were on an entirely different level. Unlike the Spanish refugees, whose religion had been suffocated by Torquemada, this second group of Jews had lived in relative peace in the German States until the eighteenth century, when Germany had ceded the province

of Alsace-Lorraine to the neighboring country of France. The Jews suddenly found themselves to be citizens of a new country, but their positive devotion to religion remained unchanged.

A clear indication of their determination to cling to their religion is the appointment of Rabbi Aryeh Leib ben Moshe, author of the *Shaagas Aryeh,* as the rabbi of Metz, one of the largest communities of Lorraine. The Shaagas Aryeh, as Rabbi Aryeh Leib was called, left his native Poland to serve as rav in Metz during the last years of his life. His great scholarship was matched by the extreme poverty in which he lived.

There is one tale that gives a clear picture of the Shaagas Aryeh's penury: He once visited Rabbi Yehoshua Falk, author of the *P'nei Yehoshua,* in Frankfurt-on-Main. The P'nei Yehoshua was a wealthy man who lived comfortably in a lavishly furnished home. The two Torah Sages spent several hours in a profound discussion of a Talmudic subject.

At one point, the P'nei Yehoshua remarked with admiration, "I cannot understand how any person could know as much as you know!" The Shaagas Aryeh, embarrassed by the compliment, looked at his host and replied, "To tell you the truth, I am wondering how a person like you could know so much!"

The P'nei Yehoshua, surprised, waited for an explanation. Smiling a little, the Shaagas Aryeh said, "You must understand, I live in very modest circumstances. I have only a tiny room with a table, a wooden bench, and my *sefarim.* I sit and learn until late at night; when I grow tired, I lie down on the hard bench and close my eyes for a few minutes. All too soon, however, the hard surface of

The Jews suddenly found themselves to be citizens of a new country, but their positive devotion to religion remained unchanged.

---

3. See Chapters 14 and 15.

The Jews of southern France were overjoyed and grateful for this welcome mat spread out to accept them as equals. They threw themselves into the progress of the Revolution, volunteered for military service, and gave freely of their means for the defense of the young republic.

the bench is painful enough to make me get up again. I sit up once more and resume my learning. Such a system can produce favorable results."

The Shaagas Aryeh glanced around the room at the soft carpet and the luxurious couches. "But you, Reb Yehoshua!" he continued. "When you get tired, you lie down on your comfortable bed, rest your head on the pillow and cover yourself with a down quilt. What could happen, G-d forbid? You could sleep all night, until the next morning! Is it not a wonder that, despite your wealth, you know as much as you do?"

The Shaagas Aryeh was known to have a rapid turnover of *shamashim,* attendants employed by the congregation to look after the needs of their rabbi. Once, one of the men in the community respectfully asked why no *shamash* lasted more than half a year in the rabbi's home.

The Shaagas Aryeh explained. "You know, of course, that the Talmud states that one should never use a scholar for personal service. That is why I always insist that my *shamash* be completely ignorant. After a while, however, I discover that my *shamash* is not ignorant at all! How can I keep him as my personal attendant?"

The answer was indeed obvious. A completely ignorant *shamash* might be hired, but constant, close association with a man as great as the Shaagas Aryeh inevitably taught the *shamash* a great deal in both theory and practice. Within six months, the ignorant man had turned into a true Torah scholar and had to be replaced!

When the question of emancipation arose, the Jews of Provence were eager to do anything necessary for the cause; the Jews of Alsace-Lorraine, however, were not willing to compromise their

religion as the price for emancipation. This resistance, coupled with the age-old prejudice against the Jews ingrained in the minds of the Gentile world, was not so easily overcome by the liberal spirit that pervaded the Revolution. For two years, the debate about this issue raged in the National Assembly. Finally, on September 28, 1791, just two days before the dissolution of the National Assembly, a decree was passed stating that the Jews in France, under the leadership of the Jacobins, would enjoy the same rights as all the other citizens, including active participation in the political life of the nation, and the right to vote and to be elected.

The Jacobins

Jacobins were members of a radical political club that played a controlling role in the French Revolution. At its onset, this group was in favor of continuing the rule of a constitutional monarchy, but with King Louis XVI's attempt to escape from France in 1791, the Jacobins turned against any form of royal rule. The National Convention, which lasted until 1795, became the ruling body of France under the Jacobins.

By and large, the Jews of southern France were overjoyed and grateful for this welcome mat spread out to accept them as equals. They threw themselves into the progress of the Revolution, volunteered for military service, and gave freely of their means for the defense of the young republic. Inevitably, this new contact with the Gentiles misled many Jews. Some compared the new laws advanced by the French leaders to the laws given on Sinai, acclaiming the philosophy of freedom as a new religion which would replace the Judaism of their fathers. The Republican calendar, which declared every tenth day as a festival, tended to do away with the observance of Shabbos as a day of rest. Extremists even went so far as to have the performance of *bris milah* forbidden by law.

The Jacobins' rule did not last very long. In their haste to overturn the old system, with no orderly transition to a new form of government, they created a chaotic situation. Into this vacuum stepped Robespierre, a Jacobin possessed of a despotic and fanatic personality. Robespierre ruled with an iron hand, using mass killings to intimidate his opponents into submission. He was particularly ruthless against members of the clergy, as well as against anyone whose religious principles he considered contrary to the new outlook of the Revolution. Jews shared the fate of other Frenchmen who were thrown into dungeons or executed by the guillotine. In this atmosphere of terror, many Jews went to extremes to renounce Judaism in a frantic effort to prove that they were worthy revolutionaries.

Eventually, Robespierre's reign of terror came to an end. France, finding itself threatened with civil war from within and military attack from the imperial countries without, eagerly looked to the military leadership of a young Corsican named Napoleon Bonaparte. Napoleon's original intention to cajole the Jews into abandoning their religion to become "Frenchmen of Mosaic persuasion" failed, but the repercussions of his attempts to rule the entire world eventually echoed across all Europe, as French soldiers spread their new ideas across the continent.[4]

Holland

The debate whether to grant full citizenship to the Netherlands' Jews was addressed in a Dutch National Assembly convened shortly after the French invasion at the end of the eighteenth century. Napoleon's scheme to erase the lines between Jew and Gentile demanded that the Jews be treated equally, whether they wanted it or not. There was no need to abolish oppressive decrees and declare the Jews entitled to basic human rights; the Jews had played a vital role in the Dutch economy for a long time, receiving humane treatment ever since the sixteenth century, when the first fugitives of Spain fled there for sanctuary. Still, despite the rights the Jews enjoyed, they were still considered aliens.

The price of citizenship was high. For centuries, the Jews in Europe had kept to themselves; their communities were close-knit structures in which the Jews collected their own taxes, financed their own educational systems, and paid the salaries of their religious leaders without interference from the government. The Jews realized that the price for full rights of citizenship would be a demand to give up the structural independence of their communities, which had given them the strength to maintain their religion and Jewish lifestyle. More religious than the Jews of southern France, Holland's Jews were unwilling to pay for their independence with their faith.

The Reform Jews of Holland, although small in numbers, were determined to rule otherwise. A splinter group of "enlightened" Jews proceeded to build their own synagogues and reform the order of their prayers. In protest, the Jewish community of Amsterdam took them to court, contending that according to established precedence, it was illegal to secede from the traditional congregational systems. In response, the French Ambassador declared that there was nothing to

4. See Chapter 31 for more details on Napoleon.

Robespierre was particularly ruthless against members of the clergy, as well as against anyone whose religious principles he considered contrary to the new outlook of the Revolution. Jews shared the fate of other Frenchmen who were thrown into dungeons or executed by the guillotine.

Chapter
32

The local government demanded compensation in a lump-sum payment of twenty times the annual special taxes they had formerly paid.

discuss. He ordered the Dutch Assembly to pass a decree that gave Holland's 50,000 Jews full civil rights. The traditionalists lost their case; henceforth, all Jews were subjects of the Dutch government and had to answer to the Dutch laws only.

Germany

Westphalia was the first German province, albeit under French rule, to grant full rights to the Jews. Napoleon established an independent government there, headed by Jerome Bonaparte, his brother. Other parts of Germany reluctantly followed, granting only partial relief from the oppressive restrictions against its Jews. Those concessions were wrested from the local authorities only after long debates and negotiations. For example, in 1812, the authorities of Frankfurt agreed to permit Jews to walk in the city parks. They canceled many of the special taxes which the Jews had to pay, allowed them to live outside of the ghetto, and agreed to let Jews found new families without restrictions. In return, the Jews had to pay a high price for these grants. The local government demanded compensation in a lump-sum payment of twenty times the annual special taxes they had formerly paid.

This hard-won independence came to an abrupt end a single year after the Jews had paid the tremendous tax. With Frankfurt retaken by the combined armies of Austria and Russia, Napoleon's concessions to the Jews vanished. By 1813, all former restrictions were restored.

With Napoleon's defeat by Austria, Russia, and Prussia, many of the concepts of

One of the representatives innocently suggested a minor amendment to the reading of the motion: "in the states" should be changed to "by the states."

equal rights and individual freedom fell quickly by the wayside. Those freedoms that did survive the upheaval were not usually granted to the Jews.

When the representatives of the different empires met in Vienna under the chairmanship of Prince Von Metternich (1814-1815), the Jews worked feverishly to restore the hard-won rights that were in danger of being abolished. As notables streamed into the city, Viennese Jews entertained the guests at lavish social affairs and presented their case. Jewish lobbyists came to Vienna from every country, expert orators with the power to persuade through words. With these and other tactics, the Jews managed to put the Jewish question before an international congress for the first time in history.

Although Metternich was favorably inclined towards the Jews, their victory proved to be short-lived. The motion before Congress was the question of whether the newly won civil rights should be preserved in the German states which had granted them. While most agreed to this measure, one of the representatives innocently suggested a minor amendment to the reading of the motion: the phrase *in the states* should be changed to *by the states*. No one recognized the importance of this apparently insignificant change until it was too late.

In most German states, the emancipation of the Jews had been forcibly imposed by the occupying French in Napoleon's ongoing campaign to win world Jewry to his side. Once the French had been defeated and the legitimate government was restored, any reforms introduced by the French were automatically invalidated. If the motion had been passed with the phrase *in the states,* this would not have mattered; since the Jews had been liberated in these German states, that alone would have been sufficient to warrant continuance of their privileges. With the new amendment reading *by the states,* however, any reform imposed by a power that was not the legitimate ruler was automatically invalidated.

Prussia had not been defeated by Napoleon, but the French spirit of liberalism did seep into the general consciousness, eventually influencing Prussian officials to abolish some of their traditional biases against the Jews. In 1812, the Prussian government officially recognized the civil rights of the Jews, with the exception of access to service in the government.

Other sections of the German Empire remained under old regimes that continued their heavy oppression of the Jews. Even in those provinces, however, a more liberal attitude began to take hold. Despite Napoleon's downfall, his attitudes and efforts had radically changed the European outlook toward the Jews. Coupled with the social and economic changes associated with the Industrial Revolution and the rise of the labor movement, the various populations of the European continent were forced, almost against their will, to revise their thinking, affecting the status of European Jews and gradually leading to their full emancipation.

The Industrial Revolution

The power of feudalism, the prevailing economic system in Middle Europe, had faded; new horizons in the Far East and West had opened channels of commerce. A new source of income developed, based on trade rather than on the cultivation and sale of agricultural products. Following the success of the Netherlands in this venture, other countries slowly adopted mercantilism as the principle means of profit. The invention of machinery and the emergence of factories changed a basic way of thinking: Wealth was no longer measured in terms of acreage and production, but in terms of money earned.

This new system proved highly beneficial to the Jews. In the feudal system, Jews were rarely allowed to own land, nor to become members of the professional guilds; essentially, they were forcibly restricted to a poor status. With no possibility of owning land or following a profession, many Jews used their ingenuity to promote and develop worldwide lanes of trade by exporting to and importing from the colonies overseas. The Jew still remained a figure to be hated and despised, but with trade assuming a major role, pragmatism asserted itself in an eagerness to employ Jewish help in the newfound economic system.

In addition, attitudes towards the laborer, who produced the goods which were traded, began to change, giving rise to the labor movement. In contrast to the feudal serf who was treated almost as a slave, the industrial worker became a "partner" in the rising affluence of the European countries. This elevation of the "third estate" to a level of importance generated sympathy for other, hitherto oppressed groups, including the Jews. The governments of Europe were forced to recognize and reckon

Wealth was no longer measured in terms of acreage and production, but in terms of money earned.

Any reform imposed by a power that was not the legitimate ruler was automatically invalidated.

The Jew still remained a figure to be hated and despised; but with trade assuming a major role, pragmatism asserted itself in an eagerness to employ Jewish help in the newfound economic system.

Chapter

32

*The emancipation
of the Jew
remained political,
not social*

*Emancipation
forced the Jews to
abandon the
independent
control that each
congregation held
over its important
public institutions.*

with this powerful movement rooted in the dignity of the common man.

All this, however, could not change one basic fact: the emancipation of the Jew remained political, not social. The governments of Europe may have reluctantly accepted the necessity of granting equal rights to the Jews, but the common man of the "third estate" still clung to the age-old prejudices ingrained by centuries of Christian hatred.

There were exceptions where social emancipation preceded political equality. In England, for example, over 150 years before the beginnings of emancipation in Europe, Menashe ben Israel failed to obtain official permission for readmittance of the Jews into the country. At the same time, however, Jewish merchants quietly moved to England and were accepted with complete equality as collaborators in the colonial expansion of the British Empire. In Holland, Jews were accepted on equal social terms even before the French Ambassador signed the decree.

The question of the common man's reluctance to accept the equality of the Jew must be coupled with another, more disturbing consideration: was the emancipation beneficial or harmful to the Jewish nation?

Daas Torah: The Wider View

It is obvious that emancipation brought many improvements to the conditions of Jewish exile. New opportunities arose to allow the Jews to live an easier, more comfortable life. On the other hand, emancipation forced the Jews to abandon the independent control that each con-

*As Jews became
gradually absorbed
into the larger city
society, many
individuals chose
to shake off the
yoke of Torah and
mitzvos.*

gregation held over its important public institutions. Gone were the exclusive communal organizations and the social ties that held the individual members of the community together. As Jews became gradually absorbed into the larger city society, many individuals chose to shake off the yoke of Torah and mitzvos. Reform Jews, who had championed the cause of emancipation, found their ranks swelled by assimilated recruits in the wake of the new tempting opportunities available.

In order to properly evaluate the impact of emancipation upon European Jewry, one must turn to *daas Torah,* the authentic opinion of our Torah leaders. Only these great Sages, with their wisdom and ability to discern the ultimate impact of current events, can advise the Jewish nation how to react.

When Napoleon, the self-styled "Great Liberator" of the Jews, marched against the Russian Czar, Rabbi Shneur Zalman of Liady, founder of Chabad, prayed for the victory of the Russian forces. As French soldiers advanced, the Baal HaTanya retreated with the Russian Army. His comments as quoted in Chapter 28[5] were of clear and pure Torah insight: physical oppression can be overcome; spiritual destruction cannot.

Rabbi Moshe Sofer, known as the Chasam Sofer, came to Pressburg, Hungary, in 1806. As rabbi of that city, he built a mighty fortress of Torah; his Yeshivah attracted students from all of Hungary and Czechoslovakia. He fought tirelessly against the Reform movement and against the heresy that had made inroads into the Jewish communities.

---

5. See page 201.

It is said that when his students rushed into his study with the exciting news that the Jews would be granted emancipation, the Chasam Sofer's eyes filled with tears. Taken aback, his students asked why the prospect of equal rights was so upsetting. The Chasam Sofer explained with a parable.

"A prince was once expelled from the king's palace. He spent years living far from home, longing for the day when his father would grant him permission to return. Finally, he heard word from the king: his father had sent workers to the prince to build a magnificent mansion for his exiled son."

The Chasam Sofer sighed. "When the prince saw the new, beautiful palace, he wept, saying, 'As long as I lived in poverty, I could hope that my father would notice my plight and would soon invite me to come home. Now that he has built me a palace in this remote exile, it seems that I have to wait a very long time until I can expect to be allowed to return home.'"

Chapter
32

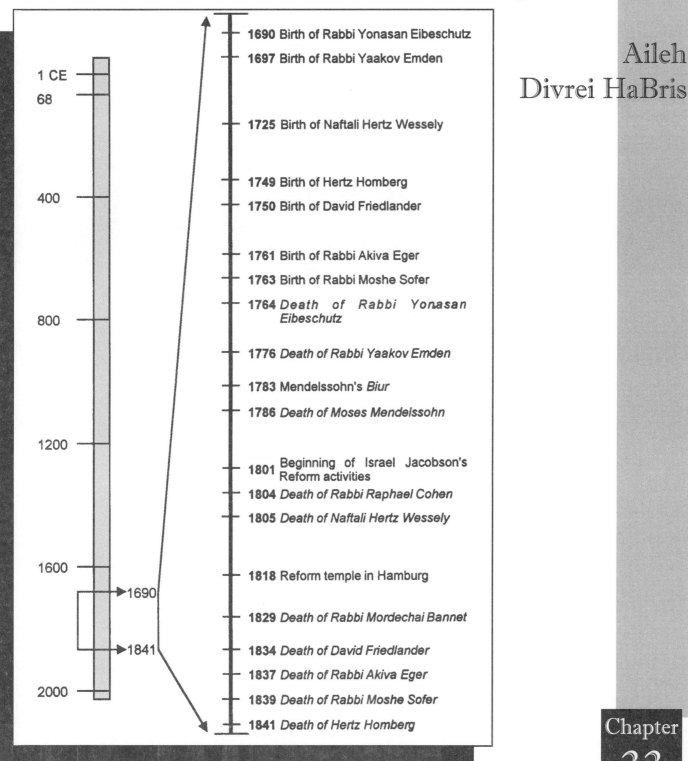

1690 Birth of Rabbi Yonasan Eibeschutz

1697 Birth of Rabbi Yaakov Emden

1725 Birth of Naftali Hertz Wessely

1749 Birth of Hertz Homberg

1750 Birth of David Friedlander

1761 Birth of Rabbi Akiva Eger

1763 Birth of Rabbi Moshe Sofer

1764 *Death of Rabbi Yonasan Eibeschutz*

1776 *Death of Rabbi Yaakov Emden*

1783 Mendelssohn's *Biur*

1786 *Death of Moses Mendelssohn*

1801 Beginning of Israel Jacobson's Reform activities

1804 *Death of Rabbi Raphael Cohen*

1805 *Death of Naftali Hertz Wessely*

1818 Reform temple in Hamburg

1829 *Death of Rabbi Mordechai Bannet*

1834 *Death of David Friedlander*

1837 *Death of Rabbi Akiva Eger*

1839 *Death of Rabbi Moshe Sofer*

1841 *Death of Hertz Homberg*

1 CE
68
400
800
1200
1600
2000

1690
1841

Chapter
33

> *Faith certainly does not come easily, but it is the Jew's duty to reinforce his faith until it becomes a strong inner conviction.*

ne of the most crucial aspects of Jewish survival is proper education. Hadrian tried to outlaw Torah learning during *Dor HaShmad*.[1] Likewise, the ignorance of many Marranos who fled from Spain led to unhappy results.[2] A much greater threat arose in the eighteenth century, both in Central and Eastern Europe, a danger whose ramifications are still felt in modern times. The Reform movement may have been induced originally by outside forces, but it reached its strongest potential within Jewish ranks. It created a rift within the Jewish people which is yet unhealed.

Reform "Enlightenment"

In the non-Jewish world, the Enlightenment began in the seventeenth century and reached its peak in the French Revolution at the end of the eighteenth century.[3] Its basic philosophy was to break away from tradition and from dogmatic belief, accepting as true and authentic only ideas that could stand the test of logic. Among its main proponents were Voltaire and Rousseau. Among the Jews, where traditionalism has been a fundamental principle of conduct throughout the ages, Enlightenment took hold much later, when this ideology was already declining among the non-Jews.

Its first enthusiastic Jewish proponents were Moses Mendelssohn and his followers. Mendelssohn, while holding fast to the discipline of religious observance, rejected the concept of faith without rationalization. In one of his main works, "Jerusalem," he expresses himself as follows: "There is not a single one of the Mosaic law's countless precepts and doctrines that says you should believe this or you should not believe this. They all say you shall do and you shall not do. For faith cannot be commanded; it accepts no orders. Doctrines change, but what Hashem requires of us is to act justly and to have mercy, and to walk humbly with your G-d, as the prophet Michah states."[4]

Mendelssohn conveniently overlooked another statement of another prophet, Chavakuk, who emphasizes that "the righteous person lives by his faith."[5] Faith certainly does not come easily, but it is the Jew's duty to reinforce his faith until it becomes a strong inner conviction. Each one of the Rambam's Thirteen Principles of Faith begins with the words *Ani maamin be'emunah sheleimah*, "I believe with a perfect faith...."[6]

Mendelssohn's fatal error was his belief that it was necessary to "modernize" the Jewish religion and to make accommodations for the emancipated Jew so that he could more easily fit into general society. The breaches he made seemed small at first, but they served as a signal to his students to allow further infringements. Eventually, the result was that the carefully preserved structure of thousands of years of Judaism broke down completely among a large portion of the Jewish world population.

With this perception, it is interesting to contrast the Christian Reformation generated by Luther and his followers and the Jewish Reform movement initiated by Mendelssohn. The Protestants were rebelling against falsifications that they claimed had been made under the leadership of the Roman Catholic Church;

---

1. See Chapter 2.
2. See Chapter 20.
3. See Chapter 30.

4. *Michah*, 6:8.
5. *Chavakuk*, 2:4.
6. See Chapter 12, where the Rambam stresses that any Jew who does not believe in any one of these thirteen principles is a heretic.

they wanted to return to what they claimed was their original Christian faith of the New Testament. The Jewish reformers were not trying to restore a corrupted religion to its original state; on the contrary, they wanted to change Jewish religion, to discard the Torah and make what they thought to be "improvements" for the ostensible purpose of allowing the Jew of the "Modern Age" to adjust to a new world.

Mendelssohn's Disciples

Mendelssohn's publication of *Biur* served an ulterior motive: to teach the Jews of Germany through the medium of Torah to understand and speak German.[7] With a knowledge of the German language, the Jew would have an entrance ticket to Gentile society. Mendelssohn's followers embraced his objectives and endeavored to accelerate the process.

First and foremost among these was Naftali Hertz Wessely, who believed in Mendelssohn's philosophy with fanatic dedication. When Emperor Joseph's Edict of Tolerance urged Jewish parents to enroll their children in secular schools, Wessely was determined to make this proposal a reality. He urged the Jews to comply by sending their children to special Jewish schools designed to provide a general, all-inclusive education. In his opinion, such a program was much more important to the Jews' general welfare than the knowledge of Torah. Wessely believed that it would be more than enough for Jewish children to learn selected parts of the Written Torah; the Oral Law and the vast tracts of *halachah* could be reserved for those who aspired to enter the rabbinate. His appeal to the Jews of Austria was published under the title *Divrei Shalom Ve'emes,* "Words of Peace and Truth," a title so innocent it

misled many readers. The abbreviation of the main part of this title is *shav,* meaning falsehood; many readers used this abbreviation as a sarcastic pun indicative of the book's true intentions.

The rabbinic leaders of Germany who raised their voices in violent protest against this destructive program included Rabbi Yechezkel Landau, Chief Rabbi of Prague, famous as the author of the *Noda B'Yehudah.* The Torah Sages demanded that the leaders of the Berlin community put Wessely in *cherem,* but the taint of the Reform movement had already contaminated Berlin to the point where the communal leaders refused to obey.

Triumphant, Wessely extended his sphere of influence as far east as Vilna in Lithuania, where his emissaries posed as religious Jews trying to improve the quality of Torah education. They were unmasked and driven out under the influence and pressure of the Gra's leadership, who personally supervised the burning of *Divrei Shalom Ve'emes.*

A second student of Mendelssohn's, Hertz Homberg, dismissed the attempt to persuade Austrian Jews to set up secular schools for their children. To his mind, force was a much better method. He went to the Austrian Imperial Government and proposed that he become an official imperial agent in charge of carrying out the imperial educational policy in Galicia. Thus, acting under official authority, Homberg attacked the Galician Jewish communities which had always guarded the education of their sons, faithful in every detail to a tradition of sanctity and purity.

Using threats, slander, and other underhanded methods, he tried to coerce the

---

7. See Chapter 30.

The abbreviation of the main part of this title is shav, meaning falsehood; many readers used this abbreviation as a sarcastic pun indicative of the book's true intentions.

Chapter
33

> *Homberg spitefully suggested that the government impose a tax on Shabbos candles as an additional pressure to force students into his school.*

Jews to convert their *Chadorim* into "enlightened schools." Homberg himself opened such schools in Galicia and staffed them with teachers who shared his outrageous philosophy. When his various efforts failed, Homberg spitefully suggested that the government impose a tax on Shabbos candles as an additional pressure to force students into his school. A tax on such a crucial item would hit everyone in the Jewish community.

A third student, David Friedlander, concentrated his efforts on the Berlin community, the cradle of Mendelssohn's Reform movement. In spite of the infectious ideology that Mendelssohn had promoted in this city, there were still a good number of Jewish families who sent their sons to the traditional *Cheder*. Friedlander hit upon the perfect method to induce the religious Jews to make the desired change: he offered those parents who could not afford to pay their *Cheder* tuition free schooling in the Reform schools. In these schools, the order of curriculum priority was as follows: language and literature of the country, then Hebrew and a smattering of Tanach. In higher grades, the emphasis was on general subjects without any study of Oral Law at all. As one might have expected, graduates from such schools became *Maskilim*,[8] drifting further and further away from true Judaism.

Friedlander, carrying the ultimate aim of the Reform movement to its most logical conclusion, went to the church in Berlin. He offered a proposal: he would

> *He offered those parents who could not afford to pay their Cheder tuition free schooling in the Reform schools.*

personally lead a group of his followers to baptism on condition that they would be exempt from accepting certain dogmas of the Christian faith which he considered irreconcilable with logic. His proposal was angrily refused. Disappointed, Friedlander turned to an all-out attempt to reform the Jewish religion instead. He offered his services to the government, suggesting they use his expertise toward granting separate status to Reform Jews.

This suggestion was made in 1812, when the Prussian government finally granted equal rights to its Jews. While Friedlander thought the time was auspicious, it also coincided with Napoleon's downfall, and the European monarchs were in no mood to "liberalize" anything. The Prussian king would recognize only two kinds of Jews: those who converted and became total Christians, and those who remained Jews in the traditional manner. Friedlander's efforts to create an official "middle ground" met with failure.

The *Maskilim* proved so brazen as to attempt to rewrite Jewish history itself. While the Congress of Vienna caused a temporary reversal of the trend towards individual rights,[9] this setback resulted in a peculiar twist to the concepts of fraternity and equality. Instead of promoting brotherhood between all peoples, a new spirit of nationalism and patriotism emerged. Each nation became fiercely aware of its own glorious significance in world events. A sudden, eager interest in history arose, as

---

8. The term *Maskilim* has the root *seichel,* the power of understanding. These groups put their own understanding ahead of strict religious beliefs. See Chapter 36 for an explanation of the differences between the *Maskilim* of the German "Enlightenment," and the *Maskilim* of the Russian "Haskalah."

9. See Chapter 32.

each nation feverishly investigated its roots to document and prove its greatness to the world at large.

The Reform Jews were not immune to the newfound fervor of discovering one's roots. But in this, as in other fields, the *Maskilim's* attempt to circumvent the religion that had shaped every aspect of Judaism since the beginning of its history proved disastrous. The true study of Jewish history demands the understanding that every event in each era is a direct result of the Jew's actions.[10] When the Reform Jews turned to the study of Jewish history, they utilized all of the scientific methods of research that they had acquired in the German universities, even as they turned a blind eye to the true causes that shape historic events.

Geiger and Graetz, the leading historians of the Reform and Liberal movements, tried to portray Jewish history as the product of a people who were driven by human impulses, ignoring the heritage of Torah and the crucial elements of faith that have always sustained the Jew in moments of crisis. It is unfortunate that Graetz's work on Jewish history remains the primary source for the majority of textbooks in use in Jewish schools. While the tremendous skill and patience he used in collecting the vast amounts of historical material and data is almost unmatched, his evaluations and judgement betray his arrogance, heresy, and ignorance, leaving his conclusions dangerously faulty.

Other disciples of Mendelssohn, among them his own daughter, abandoned not only Torah and mitzvos, but Jewish principles of morality as well. They spent their free time in the highly fashionable social salons where one could philosophize and socialize with the upper class of Christian society.

Mendelssohn's followers departed from the norm that had characterized Jewish life for millennia:

1) In education, where they trapped Jewish children in the net of heresy.

2) In religion, where they attempted to reform Judaism.

3) In their personal lives, where they tore down the boundaries of Jewish ethics and morality.

After laying the groundwork for their brazen assault on traditional Judaism in Europe, the *Maskilim* proceeded to undermine those Jews who remained loyal and steadfast in their adherence to Torah and mitzvos; the "stubborn" Jews, as the *Maskilim* derisively called them.

In Westphalia and the city of Frankfurt, for example, the *Maskilim* initiated laws forbidding Jews to pray in any synagogue except a Reform one. They forbade the use of any Chumash except Mendelssohn's *Biur*. They even had the audacity to forbid learning Chumash with Rashi, as well as prohibiting the use of traditional siddurim.

Thus began a new, painful era of oppression during exile: it was no longer merely Gentile versus Jew, but Jew against Jew. Fortunately, many of these shameful decrees were confined to isolated areas, but one can easily trace the beginning of Reform as a national movement in Germany to the establishment of the first Reform temple in the city of Hamburg in 1818.

Hamburg

Hamburg is the most important ocean harbor in Germany. Within the Confederation of German Provinces, it has special

It is unfortunate that Graetz's work on Jewish history remains the primary source for the majority of textbooks in use in Jewish schools... his evaluations and judgement betray his arrogance, heresy, and ignorance, leaving his conclusions dangerously faulty.

Chapter

33

---

10. See "Understanding Why," Chapter 25.

*A discussion
of the machlokes
between Rabbi
Eibeschutz and
Rabbi Emden
must be
approached with
the utmost caution
and respect.
Such men are
vastly beyond the
comprehension of
current times.*

status as a Hanseatic city-state established as a trade center for overseas commerce.[11] The government of Hamburg had always had a more liberal attitude towards the Jews, since it was less involved with the feudal system of the mainland, which had generated such sharp class distinctions.

The first Jews settled in Hamburg in the sixteenth century after the expulsion from Spain. They were of Sephardic stock. Ashkenazic Jews first lived in Altona, a sister city west of Hamburg, and also in Wandsbeck, on the eastern border of the city. Together, the three communities formed a united *kehillah* called A.H.W. (Altona, Hamburg, Wandsbeck), which was a bulwark of Torah and Judaism until Hitler, *yemach shemo,* destroyed these cities together with all other Jewish communities in Germany.

During the eighteenth century, the Jewish community of Hamburg was devastated by a distressing dispute with widespread ramifications. This dispute centered around two of the greatest Torah Sages of that era: Rabbi Yonasan Eibeschutz (1690-1764) and Rabbi Yaakov Emden (1697-1776). It should be noted that a discussion of the *machlokes* between Rabbi Eibeschutz and Rabbi Emden must be approached with the utmost caution and respect. Such men are vastly beyond the comprehension of current times.

Rabbi Yaakov Emden, known as the Yaavetz (an abbreviation of Yaakov ben Tzvi), was an illustrious Torah Sage who lived in the city of Altona. He was the son of Rabbi Tzvi Ashkenazi, the famous

Chacham Tzvi, known for his relentless, impassioned fight against the false messiah, Shabsai Tzvi, as well as against the subsequent cults that sprang up in his wake.[12] Like his father before him, the Yaavetz was fiercely on guard against anything that hinted of the corruption of Shabsai Tzvi.

In the year 1750, after serving as a member of the rabbinate in Prague and as Chief Rabbi of Metz, Rabbi Yonasan Eibeschutz came to Altona to serve as Chief Rabbi of the A.H.W. communities. He was honored and respected for his vast knowledge in Talmud and *halachah,* as well as his learning in Kabbalah. His reputation as a righteous Torah scholar spread far beyond the boundaries of the three communities.

During this time, an epidemic broke out in Hamburg, and childbearing women were adversely affected; many children were stillborn. Horrified and frightened, several women came to their Chief Rabbi for advice and assistance. Rabbi Eibeschutz gave these women *kameyos,* or amulets, that contained a kabbalistic text with blessings and prayers for a safe and healthy birth.

A man brought one of these *kameyos* to the Yaavetz, who carefully examined the kabbalistic text.[13] Rabbi Emden was dismayed to discover in the text a combination of letters that apparently alluded to Shabsai Tzvi. Concerned at the terrible danger of the possibility of a resurgence of such a cult, the Yaavetz denounced Rabbi Eibeschutz and had him put into *cherem.*

---

11. "Hanseatic" is a term denoting a member of a league of merchants of free cities organized to secure greater privileges in trading.

12. See Chapter 26.
13. In the wake of Shabsai Tzvi's perversions, any hint of Kabbalah was often met with suspicion. The Chassidic greats did much to dispel this distrust, but the misgivings still existed in the Yaavetz's time. See Chapter 26 for further details.

Rabbi Eibeschutz's attempts to defend his innocence met with failure; the community split in two as each member of the community rallied behind one or the other of the two scholars. The dispute spiraled out of control. The same fatal error that had been committed at other times in history occurred: Gentiles were brought into the conflict.[14] One faction appealed to the Danish king, who initially sided with Rabbi Eibeschutz before changing his mind and forcing him out of the community. In the end, the decision was reversed: the Yaavetz was forced to leave Altona and Rabbi Eibeschutz was restored to his official status.

What had begun as a *machlokes lesheim Shamayim*, a dispute for the sake of Heaven, was debased and degenerated into an ugly controversy that polarized the community and weakened the Jews of Germany at a time when a unified front was desperately needed to fight the Reform movement. Fifty-five years after Rabbi Eibeschutz's death, Hamburg reeled from a new, more horrifying scandal: the new Reform temple.

The Temple Dispute (1818)

In 1804, the last of the great rabbinic leaders of Hamburg, Rabbi Raphael Cohen, passed away. The *Maskilim* had grown in numbers and increased their pressure for reforms in the community during his tenure, but Rabbi Cohen had always managed to thwart their plans. Now, however, his passing left Hamburg defenseless against the poisonous influence of the *Maskilim.*

Israel Jacobson, a wealthy banker from Westphalia, was known and respected as a distinguished personality, deeply rooted in the Jewish faith. His spiritually empty upbringing left him without a true Torah background, but he retained a simple enthusiasm for ancient religious practices, particularly attending prayers in a synagogue. After Napoleon's downfall, Jacobson came to Berlin after the Emperor's brother was deposed from the throne of Westphalia and Jewish rights were revoked. There, in the heart of the Reform movement, Jacobson put his well-meaning but devastating plans into motion.

In an effort to revitalize attendance, Jacobson attempted to analyze the synagogue and determine ways to promote the services. He concluded that Jews were uninterested in prayer because their houses of worship were drab and lacking in aesthetics. In addition, many Hebrew prayers were unintelligible to the common Jew; who could be interested in mouthing words that were totally devoid of meaning?

While Jacobson was certainly correct in his conviction that the Jew must learn to fulfill his religious obligations wholeheartedly, his proposed solution was nothing less than disastrous. Jacobson, who had visited churches and been impressed by the stained glass and elaborate carvings, felt sure that the beauty and magnificence of the Christian services made their houses of worship more pleasing than the traditional Jewish synagogue. If the Jews would employ the same methods, Jacobson thought, surely more people would be interested in attending.

"Improvements" began in a small way at first. Even before Jacobson's appearance on the scene, the Reform movement had already abolished *Yekum Purkan,* an Aramaic section of the Shabbos prayers. Jacobson expanded these reforms by introducing the recitation of some

While Jacobson was certainly correct in his conviction that the Jew must learn to fulfill his religious obligations wholeheartedly, his proposed solution was nothing less than disastrous.

Chapter
33

14. See Chapter 16.

The Battle Against Reform:

Aileh Divrei HaBris

Orthodox leaders turned to thirty-two of the greatest scholars of the 1800's. Together, these Torah Sages created a publication of protest, significantly called Aileh Divrei HaBris, "These are the Words of the Covenant."

Tehillim in the German language. Upon his arrival in Berlin, Jacobson collaborated with another man, Jacob Beer, by holding services in their private homes. Down came the *mechitzah.* A mixed choir of men and women sang "to beautify the service." Difficult Hebrew passages were suppressed. The traditional form of Bar Mitzvah celebration was altered so as to resemble a Christian Confirmation. Most radical of all, Jacobson and Beer introduced the organ into the shul to accompany the singing of "Psalms."

This innovation caused an uproar of revulsion and horror in the Jewish community. The organ had always been associated in the Jewish mind with church services! Jacobson and Beer rationalized that the idea of having musical accompaniment to the service of Hashem had its precedent in Jewish tradition. After all, the service in the Bais HaMikdash was enhanced by instrumental music and the Levite choir. Why not enhance prayers in the synagogue in the same fashion?

The small group of traditional Jews remaining in Berlin, desperate to stop this outrage, found a surprising source of support in the Prussian government. Napoleon, who had sought to rule all Europe, was finally defeated. A backlash of protest against any hint of reform resulted as local rulers attempted to reinforce traditional institutions. Anything new and innovative reeked of the danger of possible treachery. In this suspicious atmosphere, Jacobson abandoned Berlin. The free Hanseatic city of Hamburg, which was unaffected by the restoration polices, could easily support his reforms.

Jacobson moved to Hamburg, inaugurating the first Reform Temple in 1818. The daily prayers of the Jewish longing for Tzion and the rebuilding of the Bais HaMikdash were abolished; all Jews should be loyal to their host countries alone and cease to consider themselves uprooted from their homeland. The *Maskilim* denied the Divine origin of the Torah and other mainstays of the Thirteen Articles of Faith, mixing the celebration of Jewish holidays with those of the Christians. Advertisements in newspapers of the period contained invitations to *Christnuka,* a brazen merging of the celebration of the purification of the Bais HaMikdash with Christmas. All Jewish holidays in the Diaspora were reduced to one day, as in Eretz Yisrael, to augment the understanding that the Jews no longer needed to consider themselves to be in exile.

The opening of the Hamburg Temple caused a storm of furious protest, arousing sorrow and anger among the religious Jews and the leading rabbinic leaders. The Torah Sages of the day imposed a *cherem* against Reform and their temples. One particular rabbi was shortsighted enough to approve the *Maskilim's* changes; he did not realize that the innovations of Reform Jews, while not originally violating *halachah,* were merely the beginnings of major violations of basic Torah law. Armed with this rabbinic "approval," the Reform Jews paid little attention to the *cherem.* In desperation, Orthodox leaders turned to thirty-two of the greatest scholars of the 1800's. Together, these Torah Sages created a publication of protest, significantly called *Aileh Divrei HaBris,* "These are the Words of the Covenant."

Excerpts from *Aileh Divrei HaBris*

"Therefore the Geonim, chassidim and tzaddikim arose and took a firm stand in a place where they found an 'open territory that needed fencing,' and they resolved to reiterate a public issue in three areas of flagrant violation:

1) It is forbidden to change the order and structure of our *tefillos* that have been in use in Israel throughout the ages, or to diminish them.

2) When praying, one is forbidden to recite the established body of our *tefillos* in any language other than *Leshon HaKodesh*. Any siddur that is not printed according to these guidelines is disqualified and forbidden for use.

3) It is forbidden to play a musical instrument in shul on Shabbos or Yom Tov, even if the instrument is played by a non-Jew."

Among the Torah Sages who sent their responsa to the Hamburg congregation were Rabbi Akiva Eger, Rav of the Posen *Kehillah*; Rabbi Moshe Sofer, Rav of Pressburg; Rabbi Mordechai Bannet, Rav of Nikolsburg; and Rabbi Yaakov of Lissa, author of the *Nesivos*. The following are selections from their essays.

Rabbi Moshe Sofer: "Davening in public in a language other than *Leshon HaKodesh* is absolutely out of the question. Although the Mishnah openly states, 'the following may be said in any language,' and one of the examples cited is prayer (which means that a person can fulfill the

Among the Torah Sages who sent their responsa to the Hamburg congregation were Rabbi Akiva Eger, Rav of the Posen Kehillah; Rabbi Moshe Sofer, Rav of Pressburg; Rabbi Mordechai Bannet, Rav of Nikolsburg; and Rabbi Yaakov of Lissa, author of the Nesivos.

"But to do this regularly, praying in the language of other nations, in public as a shaliach tzibbur—this is certainly forbidden."

mitzvah of prayer in any language), it applies only to an individual in an exceptional, rare incident. But to do this regularly, praying in the language of other nations, in public as a *shaliach tzibbur*—this is certainly forbidden."

Rabbi Akiva Eger: "My blessing to you for your courage and your firmness in coming out openly against davening from a siddur that contains changes from the accepted traditional text. Although the law permits prayer in any language, this is only in exceptional cases. But to establish this as the mode of davening in shul all the time, G-d forbid, one may not

Title Page of Rabbi Akiva Eger's Responsa

"Who can even imagine the depth of Anshei Knesses HaGedolah's thoughts that is contained in every word, every letter of these tefillos, both in the revealed and in the hidden interpretation of the language!"

mention this. Far be it from us to do that, especially since the Anshei Knesses HaGedolah arranged our prayers in the Holy Language which is pure and unadulterated. Who can even imagine the depth of their thoughts that is contained in every word, every letter of these *tefillos,* both in the revealed and in the hidden interpretation of the language! And if, as claimed, some of the congregants are not familiar with Hebrew, that in itself is bad and regrettable. They disregard the beautiful and pure language of our people and consider it of inferior importance, not even bothering to learn it. What a shame this is, in the eyes of the other nations! While every nation speaks its own language, honors and cultivates it, we Jews are ready to abandon it? At a time when parents hire tutors to instruct their children in French and Italian, why don't they invest at least the same effort in teaching them Hebrew? Woe to us! Is this what makes us look wise and sophisticated in the eyes of the world?"

"At a time when parents hire tutors to instruct their children in French and Italian, why don't they invest at least the same effort in teaching them Hebrew? Woe to us! Is this what makes us look wise and sophisticated in the eyes of the world?"

The publication of this appeal helped to alleviate the immediate threat of the further construction of more temples, but something more was needed to stem the threatening tide of Reform.

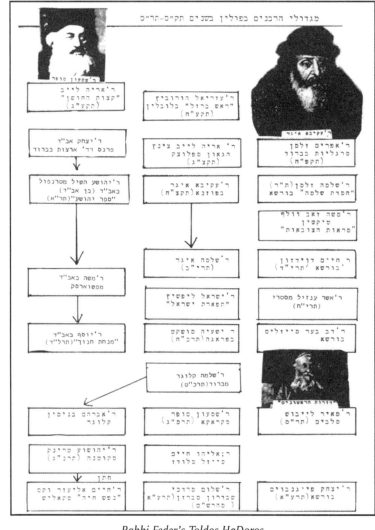

Rabbi Feder's Toldos HaDoros

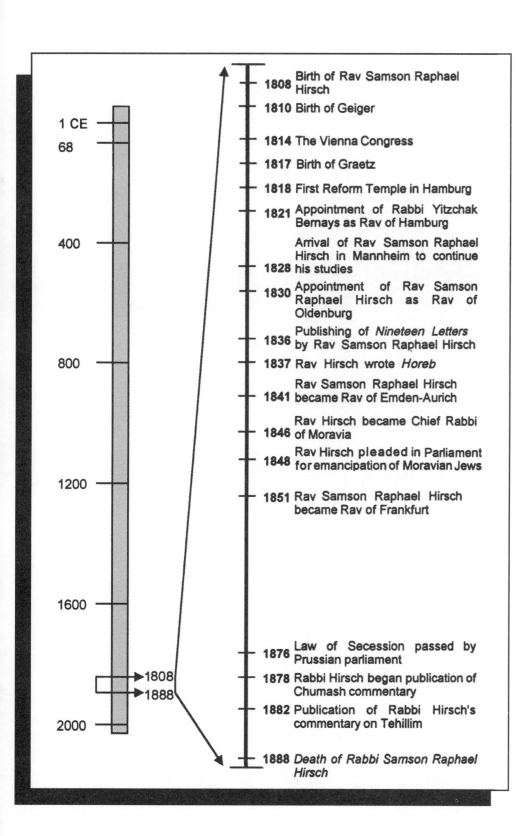

Rav Samson Raphael Hirsch:

Torah im Derech Eretz (1808-1888)

1808 Birth of Rav Samson Raphael Hirsch

1810 Birth of Geiger

1814 The Vienna Congress

1817 Birth of Graetz

1818 First Reform Temple in Hamburg

1821 Appointment of Rabbi Yitzchak Bernays as Rav of Hamburg

1828 Arrival of Rav Samson Raphael Hirsch in Mannheim to continue his studies

1830 Appointment of Rav Samson Raphael Hirsch as Rav of Oldenburg

1836 Publishing of *Nineteen Letters* by Rav Samson Raphael Hirsch

1837 Rav Hirsch wrote *Horeb*

1841 Rav Samson Raphael Hirsch became Rav of Emden-Aurich

1846 Rav Hirsch became Chief Rabbi of Moravia

1848 Rav Hirsch pleaded in Parliament for emancipation of Moravian Jews

1851 Rav Samson Raphael Hirsch became Rav of Frankfurt

1876 Law of Secession passed by Prussian parliament

1878 Rabbi Hirsch began publication of Chumash commentary

1882 Publication of Rabbi Hirsch's commentary on Tehillim

1888 *Death of Rabbi Samson Raphael Hirsch*

1 CE
68
400
800
1200
1600
2000

1808
1888

Rav Samson Raphael Hirsch:

Torah im Derech Eretz (1808-1888)

Rabbi Bernays spoke German fluently and had attended the university. With this background he was able to gain the respect of even the more "enlightened" members of the community.

av Samson Raphael Hirsch was born in Hamburg in the year 1808. His parents sent their son to a grammar school which taught secular subjects, an unusual step for religious parents adhering to Torah and mitzvos under the growing shadow of the Reform movement. At the age of ten, Samson Raphael overheard his parents discussing the desperate necessity of devising a strategy to fight against the Hamburg "Templars," who had just opened the first Reform Temple in Germany.[1] The young boy was so moved and distressed that he resolved to dedicate his whole life to the fight against Reform.

He found a worthy mentor in Rabbi Yitzchak Bernays, the Rav of Hamburg, a man of vast scholarship and piety. Until Rabbi Bernays's appointment, within two years of the opening of the Reform Temple, the *Maskilim* had been able to take advantage of a vacuum that existed in the Hamburg rabbinate. Without any knowledge of German, or enough secular knowledge to earn the respect of the more emancipated members of the community, the rabbinic leaders had been helpless to counter the actions of the Reform movement. With Rabbi Bernays's appointment, however, all this changed. He spoke German fluently and had attended the university. With this background he was able to gain the respect of even the more "enlightened" members of the community.

Rabbi Bernays made his position against the Reform movement very clear. A prime example was his refusal to accept the title of "rabbi." In his outspoken opinion, the Reform rabbis

Rabbi Raphael and Gella Hirsch, parents of Rav Samson Raphael Hirsch

who bore this title had invalidated its meaning. Instead, the community called him *Chacham* Bernays. Samson Raphael studied under *Chacham* Bernays during his teenage years, growing strongly attached to him and absorbing his powerful convictions.

In 1828, at the age of twenty, Samson Raphael left for Mannheim to continue his studies under the tutelage of Rabbi Yaakov Ettlinger, one of the great Sages of that era and author of *Oruch LaNair* and *Binyan Tzion*. Rav Hirsch, who had already received rabbinic ordination from *Chacham* Bernays, was also ordained by Rabbi Ettlinger. During the next year, he sporadically attended the famous Bonn University, determined to acquire the necessary tools with which to combat the Reform movement and to deal with the college-educated members of his community. In 1830, armed with a great store of Talmudic knowledge and with a refined secular education, Rav Hirsch was more than ready to begin the fight against what he called

Chacham Bernays

---

1. See Chapter 33.

the "crisis of civilization for the German Jews" when, at the age of twenty-two, he was appointed to the rabbinate of Oldenburg, where he also served as Rosh HaYeshivah.

At that time, Jews in Germany had reached a nadir of spiritual decay. With the Reform "Enlightenment," emancipation had become synonymous with the attempt to make Judaism as similar as possible to Christianity. "The Society of Culture," an organization that dedicated itself to establishing schools and academies for the promotion of trades, arts, and scientific research, proved to offer little more than a quick route to baptism. If Judaism and Christianity have so much in common, the Reform Jews reasoned, what difference could it possibly make? This shocking attitude influenced not only the academic youth, but the merchants and laborers of the general population as well.

At this time, with emancipation approved, and the Reform movement growing by leaps and bounds, Rav Hirsch was forced to accept the current state of affairs and had to determine the best way for religious Jewry to respond to the situation. "I welcome emancipation if Yisrael considers it not a fulfillment of its destiny, but a new phase of its many tests, one that is considerably more difficult to pass than the

> *"I welcome emancipation if Yisrael considers it not a fulfillment of its destiny but a new phase of its many tests, one that is considerably more difficult to pass than the test of suffering and enslavement."*

test of suffering and enslavement." Rav Hirsch developed a philosophy to meet the new challenge of emancipation: *Torah im Derech Eretz.*

> *Pirkei Avos (3:9) states: "A person who interrupts his study of Torah to look at his natural surroundings and exclaim with admiration, 'How beautiful is this tree!' or 'How beautiful is this furrow!' has forfeited his life." An obvious question can be posed: what is so fatally wrong with admiring the beauty of Hashem's creation?*
>
> *Rav Hirsch explains that a person who interrupts his Torah study to admire nature—one who looks upon nature, science, and the wonders of Creation as being something outside Torah—is indeed committing a great error. The Jew must understand that everything, whether it be the study of history, a slide under a microscope, or the beauty of a flower in bloom, must be used to help him recognize and gain a greater appreciation for Hashem's greatness and mastery in the universe. One who considers secular knowledge, including the admiration of nature, to be something outside the realm of Torah is truly setting foot on a dangerous and sinful path.*

Torah im Derech Eretz

Rav Hirsch uses the broadest definition for *derech eretz:* civilization. This term encompasses all activities of man in this world, including secular study, culture, the pursuit of a livelihood, and the exploration of nature. Rav Hirsch permitted, and even encouraged, the study of science and nature, *provided that this "derech eretz" was always associated with Torah.* Torah does not need secular studies, but secular studies need Torah. To approach the study of science or nature without a proper Torah background can lead only to skewed thinking.

> *"The Jew must understand that everything, whether it is the study of history, a slide under a microscope, or the beauty of a flower in bloom, must be used to help him recognize and gain a greater appreciation for Hashem's greatness and mastery in the universe."*

> *Torah does not need secular studies, but secular studies need Torah.*

Chapter

34

Rav Samson Raphael Hirsch:

Torah im Derech Eretz (1808-1888)

Derech eretz as a separate entity was a danger that could lead to assimilation, but derech eretz that was bound up with Torah, encouraged a broader appreciation of Hashem's greatness.

It is a Jew's duty to apply Torah to his current society, not to meld and dilute Torah to fit his surroundings.

Chapter
34

Unlike the Sages of Russia and Poland, whose stand against the Reform movement was strong enough to preclude any tampering with their strict standards, Rav Hirsch understood that the German Jews, exposed to emancipation and a secular world, needed something more. While Torah really does not need secular study to provide a "rounded education," the cultured Jews of Germany were unable to comprehend this. With the philosophy of *Torah im Derech Eretz,* Rav Hirsch maintained a deeply religious attitude that could still gain the respect of his "enlightened" community. *Derech eretz* as a separate entity was a danger that could lead to assimilation, but *derech eretz* that was bound up with Torah, encouraged a broader appreciation of Hashem's greatness. As Dr. Mordechai Breuer, a grandson of Rav Hirsch, observed: *"Torah im Derech Eretz* is not a physical mixture, but a chemical compound."

In 1836, Rav Hirsch expounded his ideas in his famous work, *Igros Tzafon,* nineteen letters written to a fictional college student who is utterly confused about his Jewish identity. A year later, Rav Hirsch published *Horeb,* a detailed analysis of the 613 mitzvos, which was designed to give Jewish intellectuals an understanding of the complex structure of the mitzvos and their diversified application. With these publications, Rav Hirsch's brilliance of thought and gift of writing were established and respected by all of European Jewry.

Many of today's Conservative, Reform, and so-called Orthodox Jews erroneously believe that Rav Hirsch had given his stamp of approval to the compromise of *halachah.* On the contrary! Rav Hirsch's philosophy of *Torah im Derech*

Rav Samson Raphael Hirsch

Eretz establishes the sovereignty of Torah within any given civilization. While the Jew must learn to cope with the different civilizations of his exile, it is his duty to apply Torah to his current society, not to meld and dilute Torah to fit his surroundings. This is diametrically opposite to Mendelssohn's philosophy of *Torah V'Derech Eretz,* which called for the "independent, peaceful coexistence of both realms," viewing Torah as something separate from modern-day life.[2] Rav Hirsch insisted that Torah be brought into every aspect of the Jew's daily life, including the pursuit of *derech eretz* in all its forms.

In 1841, Rav Hirsch was asked to serve as rabbi of Emden-Aurich, a prestigious position in a large district of northern Germany. Five years later, he became Chief Rabbi of Moravia with a residence in Nikolsburg. He was also appointed to be Rosh Yeshivah in the renowned

---

2. See Chapter 30.

yeshivah of Nikolsburg. At the time, Moravia seethed with suppression and anger, as the constituent rulers tried to turn back the clock and withhold the rights and privileges of emancipation. In March 1848, the common people rose in revolt and formed their own government. Rav Hirsch was appointed as the Jewish representative to Parliament, where he pleaded successfully for emancipation of the Moravian Jews. He also succeeded in abolishing many of the oppressive restrictions that had still remained in force, including the infamous "Family Law" which allowed only one child in each Jewish family to marry and live in the same city.

Frankfurt

The Reform Jews had managed to secure a majority in the Frankfurt community. According to secular law, this meant that the *Maskilim* were now the official community of Frankfurt. While many of the religious Jews bowed their heads in defeat, eleven men refused to give up. They traveled to Nikolsburg to beg Rav Hirsch—Chief Rabbi, Rosh Yeshivah, and representative to Parliament—to leave his prestigious positions and help them recreate a true religious atmosphere in Frankfurt. In 1851, two years after this underground Orthodox community had been created, Rav Hirsch came to Frankfurt, where he served as Rav for thirty-seven years, until the end of his life.

Rav Hirsch's small community, named "Kehal Adas Yeshurun," was an Orthodox congregation without compromise, a citadel of Torah of the highest quality. It became a shining example to the rest of Europe, proof that unadulterated Judaism could indeed exist and grow in the emancipated cultural climate of that era.

Rav Hirsch's first priority, even as his congregants were still praying in a private home for lack of a synagogue, was to build a Jewish day school, encompassing a total Jewish education based on *Torah im Derech Eretz*. The school grew from a few students into a large institution of over six hundred pupils. Rav Hirsch himself was principal of both the Hebrew and secular studies departments, and even taught history and literature in the secular studies department. His philosophy of *Torah im Derech Eretz* insisted that only religious Jews steeped in Torah and *shmiras ha'mitzvos* could be hired to teach any subject, including liberal arts and science. In the event that no qualified candidates could be found for the secular subjects, the vacancy could be filled by non-Jews.

On the political front, Rav Hirsch devoted his efforts to winning official recognition for his separate congregation, independent of the larger established Reform community of Frankfurt. His motto: "Separate yourself from this [evil] congregation."[3] He insisted that the community administrators should never yield their religious authority to the voting power of a non-religious majority.

As the law stood in Germany, Rav Hirsch's efforts were technically illegal. Before Rav Hirsch's time, the original Frankfurt community had already established an umbrella organization that was intended for all Jews. According to law, it was illegal for a Jew to renounce membership of his local community unless he left Judaism altogether.

Rav Hirsch found an ally in Chancellor Bismarck, a Prussian statesman who is generally regarded as the greatest European diplomat of the nineteenth century. Bismarck's dearest ambition was to

3. *Bamidbar*, 16:21.

His philosophy of Torah im Derech Eretz insisted that only religious Jews steeped in Torah and shmiras ha'mitzvos could be hired to teach any subject, including liberal arts and science.

Chapter 34

Rav Samson Raphael Hirsch:

Torah im Derech Eretz (1808-1888)

Rav Hirsch's commentary was translated from German to English and Hebrew, and is revered and studied all over the world.

see Germany united under Prussian leadership and established as the most powerful nation in Europe. Bismarck, despite occasional flashes of anti-Semitism, recognized the vital role of the Jew in Germany's ascension. He assisted Rav Hirsch in his efforts to legalize the Orthodox community. It took twenty years, but the law of secession was passed by the Prussian Parliament. As of July 1876, Orthodox Jews were permitted to leave the local Reform congregation and form their own Orthodox community organization.

There were those, however, who did not agree with Rav Hirsch's demand that the Orthodox Jews separate themselves completely from the rest of the Jews in Frankfurt. They argued that they wished to remain united with the official community of the city. The Wurzburger Rav, Rabbi Selig Ber Bamberger, believed that there were many issues, particularly in matters concerning the common welfare, in which Jews of all persuasions could work together. As long as the independence of the Orthodox in religious matters was protected, why break Jewish unity?

The two scholars conducted an exchange of open letters, but the conflict was never fully resolved. Until the genocide of the Jewish population in Germany under Hitler, *yimach shemo,* there remained two distinct types of communities: those that followed Rav Hirsch's example, such as those in Berlin and Mannheim, and others in which the Orthodox and Reform Jews remained united.

In 1878, Rav Hirsch began the publication of his greatest literary contribution, his commentary on Chumash. It is a unique presentation of both the Written and Oral Law, woven together in a fabric of extraordinary insight and orig-

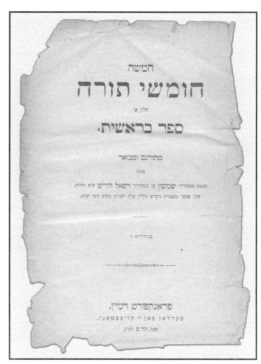

Rav Hirsch's Commentary on the Torah

inality. His commentary was translated from German to English and Hebrew, and is revered and studied all over the world. The Frankfurt community was fond of boasting, "There is no single significant statement of *Chazal* that is not mentioned in Rav Hirsch's Chumash commentary."

Rav Hirsch published another masterpiece, his commentary on *Tehillim,* in 1882. It not only translates and explains the meaning of King David's Psalms, but also applies its meanings to the situations that the Jew encounters at one time or another during his lifetime.

It is typical of the characteristic honesty of Rav Hirsch that he left a clause

"There is no single significant statement of Chazal that is not mentioned in Rav Hirsch's Chumash commentary."

Chapter

34

ספר תהלים

מתורגם ומבואר מאת

הגאון הרב שמשון בן הר״ר רפאל הירש זצ״ל

חלק ראשון : ספר א׳ וב׳

יוצא לאור בעד
חברת מפיצי ספרי הגאון רש״ר הירש זצ״ל
על ידי
בית מסחר והוצאת ספרים פ. פלדהיים
ניו יורק, תש״ך

Rav Hirsch's Psalms

in his will stating that if he should die in the middle of the secular year, any uncovered portion of his salary that he had received in advance should be returned to the community. He need not have worried; Rav Hirsch passed away on the 27th of Teves, 5649 (December 31, 1888).

With a philosophy that his congregants were capable of accepting, Rav Hirsch was able to create a generation of cultured, loyal Torah Jews. The Sages of Eastern Europe were unanimous in their praise of Rav Hirsch's leadership, even though he advocated a less concentrated Torah education than the Lithuanian and Polish Yeshivos demanded.[4] They recognized and accepted that Rav Hirsch's philosophy offered the only possible solution for Torah Judaism under the bleak reign of Reform Jewry in Germany.

---

4. Rav Baruch Ber Leibowitz (author of *Birkas Shmuel*), and other *gedolei Yisrael* considered Rav Hirsch's philosophy to be a *horaas shaah,* a temporary, emergency measure for his times. Yet Rav Shlomo Breuer, the Frankfurter Rav, and others considered Rav Hirsch's philosophy to be the proper Jewish way of life until the end of *Galus.*

Anti-Semitism in Modern Times

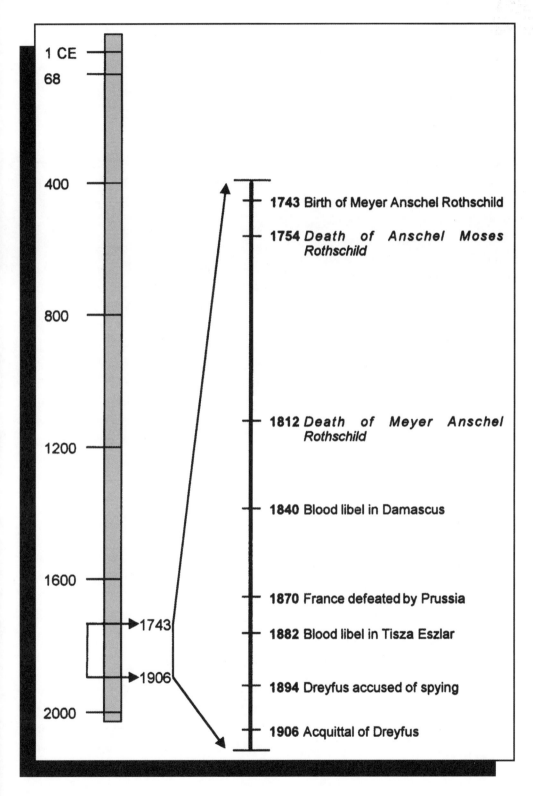

1743	Birth of Meyer Anschel Rothschild
1754	*Death of Anschel Moses Rothschild*
1812	*Death of Meyer Anschel Rothschild*
1840	Blood libel in Damascus
1870	France defeated by Prussia
1882	Blood libel in Tisza Eszlar
1894	Dreyfus accused of spying
1906	Acquittal of Dreyfus

Chapter

35

Even if the Jews themselves try to forget their origins, Hashem sends the Gentiles to remind them of the truth.

"Reasons" and the Reason

ccording to the *midrash,* the name of Mount Sinai, the mountain on which the Torah was given, is derived from the word *sinah,* hatred. The world's hatred of the Jews came down from Mount Sinai together with the Torah.

The world respects the Jews as the "People of the Book"; at the same time, the Jews are despised for their Bible and their religion. A paradox? Perhaps. Another *midrash* has the answer: *Halachah sheEisav sonei es Yaakov.* It is a law of nature that Eisav (usually explained as Rome and Christianity) hates Yaakov, the Bnei Yisrael. If one excuse no longer serves its purpose, another "reason" for this hatred cannot be far behind.

"That which comes up in your mind will not happen, that which you said, 'Let us be like the other nations, like the rest of the families of the world.' I will rule over you with a mighty hand and an outstretched arm...and with an outpouring of anger."[1]

The periodic outbreaks of hatred that have crashed over the Jews throughout history serve Hashem's purpose. The new wave of anti-Semitism in the later part of the nineteenth century arose just as the Jews, breathing the hopeful air of emancipation and equal rights, attempted to leave the Torah behind with the broken walls of the ghettos. As the century of liberty and equality degenerated into assimilation, it triggered a hatred of cataclysmic proportions. Even if the Jews themselves try to forget their origins, Hashem sends the Gentiles to remind them of the truth.

The term "anti-Semitism" was born in the nineteenth century. Until then, the

---
1. *Yechezkel,* 20:32.

hatred that every Christian harbored against the Jews was claimed to be justified because of Judas, the Jew who had betrayed their messiah and brought about his death.[2] Every Jew was just as evil as Judas had been, and every Jew deserved to be despised and hated. In addition, the Jews' stubborn refusal to change their faith was an offending, infuriating indictment against Christianity. How dare the Jews not admit that they were wrong? From a religious standpoint, the hatred of the Jew remained solid and deliberate.

By the nineteenth century, however, the religious issue had lost much of its sting. Humanism and liberalism were the new idols of Europe; religious commitments began to fall by the wayside. Nevertheless, the non-Jewish world's attitude towards the Jewish minority did not change. Instead of hating the Jews for their religion, the Gentiles now hated the Jews as a race: Jews were greedy, they controlled the economy of the world, they were murderers that drank the blood of Christian children, they were traitors that would betray their country for pennies. Since the Jews were descended from Shem while the Caucasian Europeans were descended from Yefes, the Jews were called "Semites." The new hatred unleashed on the Jews was the age-old enmity that had existed for centuries, only now it was called "anti-Semitism."

Envy and Economy

For generations, the educated, cultured Jews had served as the managers of nobles' estates and in other official capacities. The illiterate peasants were incapable of such tasks, and the nobles were usually more intent on drinking and hunting than on their duties to their

---
2. See Chapter 13.

vassals. As a result, the Jews became trapped in the middle, the peasants' visible figure of resentment against their masters.[3]

The concept of nobles and peasantry had largely disappeared by the latter part of the nineteenth century,[4] but the Jews still played a prominent role in business and the economy. The nation that had been called the "People of the Book" rose to meteoric heights in the world of finance and politics. Inevitably, the power wielded by Jewish businessmen gave rise to fierce pangs of envy and resentment.

The Rothschild family serves as an excellent example of the role the Jews played in world finance. The power they wielded in the nineteenth century was such that they could actually influence nations towards war or peace.

The Rothschilds trace their origin to 1585 in Frankfurt, Germany, where the first Rothschilds occupied a house on Jews' Street #148. The house had a red shield, called "rotschild" in German, which the occupants later adapted as their surname. Anschel Moses Rothschild, who died in 1754, sold provisions from the attic room where he and his family lived.

With Anschel Moses's death, his eldest son, eleven-year-old Meyer Anschel, was forced to abandon his plans for a Yeshivah education and had to step into his father's role as family breadwinner. He found employment in Hanover in the Oppenheimer banking house, where he gained enough experience to return to Frankfurt and open up a business of his own. He soon acquired a reputation for honesty and reliability, until many of the German noblemen trusted him with their financial problems.

When Napoleon marched into Germany, young Prince Wilhelm of Essen, one of the richest heirs in all Germany, left his fortune with Rothschild. On his return from an exile that he had never expected to survive, the prince returned to Rothschild and discovered that the Jew had not only faithfully guarded his wealth, but had managed Wilhelm's monies so well that he had amassed a tremendous profit. Rothschild's reputation, both as a financial genius and a man of true integrity, spread throughout Europe.

Both Rothschild and his wife were strictly Orthodox Jews. He never learned to speak German; instead, he made himself understood with his native "Yiddish." His philanthropic acts and generosity have become legendary. Despite his great wealth, his lifestyle remained modest and simple. Until the end of his life in 1812, he lived in the original Rothschild home on Jews' Street. Even after his death, his wife, who survived him by many years, refused to leave the dark, old house which she associated with the family's good fortune.

Rothschild's children went into the family business. The eldest remained in Frankfurt, but the other four sons were sent to other European trade centers,

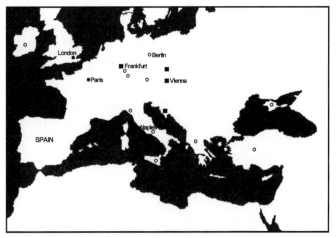

The Rothschild Banking Empire

3. See Chapter 25.
4. But not completely; see Chapter 25.

Rothschild's reputation, both as a financial genius and a man of true integrity, spread throughout Europe.

Chapter
35

In the late 1800's, there was a resurgence of one of the most dreaded and horrifying accusations of all time: the blood libel.

eventually founding branches of the Rothschild Bank in Naples, Vienna, Paris, and London. With five brothers situated in key European locations, they could send vital information discreetly and quickly to each other. The Rothschild banking complex grew into a world power that wielded its influence on major government policies throughout the nineteenth century. Their power was such that when the Russian government requested a loan from Great Britain to bolster its sagging finances, the Rothschild who was then head of the London branch attached a condition to the loan: the excesses against the Russian Jews must stop before negotiations could begin. When the persecutions continued, the bank broke off its relations with Russia.

The Industrial Revolution brought prosperity in its wake. Most European countries, with the exception of Russia,[5] participated in this surge towards capitalism. In reality, the majority of banks were controlled by Gentiles; while the Jews did and always have maintained a high profile in world events, they were not really in control of the world's economy.

Despite overwhelming evidence to the contrary, the concept that the Jews were determined to rule Europe persisted. One of the most outrageous yet most commonly propagated lies was published in *The Protocols of the Elders of Zion*. This pamphlet, originally written in France, claimed to be the secret notes, recorded at a meeting of an international Jewish conspiracy to take over the world. Czar Nicholas II actually contributed over twelve million rubles from his private funds in the early 1900's for the publication of this pamphlet in Russia; Henry Ford, the inventor of the motorcar and a

_____
5. See Chapter 36.

rabid anti-Semite, funded a similar publishing enterprise in America. Copies of the *Protocols,* picturing a spider with a Jewish face grasping the world in its legs, are still circulated today.

Anti-Semitism does not depend on logic. Isolated situations are blown out of proportion and generalized; if one Jew does wrong, all Jews are suspect. One wrongdoing committed by a single Jew could easily lead to widespread persecutions against all European Jewry. In the late 1800's, there was a resurgence of one of the most dreaded and horrifying accusations of all time: the blood libel.

Blood and Matzos

The vicious fabrication that Jews commit "ritual murder" was not new.[6] The first recorded blood libel took place in England in 1144, when Jews were accused of abducting, torturing, and slaughtering a Christian child in order to use his blood for Pesach. In 1181, witnesses in Austria swore they had seen the Jews slaughtering three Christian boys who were last seen playing on a frozen river. By the time the unmarked bodies were recovered in the thaw of spring, three hundred innocent Jews had already been burned at the stake. Other blood libels arose through the years; in 1255, nineteen Jews were hanged in England without the benefit of a trial when a missing child was found dead the day after a Jewish wedding.

Even if the Jews in a particular case were proven innocent, the Christian world never doubted the validity of such an accusation. In time, the bloodthirsty, murdering Jew was as much a part of Christian dogma as the Jews' betrayal of their savior. The few Emperors and Popes enlightened enough to declare

_____
6. See Chapter 15.

The blood libel revived in "The Ritual Murder," in the Nazi newspaper "Der Stürmer"

The blood libel took on new ramifications as the advancements in communications and the press brought events to the attention of the entire world.

their blood. All Jews were to believed to be evil, bloodthirsty creatures. Even if the blood libel was unknown in one area, helpful Christians would introduce the concept, as was the case when an official opinion was submitted to the Russian Czar in 1799 to inform him that the Jews, who were part of his realm, did indeed murder innocent Christians. In later centuries, however, the blood libel took on new ramifications as the advancements in communications and the press brought events to the attention of the entire world.

In 1840, a Christian monk in Damascus, Syria, which was then under Muslim rule, disappeared. The Jews were not immediately accused; the blood libel was a Christian fabrication that had never been circulated among the Muslims. The French consul, determined to correct

that the concept of the blood libel was false, did as little good as the vehement denials of the most respected Sages. Of course the Jews killed Christian children; everyone knew it.

Blood libels continued to erupt periodically. In 1475, a Jew in Italy found a dead child by the river. He brought the body immediately to the bishop in an effort to escape accusations, but several Jews were immediately arrested and tortured until they "confessed" to the crime. The child's embalmed body became a shrine; the child was canonized as a saint in the sixteenth century, and it was not until 1965 that the Church canceled the child's sainthood for his supposed martyrdom.

Torquemada arranged for a blood libel to encourage Ferdinand and Isabella to expel the Jews from Spain.[7] Wherever the Jew fled in exile, the ugly fabrication followed him: the Jews killed Christians for

7. See Chapter 19.

The Blood Libel (partial list of cases)			
Year	Place	Country	Results
1144	Norwich	England	
1171	Blois	France	31 Jews burned
1199	Erfurt	Germany	3 Jews hanged
1235	Wolfsheim	Germany	18 Jews hanged
1285	Munich	Germany	90 Jews killed
1286	Oberwesel	Germany	40 Jews killed
1288	Troyes	France	13 Jews burnt
1407	Cracow	Poland	
1494	Tyrman	Hungary	12 Jews, 22 Jewesses burned
1505	Budweis	Bohemia	13 Jews drowned themselves
1691	Wilna	Lithuania	4 Jews executed
1801	Bucharest	Rumania	128 Jews killed
1823	Velia, Vitebsk	Poland	lasted 12 years
1840	Damascus	Syria	13 Jews arrested and tortured
1882	Tisza-Eszlar	Hungary	
1887	Telse	Russia	
1899	Polna	Russia	
1911-13	Beilis Case	Russia	
1934		Nazi Germany "Der Sturmer" Spreading Anti-Jewish propaganda	

(Gleaned from *The Jewish Encyclopedia*)

Beilis was arrested and imprisoned under harsh conditions that dragged on for years until the actual trial took place in the autumn of 1914.

this oversight, advised the authorities that the Jews had probably murdered the monk for his blood.

The leaders of the Damascus Jewish community were promptly arrested and brutally tortured. Mobs swarmed through the streets, attacking the entire Jewish population at will. Thanks to the more modern methods of communication, the horror story reached Europe, where prominent Jews, including Sir Moses Montefiore, protested the outrageous accusation. With the intervention of the British government, which dispatched a committee of three prominent Jewish statesmen to investigate the affair, many Jewish lives were spared. But the accusation had taken root, and the belief in blood libels still exists in the Arab world today.

Under Czar Nicholas I of Russia, blood libels were stamped with government approval. A document was issued in 1844, detailing exactly how the Jews used Christian blood. In 1853, two Jews were convicted in a "fair trial" for ritually murdering two Christian children.[8]

In 1882, the blood libel was revived once more, this time in a small Hungarian village. Shortly before Pesach, a Christian girl disappeared. The rumor spread like wildfire: local Jews had murdered her in their synagogue in order to bake matzos with her blood. Under torture, they obtained testimony from the son of the *shamash* of the synagogue, blaming the murder on fifteen Jews. Hate for the Jews flared up in the entire country and bloody attacks were mounted on Jews in other communities. It did not matter if a Jew lived elsewhere and could not have been guilty of slaughtering the murdered girl; the crime of being a Jew was enough. After a prolonged investigation,

the charge was dropped and the suspects set free, but the hatred and suspicion still remained—and still does.

Incredibly, belief in the blood libel still lingers. As late as 1912, Menachem Mendel Beilis was accused of murdering a Christian child to use his blood to bake matzos for Pesach in Kiev, Russia. Despite overwhelming evidence that a Russian woman and three of her henchmen had killed the child, Beilis was arrested and imprisoned under harsh conditions that dragged on for years until the actual trial took place in the autumn of 1914. Witnesses offered ample proof that Beilis was innocent, while other witnesses made statements that were confirmation of the true murderers' guilt.

The jury eventually decided that, while the child had been murdered in the factory where Beilis had been superintendent, the Jew had not been the actual murderer. The government was infuriated—Beilis wrote in his autobiography that he had been told that the Czar had thanked G-d that a Jew was accused of the murder in the first place—and arranged for a book to be published, accusing Beilis of the murder, despite the outcome of the trial.

The Dreyfus Affair

Napoleon's defeat at Waterloo, in 1815, proved to be only the beginning of a series of setbacks for France. In 1870, France suffered a humiliating defeat at the hands of the Prussian army. With the economy in ruins and a bleak political future, the people split into factions that blamed each other for the country's woes.

The Liberals, one of the two leading political parties, claimed that their opponents, the Conservatives, were responsible for

---

8. See Chapter 36 for more on Czar Nicholas I.

Chapter
35

the military and economic disaster. The Conservatives, desperate to find a convenient defense, seized upon the classic scapegoat that had served the Gentiles so well throughout history: the Jew. France's population at that time was numbered at forty million; there were only approximately 100,000 Jews. With such few numbers and consequently little political influence, the Jews could easily be blamed, with small chance of repercussions. France, the country that prided itself on equality and fraternity, was out for blood.[9]

In 1894, a cleaning woman in the German embassy in France found a sheaf of papers carelessly thrown in a wastebasket. The cleaning woman was actually a French secret agent in counter-espionage. She brought the papers, a *bordereau* (catalogue or register), to her superiors. The *bordereau* listed a number of French military secrets which had been sold to German Ambassador Schwartzkoppen. The French Secret Service realized that secrets of such magnitude could only have been leaked by a traitor who was an officer of the general staff. Such treachery needed to be quickly exposed and publicly condemned. The search for the renegade was on.

At that time, there was only one Jew on the general staff, Captain Alfred Dreyfus. Only thirty-five, he had enjoyed a meteoric rise in the military with his brilliance as a soldier and his loyal patriotism for France. He came from a rich, completely assimilated family and was happily married to a millionaire's daughter. Nothing in his career had ever hinted at anything remotely resembling treachery, but his status as a Jew was enough. When the *bordereau* was found, a feverish search began for evidence

that would prove that Dreyfus, the Jew, was a traitor to his country.

The *bordereau* contained some messages handwritten by the traitor to Schwartzkoppen. The investigators summoned experts and urged them to prove that the writing matched samples written by Dreyfus. Frustratingly enough, the experts could not agree on positive proof.

Dreyfus remained untouchable until a member of the army, Colonel Henry, brought the prosecutor a crucial piece of evidence: a telegram in which Schwartzkoppen referred to a man, "D.," who had helped the Germans conquer Nice's fortifications. Here was the proof they had been seeking! "D." was obviously Dreyfus. Alfred Dreyfus, the Jew, was the traitor who had betrayed France to the German ambassador. Dreyfus protested and insisted that he was innocent of any treachery, but everyone knew better: the Jew was guilty.

In a highly publicized, humiliating court-martial, Dreyfus was dishonorably stripped of his rank and sentenced to lifetime imprisonment on Devil's Island off the coast of South America. Dreyfus stood still as they ripped his military insignia off his uniform and broke his sword in half. Throughout the ceremony, he maintained his posture and dignity, even as the anti-Semitic jeers of the public rang in his ears.

The Conservatives were satisfied with their Jewish scapegoat. Edward Frumond, a notorious Jew-hater, incited the masses with inflammatory articles against all French Jews in his newspaper, *La Libre Parole*. At the same time, however, others argued that Dreyfus was innocent. Even as Dreyfus was sent to exile

Dreyfus protested and insisted that he was innocent of any treachery, but everyone knew better: the Jew was guilty.

9. See pages 257-258 for the French attitude towards the blood libel.

Chapter

35

*To everyone's
astonishment,
Dreyfus was not
acquitted at all.
The French
government simply
could not admit to
such a grave error.*

on an island notorious for its harsh climate and primitive conditions, France split in two factions, unable to resolve whether the Jew had actually betrayed his country. With time, two factions arose, the Dreyfusards and the Anti-Dreyfusards. The controversy reached its height as the government was forced to dissolve for new elections.

Meanwhile, Dreyfus's family hired the best lawyers to prove his innocence. Colonel Picquart, a non-Jew whose sense of honor and justice was affronted by the dishonesty that permeated Dreyfus's trial, offered his assistance. He had examined the dossier of the Dreyfus case and pinpointed the inconsistencies and falsifications used in condemning Dreyfus. Determined to discover the truth about his former colleague, Picquart spent days researching the evidence.

Picquart was still studying the dossier when a letter requesting admittance to the general staff arrived in his office. As Picquart read the application, he was struck by the resemblance of the handwriting to the documents found in the German Embassy. Picquart glanced at the signature at the bottom of the letter: Colonel Esterhazy. Intrigued, he began to ask questions. Esterhazy had an unsavory reputation as an alcoholic who was always in desperate need of money. Could this man be the true culprit?

Picquart reported his findings to his superiors, but he was met with stubborn insistence. Dreyfus was guilty. Dreyfus *must* be guilty! When Picquart insisted, his immediate superior, a close friend of Esterhazy's, had the troublesome colonel transferred to Tunis, safely out of the way. Esterhazy's handwriting may have resembled the traitor's, but the telegram with the initial "D." was all the proof they needed.

Many of France's greatest minds came to the defense of Dreyfus, convinced that a colossal injustice had been done to an innocent man. One famous writer, Emile Zola, publicized his letter to the French President titled *J'accuse!* ("I Accuse!"), in which he indicted the French system for having allowed such a colossal travesty of justice to take place. When the tribunal reconvened to reconsider the Dreyfus case, the whole world waited expectantly, sure that Dreyfus would be acquitted.

Then, without warning, the case against Dreyfus shattered. Colonel Henry, the man who had "discovered" the incriminating telegram, confessed that he had forged the telegram himself, and then committed suicide. The military tribunal was forced to recall Dreyfus from Devil's Island and have him retried.

To everyone's astonishment, Dreyfus was not acquitted at all. The French government simply could not admit to such a grave error. Instead, his life sentence was reduced to a ten-year imprisonment; the President of the French Republic granted him a pardon the following day. Alfred Dreyfus was now a free man, but he was still branded a traitor, his name still disgraced. Disillusioned by the treatment he had received from the country he had so selflessly served, Dreyfus accepted the verdict with resignation and returned home.

It took a decade for the French government to change its mind. In 1906, France's highest court invalidated the verdict against Dreyfus and unanimously declared him innocent of all charges, reinstating him in the army. The former captain was promoted to major and awarded the Legion of Honor. Colonel Picquart was promoted to general and eventually became the Minister of War in

Georges Clemenceau's cabinet. Despite this final admission of the truth, anti-Semitism in France still persisted, lying just beneath the surface. The enthusiasm with which the Vichy regime collaborated with the Nazis during World War II serves as ample proof that the ingrained animosity of Gentile towards Jew needs little incentive to flare into open hatred.

Aside from the direct ramifications of such a miscarriage of justice and such blatant anti-Semitism, the Dreyfus Affair came as a rude shock to many Jews. Moses Mendelssohn had preached that if the Jew would break down the barriers of the ghetto and act with culture and enlightenment, hatred for the Jews would surely fall by the wayside.[10] Most assimilated Jews truly believed that once they abandoned their external Jewishness to act, speak, and dress like Gentiles, prejudices would crumble and the Jews would be respected and loved (or at least tolerated) by all Europe.

Captain Alfred Dreyfus was a paragon of the assimilated Jew. Not only was he outwardly identical to his Gentile associates, but he had shown extraordinary readiness to serve his fatherland with the greatest patriotism and dedication. Nevertheless, when he stood accused of treason, his culture and enlightenment had not helped him at all. All the assurances of protection by law, of fairness and honesty, had been cast aside by a wave of open, vicious Jew-hatred. It hadn't mattered that Dreyfus was "enlightened"; he was a Jew, and that had been enough to brand him a traitor.

Reform Jewry was thrown into a state of distress and turmoil. They had turned their backs on Torah and refused to admit that no other answer existed. Instead, they posed a new question: if assimilation could not assure tolerance and freedom from prejudice, how could the Jew better his situation in exile? The *Maskilim* of Russia tried a different approach by becoming "cultured" but still retaining their Jewish identity, but this, too, met with failure as pogroms devastated Russian Jewry at the turn of the twentieth century.[11]

One Jew, whose assimilated background was similar to Dreyfus's own, watched the trial and court-martial from the news reporters' balcony. Dismayed by the travesty of justice, the reporter determined to devise a solution of his own; but the new concept of "Zionism" that Theodore Herzl developed would prove to be just as damaging to the Jewish nation.

All the assurances of protection by law, of fairness and honesty, had been cast aside by a wave of open, vicious Jew-hatred.

Chapter

35

10. See Chapter 30.

11. See Chapter 37.

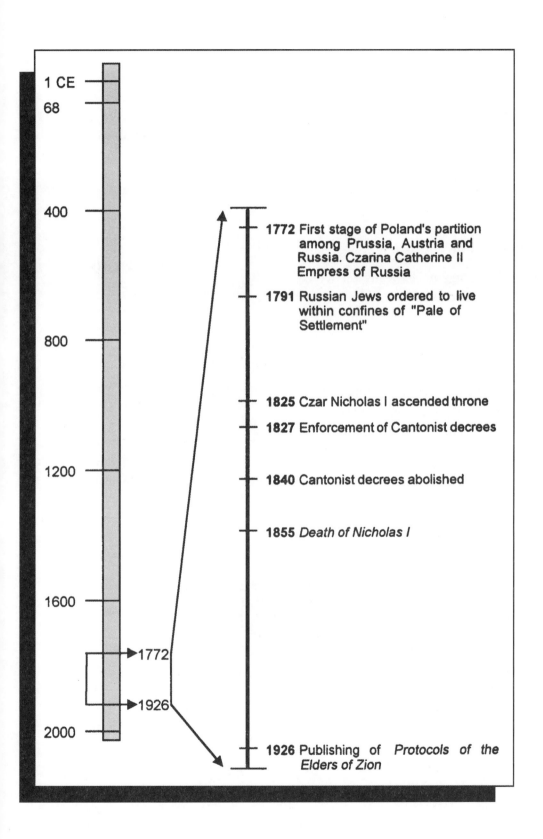

1 CE

68

400

800

1200

1600

2000

1772

1926

1772 First stage of Poland's partition among Prussia, Austria and Russia. Czarina Catherine II Empress of Russia

1791 Russian Jews ordered to live within confines of "Pale of Settlement"

1825 Czar Nicholas I ascended throne

1827 Enforcement of Cantonist decrees

1840 Cantonist decrees abolished

1855 *Death of Nicholas I*

1926 Publishing of *Protocols of the Elders of Zion*

Chapter

36

Polish Jewry thrived for nearly one hundred forty years before the Cossacks swept across the country, utterly destroying a vibrant society.

In the aftermath of the expulsion from Spain, Poland and Lithuania welcomed the Jews into their lands, eager for assistance in leading their backward countries to economic stability (and in contributing to the coffers of the nobility). While the Jews were still forced to cope with Christian hatred and bigotry, they established a rich spiritual entity supervised by an effective self-government, the Vaad Arba Aratzos. Polish Jewry thrived for nearly one hundred forty years before the Cossacks swept across the country, utterly destroying a vibrant society.[1]

The Polish kings never really recovered their original power, nor did the Jews ever regain their favorable political status. Instead of economic well-being, the Jews struggled with poverty and more frequent persecutions. In 1792, Poland was preemptively divided between its three powerful neighbors, Prussia, Austria, and Russia.[2] To their dismay, over one million Jews suddenly found themselves living under the rule of the despotic Czars.

Until the annexation of Poland, there were probably fewer than 100,000 Jews in all of Russia's vast territory. Russia was not kind to the Jews. The country's civilization lagged far behind the rest of Europe's; the social and intellectual development that had blossomed after the Crusades did not touch the huge tracts of Russian land and its peasantry. The same bigotry and hatred that was beginning to fade in Western Europe still thrived in still-medieval minds. The Czars were fer-

_____
1. See Chapter 23 and Chapter 25.
2. Poland remained under foreign rule until 1918.

vent Greek Orthodox Christians and fiercely anti-Jewish.

Catherine (1762–1796)

With Russia's annexation of Poland, the ruling Czarina, Catherine II, determined to awaken her stagnant country and lead her people away from the dormancy of centuries. She was pragmatic enough to realize that these unwanted Jews could

The Czars were fervent Greek Orthodox Christians and fiercely anti-Jewish.

probably fulfill a purpose in improving the primitive agriculture and lack of modernization that characterized her people. Ironically enough, even as Mendelssohn and others struggled to introduce the concepts of emancipation and equal rights in Western Europe, Catherine offered tremendous opportunities to the Jews of Russia, including the option to enter many professions and businesses that had long been taboo for the Jews in Europe. They were allowed to vote and were given administrative

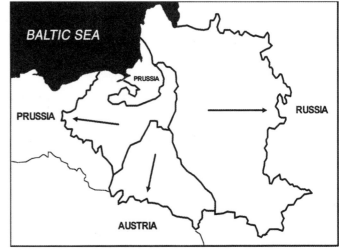

Polish Partition

positions in the government. Most importantly, Catherine, recognizing the benefits of strong central organizations, permitted the Jews to maintain their close-knit *kehillos,* the communities that kept the Jewish people together.

Catherine's good intentions did bear fruit; historically, she is credited with opening the "windows to the west" for her people. Almost inevitably, however, Catherine's initial benevolence transformed itself into harsh measures. News of the French Revolution alarmed her into theorizing that the trend towards modernization would ultimately backfire and only create social unrest. She resolved to reverse the course and restore the old, safer system of a centralized power maintained by brute force. As a kind of safety valve against unrest, Catherine began to incite the common people against the Jews; she wanted her people to hate something other than her regime. The rabid, almost primitive anti-Semitism of the Russian people exploded once again with the Czarina's active encouragement.

The Pale of Settlement

One of Catherine's first steps was to herd the Jews into one region. A well-defined area was soon mapped out, which would eventually be called the "Pale of Settlement." Essentially, the Pale was a large ghetto-like area, composed of twenty-five districts on the former Russian-Polish border. Only a few thousand highly-cultured Jews and specialist workers could obtain a pass which enabled them to travel outside the Pale. Even within the Pale itself, life was restricted; Catherine ordered all Jews to leave villages and rural areas and live in the cities. Jews were forced to abandon their homes and livelihoods to

crowd into small areas in unsanitary conditions. They were not permitted to sell alcohol, work as innkeepers, or operate the postal stations where the overland coaches would stop to disembark and load passengers. Begging soon became a legitimate calling.

When Napoleon's armies swept across Europe and into Russia, many restrictions were relaxed. Czar Alexander I preferred his Jews to remain loyal, especially as news of Napoleon's "Sanhedrin" had given rise to wistful hopes of redemption.[3] Indeed, many of the Jews supported the Czar, all too aware that it was better to live under harsh circumstances

Catherine began to incite the common people against the Jews; she wanted her people to hate something other than her regime.

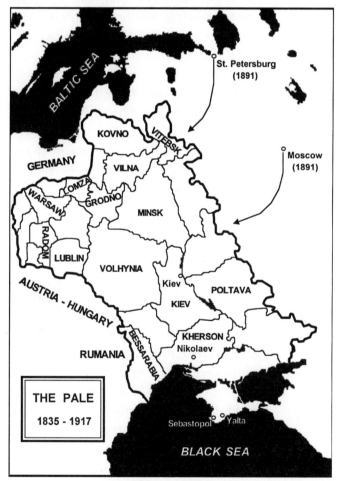

The Pale of Settlement

—————
3. See Chapter 31.

Chapter
36

Russia seemed to watch the rest of Europe. When most countries made a temporary reversal in policies, replacing liberal policies with more reactionary ones, Russia followed suit.

Their religion transcended the severity of their exile and gave them the will to survive.

than to face the dangerous twin challenges of emancipation and assimilation.[4] After the war ended and Napoleon was driven back, the more lenient policies continued for some time, perhaps in appreciation of the Jews' loyalty. But Alexander, afraid that his totalitarian rule might be threatened if he proved too indulgent, issued decrees that were designed to destroy any chance of opposition. The Jews found themselves driven back to the Pale with its restricted space and subjected to even harsher legislation than before.

Russia seemed to watch the rest of Europe. When most countries made a temporary reversal in policies, replacing liberal policies with more reactionary ones, Russia followed suit. Alexander ruled that Jews were banned not only from the villages, but also from the western territories close to the border; this ensured that they would not escape to the "free" countries of the West. Sources of income that had survived the initial edicts were subsequently banned, resulting in a poverty more pronounced than the Jews had ever known.

Jews could no longer rent an apartment of their own, or even part of one; in cities such as Cracow, Lodz, Lemberg, Odessa, and Vilna, it became common for four families to share a single room. There was usually no furniture. Children died of starvation in these crowded conditions as often as they did of typhus and other diseases.

Somehow, with inborn ingenuity, the Jews invented new trades to replace those that had become forbidden.

4. See Chapter 28.

In cities such as Cracow, Lodz, Lemberg, Odessa and Vilna, it became common for four families to share a single room.

Any other people would have eventually smothered under such oppression. But the Jew has one crucial asset: Torah.

Those fortunate enough to possess good voices became cantors, while others were hired to serve as *shamashim* in synagogues. Marriage brokers flourished. With the inbred infinite patience of the Jew in exile, many became traveling peddlers, carrying bulging knapsacks of goods as they wandered from city to city, hawking their wares. One way or another, the Russian Jews managed to scrape together enough money to survive.

Any other people would have eventually smothered under such oppression. But the Jew has one crucial asset: Torah. The Jews lived from week to week for the sake of Shabbos; prayer was a central factor of their lives; they treasured those sons that were clever enough to learn. Their religion transcended the severity of their exile and gave them the will to survive.

This phenomenon did not go unnoticed. The Czars, frustrated in their efforts to destroy the Jews, added new restrictions and edicts even as they offered rewards and enticements to those that would accept baptism. Nothing helped; only a few individuals converted. Even worse, despite a law that forbade Christians to have any social contacts with the Jews, the numbers of conversions to Judaism actually multiplied.

The Cantonists

Nicholas I (reigned 1825-1855) ascended the throne on his father's death. Like Alexander, he was determined to ensure that the despotic reign of the Czars would not be threatened by the more enlightened attitudes of Western Europe. The irritating problem of the Jews would have to be solved, one way or another.

The thirty years of Nicholas's reign were filled with unremitting persecution. He continued to oppress the impoverished Jews even as he considered different methods of destroying them. Jews could apparently thrive in poverty and hold their heads high, but there were other, more fiendish ways to break their resistance and turn them into Christians, whether they wished it or not.

In 1827, Nicholas instituted one of the most horrific decrees of Czarist Russia: the forced conscription of Jewish children into the Russian army. Until his time, the Jews had not been deemed worthy of serving in the Russian army; instead, they paid a "recruiting tax." Now, however, Nicholas demanded their service with a vengeance. Unlike the common people, who were drafted into the army at age eighteen for a period of twenty-five years, Jewish children were snatched at the age of twelve and forced to spend additional years in "training." Those that survived to reach their eighteenth year would then be forced to serve in the army for the next twenty-five years, just like their Russian counterparts.

Imperial decree demanded that each Jewish community provide a set number of boys. These hapless children were eventually called "Cantonists," a term which had originally referred to the sons of professional soldiers who were taken out of their home environment to be groomed for a lifelong career in the Russian army.

Jewish children were snatched at the age of twelve and forced to spend additional years in "training." Those that survived to reach their eighteenth year would then be forced to serve in the army for the next twenty-five years, just like their Russian counterparts.

In this instance, however, Nicholas was more interested in forcing these young boys to convert to Christianity than in turning them into soldiers.

The Jews were ordered to deliver "recruits" to the military service. The government held the leaders of the Jewish communities responsible for filling their quotas; if they failed to do so, the authorities conscripted the leaders of the community.

The unfortunate victims, often only eight or nine years old, were marched to distant provinces where they were "trained" by brutal, sadistic officers. Many of the children could not make the long trip and died along the way. Those who did survive were condemned to a harsh existence of constant drills, torture, and harassment. Persistent priests preached to them about baptism as the only way out of their misery. If the children remained stubborn, the next step would be torture by starvation.

The boys were forced to eat pork and to violate other commandments of the Torah. When the Jewish boys refused to eat the pork, they were given salted fish with no water to quench their thirst. Failure to obey was met with brutal beatings and abuse. Frequently, a stubborn Jew

The boys were forced to eat pork and to violate other commandments of the Torah. When the Jewish boys refused to eat the pork, they were given salted fish with no water to quench their thirst. Failure to obey was met with brutal beatings and abuse.

Chapter

36

With Nicholas looking on, the young soldiers were marched towards the river where the baptism would take place. When the bishop ordered them to enter the river to be baptized as Christians, the entire company stepped forward, entered the river —and kept going. No one came back. Before the stunned eyes of the Czar, the entire company of young Jews fearlessly gave up their lives al kiddush Hashem.

would be punished with the order to remain kneeling all night. If he fainted from fatigue, his tormentors would pour cold water over their victim and force him to continue his ordeal.

Cut off from their families and forbidden all contact with their former lives, most of the children succumbed and converted. Two decades of harsh, rough army life obliterated the faint childhood memories of their lives as Jews. Those few who managed to cling to their faith returned home with broken hearts and bodies, recounting tales of unmitigated horror, yet unprecedented heroism.

One of the cruelest aspects of the Cantonist edict was Nicholas's sadism in forcing the established Jewish leadership to soil their hands by holding them responsible to fulfill the quota of conscripted children.

Since no parents would willingly surrender their child to the horror of conscription and inevitable baptism, many leaders were forced to resort to trickery to fulfill the quota.

One of the most famous stories relates how an entire company of young Jewish "soldiers" underwent constant torture before they finally capitulated and declared that they were ready to accept baptism. Arrangements were made for an elaborate ceremony, to be witnessed by Czar Nicholas himself. After all, this would be a personal triumph for Nicholas, proof of the success of his policy.

With Nicholas looking on, the young soldiers were marched towards the river where the baptism would take place. When the bishop ordered them to enter the river to be baptized as Christians, the entire company stepped forward, entered the river—and kept going. No

one came back. Before the stunned eyes of the Czar, the entire company of young Jews fearlessly gave up their lives *al kiddush Hashem*.

Impoverished families saw their children disappear, kidnaped by their fellow Jews to take the place of wealthier children. Frightened parents locked their children behind barred doors at conscription time; any boy roaming the streets might be considered fair game. Worse, Jews accepted employment as child-snatchers, kidnaping young boys from their homes and sending them to probable death. More than anything else, the involvement of the communal leaders and the terrible willingness of other Jews to snatch the children undermined the cohesiveness of the Jewish community at a time when unity was desperately needed.

The rabbinic leaders of Russia spared no effort in their attempt to stop the horror of one Jew sending another to forced conversion and death. It is said that Rabbi Eliyahu Shik came to the city of Horodna and was told that the assembly hall of the Jewish community was filled with Jewish boys who had been rounded up for shipment to distant barracks. The rabbi picked up an ax, went out in the streets, and shouted, "What is the reason that the Jews are tramped upon in exile? It is because the Jews themselves are the kidnappers!"[5] A large crowd gathered around Rabbi Shik, who demanded, "My brothers and fellow Jews, why are you silent? Come with me and let us save Jewish souls!" The crowd followed Rabbi Shik's lead. Grabbing axes and crowbars, they marched to the community hall. Within minutes, the doors were broken and the imprisoned children were freed.

Hope lay in the few loopholes through which Jewish children could escape the

---

5. Based on *Yeshayah*, 42:24.

terrible fate of the Cantonists. Wealthier Jews were able to bribe officials and render their children exempt. An only child would not be conscripted, so many families registered each boy under a different surname. Many were successful in evading the terrible draft, but there were probably 60,000 innocent victims over the years, boys snatched from their homes and condemned to a hopeless life in the Russian army.

"Changes" in Policy

Fifteen years had passed since Czar Nicholas had ascended the throne and begun his infamous rule, but the Jews stubbornly clung to their faith. If the Cantonist conscription could not compel the Jews to abandon their way of life, some new approach would be necessary. This time, Nicholas decided, he would offer the hand of "friendship." Perhaps he did not realize that a false mask of kindness would do little to obscure the brutality of his regime.

Nicholas invited Yitzchak Levinson, a prominent assimilated Jew, to set up a new educational system in Russia. The trend of assimilation leading to eventual baptism had already begun in the West; Nicholas surmised that a similar program in his country might also accelerate the process of converting his stubborn Jews to loyal Christians.

Levinson, pleased with the opportunity, suggested that his task would be easier with governmental assistance. The Jews would be stubborn at first, so it would be necessary to weaken their resistance by ensuring that their only source of education would be the modern, enlightened sort of the Reform movement. He pushed the Czar to issue a law censoring Torah literature and Chassidic

books. Tens of thousands of *sefarim* were burned.

When Nicholas decided that Levinson was too slow to achieve results, he found a second Jewish collaborator, Dr. Max Lilienthal, who would help him force "enlightenment" on the Jews. At Lilienthal's direction, a new decree was issued, ordering the establishment of two teachers' seminaries in 1844. The Jews were graciously "allowed" to pay for these seminaries with a special tax levied on kosher meat and Shabbos candles. The new program of studies, as taught in these seminaries, would surely help the Jews see the error of their ways and become first loyal Russians, then Christians.

Frustratingly enough, no Jews seemed interested in attending the seminaries. Nicholas wanted to close all *Chadorim* and Yeshivos in Russia to force attendance, but with the combined efforts of Rabbi Yitzchak of Volozhin[6] and the Lubavitcher Rebbe, Reb Menachem Mendel, the terrible edict was rescinded.

As the seminaries' halls remained empty, Lilienthal traveled throughout Russia, hawking his brand of education in Jewish communities. To his dismay, he was met with stony rejection. It was simply too obvious that the Czar had baptism, not education, in mind; after all, Jewish children could already read and write fluently, while most of the Russian population were completely illiterate. The "mask of kindness" slipped off much too easily to fool the Jews.

Nicholas was eventually forced to admit that this ploy had failed. The new schools had virtually no students. Even during his reign, the authorities started to close the schools. Lilienthal himself

---

6. See Chapter 40.

> *Jews were graciously "allowed" to pay for these seminaries with a special tax levied on kosher meat and Shabbos candles. The new education package, as taught in these seminaries, would surely help the Jews see the error of their ways and become first loyal Russians, then Christians.*

Chapter
36

By allowing the Jews to attend the Russian universities instead of instituting special seminaries for their use, Alexander managed to succeed where his father had failed. By exposing the Jews to the outside world, the same insidious cycle that had occurred in Germany and France began.

abandoned his efforts and emigrated to America. The Czar threw off the image of benevolence and reverted to brutality, devising new schemes to destroy the Jews once and for all.

Deadly Classifications

The conscriptions continued, growing more frequent when Russia entered the Crimean War. Nicholas encouraged blood libels and published a government booklet, explaining exactly how and why Jews slaughtered innocent Christians before Pesach.[7] Towards the end of his reign, Nicholas issued a new decree, one that could have easily destroyed more than half the Jewish population in Russia.

All Jews would be divided into two categories; those Jews who had no useful trade or profession and were not registered as workers or businessmen would be in the category of "non-useful Jews," while those who offered some degree of benefit to Russia would be "useful Jews." "Useful Jews" would still be restricted to the Pale of Settlement, laboring under the many decrees that Nicholas saw fit to impose on them; but at least they would be alive, and entitled to some small measure of protection. "Non-useful Jews" would be completely outside the law, with no right to live anywhere and exposed to starvation, robbery, assault, and murder. If this edict had gone into effect, it would have doomed hundreds of thousands of Jews within Russia.

Fortunately, Nicholas did not live long enough to put the decree into effect. With his death in 1855, the Jews breathed a grateful sigh of relief and offered prayers of thanksgiving that the fanatical despot could no longer threaten the lives of millions of Russian Jews.

_____
7. See Chapter 35.

Temporary Reforms: Alexander II (1855–1881)

Alexander II, Nicholas's son, became Czar after his father's death. He was more intelligent and less narrow-minded than his despotic father, but he was still a true son of the vindictive spirit of the Romanov Dynasty. He was called the "great reformer" for his emancipation of the serfs in 1861 and for other benevolent policies, but his true nature eventually emerged.

Like his father, Alexander wanted his Jews to become Christians, but he thought a milder policy would achieve his goals more quickly. He replaced the terrible Cantonist edict with a general draft; thousands of Jews were still forced to serve in the Russian army, but for a period of only four years. The Pale was enlarged and Jews of certain categories were given permission to live outside of the boundaries and even attend the universities. Such permissiveness was actually designed to hasten assimilation, but many Jews seized the opportunity to better their miserable lives. Still, the majority of the Jewish population remained confined to the squalid conditions of the Pale.

By allowing the Jews to attend the Russian universities instead of instituting special seminaries for their use, Alexander managed to succeed where his father had failed. By exposing the Jews to the outside world, the same insidious cycle that had occurred in Germany and France began. With the easing of physical hardships under Alexander's rule and with greater social access to the secular world, the influence of the *Maskilim* grew in proportion.

In Russia, the movement for Reform was called "*Haskalah*,"[8] not "enlightenment."

There was no "religious" Reform as there was in Germany—*Haskalah* was totally anti-religious. Unlike their German counterparts, Russia's young Jews did not aspire to abandon their ethnic attachment to the Jewish people; there was no movement to speak Russian instead of Hebrew or Yiddish, as Mendelssohn had done with the infamous *Biur* in Germany.[9] While Mendelssohn had enjoyed the company and culture of the refined Germans, the Russians were peasants who were wholly devoted to pursuing the elementary needs of their mundane existence. Instead of advocating fraternization with their fellow Russians, the *Maskilim* in Russia determined to create a new, modern culture of their own, more attuned to the secularism that seemed to hold the key to social acceptance. They wanted to remain Jews, but not old-fashioned, Torah-oriented Jews.

The intelligence and talents that had been used for Torah study were diverted to the fields of art and theater, creating a new type of literature and entertainment injected with Jewish witticisms and biting self-criticism. Unhappily enough, the leaders of the movement often came from the ranks of the Yeshivos. Writers like Chaim Nachman Bialik and Mendele Mocher Seforim had a Talmudic background. The disease crept into the Yeshivos, until it was not unusual to find Yeshivah students who kept a secular book under their holy *sefarim*. This type of subversive secularism was a greater threat to the survival of Judaism than the German Reform movement.

Berlin suggested that anti-Semitism could be abolished by assimilation; the Russian *Maskilim* theorized that a secular culture which still remained distinctly Jewish would abolish persecution without destroying the Jewish entity as a nation. The Dreyfus affair and the rampant hatred in Western Europe proved the assimilationists wrong; events in Russia proved to be equally disastrous.

The Maskilim in Russia determined to create a new, modern culture of their own, more attuned to the secularism that seemed to hold the key to social acceptance. They wanted to remain Jews, but not old-fashioned, Torah-oriented Jews.

---

8. From the same root that the word *Maskilim* is derived.
9. See Chapter 30.

Chapter
36

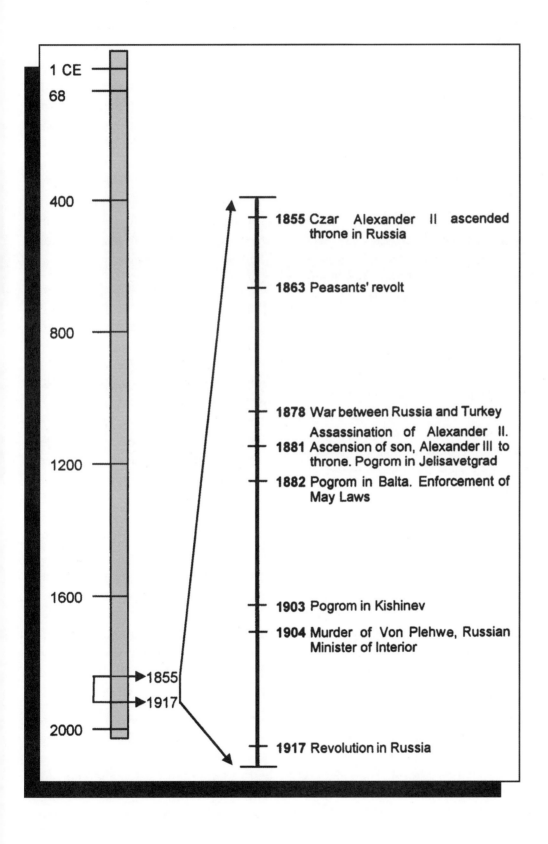

1855 Czar Alexander II ascended throne in Russia

1863 Peasants' revolt

1878 War between Russia and Turkey

1881 Assassination of Alexander II. Ascension of son, Alexander III to throne. Pogrom in Jelisavetgrad

1882 Pogrom in Balta. Enforcement of May Laws

1903 Pogrom in Kishinev

1904 Murder of Von Plehwe, Russian Minister of Interior

1917 Revolution in Russia

1855
1917

Chapter
37

Assassination

 Alexander's benevolence towards the peasants backfired. Despite the reforms that granted partial freedom to the peasants, Russia essentially remained a feudal society ruled by a corrupt Czar who still believed in the divine right of kings. In 1863, the unrest exploded into a dangerous uprising. Infuriated, the Czar canceled all reforms and instituted reactionary policies. The habitual tyranny of the Romanov Dynasty was clearly exposed.

As so often happens in cases of social conflict, the Jews were caught between the two factions. Even the Jews themselves were divided. Some of the younger, more radical elements openly sympathized with the peasants' revolt and joined the revolutionary "Nihilists," who believed that conditions in Russia had reached the point that all acts of terrorism, and even assassination, were justified to force a change. Others supported Alexander, all too aware that a true revolution would leave the Jews open to attack from both sides.

In March of 1881, Alexander agreed to sign a decree which would be the first step towards a constitutional government in Russia. Anxious to publicize this concession personally, the Czar rode an open carriage in a grand parade. The police warned Alexander that the Nihilists would take advantage and attempt assassination, but the Czar ignored the warning.

The first bomb missed Alexander, killing several of his attendants. Triumphant in his escape from assassination, the Czar descended from the imperial carriage to inquire about the injured. The Nihilists seized the opportunity and threw their second bomb, which exploded almost at his feet. His mutilated body was carried to the Winter Palace, where he died a few minutes later. His son, Alexander III, ascended to the throne.

Alexander III (1881–1894)

Alexander III was bent on the continuation of his absolute rule over the peasantry by methods of brutality and despotism. After all, the few reforms his father had instituted had led to unrest and eventual assassination. Fanatically religious, Alexander was determined to convert his entire country to the Greek Orthodox Church and rid Russia of any alien influences. The growing population of over five million Jews only served to increase his resolve. The Jews must be destroyed.

All reforms were abandoned. Alexander spread the idea that the Jews, not the Czars, were responsible for the suffering of the peasantry. Once again, the Jew was the scapegoat for political and social unrest. Such allegations were reinforced by the Jews' increasingly prominent positions in the fields of industry and commerce; resentful Gentiles claimed that the Jews were stealing their business. In addition, a wartime scandal involving a few Jews was blown out of proportion: the saying was "If one Jew does wrong, all Jews are suspect." The stage was set for Alexander's plan to force one-third of his Jews to assimilate, one-third to emigrate, and the final third to die of starvation. Streams of Jews did flee to America and other havens, but not enough to satisfy the Czar. When starvation proved to be taking too long, Alexander devised a new method to speed up the progress: the pogrom.

Pogrom is the Russian word for "destruction," but it is now used only in reference to the violent, government-sanctioned anti-Semitic outbreaks at the end of the nineteenth century and the beginning of the twentieth. The sadism of deliberate incitement by a government that should have protected its helpless citizens was heightened when Alexander blamed the Jews, saying that they had brought the pogroms upon themselves.

In most cases, the pogroms appeared as spontaneous expressions of popular sentiment; in truth, they were actually encouraged by the authorities. Alexander had sent secret orders from St. Petersburg with detailed instructions indicating when "popular indignation" against the Jews should explode into violence. The government never admitted its involvement, but the regularity of the pogroms and the uniform lack of police intervention left little doubt of the truth.

The first attack on the Jews erupted in Jelisavetgrad, a city with 1,500 Jews. For two days, the Jewish streets ran with blood, as a howling mob ran rampant. Policemen strolled by, watching the destruction with idle interest. On the third day, the police and army finally intervened to restore order.

The pogrom in Jelisavetgrad was just the prelude to a conflagration that would engulf hundreds of Jewish settlements with the same unbridled fury. A few weeks later, a pogrom erupted against the Jewish community of Kiev, the capital of the Ukraine, where Jews had lived since the early Middle Ages. Unlike officials in other cities, Kiev's police department gave the Jews warning of the onslaught, but the Jews refused to believe that such a thing could possibly happen. Most remained in the city instead of escaping. When Sunday morning arrived, it was too late.

Podol, the Jewish section of Kiev, swarmed with looting, bloodthirsty peasants. Women were attacked and several men were killed or wounded. The synagogue was stormed; the mob dragged the Torah scrolls out of the ark and trampled them into the mud. Christian inhabitants even

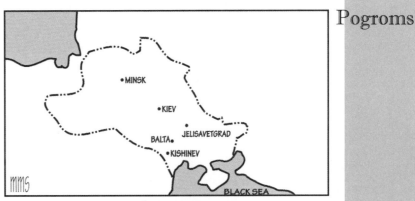

The Pogroms

took the precaution of placing statues of saints in their windows to avoid ransacking. During the looting, Cossack soldiers indifferently patrolled the streets, watching the carnage that they were supposed to stop. A few officers rode past to inspect the progress of the "operation." The storm raged for three days until soldiers were commanded to chase the drunken hoodlums out of the city.

In April of 1882, the Jews of Balta, a town in the province of Podolia, resolved to defend themselves against the mob. The police split the defense in two by cutting off a bridge, leaving one sector of the town completely isolated and helpless to repel the pogrom. Five thousand rioters stormed a bar and drank themselves into a state of drunken courage before scattering through the streets to attack and murder Jews by the score. Over twelve hundred homes and shops were destroyed, leaving some 15,000 Jews penniless.

With Balta, the first round of pogroms was over. The stunned Jews now had to cope with Alexander's accusation that they had brought the pogroms upon themselves. The violent attacks, Alexander declared, were only the understandable expressions of frustration by the Christians who had been financially exploited by Jewish businessmen and forced

Alexander had sent secret orders from St. Petersburg with detailed instructions indicating when "popular indignation" against the Jews should explode into violence.

Chapter

37

> *Until Alexander's death in 1894, the Jews suffered from "cold" pogroms, a series of successive edicts aimed at impoverishing the Jews.*

into poverty. As a result, the government was "forced" to pass a series of restrictive laws which would protect the Russians against the menace of Jewish takeover.

Until Alexander's death in 1894, the Jews suffered from "cold" pogroms, a series of successive edicts aimed at impoverishing the Jews. The May Laws of 1882, seen as a repercussion of the Balta pogrom and the Jews' role in "causing" the pogrom in the first place, crammed the already-crowded Jews into even smaller areas than before. Most Jews attending universities were expelled. Many of these completed their degrees in Western European universities, only to be told on their return that foreign professional licenses would not be recognized in Russia. With each successive decree, the weight of oppression increased. A terrible famine in 1891 left the Jews in even more desperate straits. When Alexander III died in 1894, the Jews were relieved. They had no way of knowing that his son, Czar Nicholas II and the last ruling Czar of Russia, would be even worse.

Nicholas II (1894–1917)

The tyranny of the Czars had turned ignorant laborers into a seething mass of anarchists, terrorists, socialists, and other radicals. Many Jews were attracted to these extremists, dreaming of a new era of equal rights beginning with the Czar's downfall. Nicholas desperately seized on this to proclaim that the Jews, besides being money-hungry, bloodthirsty, and evil, were also subversive revolutionaries. The radicals promptly turned on their Jewish colleagues. Once again, everyone looked on the Jew as the culprit for everything that occurred.

On Easter Day in 1903, tragedy struck Kishinev, the capital of Bessarabia. The savagery of this attack surpassed anything that had happened before. The drunken mob went berserk, incited by passionate

sermons to attack the nation that had once destroyed their savior. They fell upon the Kishinev Jews, armed with sticks and hatchets, smashing skulls, slashing people in two, gouging out eyes, throwing infants into the street, and committing similar unspeakable atrocities. Even those Russians who had not participated in the first wave of the attack joined the mob to loot and plunder what was left of the Kishinev Jewish community.

The government openly supported these excesses, accusing the Jews of bringing the bloodbath on themselves. It was a poorly guarded secret that the Minister of the Interior, the notorious Von Plehwe, had been behind the Kishinev pogrom, although Von Plehwe's murder by the Nihilists in 1904 did little to stop the violence.

In 1905, after thousands of peasants had been massacred when they presented a petition for a constitution, the workers finally revolted and organized a strike. The Czar was forced to grant a limited constitution, but neither side was satisfied with the situation. Desperate for a scapegoat, Nicholas began to arrange for the publishing of anti-Semitic literature. In the last months of 1905, 650 Jewish communities were attacked and the Czar honored those who had begun the pogroms. By 1906, Nicholas had the members of his army participating openly in the attacks.

World Reaction — and Non-Reaction

Despite the very tight censorship in Russia, news of the horrific events leaked out. For the enlightened minds of the West, who had prided themselves on the progress of civilization in the modern age, the news that brutality and torture still thrived in Russia came as a shocking, rude awakening.

One of the main harbingers of the devastating news was Rabbi Yitzchak Elchanan Spector of Kovno, one of the greatest Sages of his day. He smuggled secret reports of the pogroms to the rabbinic leaders in the West, among them Rav Hirsch because of his political connections in Germany. Appalled, the Torah leaders mobilized to perform any action possible to help the Russian Jews. In Paris, London, New York, and Philadelphia, mass assemblies were organized to proclaim a worldwide protest against the genocide.

The largest assembly was held in London, at the mayor's initiative. They demanded that British Prime Minister Gladstone lodge an official protest in Moscow against the inhuman acts of the Russian people against its Jews. But Gladstone refused to act, claiming that the conduct of the Russian government towards the people in its country was an internal affair of the Russians and that His Majesty's government had no right to intervene. President Harrison of the United States, on the other hand, agreed to send a message of protest to the Czar. The gesture was politic, but Nicholas ignored it completely.

While little could be done to halt the onslaught, England and America did agree to receive refugees. Russian Jews emigrated *en masse* to the West, traveling by train, boat, wagon, or foot if necessary. There was no organized planning or system; the Jews just wanted to escape. Most went to the United States, the "land of opportunity." Together with refugees from Germany in the mid-nineteenth century, they formed a large segment of the Jewish population in North America, settling in New York, Philadelphia, Montreal, and other cities.

Once the doors for emigration were officially open, efforts were made to set up a resettlement foundation that would enable the Jews to live independently and with dignity. One novel idea for resettlement is credited to an extremely wealthy Jewish philanthropist, Baron Hirsch. Hirsch set aside a good part of his fortune for the relief of the crisis in Russia and secured the cooperation of the Russian government in his large-scale emigration program. He planned to acquire a large piece of land in Argentina, South America, which contained sufficient space for thousands of immigrant families. Argentina was largely uncultivated and relatively uninhabited; the Jews would be welcome in this part of the world, free of the prejudice that had haunted their footsteps for centuries.

Initially, Hirsch hoped to resettle 25,000 people in the first year, increasing the number of newcomers every year, so that, within a period of twenty-five years, three million Jews would find a new home in Argentina. But the plan, which seemed so plausible on paper, failed to materialize. Jews were more than ready to leave Russia, but they were uninterested in moving thousands of miles away from civilization to a country where there were no other Jews and little chance of financial success.

The thrust of Jewish emigration had to be directed elsewhere. Eretz Yisrael was an obvious choice, but how—and under whose direction—would they get there?

> *One of the main harbingers of the devastating news was Rabbi Yitzchak Elchanan Spector of Kovno, one of the greatest Sages of his day, who smuggled secret reports of the pogroms to the rabbinic leaders in the West.*

> *One novel idea for resettlement is credited to an extremely wealthy Jewish philanthropist, Baron Hirsch. Hirsch set aside a good part of his fortune for the relief of the crisis in Russia and secured the cooperation of the Russian government in his large-scale emigration program.*

Chapter
37

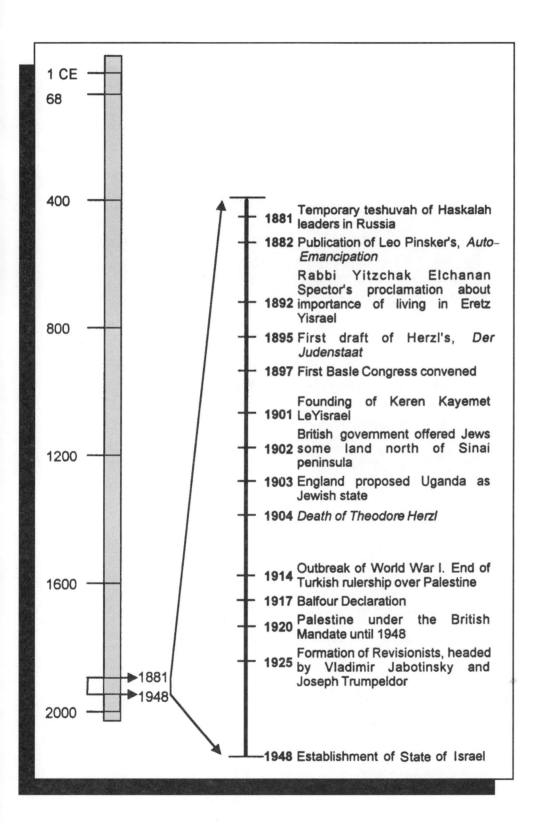

1881	Temporary teshuvah of Haskalah leaders in Russia
1882	Publication of Leo Pinsker's, *Auto-Emancipation*
1892	Rabbi Yitzchak Elchanan Spector's proclamation about importance of living in Eretz Yisrael
1895	First draft of Herzl's, *Der Judenstaat*
1897	First Basle Congress convened
1901	Founding of Keren Kayemet LeYisrael
1902	British government offered Jews some land north of Sinai peninsula
1903	England proposed Uganda as Jewish state
1904	*Death of Theodore Herzl*
1914	Outbreak of World War I. End of Turkish rulership over Palestine
1917	Balfour Declaration
1920	Palestine under the British Mandate until 1948
1925	Formation of Revisionists, headed by Vladimir Jabotinsky and Joseph Trumpeldor
1948	Establishment of State of Israel

Chapter

38

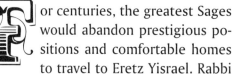

An organization called Chovevei Tzion purchased land that could be used for agriculture; by offering a livelihood as well as a home, Chovevei Tzion promoted immigration to Eretz Yisrael.

or centuries, the greatest Sages would abandon prestigious positions and comfortable homes to travel to Eretz Yisrael. Rabbi Yehudah HaLevi was killed shortly after arrriving on Eretz Yisrael's holy soil;[1] the Ramban spent the last years of his life in Yerushalayim, establishing a synagogue in the midst of the ruins of the city;[2] Sephardic greats such as Rav Yosef Saragossi, Rav Yaakov Berav, and Rav Yosef Karo, author of the *Shulchan Aruch,* left Spain and eventually settled in Tzefas;[3] Rabbi Ovadiah of Bartenurah, Italy, made the journey to Yerushalayim in 1488; the Vilna Gaon departed for Eretz Yisrael, only to return to Vilna without explanation.[4] Many of the students of the Gaon and the Baal Shem Tov traveled to Eretz Yisrael, struggling to survive in a foreign land, with no livelihood.

The longing to return to Eretz Yisrael is

The Netziv

an integral part of the Jew's exile.[5] According to the Ramban, the mitzvah of living in Eretz Yisrael is one of the 613 commandments incumbent on all Jews, even during times of exile; living outside Eretz Yisrael can only be justified by substantial cause.[6] Many Torah scholars and rabbinic leaders, such as the disciples of the Gaon and the Baal Shem Tov, encouraged emigration to Eretz Yisrael. In the year 1892, the venerable Sage Rabbi Yitzchak Elchanan Spector published a proclamation about the importance and viability of the mitzvah to live in Eretz Yisrael; the Netziv, Rav Naftoli Tzvi Berlin, also approved of the effort to journey to Eretz Yisrael, and attempted to go himself.[7]

In the nineteenth century, things suddenly changed, as massive immigration to Eretz Yisrael was prompted by something other than religious fervor. The pogroms in Russia, combined with the vicious upsurge of anti-Semitism in Western Europe, drove the Jews to a desperate search for refuge. America, the land of "golden opportunity," offered a haven, as did the possibility of settling in the barrens of South America. But refugees from Eastern Europe in increasing numbers turned to the possibility of settling in Eretz Yisrael.

Thanks to the efforts of wealthy Jewish philanthropists, living in Eretz Yisrael was no longer the impossibility that had been courageously faced by determined Jews throughout the generations. An organization called *Chovevei Tzion* purchased land that could be used for agriculture; by offering a livelihood as well as a home, *Chovevei Tzion* promoted immigration to Eretz Yisrael. Those who

---

1. See Chapter 11.
2. See Chapter 17.
3. See Chapter 22.
4. See Chapter 29.

5. See Chapter 1 [Rabbi Tzadok].
6. *Tosafos, Kesubos,* 110b.
7. See Chapter 40.

escaped from the Russian pogroms joined the Sephardic Jews that had lived there for centuries, the descendants of the disciples of the Vilna Gaon and the Baal Shem Tov, and others who had abandoned the questionable comforts of Europe to live on the sanctified land of Eretz Yisrael. Another group of active pioneers had begun to settle in various parts of Eretz Yisrael under the name *"Bilu,"* an abbreviation for *Bais Yaakov Lechu Venailcha.*[8] Overcoming tremendous odds, they built the early *yishuvim,* or settlements, in the Holy Land.

There was little conflict between those who immigrated out of religious piety and those who came to Eretz Yisrael to escape a bleak future in Europe—they all shared an appreciation for the holiness and purity of the land. The new wave of settlers in the early 1900's, however, came with a different thought in mind: a love for the country of their ancestors, which eventually turned into the ideology called "Zionism."

Dr. Pinsker's "Diagnosis"

The French Revolution had proclaimed the principles of freedom to the medieval world. The walls of the ghettos had been torn down, and the Jews had gradually breathed the air of emancipation and, inevitably, assimilation. In the initial stages of this long-awaited liberation, many Jews became convinced that anti-Semitism no longer existed in the modern, enlightened world, but the pogroms of Russia taught them otherwise. Government-sponsored slayings and the proliferation of the absurd blood libel taught a bitter lesson: assimilation does not

work. The Jews had no hope for any future among the Gentiles.

Rather than admit they were wrong to turn their backs on Torah, the *Maskilim* racked their brains for some other solution. Political and social emancipation in Russia and any other European country were not the answer, but perhaps there could be another kind of emancipation?

Leo Pinsker, a Jewish doctor in Odessa, formulated the solution in a book which he called *Auto-Emancipation.* In this book, Pinsker claims that the Jews' current status is "ill." As long as the Jews are in exile, they are not a living nation but only the shadow of a people. The Jews must free themselves by their own strength and find a territory, either in Palestine or in some other country (the place was immaterial to Pinsker at that time), with room for the millions of homeless Jews from all over the world. This land must be guaranteed to the Jews by international help, so that the people could settle there and develop in freedom.

Pinsker's concept of a national homeland bore no resemblance to the Holy Land for which the Jews pray three times a day. His theories contained the essence of Zionist ideology, "Let us be like all other nations." To the religious Jew, "Eretz Yisrael without Torah is like a body without a soul," but Pinsker wasn't interested in the soul; all he wanted was a country where the Jews could develop a land of their own.

Even as Pinsker developed his diagnosis of the "illness" that plagued Jewry, an assimilated Western Jew was developing ideas of his own.

To the religious Jew, "Eretz Yisrael without Torah is like a body without a soul."

Leo Pinsker formulated the solution in a book called Auto-Emancipation

8. *Yeshayah,* 2:5.

Chapter
38

> *Herzl dismissed these anti-Semitic incidents as nothing more than scar tissue left over from a generation that was no longer of any concern.*

Theodore Herzl

Born in Hungary and raised and educated in Vienna, Theodore Herzl had no knowledge of his Jewish heritage. As a newspaper reporter, he had experienced a series of anti-Semitic rejections, but he dismissed these incidents as nothing more than scar tissue left over from a generation that was no longer of any concern.

Herzl's views and beliefs turned to ashes when he accepted an assignment from a Viennese newspaper to serve as a reporter at the infamous Dreyfus case. The brutal reality of anti-Semitism stunned him as the scream, "Death to the Jews!" echoed in the streets of France, the cradle of human rights and equality. Dreyfus came from an assimilated background like Herzl's; he was educated, ignorant of his Jewish background, fiercely loyal to his homeland, but his status as Jew was enough to make Dreyfus a despised, dishonored creature. Herzl was shattered at the realization that even when the Jews have assimilated, the old prejudices and hatreds remained.

Herzl left France, determined to find some solution to the dilemma of the Jews throughout the world. The prospect of returning to his roots never even occurred to him; he knew nothing about religion in the first place. Instead, he used his brilliant mind and organizational talent to create a new plan. On June 13, 1895, Herzl began the first draft of *Der Judenstaat,* "The Jews' State." In this book he established his definition of a "nation" as a group of people bound together by common suffering and persecution.

Herzl believed that no one but the Jews themselves could solve the Jewish problem. The great powers of the world must be persuaded to provide space for a Jewish homeland. He disapproved of the gradual infiltration and piecemeal colonization of Eretz Yisrael that had been undertaken by the Jewish philanthropists, Barons Hirsch and Rothschild. Instead, he was convinced that the Jews ought to enter their new country in large, organized groups with their heads held high.

Herzl dedicated his talents as a writer, politician, and organizer to translate his dream into reality. He negotiated with the German Emperor and the heads of other involved governments, hoping to intrigue and interest them in his ambitious plan. Above all, he mobilized and galvanized Jewish leaders in the various European countries in an attempt to rally them to his side.

The Basle Congress

Before Herzl could persuade the leaders of the great powers to grant the Jews a homeland, he first needed the approval of the Jews in order to act on their behalf. With great difficulty, he convened a world assembly of Zionists. This initial effort proved more complicated than he had anticipated.

Reform rabbis in Germany opposed him for fear of losing their hard-won emancipation rights. What would the governments think of Jewish loyalty in the light of a national movement to encourage a Jewish state? When the city of Munich was chosen as a suitable location for a Zionist Congress, the local Jewish community rented all available halls for the day the convention was supposed to be held. At the last moment, the Congress had to be transferred to Basle, Switzerland.

Opposition to Herzl's program also came from deeply religious Jews who felt that it was presumptuous to initiate mass immigration to Eretz Yisrael without a signal from Heaven.[9] Above all, the rabbinic leaders viewed the idea of recreating the Jewish nation on a secular basis as completely opposed to the Torah's teachings—indeed it was tantamount to idol worship.[10] They issued statements against the new movement and called for strong opposition to it.

Despite the lack of solidarity, on August 27, 1897, the first Basle Congress finally met in what was intended to become an annual session. Later on, it convened biannually until World War II.

The Congress functioned as a temporary Zionist Parliament which formulated the policies of the Zionist movement. It consisted of two hundred and four delegates from an equal number of Jewish communities. From the first opening moments it seemed impossible to reconcile the different factions. Whatever results were achieved at all, were due solely to Herzl's ability to dominate the proceedings.

The religious delegates, mostly from the East, Poland and Russia, rallied under the name of *Chovevei Tzion,* "Lovers of Zion." These interpreted the writings of Rabbi Yitzchak Elchanan Spector and the urgings of the Netziv as encouragement to participate in the Zionist project of rebuilding Eretz Yisrael, not realizing that these selfsame leaders were vehemently opposed to the nationalistic concepts of Zionism and their vision of a secular, non-religious homeland. Representatives of *Bilu,* the settlements already in Eretz Yisrael, were reluctant to accept Herzl at all. They

were uninterested in the leadership of a man so lacking in religious motivation, although the members of *Bilu* themselves were not religious at all.

Other groups preferred a more practical method which could produce faster results, albeit on a smaller scale, by directly purchasing tracts of land in Eretz Yisrael. Others, particularly the Russian *Maskilim,* were more interested in promoting Eretz Yisrael as the essence of Jewish culture. One more radical group, called the "Territorialists," followed Pinsker's line of thinking that any land, not necessarily Eretz Yisrael, would serve their purpose.

Eventually, Herzl was able to engineer a compromise which allowed each faction to pursue its particular policy under the umbrella of the Zionist movement. Generally speaking, the assembled delegates split into three factions: political Zionists, led by Herzl, who sought to achieve a Jewish homeland through political action; practical Zionists, who would concentrate on immigration of pioneers to Eretz Yisrael after tracts of land were purchased from the Turkish government with the help of the Rothschilds, Sir Montefiore, and other philanthropists; and cultural Zionists, who focused on making Eretz Yisrael a cultural center of the world, led by Russian *Maskilim,* poets, and historians.

At first, the religious Zionists did not form their own distinct group; they still hoped that the concept of holiness would naturally prevail and permeate the entire movement. When a Rumanian Zionist, a rabbi, stood up and chanted the *shehecheyanu* blessing, many of the

---

9. Chazal in *Kesubos,* 111a state that Hashem imposed three oaths upon the Jews and the nations of the world concerning the exile, including the promise that the Jews will not attempt to storm Eretz Yisrael by force.

10. See Rabbi Wasserman's *Epoch of the Messiah,* page 12.

The assembled delegates split into three factions: political Zionists, led by Herzl, who sought to achieve a Jewish homeland through political action; practical Zionists, who would concentrate on immigration of pioneers to Eretz Yisrael after tracts of land were purchased from the Turkish government with the help of the Rothschilds, Sir Montefiore, and other philanthropists; and cultural Zionists, who focused on making Eretz Yisrael a cultural center of the world.

Chapter
38

A national fund was set up, the Keren Kayemet LeYisrael (KKL), to buy collective land in Eretz Yisrael.

At collection time, the contents of these boxes added up to enormous sums of money.

delegates felt deeply moved. The religious Zionists remained in the Congress, hoping for further developments.

At that Congress the Basle Progam was proclaimed, stating Zionisism's main goal to be: "Establishing a home for the Jewish people in Palestine, secured under public law." After its conclusion Herzl wrote in his diary, "If I were to sum up the results of this Congress in a few words, I would say I founded the Jewish State in Basle." As it turned out, this statement was premature. Herzl lived for eight more years, but he never saw a Jewish State.

What's Wrong with Uganda?

Zionism's organization grew as the Congress met regularly. Every Jew who paid his *shekel,* a special ticket, the name of which was adopted from the currency mentioned in the Torah, had a vote. (At that time, the *shekel* was valued at one German mark, or a half-dollar.) Financial foundations were established; as early as 1901, a national fund was set up, the *Keren Kayemet LeYisrael* (KKL), to buy collective land in Eretz Yisrael. Collections for this fund came from thousands of donation boxes which were distributed to Jewish households all over the world. At collection time, the contents of these boxes added up to enormous sums of money.

In 1902, it seemed as if political Zionism would produce results. In response to the horror of the Russian pogroms, the British government offered to give the Jews self-government on a strip of land to the north of the Sinai Peninsula. However, it was found impossible to provide enough water for cultivation of the desert area.

The following year, England proposed Uganda, in the colony of British East Africa, as the site for a Jewish state. This plan caused a major uproar among the

Zionists. The Territorialists, as well as Herzl, were prepared to accept it, but the majority of the East European delegates were up in arms. A major crisis arose, to the point where one fanatic actually tried to murder Max Nordau, one of Herzl's closest friends. The delegates voted to postpone the decision; two years later, the Uganda Plan was abandoned.

Herzl left the Congress in a state of depression. When he died on July 3, 1904, he was mourned as a hero by all the Zionist factions. In retrospect, however, an honest look at Herzl reveals an assimilated Western Jew who had completely forgotten his Jewishness. A man with an anti-Torah background cannot lead the Jewish people.

Religious Efforts

After Herzl's death, the efforts of the Zionists were continued, albeit at a somewhat slower pace. Some prominent rabbinic leaders, including Rabbi Zirelson, Rabbi Cohn of Basle, Rabbi Chaim Israel Eis, and the Poltaver Rav, remained within the Zionist system in the hope that it would still be possible to retain Orthodox Judaism as a fundamental necessity. They still clung to the hope that the Zionists would abandon their slogan of "Eretz Yisrael is in Asia, not in Heaven." They rallied under the name *Mizrachi,* hoping they could still unite the banner of Torah and the banner of nationalism.

These last hopes were dashed at the Tenth Congress. The majority passed a motion that all cultural and educational activity in Eretz Yisrael should be combined under the direction of the Zionist organization, which was dominated by anti-religious elements. The Zionist leadership consistently vetoed all attempts to yield to the demands of the religious group; the resolution passed in its original version. Most Orthodox leaders abandoned their efforts to bring the Zionists back to religious considerations from within their own system. They retreated and founded Agudas Yisrael, ready to combat anti-religious proposals with their own organization.[11] Those that remained in the Mizrachi group found themselves forced into concession after concession, without any real religious gain.

With time, the Zionist party became permanently divided into four separate groups:

The Socialists, or Labor Party, adopted the program of the Marxist Socialist movement. The Socialists are dedicated to improving the material lot of the working class and are strongly opposed to any religious orientation in Eretz Yisrael.

The General Zionists, or middle class, as a group are oriented towards a capitalistic economy.

Religious Zionists, or Mizrachi, retain Torah and mitzvos, but do not necessarily accept *daas Torah* in matters concerning political issues and the common welfare.

The Revisionists, a splinter group formed in 1925, during the era of the British Mandate,[12] protested the acquiescence of the Zionist leaders to the restrictive immigration policies of the British government. Its members insisted on capturing Eretz Yisrael for the Jewish people by any means. This party was headed by Vladimir Jabotinsky, a

lawyer, writer, and one of the world's foremost orators.

The Balfour Declaration

Palestine remained under the rule of the Ottoman Empire until World War I, when the British army, assisted by Jews and Arabs, defeated the Turks. In 1917, the British government issued a declaration that formally acknowledged the Jews' claim to Palestine. In actuality, the Balfour Declaration is a marvelous example of diplomatic double-talk. It was published in the form of a letter by the British Foreign Secretary, Lord Balfour, to a member of the Rothschild family in England:

"Dear Lord Rothschild,

I have much pleasure in conveying to you, on behalf of His Majesty's Government, the following declaration of sympathy with Jewish Zionist aspirations which has been submitted to, and approved by, the Cabinet.

"His Majesty's Government view with favor the establishment in Palestine of a national home for the Jewish people, and will use their best endeavors to facilitate the achievement of the object, it being clearly understood that nothing shall be done which may prejudice the civil and religious rights of existing non-Jewish communities in Palestine, or the rights and political status enjoyed by Jews in any other country."

> *The Socialists, or Labor Party, adopted the program of the Marxist Socialist movement.*

> *Religious Zionists, Mizrachi, retain Torah and mitzvos, but do not necessarily accept daas Torah in matters concerning political issues and the common welfare.*

> *The Revisionists, a splinter group formed in 1925, during the era of the British Mandate, protested the acquiescence of the Zionist leaders to the restrictive immigration policies of the British government. Its members insisted on capturing Eretz Yisrael for the Jewish people by any means.*

> *The General Zionists, or middle class, as a group are oriented towards a capitalistic economy.*

11. See Chapter 39.
12. A Mandate refers to territory granted to a nation for the purpose of establishing a government and educating the people, until eventually the country can rule itself. In the case of Palestine, the League of Nations granted it as a Mandate to Great Britain because the English had conquered Palestine from the Turks.

Chapter

38

The Zionists, wary of jeopardizing the expected wave of sympathy that would surely come after the war, refused to use illegal methods to save the lives of European Jews.

At first glance, this declaration seems to be a triumph for the Zionists. Great Britain had publicly declared that it approved of the concept of a national homeland for the world's Jews and wanted to help this homeland come into being. When World War I ended, this declaration became part of the mandate granted to Great Britain by the League of Nations,[13] based on the assumption that the British would assist the Jews in creating a homeland for themselves.

A closer look at the diplomatic language, however, reveals that the Balfour Declaration was little more than a pretty collection of words. England needed the support of the Jews for her role in the Middle East, so Lord Balfour offered "best endeavors" without concrete details, which could have jeopardized Britain's friendship with the Arabs; since "nothing shall be done which may prejudice the civil and religious rights of existing non-Jewish communities in Palestine," the whole offer was virtually invalidated.

1948: A New Kind of Israel

For the duration of their mandate (1920–1948), Great Britain made an unsuccessful attempt to keep a delicate balance between Jewish hopes and Arab protests. When the diplomatic and economic conditions advised a closer relationship with the Arab countries, the British openly reneged on their professed sympathy with the Zionists.

The infamous White Paper, which placed a ridiculously low limit on the number of Jews permitted to immigrate to Palestine each year, left millions of Jews stranded

---

13. Following World War I, the victorious allies founded an international body called the League of Nations, similar to the United Nations founded after World War II. It was the League of Nations that decided which nations should rule over the countries that had been conquered by the allies during the war.

A closer look at the diplomatic language, however, reveals that the Balfour Declaration was little more than a pretty collection of words. England needed the support of the Jews for her role in the Middle East, so Lord Balfour offered "best endeavors" without concrete details, which could have jeopardized Britain's friendship with the Arabs.

in Europe during World War II while Hitler, *yimach shemo,* carried out his systematic genocide. The Zionists, wary of jeopardizing the expected wave of sympathy that would surely come after the war, refused to use illegal methods to save the lives of European Jews.

In 1948, as the Zionists had expected, Britain relinquished its mandate and the State of Israel, a country based not on religion but "like all other nations," came into being. Religious Jewry now had to decide how to react to the State and its irreligious leaders.

Ideologically, Agudas Yisrael remained as opposed to Zionism as before; indeed, Rabbi Elchonon Wasserman had denounced Zionism as a modern version of idol-worship. Those Torah leaders who had walked out of the Zionist Congress in protest of the anti-religious policy of the Zionist Congress had done so because of

Credit of OJ Archives of Agudath Israel of America

Rav Reuven Grozovsky

the Torah's warning: *Al toshes yadcha im rasha,* "Do not join hands with a wicked person."[14] In what way would Agudas Yisrael relate to the new country in which the anti-religious Zionist party wielded a controlling influence?

In line with the policy of Agudas Yisrael, the question was put to *daas Torah*; the *Moetzes Gedolei HaTorah* had to determine the answer. At that time, the chairman of the Rabbinic Council was the great Sage, Rav Reuven Grozovsky, son-in-law of Rav Baruch Ber Leibowitz. At an Agudah conference, Reb Reuven explained:

"One is part of it whether he likes it or not.... The only way to eliminate or alleviate any bad laws is through the legislative or judicial way. The rule 'do not associate yourself with the wicked' does not apply here, since, even unwillingly, everyone is associated. We must make every effort to utilize the democratic privileges, which the state grants us, to battle for our rights. There is a difference between a state and a movement. In a state, for example, should we not participate in the election, it would mean relinquishing our basic rights and even assisting them to rule over us with an even greater power. The participation in the election cannot be considered an approval of their government, their laws, or their ideals."[15]

On the basis of this ruling, Agudas Yisrael reluctantly cooperated with the new State. Many original members of the Agudah protested, fearing a reversal of its earlier anti-Zionist position. They were more inclined to accept the position taken by the *Neturai Karta,* a movement started by the original residents of the old *yishuv* in Yerushalayim, who completely reject the concept of a Jewish State and fight against its existence. Despite these protests, Agudas Yisrael acted, and continues to act, in line with its constitutional position that the Rabbinic Council is the final arbiter of any ruling.

Events in Jewish history can move at a bewilderingly rapid pace. One must look back towards the past to understand current issues: *maaseh avos siman levanim,* events that happened to past generations are a portent for future generations. History will continue to move, but with faith in Hashem and the acceptance of *daas Torah* as the guide towards understanding, the Jewish people will survive.

The Moetzes Gedolei HaTorah had to determine the answer. At that time, the chairman of the Rabbinic Council was the great Sage, Rav Reuven Grozovsky, son-in-law of Rav Baruch Ber Leibowitz.

14. *Shemos,* 23:1.

15. *A History of Agudas Yisrael,* by Joseph Friedenson.

Chapter

38

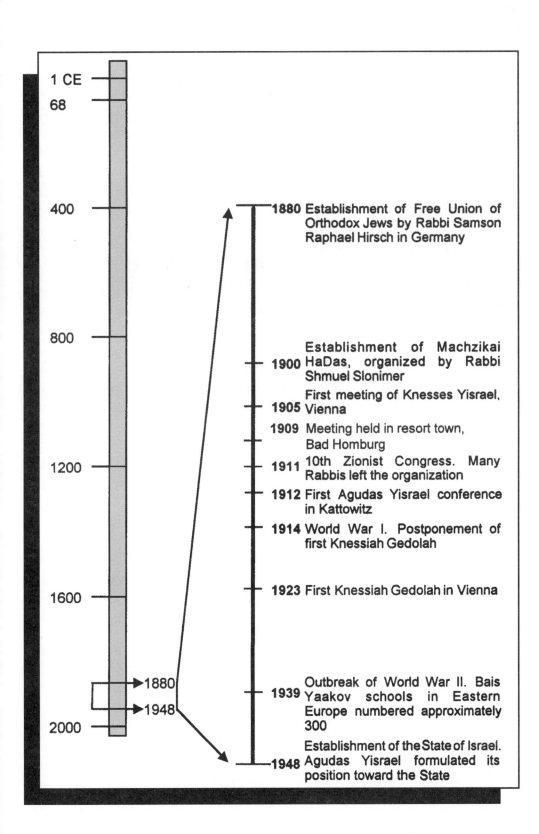

1 CE	
68	
400	**1880** Establishment of Free Union of Orthodox Jews by Rabbi Samson Raphael Hirsch in Germany
800	
	1900 Establishment of Machzikai HaDas, organized by Rabbi Shmuel Slonimer
	1905 First meeting of Knesses Yisrael, Vienna
	1909 Meeting held in resort town, Bad Homburg
1200	**1911** 10th Zionist Congress. Many Rabbis left the organization
	1912 First Agudas Yisrael conference in Kattowitz
	1914 World War I. Postponement of first Knessiah Gedolah
1600	**1923** First Knessiah Gedolah in Vienna
1880	
1948	**1939** Outbreak of World War II. Bais Yaakov schools in Eastern Europe numbered approximately 300
2000	**1948** Establishment of the State of Israel. Agudas Yisrael formulated its position toward the State

Chapter

39

Reaction
of the Gedolim
to the Secular
Movements

Torah leaders realized that a compromise was impossible; a worldwide movement like the Zionists required a worldwide counter-movement.

ith emancipation and the subsequent exposure to the outside world, nineteenth-century Jewry found its religion assaulted from within. In each region, as a new movement arose to poison the minds of the Jewish people, a counter-movement began to combat assimilation. In Germany, where Reform strove for complete assimilation, Rav Samson Raphael Hirsch introduced the philosophy of *Torah im Derech Eretz;*[1] in Russia, where the *Maskilim* tried to introduce a new, more "cultured" Judaism, the Chassidic movement lent strength to religious resistance;[2] in Lithuania as well as Russia, the Yeshivos and the mussar movement checked the cancerous influence of Haskalah within the Yeshivah halls;[3] and in Hungary, the Chasam Sofer's leadership frustrated the *Maskilim's* efforts.[4]

At the turn of the twentieth century, however, a new danger arose that encompassed all of European Jewry. The new Jewish nationalism that Herzl had created in Zionism, coupled with the fascinating temptation of Socialism and its promise of equality, were combined to form a dangerous new religion of its own. Zionism's call for a "Jewish homeland" and "Jewish unity" initially seemed so innocent that many Jews failed to recognize the secular, irreligious tone of a group of Jews who would have been equally content to win either Uganda or Eretz Yisrael as the Jewish homeland.[5]

The leaders of Torah-observant Jewry were reluctant to openly oppose the new Zionist movement, despite alarm and apprehension regarding Zionism's true intentions. At first, attempts were made to negotiate from within; by initially

1. See Chapter 34.
2. See Chapter 36.
3. See Chapter 40.

participating with the Zionist Congress, rabbinic leaders hoped to guide and persuade the Zionist leaders to follow the true path of Torah. When events proved this to be a hopeless undertaking, Torah leaders realized that a compromise was impossible; a worldwide movement like the Zionists required a worldwide counter-movement. Religious Jews, regardless of their differences in outlook and ideology, united to combat the new heretical ideas and to guard the integrity of the Torah front with an organization of their own: Agudas Yisrael.

Humble Beginnings

Rav Samson Raphael Hirsch of Frankfurt had stepped fearlessly into a cesspool of Reform and created a small Orthodox community.[6] All too aware of the vast might of the Reform movement, Rav Hirsch attempted to expand his influence beyond the boundaries of his community. He sponsored the "Free Union of Orthodox Jews in Germany" to serve as a consolidation of all separatist communities in cities where the Reform Jews had the majority of votes. This organization, one of the last projects of Rav Hirsch before he died in 1888, never really came into being, but the concept was born, ready to be picked up by his successor and students and to be revised to create a worldwide Torah organization.

In 1900, Rabbi Shmuel Slonimer undertook to create an organization that would rally religious Jews to combat the *Maskilim* in Russia. The Haskalah movement in Russia, which was more interested in creating a "new, more cultured" Judaism than in causing complete assimilation, had set up an organization with the express intention of

4. See Chapter 40.
5. See Chapter 38.
6. See Chapter 34.

undermining religious education. In order to entice unsuspecting parents to send their children to their schools, they called their educational institutions "improved *Chadorim*" rather than "enlightened" or "reformed" schools. This deceived the simple Jew, as well as a government which opposed any change of the status quo, into believing that the "improved *Chadorim*" followed the traditional pattern with only minor modifications, when the true intent was actually systematic indoctrination of secularism.

Rabbi Shmuel Slonimer knew that a combination of all Orthodox groups under a single umbrella organization would be necessary to wage a successful battle against the "improved *Chadorim*." He joined hands with the Lubavitcher Rebbe, Reb Sholom Dov Ber, and appealed to all Jewish communities to create chapters of a new union called *Machzikai HaDas,* or "Supporters of Religious Traditions." The objective would be to rescue the study of Torah and the observance of mitzvos from the attacks of the Haskalah movement.

In the year 1905, a group of rabbinic leaders from Russia, Poland, and Lithuania met in Vienna to organize a worldwide body which they named *Knesses Yisrael.* The Torah world greeted this announcement with enthusiasm, but other, unfriendly eyes disapproved. Czar Nicholas II of Russia, faced by continuous unrest and periodic uprisings, and possessed by an almost psychotic fear of losing his throne, quashed the new organization as a potential threat to his empire. Initial efforts had failed, but the seeds planted by Rabbi Shmuel Slonimer in the East and Rav Hirsch in the West were destined to be combined to form a single union of Orthodox Jewry.

East meets West: Bad Homburg

In order to create a worldwide Torah organization, it would be necessary to put aside all differences that existed between the various factions, as well as the regional distinctions that characterized religious Jewry. The vast gulf that separated the Jews of Eastern Europe from those that lived in the West made such a task seem almost impossible.

To the German or French Jew, for example, the Jews of Eastern Europe appeared to be almost uncouth in their ignorance of the modern world. The religious Jew in Western Europe was deeply religious and observed all the mitzvos, but he was also civilized, educated in secular subjects, and fluent in the language of his country. The Jews of Russia, Poland, and Lithuania, on the other hand, had little or no dealings with their Gentile counterparts and spoke Yiddish, which to the Western Jews was "inferior" from a linguistic and grammatical point of view. Ill-concealed contempt for this lack of culture made it difficult for German and French Jews to deal with their Eastern European brethren.

The Jews of Eastern Europe harbored a similar disdain for the Jews of Germany. In Poland, Russia, and Lithuania, the Jews devoted all their education to Torah; in their eyes, Western Europeans had contaminated their Torah studies with secular lessons, and shamelessly adulterated their religious convictions in their eagerness to make concessions to the non-Jews. The Eastern Jews, unlike those of Germany, had met the Reform movement with blunt, unyielding rejection. They were not only unashamed, but proud to show themselves as Jews, while to their disgust, the Germans dressed in the fashions of the day.

The growing threat of Zionism and the ever-increasing efforts of the *Maskilim*

Rabbi Shmuel Slonimer knew that a combination of all Orthodox groups under a single umbrella organization would be necessary to wage a successful battle against the "improved Chadorim."

Chapter
39

Reaction
of the Gedolim
to the Secular
Movements

East and West
finally met in Bad
Homburg, a small
health resort near
Frankfurt,
Germany, where
Rav Yitzchak Isaac
HaLevi, one of the
great rabbinic
leaders of
Lithuania, spent a
few weeks each
summer.

demanded that such differences be put aside. But who could possibly convince the Jews of Germany and France to work together with those of Russia, Poland, and Lithuania? Who could cajole Chassidim and Misnagdim to set aside ideological differences to work for a common cause?

East and West finally met in Bad Homburg, a small health resort near Frankfurt, Germany, where Rav Yitzchak Isaac HaLevi, one of the great rabbinic leaders of Lithuania who had been brought to Hamburg to spread Torah knowledge, spent a few weeks each summer. Rav Yitzchak Isaac HaLevi authored *Doros HaRishonim,* an outstanding work on many eras of Jewish history. He used this work to disprove the heresies of the Reform historian Graetz and his colleagues, pointing out Talmudic

A close, honest look at themselves revealed that both factions possessed different qualities that could be combined for mutual benefit.

Credit of OJ Archives of Agudath Israel of America

Rav Yitzchak Isaac HaLevi (Rabinowitz)

sources that they had misinterpreted and using clear-headed analysis to prove that Graetz's statements were often ill-conceived and full of contradictions.[7] In addition to his tremendous work with Jewish history, Rav Yitzchak Isaac served as a staff member of the great Volozhiner Yeshivah and was a close friend of Rav Chaim Soloveitchik, the Brisker Rav.[8]

Another great rabbinic scholar who helped bridge East with West was Rav Shlomo Breuer who was originally from Hungary and a student of the K'sav Sofer. He became the Frankfurter Rav being the son-in-law of Rav Samson Raphael Hirsch.

Rav Yitzchak Isaac and other Torah Sages of the East were astonished when they met Western Jews who were college graduates and professionals and still possessed a genuine understanding and deep love for Torah. At the same time, the Western Jews came to the humbling realization that their knowledge of Torah was largely inferior to that of the towering Talumudic geniuses of the East. A close, honest look at themselves revealed that both factions possessed different

Rav Yitzchak Isaac and other Torah Sages of the East were astonished when they met Western Jews who were college graduates and professionals and still possessed a genuine understanding and deep love for Torah.

7. See Chapter 33.

8. See Chapter 40.

qualities that could be combined for mutual benefit. German Orthodoxy needed the warmth and depth of Eastern Torah life; the Eastern Jews needed the organizational skill and the clarity of outlook developed within the German community. With mutual respect, the idea for Agudas Yisrael was born.

Although several meetings were held in Bad Homburg in 1909, many German rabbis were reluctant to put themselves officially on record as opponents of the Zionists who had captured the fancy of world Jewry with their visions of rebuilding Eretz Yisrael. After the Tenth Zionist Congress in 1911, however, when the Zionists adamantly refused to allow religion to become an integral part of Eretz Yisrael's future, most Orthodox rabbinic leaders abandoned any lingering hopes of guiding the Zionists back towards a more religious outlook.[9] The only hope of a worldwide battle against secularism was Agudas Yisrael.

Meeting at Kattowitz

Rav Yaakov Rosenheim, the communal leader of Frankfurt, was chosen by the Torah leaders at Bad Homburg to implement the plan of organizing world Orthodoxy by creating Agudas Yisrael. Rav Rosenheim was a gifted writer, a clear thinker, a brilliant organizer, and an apt spokesman. As a disciple and follower of Rav Samson Raphael Hirsch, Rav Rosenheim personified *Torah im Derech Eretz* by relating every activity, no matter how

> *Rav Rosenheim was a gifted writer, a clear thinker, a brilliant organizer, and an apt spokesman.*

Rav Rosenheim and his wife

insignificant or mundane it might seem, to Torah. Now, with the mandate to create Agudas Yisrael, Rav Rosenheim threw all his considerable talents and energy into creating an organization to represent all Orthodox Jewry.

Rav Rosenheim sent out invitations to an introductory conference in Kattowitz, intended to serve as preliminary working sessions towards the larger goal of setting up the organization of a world party. Optimistically speaking, no one anticipated more than a maximum of two hundred delegates at Kattowitz. To Rav Rosenheim's delighted surprise, the tremendous enthusiasm which greeted this first conference surpassed all expectations; the actual number of delegates who came to Kattowitz, including leading Torah Sages, rabbis and lay leaders, was over three times the number expected.

The conference opened on the 12th of Sivan in 1912 and lasted two days. In this

> *German Orthodoxy needed the warmth and depth of Eastern Torah life; the Eastern Jews needed the organizational skill and the clarity of outlook developed within the German community. With mutual respect, the idea for Agudas Yisrael was born.*

Chapter
39

9. See Chapter 38.

Reaction of the Gedolim to the Secular Movements

Chapter

39

Credit of OJ Archives of Agudath Israel of America

Chofetz Chaim

Credit of OJ Archives of Agudath Israel of America

Rabbi Chaim Ozer Grodzenski

short time, the organization defined its fundamental policies. The final resolution declared that Agudas Yisrael would serve to resolve all difficulties facing Jews and Judaism on the basis of Torah, without any political considerations. The *Moetzes Gedolei HaTorah,* the Rabbinic Council, would be the supreme governing body and final authority in all decisions. A more detailed program would be de-signed and ratified at a *Knessiah Gedolah,* or Grand Assembly, which would take place within the next two years.

The *Moetzes Gedolei HaTorah* remains one of the most distinctive features of Agudas Yisrael. It offers ample proof that Agudas Yisrael is committed to *daas Torah,* deci-sions based on a Torah view only. Only the most outstanding spiritual leaders of each era were eligible to serve on the *Moetzes Gedolei HaTorah.* Candidates for the Council did not campaign for elec-tion, but were granted membership in recognition of their universally acclaimed status as the greatest Torah leaders of their day. Members of the *Moetzes Gedolei*

HaTorah have included Reb Chaim Ozer Grodzenski, the Chofetz Chaim, the Tschebiner Rav, Rav Dov Berish Weiden-feld, Rav Zalman Sorotzkin, the Brisker Rav, the Sadigurer Rebbe, and Rav Reuven Grozovsky.

The First *Knessiah Gedolah*

The original date for the first *Knessiah Gedolah* was indefinitely postponed with the outbreak of the First World War (1914–1918). Despite fears that the elab-orate groundwork already laid would prove futile, the efforts of emissaries from Germany to Poland during the war years earned Agudas Yisrael the support of Polish Chassidic Jews and their leaders.

With the end of the war, Agudas Yisrael began making new plans. In Elul of 1923, over nine hundred delegates attended the first *Knessiah Gedolah,* which took place in Vienna. For possibly the first time since the Talmud had been com-pleted in Babylonia (circa 500 C.E.), an international convention of religious

Jewry came together: Jews from Eastern and Western Europe, Chassidim and Misnagdim, put aside all disagreements, animosity, and distrust, for the holy purpose of maintaining the Jewish nation as a pure and righteous nation.

The high point of the session came when the saintly Chofetz Chaim, who was then eighty-five years old, made his entry into the hall and gave his blessing for the entire undertaking. Great orators expressed the sentiments of this historical moment and brought their listeners to a high pitch of inspiration. Rav Meir Shapiro, the Lubliner Rav, set the words of *Tehillim* to a stirring melody and taught it to the entire convention: "*Im amarti matah ragli, chasdecha Hashem yisadaini,* If I said [in despair] my strength is gone, Your kindness, Hashem, lifted me up."[10]

Aside from the emotional experience of the gathering, there were a number of tangible results. The organization moved from generalities to specifics; separate branches were established to deal with certain problems, particularly that of strengthening Torah. *Keren Ha-Torah,* a fund dedicated to supporting Torah institutions in danger of financial collapse, did as much as possible to assist the hundreds of Yeshivos left indigent after the war.

Daf Yomi

During the first *Knessiah Gedolah,* Rav Meir Shapiro, an outstanding orator and great scholar, offered an innovative proposal: *Daf Yomi,* literally "daily page," a system for uniting Jewry through Torah study, by setting up a calendar of daily study. Every day, the same *daf* of Gemara would be studied by all Jews throughout the world, thus completing the entire Gemara every seven years.

10. *Tehillim,* 94:18.

The concept of *Daf Yomi* enforces diligence even as it encourages unity. One can not afford to miss even a single day of learning, for this would disrupt the entire cycle; at the same time, the idea that a Jew could travel halfway across the world and be able to join a Torah lecture on the same subject he is learning in his hometown offers support, fellowship, and solidarity.

This *Daf Yomi* method was not in any way initiated to hinder the in-depth learning that was the backbone of the Yeshivah way of learning. Those who were engrossed in learning in a Yeshivah atmosphere were not encouraged to learn *Daf Yomi,* which tends to be more superficial, but to rather delve into the depths of every subject and to work on fully understanding every line, according to each individual's capabilities. The *Daf Yomi* was encouraged mainly for those who were limited in their time for studying Torah and therefore created a

Credit of OJ Archives of Agudath Israel of America

Rav Meir Shapiro

Every day, the same daf of Gemara would be studied by all Jews throughout the world, thus completing the entire Gemara every seven years.

Chapter

39

Reaction
of the Gedolim
to the Secular
Movements

Their love of Torah and Judaism and their desire to impart this same love to Jewish women all over the world is the legacy that Sarah Schenirer left for posterity.

continuous regimen of diligent Torah study to fulfill each day to its utmost potential.

The ongoing *Daf Yomi* program is responsible for a remarkable increase in the study of Gemara by laymen. The twentieth century has witnessed seven complete cycles of Gemara, learned one day at a time, by Jews all over the world.

The Bais Yaakov Movement

Until the earlier twentieth century, the influence of the home was the only education Jewish women ever received. Girls were supposed to absorb Jewish values from watching and emulating their parents and patterning their lives after the religious atmosphere of their homes. There were the few exceptional daughters who stood by the door and listened while their fathers and brothers studied Gemara; a few more radical parents might have actually sat down with their daughters and taught them a few words of Chumash, but organized education for girls was largely nonexistent.

This method had proved satisfactory for centuries, but it left Jewish girls dangerously vulnerable to the Haskalah movement. With attendance of public schools a requirement by law, Jewish girls were exposed to the poison of socialism and "enlightenment" without an extensive Torah background to lend them support in refuting the *Maskilim's* arguments. Many parents did not even realize what was happening until their daughters openly began to question their religious practices. In that critical situation, Sarah Schenirer, a "simple" Jewish woman, stepped forward to fill this dangerous gap with the Bais Yaakov movement.

Sarah Schenirer

Sarah Schenirer, a native of Cracow, was a seamstress by profession. The inspiration for Bais Yaakov came while she listened to an inspiring sermon based on Rav Hirsch's writings in a Viennese synagogue. If she could invoke the same eloquence to speak to her friends back in Cracow, surely they would understand and appreciate the beauty of living as a loyal daughter of the Jewish people. She determined to return to Cracow and start a religious school for girls. She is quoted as saying, "Instead of sewing garments for the body, I will sew garments for the soul."

With the enthusiastic approval of the Torah Sages of her era, Sarah Schenirer began her school with a small class of twenty-five girls. These first students eventually graduated to become Bais Yaakov teachers themselves. Their love of Torah and Judaism and their desire to impart this same love to Jewish women all over the world is the legacy that Sarah Schenirer left for posterity.

"Instead of sewing garments for the body, I will sew garments for the soul."

Reaction
of the Gedolim
to the Secular
Movements

Within a few years, Bais Yaakov had brought about a revolution in the Jewish home. Bais Yaakov students became living examples of the Talmudic statement regarding Jewish women: "Why do they merit the reward of the World to Come, even more than the men who study the Torah? Because they encourage their husbands and sons to study in the Bais HaMidrash and they stay up late at night to greet their husbands when they return home from learning."[11]

Today, the legacy of Sarah Schenirer lives in the hundreds of Bais Yaakov schools throughout the world.

As Bais Yaakov expanded into a large network, Agudas Yisrael undertook its financial backing. By the outbreak of World War II, there were almost three hundred Bais Yaakov schools in Poland and Lithuania. In Cracow, where Sarah Schenirer began her historic work, a huge teachers' seminary saw hundreds of graduates leave its halls each year to spread the message of Torah across the continent. Today, the legacy of Sarah Schenirer lives on in the hundreds of Bais Yaakov schools throughout the world.

11. *Berachos,* 17a.

Chapter
39

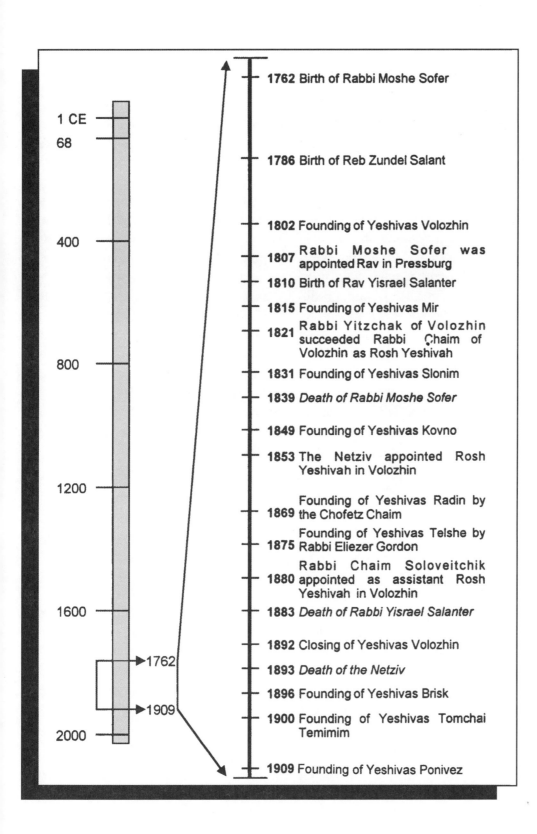

1 CE
68
400
800
1200
1600
2000

1762
1909

1762 Birth of Rabbi Moshe Sofer

1786 Birth of Reb Zundel Salant

1802 Founding of Yeshivas Volozhin

1807 Rabbi Moshe Sofer was appointed Rav in Pressburg

1810 Birth of Rav Yisrael Salanter

1815 Founding of Yeshivas Mir

1821 Rabbi Yitzchak of Volozhin succeeded Rabbi Ç̣haim of Volozhin as Rosh Yeshivah

1831 Founding of Yeshivas Slonim

1839 *Death of Rabbi Moshe Sofer*

1849 Founding of Yeshivas Kovno

1853 The Netziv appointed Rosh Yeshivah in Volozhin

1869 Founding of Yeshivas Radin by the Chofetz Chaim

1875 Founding of Yeshivas Telshe by Rabbi Eliezer Gordon

1880 Rabbi Chaim Soloveitchik appointed as assistant Rosh Yeshivah in Volozhin

1883 *Death of Rabbi Yisrael Salanter*

1892 Closing of Yeshivas Volozhin

1893 *Death of the Netziv*

1896 Founding of Yeshivas Brisk

1900 Founding of Yeshivas Tomchai Temimim

1909 Founding of Yeshivas Ponivez

Volozhin, "Mother of Yeshivos," and the Mussar Movement

Volozhin,
"Mother of
Yeshivos,"
and the
Mussar
Movement

*Reb Chaim of
Volozhin wanted
to create an
institution that
would provide the
best minds of the
country with
comfortable
housing and
regular meals; a
school that would
teach Torah with
dignity in a central
location where
daily lessons would
be given by the
leading Roshei
Yeshivah; where
the Gemara would
be taught in a
systematic, orderly
fashion.*

Chapter

40

In the fourteenth century, Yeshivos flourished in Eastern Europe under the watchful eyes of the Vaad Arba Aratzos.[1] The Yeshivos of that era bore little resemblance to the Yeshivah of today. The Rav in every community maintained a Bais HaMidrash, or study hall, and personally taught Torah to the local Jewish boys. The more promising boys in smaller villages were usually sent to a large city when they reached Bar Mitzvah.

In the city, the local rabbi would arrange for them to receive *teg* (literally, "days" in Yiddish), which meant that the boys were given a list of families who were willing to share meals with them on different days of the week. All too often, *teg* covered only one meal a day, or even a few meals a week. There was no dormitory, but a place to sleep was no problem: the *seder,* or learning period, lasted late into the night, and when the young men felt too sleepy to continue, they would simply stretch out on a back bench in the Bais HaMidrash.

Reb Chaim of Volozhin, the Vilna Gaon's most prestigious disciple, envisioned a different kind of Yeshivah. He wanted to create an institution that would provide the best minds of the country with comfortable housing and regular meals; a school that would teach Torah with dignity in a central location where daily lessons would be given by the leading Roshei Yeshivah; where the Gemara would be taught in a systematic, orderly fashion. Reb Chaim wanted nothing less than to create a generation of spiritual leaders for the entire country.

Such an institution, unlike the makeshift Yeshivos of two centuries before, would require financial backing; Reb Chaim did not want his students to have to concern

themselves with the worry of material sustenance. By providing the members of such a Yeshivah with all their needs, all their energy and concentration could be devoted to Torah.

Reb Chaim founded the Volozhiner Yeshivah shortly after his mentor's passing. It quickly developed into a world-famous institution, attracting the elite of the world's scholars. Initially, Reb Chaim, who was independently wealthy, supported his students himself. With time, however, the number of scholars studying in the Yeshivah had increased to the point where Reb Chaim could no longer carry the financial burden alone. He turned to communities throughout Lithuania, appealing for help. The Jews of Eastern Europe, who understood that the Yeshivah played a crucial role in shaping Torah leaders for future generations, responded with generosity. Reb Chaim was able to build a separate building for his Yeshivah and develop it into a major Torah center.

Volozhin followed the Gaon's approach to learning. Reb Chaim himself delivered a daily Torah lecture. The Yeshivah's program called for a systematic coverage of all Shass, from beginning to end. The Roshei Yeshivah gave a daily discourse; in addition, each student learned a second *masechta* of his own choice. Reb Chaim stressed the necessity of constant learning. Twenty-four hours a day, the study hall rang with the words of Torah. Holidays and vacation made no difference. Volozhin never stood empty.

With Reb Chaim's passing in 1821, his son, Rabbi Yitzchak, succeeded him as Rosh Yeshivah. During his tenure, Czar Nicholas I threatened to close all Yeshivos. The desperate necessity of stopping this terrible edict forced Rabbi Yitzchak

1. See Chapter 23.

to leave the Yeshivah for long periods of time in order to deal with the Czar. His efforts took him away from his commitment to his daily lectures and he was compelled to give over the spiritual leadership of the Yeshivah to the Netziv, Rabbi Naftoli Zvi Yehudah Berlin, his son-in-law. The Netziv authored many Talmudic works, including a commentary on Chumash, *Hamek Davar,* and a commentary on the questions of Rav Achai, as well as responsa, *Meishiv Davar.*

After the death of Rabbi Yitzchak, the question arose: who would succeed him as Rosh Yeshivah? The Netziv was acknowledged for his vast *bekius,* his widespread knowledge of Talmud, but Rav Yosef Dov Soloveitchik, a profound scholar of superior intellect and author of the *Beis HaLevi,* was also worthy of the post. The two Torah giants brought the matter to a *Din Torah* and awaited a decision.

The *Din Torah* decided in favor of the Netziv. The Beis HaLevi quietly left Volozhin and eventually became Rav of Brisk. Later, when the Netziv found himself overwhelmed by the demands of leadership, he asked Rav Chaim Soloveitchik, the Beis HaLevi's son and his own granddaughter's husband, to return to Volozhin and serve as assistant Rosh Yeshivah.

The Volozhin Yeshivah fulfilled the role Reb Chaim had envisioned; it attracted the greatest scholars of Lithuania, young men who became the Torah leaders and Roshei Yeshivah of future generations. As early as 1815, during Reb Chaim's own lifetime, one of his former students established a Yeshivah in Mir, near the Polish-Russian border, which flourished for over 120 years, until the Second World War.[2] Unfortunately, it also attracted the unwanted attention of the Haskalah movement, whose activists rightfully saw the Yeshivah as a major threat to their efforts to rob Lithuanian Jewry of its precious heritage.

The *Maskilim* could not allow the Yeshivah, with its tremendous impact and vast influence for Torah, to continue flourishing. With the willing ear of the Russian authorities, they accused the Yeshivah of being a backward, insubordinate, and even subversive institution. As a result, Czar Alexander III issued an edict requiring the Yeshivah to change its curriculum to include secular studies. If Volozhin refused to comply, it would be forced to close its doors.

The decision was painful, but the Netziv and Rav Chaim knew that they had no choice. The introduction of secular studies would destroy the character of the Yeshivah. Volozhin would have to close.

On Wednesday, the 5th of Shvat, 1892, a detachment of police surrounded the building. In the presence of the entire Yeshivah and a crowd of onlookers, an official order was read: all students must immediately vacate the Yeshivah and leave town within three days. After the Sifrei Torah and other *sefarim* were removed from the building, the doors were padlocked and sealed. As they locked the doors, the Netziv collapsed, unconscious. His weeping students carried him home. Eyewitnesses later testified that the forced closing of the Yeshivah was the most tragic, emotionally devastating experience in their lives. (Some years later, Volozhin reopened under the leadership of Rav Raphael Shapiro, but it never regained its leading role.)

The Netziv, broken in spirit by this tragedy, left Lithuania to go to Eretz Yisrael, with

The Volozhin Yeshivah fulfilled the role Reb Chaim had envisioned; it attracted the greatest scholars of Lithuania, young men who became the Torah leaders and Roshei Yeshivah of future generations.

2. See below.

Volozhin,
"Mother
of Yeshivos,"
and the
Mussar
Movement

the hope that he would find comfort on its holy soil. On his way he became ill and was forced to stop in Warsaw to consult with a doctor. He succumbed to his sickness the following year, in 1893, without reaching his destination.

Rav Chaim Soloveitchik returned to Brisk, where he accepted his father's position as Rav. In addition to his duties as rabbinic leader of the city, he gathered a number of students, many of whom became Roshei Yeshivah all over the world. Brisk soon became the focus of attention in the Torah world. Any scholar of note would make an effort to visit the Brisker Rav and offer his analysis of the Gemara; it was considered a mark of distinction if Reb Chaim gave his approval, or at least did not shrug it off as irrelevant. Reb Chaim Brisker, as he was reverently called, became the recognized rabbinic authority of world Jewry.

Volozhin's Legacy

The Yeshivah of Volozhin lasted ninety years, from 1802 to 1892, through three generations. While its demise was a tragic loss for the Torah world, an entire network of new Yeshivos sprung up in its wake. Czar Alexander had forced Volozhin to close, but the typical corruption of the Russian bureaucracy allowed other Yeshivos to flourish. The founders and leaders of these Yeshivos were the selfsame scholars that Reb Chaim of Volozhin had groomed in his Yeshivah. Volozhin has been called *Em HaYeshivos,* "Mother of Yeshivos"; the modern concept of the Yeshivah, as well as of Roshei Yeshivah who guide their students, are Reb Chaim's legacy.

The Mirrer Yeshivah, established during Reb Chaim's lifetime, was one of the largest of all Lithuanian Yeshivos. During World War II, the Mirrer Yeshivah was forced to escape the twin threats of Communist Russia and Nazi genocide. After a long, miraculous odyssey through Russia and Siberia, the Mirrer Yeshivah found temporary refuge in Shanghai, China. Today, branches of the Mirrer Yeshivah are in New York and Yerushalayim.

Another Yeshivah was founded in Telshe (Telz) at the Prussian border by Rabbi Eliezer Gordon, another former student of Volozhin. His son-in-law, Reb Yosef Leib Bloch, eventually became the head of the Yeshivah. With Reb Yosef Leib's passing, the leadership passed to his sons. Although the Yeshivah was destroyed in World War II, Reb Eliyahu Meir Bloch survived the war and replanted the Telshe Yeshivah in Cleveland, Ohio.

Other Yeshivos of fame were the Yeshivah of Radin, founded by the saintly

Credit of OJ Archives of Agudath Israel of America

Rav Elchonon Wasserman

Chofetz Chaim in 1869, and the Yeshivah of Ponivez, founded in 1909. The Ponivezer Yeshivah eventually came under the leadership of Rav Yosef Kahaneman, the Ponivezer Rav. Rav Elchonon Wasserman, the great Torah Sage who was killed by the Nazis in World War II, founded another great Yeshivah in Baranowitz.

Each of these post-Volozhin Yeshivos had its own approach to learning and outlook. Volozhin could never be duplicated, but the new, vast horizons of Torah learning that Reb Chaim opened are still being explored today.

Timetable of Yeshivos Established in Russia / Lithuania	
1802	Yeshivas Volozhin
1815	Yeshivas Mir
1831	Yeshivas Slonim
1849	Yeshivas Kovno
1869	Yeshivas Radin
1875	Yeshivas Telshe
1900	Yeshivas Tomchai Temimim
1909	Yeshivas Ponivez

The list of higher-ranking Yeshivos of Europe in the nineteenth century would be incomplete without Pressburg, Hungary, one of the oldest Jewish communities in Europe. Under the spiritual leadership of Reb Moshe Sofer, one of the greatest Sages of his day, the Pressburg community and its Yeshivah became a world center of Torah.

Reb Moshe Sofer, known as the Chasam Sofer, was born in Frankfurt, Germany, before this illustrious Jewish community was poisoned by the Reform movement. At that time, the Rav of Frankfurt was the famous Rav Pinchas Horowitz, who had studied in Poland under the Maggid of Mezerich.[3] Rabbi Nassan Adler, revered as a giant of Torah and a master of Kabbalah, lived in Frankfurt as well. With young Moshe's superior intellect and refined character, the boy soon became the prized pupil of both Rabbi Horowitz and Rabbi Adler.

When Moshe was in his teens, the community's distrust of Rav Adler's kabbalistic customs compelled the Rav to leave Frankfurt. Moshe followed his mentor to the east, where he developed his great abilities and eventually began a long, illustrious career. In 1807, he was offered the prestigious position of Chief Rabbi in Pressburg, where he resided until the end of his life.

The range of his Talmudic knowledge was phenomenal, while his magnetic personality and knowledge of secular subjects enabled him to combat the *Maskilim's* efforts to bring the "enlightenment" to Hungary. When Jewish issues were involved, including the question of Emancipation, the Chasam Sofer was willing to enter the corridors of Austrian politics. Even the Austrian Emperor recognized his authority.

His halachic responsa numbered in the thousands, covering an infinite variety of problems that were submitted to him from all parts of the globe. It is no wonder that, under his leadership, the Pressburg Yeshivah achieved recognition as a center of Torah comparable to the Volozhiner Yeshivah in Lithuania.

Chasam Sofer

3. See Chapter 28.

Under the spiritual leadership of Reb Moshe Sofer, one of the greatest Sages of his day, the Pressburg community and its Yeshivah became a world center of Torah.

Chapter 40

Mussar puts emphasis on the effort to ennoble one's character, to break negative character traits, and to develop love of Hashem and fear of Heaven. The founder of this movement was an extraordinary personality, a combination of a genius in Torah and a paragon of piety, Rav Yisrael Salanter.

The Yeshivah of Pressburg

With Reb Moshe's guidance, the enrollment in the Yeshivah of Pressburg rapidly rose to an average of 300 students. The Chasam Sofer delivered a daily Torah lecture from 11:00 to 12:30, following the order of the Gemara; tests were given to the students on a weekly basis. In the evenings, lectures were delivered in *halachah* and Chumash with the commentaries. From time to time, the Rav would also give a *shiur klali,* a public discourse on a specific topic. These usually consisted of a thorough analysis of the various aspects of a subject in the Gemara. In contrast with the regular daily lecture, this presentation could cut across every section of the Gemara, Rishonim, and Acharonim. After a thorough analytic overview, the Rosh Yeshivah explained the actual *halachah.*

In addition to Talmudic studies, the students of the Pressburg Yeshivah were educated and trained for their future role as rabbis, including ways to fight against the Reform movement and how to cope with social and halachic questions as they arose.

The Chasam Sofer's strong hand on the Yeshivah was matched by his determination to keep the destructive influence of

Yeshivos and Chassidic centers in Eastern Europe

the *Maskilim* in Hungary to an absolute minimum. The crisis that caused the tragic downfall of Volozhin could not have happened in Pressburg; the singular influence of the Chasam Sofer created a bulwark of strength against the onslaught of Haskalah. In addition, Reform Jewry's infiltration of the ranks of Hungarian Jews could not achieve the same results as they did in Poland and Germany. The Jews in Hungary were comparatively well off, and mingled easily with the Gentiles without giving up any of their religious practices, while the Hapsburg Dynasty was conservative enough and religious enough to dislike any form of liberalism, even among the Jews. Promises of an "easier life" and "social acceptance" had no power in Hungary. Faced by an unhelpful government and the powerful personality of the Chasam Sofer, the *Maskilim* lost much of the battle.

The Mussar Movement

One of the greatest weapons of the *Maskilim* was their ability to point to religious Jews and denounce dishonesty and lack of character, particularly in Russia, where the government had cut off almost every means for Jews to be able to make a living.

Mussar is roughly translated as "Torah ethics." It puts emphasis on the effort to ennoble one's character, to break negative character traits, and to develop love of Hashem and fear of Heaven. The founder of this movement was an extraordinary personality, a combination of a genius in Torah and a paragon of piety, Rav Yisrael Salanter.

The small Lithuanian town of Salant was home to a remarkable man who refused any titles and was simply called "Reb Zundel." Born in 1786, Reb Zundel received his education in the Volozhiner

Yeshivah. After Reb Chaim's passing, he traveled to Posen to study under the great Rabbi Akiva Eger. On his return to Lithuania, he dedicated his life to perfection, not only in the learning of Torah, but in developing his character traits and becoming a total servant of Hashem. He shunned publicity, deliberately choosing to live in the tiny village of Salant, where he could live in quiet obscurity. His unusual piety and boundless faith in Hashem were legendary.

A young Torah student named Yisrael studied in the Beis HaMidrash in Salant. Yisrael, a promising scholar who was fluent in all Shass, was fascinated with Reb Zundel and tried to emulate him. Reb Zundel often went on solitary walks into the woods in order to learn mussar and to meditate in seclusion. Yisrael followed him and watched his actions from a distance. Once, when Yisrael was about fourteen years old, Reb Zundel suddenly turned around and faced the young man. "Yisrael!" Reb Zundel said. "Learn mussar and become a *yerei Shamayim*, a G-d fearing person!"

Later Reb Yisrael declared, "This remark became the turning point in my life." He resolved to make the study of mussar the main purpose of his own life, and to disseminate the importance of mussar among Jewry at large.

Rav Yisrael Salanter followed in the Vilna Gaon's footsteps in recommending *Mesillas Yesharim* (Path of the Righteous) as the perfect textbook of mussar.[4] Its author, Rabbi Moshe Chaim Luzzatto, remarks in its introduction that the work contains no novel ideas, but simple, fundamental concepts that a reader might consider superfluous to study. In reality, these principles demand closer study *because* they are so basic. A superficial study of

4. See Chapter 26.

Mesillas Yesharim will have little impact on the student; repetition, dedication, and concentration will cause the scholar to realize that the subjects discussed in *Mesillas Yesharim* are not impersonal topics, but personal lessons in Torah values and ideals.

Reb Yisrael traveled through Lithuania and Poland to spread his mussar ideas. First, he established his reputation as a brilliant Torah scholar who could mesmerize his audience with his Talmud lectures. One famous story offers proof of his quick wit:

It was customary for a speaker to post a list of sources that would be cited during his discourse; in this manner, those who attended the lecture would be prepared. A man with a rather malicious sense of humor replaced Reb Yisrael's list of sources with a list, instead, of Talmudic references picked at random with no apparent connection. Reb Yisrael arrived at the podium and discovered the bogus list; on the spot, he composed a new lecture that brilliantly wove all the sources together.

Once Reb Yisrael had established his reputation and gained the respect of the Torah community, he moved to Vilna, where his philosophy of mussar grew into a mass movement. Disturbed by this new weapon of Torah, the Russian government and the *Maskilim* eventually forced Reb Yisrael to leave the city. As Reb Yisrael once quipped, "The *Maskilim* want to reform Judaism, but I want to reform the Jews." Reb Yisrael left Vilna and traveled to Kovno.

A famous story is told of a businessman who asked Rav Yisrael Salanter: "I have only a half hour a day to learn. What shall I do? Learn Gemara or mussar?"

Rav Yisrael Salanter followed in the Vilna Gaon's footsteps in recommending Mesillas Yesharim (Path of the Righteous) as the perfect textbook of mussar.

Volozhin,
"Mother
of Yeshivos,"
and the
Mussar
Movement

*While mussar was
certainly not a
replacement for
learning Gemara,
it supplemented
learning with the
ethical behavior
that behooves a
true Torah scholar.*

"Learn mussar," advised Reb Yisrael, "and you will realize that you can find much more time to learn Gemara."

With the help of a wealthy philanthropist from Germany, he founded a great Yeshivah of Torah and mussar in Kovno. He attracted a number of devoted followers who eventually spread the mussar idea in various Yeshivos in Lithuania; mussar soon became a vital accessory to the daily program of Torah learning. While mussar was certainly not a replacement for learning Gemara, it supplemented learning with the ethical behavior that behooves a true Torah scholar. As time passed, the new system of learning mussar developed: there was a daily learning period, usually at the end of the day, in which two students would study a mussar work together; there was also a weekly lecture, called a *shmuess,* delivered to the entire Yeshivah. Today, it is common to have a separate learning period for mussar in almost every Yeshivah.[5]

The study of mussar was guided and regulated by a member of the staff called the *mashgiach,* or supervisor. The *mashgiach* delivered the weekly *shmuess* and supervised the development of each student's character and outlook. He acted as rebbe, counselor, and advisor, directing the growth of a young teenager into a mature Torah scholar of exemplary moral conduct.

Among the more famous disciples of Rav Yisrael Salanter and his disciples were Rabbi Yitzchak Blazer, known as Rabbi Yitzchak Petterburger; Rabbi Simcha Zissel Kelmer, who presided over Yeshivas Kelmer Talmud Torah; Rabbi Nosson Zvi Finkel, reverently known as *Der Alter* of Slobodka; Reb Yeruchom Levovitz, the Mirrer Mashgiach; and others.

At the age of seventy, Reb Yisrael left Lithuania and traveled to Western Europe. No explanation was offered, although many have been suggested. Perhaps he wished to avoid the wide recognition and prestige he had gained in the land of his birth; perhaps he felt that the message of mussar was needed in Western Europe. It was certainly true that the Western European Jews had drifted further away from Orthodox Judaism than the Jews of Russia, Poland, and Lithuania.

Reb Yisrael stayed in Paris for nearly two years, leaving a profound spiritual impact on the Jews of that city. He returned to Koenigsberg in East Prussia, where he died in 1883, leaving the world of Yeshivos profoundly touched and enhanced by his message of true Torah ethics.

---

5. In Reb Yisrael's time, some prominent Roshei Yeshivah objected to the idea of mussar as a separate subject. They argued that training in ethics and Torah values was an integral part of learning; every page of the Chumash and Gemara contain elements of mussar which should be studied as an integral part of Torah education.

Index

Index

Index

Index